The Crime of Aggression

Human Rights and Crimes against Humanity
Series Editor: Eric D. Weitz

*A list of titles
in this series
appears at the
back of the book.*

The Crime of Aggression

The Quest for Justice in an Age of Drones,
Cyberattacks, Insurgents, and Autocrats

Noah Weisbord

PRINCETON UNIVERSITY PRESS

PRINCETON AND OXFORD

Copyright © 2019 by Noah Weisbord

Requests for permission to reproduce material from this work should be sent to permissions@press.princeton.edu

Published by Princeton University Press

41 William Street, Princeton, New Jersey 08540

6 Oxford Street, Woodstock, Oxfordshire OX20 1TR

press.princeton.edu

All Rights Reserved

Library of Congress Control Number: 2019930186

ISBN 978-0-691-16987-3

British Library Cataloging-in-Publication Data is available

Editorial: Brigitta van Rheinberg, Eric Crahan, Pamela Weidman and Thalia Leaf

Production Editorial: Jenny Wolkowicki

Text design: Leslie Flis

Jacket design: Amanda Weiss

Production: Jacqueline Poirier

Publicity: James Schneider and Caroline Priday

Copyeditor: Maia Vaswani

This book has been composed in Sabon LT Std

Printed on acid-free paper. ∞

Printed in the United States of America

10 9 8 7 6 5 4 3 2 1

For Auntie Merrily

Contents

Acknowledgments   ix

Introduction   1

CHAPTER 1   Is Law Dead?   9

CHAPTER 2   Timeslip: Invasion of the Crimea,
Collapse of the League of Nations   21

CHAPTER 3   The Nuremberg Avant-Garde Moment   45

CHAPTER 4   Cold War *Jus ad Bellum*: Law of Force
vs. Rule of Law   53

CHAPTER 5   Nuremberg Renaissance: The 1990s   71

CHAPTER 6   The Crime of Aggression: From Rome to Kampala   89

CHAPTER 7   Judging Wars   113

CHAPTER 8   Sci-fi Warfare   133

CHAPTER 9   You're under Arrest, Mr. President   151

CHAPTER 10   Activation   169

Notes   179

Index   247

Acknowledgments

I'm grateful to Martha Minow (SJD supervision), Peter McFarlane, Charles Jalloh (ideas and editing), Ben Ferencz, Don Ferencz, Roger Clark, Claus Kress, David Scheffer, Bill Schabas, Christian Wenaweser, Stefan Barriga, Astrid Reisinger-Coracini, Jürg Lindemann, Carrie McDougall, Päl Wrange, Jutta Bertram Nothnagel, Jennifer Trahan, Leena Grover, Wolfgang Danspeckgruber, Robbie Manson (and the Special Working Group on the Crime of Aggression), Kevin Droz, Alysha Flipse, Michael Pego, Gregg Strock (research), Brigitta Van Rheinberg, Eric Weitz, Eric Crahan, Pamela Weidman (editing), Jenny Wolkowicki (production), Maia Vaswani (copyediting), Rick Broadhead (agent), Peter Leuprecht, Tim Weisbord, Bonnie Theriault-Weisbord, Arnie Gelbart, Sandor Klein, Mona Klein, Marc Tasman, Bonnie Klein-Tasman, Cleo Paskal, Anna Paskal, Jim Thomas, Kim Kachanoff, Robbie Heft, Riva Heft, Phillis Amber-Weisbord, Thomas Park, the Weisbord Acres community. And, of course, brilliant Alana Klein.

The Crime of Aggression

Introduction

> To initiate a war of aggression . . . is the supreme international
> crime differing only from other war crimes in that it contains
> within itself the accumulated evil of the whole.
> —Judgment of the Nuremberg tribunal, 1946[1]

I first met former Nuremberg prosecutor Benjamin Ferencz in The Hague
in 2004. International Criminal Court (ICC) prosecutor Luis Moreno Ocampo, whose law clerk I had just become, introduced us in the doorway
to his office. Ferencz was livid and Moreno Ocampo found this amusing.

Five foot tall and eighty-four years old, Ferencz stood three inches
from my face bellowing: "Why aren't you screaming? Why aren't you
screaming? This is the job for the young people to do." What made
him especially angry was that the United States had lobbied forcefully
to exclude the crime of aggression—individual criminal responsibility
for aggressive war—from the ICC's code of crimes, or—if aggression
were included—that US leaders would not be prosecuted. Then the
United States had illegally invaded Iraq without any leadership accountability and undermined his life's work: criminal accountability for aggressive war.

"Conservatives intent on destroying the International Criminal Court
have misstated the facts and have done a disservice to the United States
and its military personnel," Ferencz raged. "How much more suffering
must the innocents of this planet endure before decision-makers recognize
that law is better than war?"

After the Second World War, Ferencz had prosecuted the *Einsatzgruppen Case*, a trial of twenty-two Nazi death-squad leaders who had killed
over a million victims and claimed self-defense. Ferencz spent the rest of
his life campaigning to create a permanent ICC modeled on the Nuremberg precedent, capable of punishing leaders who committed any of the
four core international crimes: genocide, war crimes, crimes against humanity, and aggression. For him, a proud American, the US invasion of
Iraq, based on falsified information about a future attack, signaled a Bush
administration campaign to undermine international law. "They are entitled to their opinion but they are not entitled to lie to the American
public and get away with it," he fumed. For Ferencz, lying to justify war
and exempting American leaders from the Nuremberg precedent were
shortsighted hypocrisy. If legal accountability was not equally applied to

all, Ferencz believed it would undermine the rule of law and destroy the world.

I had just been admitted to a doctoral program at Harvard Law and was trolling for a dissertation topic. Moreno Ocampo told Ferencz he was encouraging me to study the so-called peace-versus-justice dilemma. "You wanna talk about peace versus justice?" Ferencz nudged. "Imagine prosecuting the Germans while we needed them to fight the Cold War against the Russians!"

Moreno Ocampo was silent. He was sympathetic to the Nuremberg principle that aggressive war must not be tolerated, but he was overloaded and a new law meant more prosecutions.

The dilemma landed on me.

Would criminal accountability for aggression set back alternative avenues for peace? Or was there no lasting peace without justice? Was Ferencz overzealous, or was he right?

I decided to study the crime of aggression and find out.

Ferencz advocated for my inclusion as a nonstate delegate to the Special Working Group on the Crime of Aggression, charged with drafting the crime by the Assembly of States Parties to the ICC. I started as a note taker, beginning my journey to understanding the way modern war is conceptualized and judged. In time, I earned a place as an independent expert wrestling with the design of international law's supreme crime, a crime one scholar pessimistically dubbed "a Gordian knot in search of a sword."[2]

The crime of aggression would provide domestic and international courts with a powerful check on authoritarian power. After a decade of negotiations and against all expectations, in 2010, the signatory states of the ICC convened a multilateral conference in Kampala and added aggression to the list of crimes the court and its signatory states are empowered to prosecute. Comprising 123 states, the Assembly of States Parties scheduled the activation of the law for 2017, enough grace time for governments and militaries to revise their policies. Waging war, the traditional prerogative of presidents and princes, was about to become an international crime.

A prosecutable crime of aggression would strengthen the prohibition on war by making leaders—rather than their populations—personally responsible for the wars they start. The crime of aggression allows domestic and international courts to make principled, as opposed to political, determinations on whether a war is legal or illegal. It is based on the Nuremberg precedent, the UN Charter, and customary international law binding on all states. Aggressive acts enumerated in the definition of the offence include invasion, bombardment, blockade, and armed attacks on another state's forces. If a state ratifies the crime of aggression—as fifteen

NATO states have already done—and incorporates it into domestic law, its courts have the authority to prosecute rogue leaders. If states falter, the ICC can step in and prosecute perpetrators, as it currently does in cases of genocide, crimes against humanity, and war crimes.

The basis of the crime of aggression is the conviction that leaders bring their populations to war, not the reverse, and it is with leaders that responsibility should lie. Languishing in his prison cell in Nuremberg, Hermann Goering, Hitler's second-in-command, explained the relationship to Gustave Gilbert, his prison psychologist:

> Why, of course, the *people* don't want war. . . . Why would some poor slob on a farm want to risk his life in a war when the best that he can get out of it is to come back to his farm in one piece. . . . But, after all, it is the *leaders* of the country who determine the policy and it is always a simple matter to drag the people along, whether it is a democracy or a fascist dictatorship or a Parliament or a Communist dictatorship.[3]

When Gilbert argued that democracies are different because the people have a say, Goering had a ready reply:

> Voice or no voice, the people can always be brought to the bidding of the leaders. That is easy. All you have to do is tell them they are being attacked and denounce the pacifists for lack of patriotism and exposing the country to danger. It works the same way in any country.[4]

Today, with unprecedented means to disseminate, measure, and control propaganda, the capacity of leaders to bring their populations to war has increased exponentially. The crime of aggression offers an opportunity to assign responsibility where it belongs.

State responsibility suffers from two frustrating deficiencies. It targets only states and fails to effectively leverage the potential of international law. The Nuremberg tribunal was prescient in its 1945 judgment: "Crimes against International Law are committed by men, not by abstract entities, and only by punishing individuals who commit such crimes can the provisions of International Law be enforced."[5] Sidelined during the Cold War, individual responsibility has made a comeback.

It has become increasingly clear that twentieth century notions of state responsibility underlie contemporary international law and frustrate enforcement. The UN has no standing army and relies on cooperative states to pressure rogue states into compliance. Had the drafters of the UN Charter focused their energy on individuals instead, they may have leveraged their force and more effectively compelled compliance. At the turn of the millennium, dissatisfied states have resurrected the Nuremberg precedent, hoping to fix the defect. Beyond dispensing just deserts and vindicating the suffering of victims, retributive justice can have a deterrent effect on political and military leaders and change the rules of international relations. Criminal accusations can seriously undermine the political ambitions of existing or aspiring leaders.[6]

Furthermore, al Qaeda's attacks all over the world, and now those of the Islamic State (IS, or ISIS), have demonstrated that states are no longer the only, or even the primary, threat to the peace. Technology is culminating in the ability of one person to wage war on the world and win.[7] Corporations have adjusted to the emergence of the individual as a global threat and are fast-tracking the development of military technologies, including drones and cyberweapons, designed to target individuals from afar. International lawyers have taken the hint. By regulating the individual, they hope to better capture the sociological dimensions of modern war and, in this way, make international law more effective.

Criminal accountability will not end war, but has the potential to influence the practice of domestic and international politics so that aggressive war is no longer a tempting option. Even when countries do not sign on to the law or opt out, an activated crime of aggression will provide opponents of authoritarian leaders with the legal leverage to curtail impulsive wars. Had the crime of aggression been law in 1990, Iraqi president Saddam Hussein could have been punished for the invasion of Kuwait (as US President George H. W. Bush and UK Prime Minister Margaret Thatcher discussed), perhaps precluding the 2003 Iraq War and saving Hussein's civilian population from crippling sanctions. Arguably, had aggression been a prosecutable crime in 2003, UK Prime Minister Tony Blair—who relied heavily on the legal advice of his attorney general—would not have brought his country to war in Iraq. And without the Iraq War there would be no ISIS. The law can also be used to defend cases involving the legitimate use of force. A clear legal standard provides legitimacy for leaders unfairly maligned for using necessary and proportional self-defense in response to an armed attack on their territory.

The enforcement of international criminal law has been more successful than most people realize, although prosecution occurs more often domestically than in The Hague's courts. But even The Hague has had success. Once-powerful presidents, prime ministers, and vice-presidents have been brought before the ICC. Every one of the 161 Yugoslav war criminals indicted by the International Criminal Tribunal for the Former Yugoslavia (ICTY) was captured or killed. The Rwanda Tribunal (ICTR) had similar success.

The crime of aggression holds the promise of buttressing the rule of law when it works, and revealing the futility of the rule of law when it fails. The ideal of law is that reason can constrain violence. Yet violations such those of the United States and Russia, unending warfare in Iraq and Syria, state-sponsored terrorism, and paralysis of the UN Security Council challenge this conviction. The crime of aggression embodies a beleaguered hope that the rule of law can help create a more stable, peaceful world.

Although international law may sometimes seem meaningless as a means of opposing powerful leaders, it is the most reliable set of objective standards for checking unbridled greed and nationalism. By setting benchmarks for behavior, and rules of evidence and procedure, it allows government officials, lawmakers, courts, media, and civil society to evaluate the legality of their leaders' propaganda for waging war. The rule of law is the most effective resistance tool to sway institutions and to keep authoritarian leaders in check.

The revival of the crime of aggression is an overdue response to deepening dissatisfaction with the way wars are started and judged. Particularly frustrating was contemporary international law's emphasis on collective responsibility of states rather than individuals, its reliance on a biased political process to judge wars, and patchy enforcement. After a century of failed attempts and false starts, the impulse to hold individuals accountable for aggressive war resurfaced after the US-led invasion of Iraq, and, even more surprisingly, gained newfound traction. It emerged alongside preexisting, competing practices for managing interstate conflict, such as negotiation, collective security, and balance of power.

Under the current UN regime, states are responsible for judging other states. Their decisions are influenced by politics as much as principles. The UN Security Council, a political body consisting of five permanent members—Britain, China, France, Russia, and the United States—and ten elected members sitting for two-year terms, has primary responsibility for determining whether aggression has occurred, and for mustering a collective response.[8] Any one of these states, granted permanent seats on the council after World War II, can veto a decision of the other fourteen members of the council at will and without justification, leading to seventy years of chronic deadlock and biased decision making. Five powerful nations control determinations of aggressive war in a political process that favors the aggressors, leading victims of international aggression to conclude that the system is rigged.

The crime of aggression is a legal response to these frustrating deficiencies. Tools to identify breaches of widely accepted international standards give government officials, lawmakers, the courts, the media, and civil society the means to hold perpetrators to account. In regulating the individual, the new law has the potential to make international law fairer and more effective.

The new law responds to loss of faith in the Security Council's politicized decisions and to demands that justifications for armed force be tested against a universal standard by impartial judges. International, regional, and domestic courts are meant to serve as a check on the frivolous claims of leaders who would frighten their populations with vague threats to their safety or the safety of others in order to justify aggressive war.

Whether or not criminal law deters aggressive war, the crime of aggression also has an important retributive function. When a criminal court punishes a perpetrator, it is inflicting a publicly visible defeat on behalf of the community meant to correct "the wrongdoer's false message that the victim [is] less worthy."[9] Punishment serves to recognize wrongdoing even when it fails as a deterrent, and regardless of the effects of that punishment.[10] The Nuremberg tribunal, for example, systematically debunked the alibis of the Nazi leaders and revealed to the world, beyond a reasonable doubt, the extent of their depravity. The crime of aggression provides the legal basis for judges hearing an aggression case to reveal the defendant's true reasons for war and hold wrongdoers to account.

The new law responds to the perception that unbridled politics has failed to advance international peace. The drafters of the crime wager that the new law will infiltrate institutional practices and become a more compelling safeguard against reckless leaders intent on bringing their nations to war.

Critics worry that the crime of aggression will destabilize international relations by impeding negotiated solutions to international disputes. Andrew Natsios, President George W. Bush's special envoy to Sudan, argues that the threat of arrest for international crimes increased Sudanese President Omar al-Bashir's incentive to cling to power as the only means of avoiding punishment.[11] Natsios favored a political deal between the north and south "based on a realistic appraisal of what is achievable under the current unfavorable circumstances."[12] But with ruthless leaders still in power in Sudan and South Sudan, the peace deal unraveled, resulting in mass atrocities and perpetual war.[13] What Natsios overlooked is that justice can also contribute to sustainable peace by discrediting and marginalizing destabilizing political leaders. Serbian President Slobodan Milošević's fall from power is a prime example.[14] Following indictments issued by the ICTY, the Serbian people forced the authoritarian, internationally marginalized Milošević out of office, achieving peace without amnesty.[15] It is leaders who invade other states who threaten international peace, not the laws enacted to check them.

Other critics worry that the crime of aggression will put a chill on humanitarian intervention.[16] They warn that the prohibition will be *too* effective, stymying the use of force for humanitarian ends, preventing states from cooperating to stop mass atrocities where the legality of military action is contested.[17] In fact, the new law finally makes it possible to transparently evaluate the veracity of a leader's claim that an unauthorized war was undertaken for humanitarian ends, and distinguish genuine humanitarian intervention from spurious self-interest under the guise of "Responsibility to Protect."

Cynicism about legal rationality undermines the logic of institutional checks and balances on the arbitrary exercise of political and military power and concedes defeat to the forces critics claim to oppose. Empty calls for "ethical choice and responsibility" in politics are, unfortunately, vulnerable to the same critiques leveled at law, without law's institutional leverage.[18] Exaggeration of law's indeterminacy results in the paralyzing conclusion that legal norms never trump self-interest.[19] It is true that ambiguities in the law create opportunities for strategic lawyering, but this is an argument for skillful drafting and adjudication, not for jettisoning the law.

The League of Nations collapsed because nations failed to enforce its prohibition on aggressive war. International justice, however, is not the same as collective security. Key differences create new possibilities to advance the rule of law in matters of war and peace. Although states' refusal to arrest powerful leaders could reveal the ICC's impotence and snuff out the court's authority, political and military leaders, even the leaders of great powers, are more vulnerable to enforcement than entire states. Perpetrators of international crimes face the possibility of arrest at home or abroad. Domestic political opponents, successor regimes, the legislature, or the judiciary may spearhead an arrest and trial for the crime of aggression. Foreign militaries, foreign police, UN peacekeepers, regional peacekeepers, and even private contractors have arrested fugitives for international crimes.

The peace versus justice dilemma raised by Ferencz led me to a decade of research and study. I came to believe that abstract forces and state competition are the tinder of war, but pyromaniacs are required to light the fire. Law provides institutional possibilities to resist the human decision to set the world ablaze. The cynical view that war is inevitable creates space in which leaders can harness dangerous forces and shirk responsibility for their aggression. It seemed to me that the Nuremberg judgment's breakthrough conclusion that wars are caused by individuals and that those individuals are personally accountable embodied the future's most hopeful approach to peace.

CHAPTER 1

Is Law Dead?

> At his best, man is the noblest of all animals; separated from law
> and justice he is the worst.
> —Aristotle, *Politics*, fourth century BCE

> If you must break the law, do it to seize power: in all other cases
> observe it.
> —Julius Caesar, 100–44 BCE

> "Where has God gone?" he [the madman] cried. "I shall tell you.
> We have killed him –you and I. . . . Whither are we moving now?
> Away from all suns? Are we not perpetually falling? Backward,
> sideward, forward, in all directions? Is there any up or down left?
> Are we not straying as through an infinite nothing?"
> —Friedrich Nietzsche, *The Gay Science*, 1882

Law is neither dead nor irrelevant. It has permeated the bureaucratic,
legalistic structure of the modern war machine.[1] All world leaders acknowledge the post–World War II legal basis for waging war. What differ
among leaders are their strategies in contending with the law, which is as
distinct and demanding a battlefield as are desert, jungle, or urban ter-
rains. Leaders, powerful or not, must negotiate the legal terrain in order
to wage war, including persuading the population of the justice of the
war, persuading allies, persuading domestic and international courts, pur-
chasing weapons, negotiating leases on foreign bases. Law is not simply
an effective formal constraint on power. It can slow leaders or assist their
military goals. Leaders' strategies range from attacking the law, vacu-
ously interpreting the law to justify force, or ignoring the law entirely
unless stopped. This choice of strategies can be seen in reference to the
legal maneuvers of US presidents George W. Bush, Barack Obama, and
Donald Trump. All three leaders have had to deal, in their own way,
with the post–World War II legal order, the basis for the modern crime
of aggression.

BUSH: ATTACKING THE LAW

According to George W. Bush, the 9/11 attacks were a harbinger of "un-precedented dangers" posed by interconnected terrorists including Hamas, Hezbollah, and murky groups in remote deserts and large cities. Bush linked these nonstate groups to an "axis of evil," including North Korea, Iran, and Iraq, which could supply terrorists with weapons of mass destruction in order to attack the United States. The post-9/11 emergency provided Vice-President Dick Cheney and a cadre of militant lawyers with an opportunity to implement their "unitary executive" theory of presidential power.[2] In a legal memorandum to the president, John Yoo argued, "The historical record demonstrates that the power to initiate military hostilities, particularly in response to the threat of an armed attack, rests exclusively with the President."[3] To free the president from international law checks and balances, hard-liners attacked the legitimacy of the post–World War II order. "All international laws are invalid, meaningless attempts to constrict American power," said John Bolton, President Bush's ambassador to the UN.[4]

The Preparatory Commission of the Assembly of States Parties to the ICC was wrestling with the definition of the crime of aggression and its jurisdictional reach at the same time as the United States invaded Iraq.[5] The special working group dissected and reassembled post–World War II legal precedents as President Bush used falsified intelligence about a terrorist attack with weapons of mass destruction to justify the invasion. Bush attacked international law by denying legal protection to detainees the United States unilaterally labeled "terrorists," authorizing torture in violation of international and domestic law, ordering extrajudicial killing, "unsigning" the treaty establishing the ICC, and successfully passing an act authorizing the invasion of The Hague should the ICC seek to prosecute an American for torture or other international crimes.[6] Bush's battlefield strategy was to attack international law into oblivion and wage unrestrained war.

The self-serving lesson of a cadre of "realistic," nationalistic American international law and relations scholars was that international law had been ineffective and should be abandoned when it came to regulating force. For Ferencz, who had experienced Germany's descent into authoritarianism and war, the Bush administration had demonstrated the urgency of a robust post–World War II legal prohibition on force that could check the abuse of executive power. "As long as militants—whether individuals, groups or nations—insist that they alone can determine the legality of their actions," he said, "their military power is not a safeguard but a menace."[7]

One of Bush's prisoners in Iraq was Abu Bakr al-Baghdadi, a "civilian internee" at Camp Bucca. His captors didn't know or care, but Doctor Baghdadi held a PhD from the Islamic University of Baghdad, graduating in Islamic history and law. Rumors suggested he was radicalized early under Saddam Hussein, but forged an alliance with Baathists he met at Camp Bucca. "He was a street thug when we picked him up in 2004," a Pentagon official recalled. "It's hard to imagine we could have had a crystal ball then that would tell us he'd become head of ISIS."[8]

In 2008, Barack Obama became president and inherited Bush's catastrophic illegal war, the broad executive powers Bush had commandeered, and Abu Bakr al-Baghdadi.

OBAMA: NEGOTIATING THE LAW

Bush's Iraq legacy left President Barack Obama in a bind. Al-Baghdadi's fundamentalist jihadist army, ISIS, had swept into Iraq from Syria, threatened to flood Iraq's second largest city by detonating an upstream hydroelectric dam, condemned an ancient religious minority to extermination, beheaded two American journalists on video, and seized a vast swath of the border between Turkey and Syria. The president struggled to find a legal justification to allow the United States to intervene with armed force, but none of the post–World War II legal categories authorizing war fit. Without a dependable legal rationale, the president risked leading the United States into an illegal war like that of his predecessor. As a legal scholar, he must surely have considered the place of law in the gathering war—ennobling beacon, obstacle on the route to power, or infinite nothing.

Complicating matters as Obama considered his options was Major General Charlie Dunlap's influential twenty-first century concept of "lawfare," the use of law as a weapon of war. In 2001, Dunlap argued that international law was becoming part of the problem, not the solution, for humanizing modern war.[9] Dunlap had captured the American legal imagination by taking a powerful set of insights developed by legal scholars in the 1960s and 1970s civil-rights, woman's-rights, and antiwar movements and weaponizing them. These "critical legal scholars" argued that most legal rules are easily manipulated, judges and other officials interpreting the law possess hidden discretion, and the rule of law is a myth. They argued that the law tends to serve the interests of powerful classes entrenched in government and the judiciary. The critical legal scholars never expected their insights about the law to be plundered by the military.

Dunlap's concern was that clever enemies of the United States would manipulate the law to subvert American and humanitarian goals, but other legal scholars saw an opportunity, not a concern. Top Bush-administration lawyer, John Yoo, who had used legal interpretation to increase presidential power to authorize torture and permit warrantless surveillance, called his memoir *War by Other Means*.[10] Scholars of other stripes harnessed the lawfare concept for humanitarian ends. David Krane, the American war-crimes prosecutor who used international law to indict and imprison brutal Sierra Leonean President Charles Taylor, argued that law can be used as a weapon.[11] Once law was depicted as a partisan weapon, its spell was broken, and its authority as arbiter of justice dissipated.

Would Obama, elected to end Bush-era abuses, vindicate the rule of law? Or would the emergency in Iraq and Syria, the temptations of American power, and Dunlap's decoupling of law and justice influence his thinking? ISIS would test the relevance and claim to justice of international law.

Searching for a persuasive legal justification for war, Obama tested a number of judicial interpretations against the facts on the ground. For the war to garner widespread support, which was a strategic imperative, he needed a viable legal rationale.

On the day ISIS captured the Mosul dam, Obama's first air strikes targeted non-dam ISIS positions. In his August 7 address to the nation, Obama announced a renewed war in Iraq and stated his preliminary justifications for war. He said the air strikes were necessary to protect the American Erbil consulate and personnel and at the request of the Iraqi Government, the United States had initiated "a humanitarian effort to help save thousands of Iraqi civilians who are trapped on a mountain without food and water and facing almost certain death."[12] The official request by the Iraqi Government for US assistance put the air strikes on firm international legal ground. But Obama's September 11 vow to expand the war into Syria without a formal invitation was more legally controversial.[13] With a mushrooming list of moral and strategic reasons to wage war against ISIS in Syria, all Obama lacked was a persuasive legal justification.

Obama turned to the deceptively simple post–World War II law of war, applicable in 2014 to states, but not yet to individuals. The blanket prohibition on the use of armed force enshrined in Article 2(4) of the UN Charter has two exceptions. The first is collective action to maintain international peace and security.[14] Only the UN Security Council can authorize a collective response. A textbook example is the 1990 *Operation Desert Storm*, in which the UN approved the use for force against Iraq after Saddam Hussein invaded and annexed Kuwait. The second exception is self-defense in response to an armed attack.[15] The use of force by the United States in Afghanistan following the 9/11 attacks is an oft-repeated example. For the use of armed force to be legal without an invitation, it needs to fulfill the criteria of either exception. Obama had to explain how America's war against ISIS in Syria was an exception to the blanket prohibition against the use of armed force without an invitation.

A year before, when evidence had emerged that Syrian President Bashar al-Assad was testing chemical weapons in Damascus and Aleppo neighborhoods, Obama had drawn his line in the sand. "[A] red line for us is we start seeing a whole bunch of chemical weapons moving around or being utilized," he said.[16] He threatened military engagement if Assad used chemical weapons against his people.

The next day, rockets containing sarin gas were fired into the Ghouta neighborhood of East Damascus, killing over a thousand civilians, including many children.[17] Over sixty states and one hundred civil-society groups demanded the Security Council initiate an ICC investigation.[18] Obama began to plan targeted air strikes in Syria to deter and punish Assad. Syrian and Russian authorities claimed it was fake news, and Russia threatened to veto any ICC accountability or Security Council peace enforcement in Syria.

Faced with the Russian veto, Obama argued that to uphold international law, the United States would need to violate it. Assad's use of chemical weapons was such a heinous violation of fundamental international rules that Obama was prepared to invade Syria. "I'm comfortable going forward without the approval of a United Nations Security Council that, so far, has been completely paralyzed and unwilling to hold Assad accountable."[19] This Orwellian manipulation of the legal norms begged for an independent legal assessment.

Putin countered Obama's argument for war in Syria with an op-ed in the *New York Times*: "Under current international law, force is permitted only in self-defense or by the decision of the Security Council. Anything else is unacceptable under the United Nations Charter and would constitute an act of aggression." Putin blamed the collapse of the League of Nations on flimsy enforcement, and praised the drafters of the UN Charter: "The profound wisdom of this has underpinned the stability of international relations for decades." Putin's credibility was questionable since Russia had invaded Georgia in 2008 and would annex the Crimea in 2014. Interestingly, both Obama's legal dance and Putin's rendition of international law illustrate how law has permeated the war machine and how contradictory legal strategies vie for primacy without an independent institution to assess their claims. "The law is still the law," Putin admonished, "and we must follow it whether we like it or not."[20] But whose law?

In 2014, al-Baghdadi entered the fray with his own legal arguments for war. He summoned *mujahideen* from around the world to join the fight and create a caliphate uniting Islamic peoples.[21] Claiming to be a descendant of the Prophet Mohammed, al-Baghdadi took the title of Caliph Ibrahim. As caliph, he claimed legal authority to order jihad. In response, thousands of foreign jihadis galvanized by a perceived American war on Islam flooded Iraq and Syria. Obama and al-Baghdadi, both legal scholars, understood the essential lesson that law is not a gentle civilizer, it is on a continuum with war—means to the same end.

By the end of summer 2014, Obama was noticeably shaken by the escalating violence in Syria and its destabilizing effect on Iraq. He had witnessed the Syrian president gassing his own people, the meteoric rise of a self-proclaimed caliph, floods of fresh foreign jihadis, and a desperate plea for assistance from Iraq. It seemed to him that the United States and its allies had no choice but to enter Syria in order to defeat ISIS. They could not stop at the Syrian border while jihadis flowed back and forth, recuperating, rearming, and resuming hostilities in Iraq. Dismissing al-Baghdadi's Islamist legal justifications for war, Obama struggled to articulate his own international legal rationale for the use of force.

He tried to use the humanitarian intervention rationale to save the Yezidi from genocide.[22] This had worked in Iraq because of the government's invitation, but not in Syria because most states did not consider humanitarian intervention a stand-alone legal justification in 2014.[23]

He considered "armed reprisals" for ISIS's execution of James Foley as a rationale, but under the 1928 General Treaty for Renunciation of War and the 1945 UN Charter, armed reprisals ceased to be a legal justification for war.[24]

He tried traditional self-defense as a justification, but there had been no armed attack against the United States,[25] and the execution of James Foley did not qualify.[26] The attacker in Iraq was not another state or guerillas sent on behalf of a state. Neither would a potential future attack on the United States by ISIS trigger the right of self-defense.

With no Security Council resolution, humanitarian intervention debatable, reprisals an antiquated justification, and inadequate self-defense criteria, Obama was running out of legal options for the use of force in Syria. He finally settled on a controversial new interpretation of the right of self-defense, an incremental evolution of existing law. Samantha Power, Obama's ambassador to the UN, presented his justification to the Security Council:

> States must be able to defend themselves, in accordance with the inherent right of individual and collective self-defence, as reflected in Article 51 of the Charter of the United Nations, when, as is the case here, the government of the State where the threat is located is unwilling or unable to prevent the use of its territory for such attacks.[27]

Russian Permanent Representative to the UN Vitaly Churkin said "No." He cautioned that armed intervention without Syrian authorization "will pose problems for Russia as well as for many other countries respecting international law, including China."[28] Citing the *Nicaragua Case* and two other important *jus ad bellum* precedents, legal scholar Kevin Jon Heller concurred, "the Court [ICJ] has consistently held that Article 51 of the UN Charter limits self-defensive acts against non-state actors to situations in which the non-state actor's armed attacks are in some way imputable to the state whose territorial sovereignty is being violated."[29] He cited a major academic study by Tom Ruys that concluded, "The only thing that can be said about proportionate transborder measures of self-defence against attacks by non-State actors in cases falling below the *Nicaragua* threshold [i.e., the state has 'effective control' over the nonstate actors] is that they are 'not unambiguously illegal.' "[30]

French Foreign Minister Laurent Fabius expressed doubts about the legality of Obama's argument.[31] The strategic repercussions of this new interpretation of the law of self-defense became apparent. States including France, Belgium, Denmark, and the Netherlands were willing to fight ISIS in Iraq, since the legal justification for war was sound, but not in Syria, where the justification was untested.

Obama's choice of legal strategy, as is usual in modern conflict, shaped the way he conducted war. Obama's choice restricted the United States to an "Iraq first" strategy that targeted ISIS and did not justify force against Assad's use of chemical weapons or against other jihadist groups spreading throughout Syria.

Whether or not self-defense in response to an armed attack by a nonstate entity was permissible when the host state was unwilling or unable to prevent the attacks would remain controversial in international law until an independent, impartial judicial institution was empowered to establish the contours of the law of war. Given this institutional lacuna, Obama made his own legal determination and US special forces and drones spread throughout Syria.

TRUMP: NEGATING THE LAW

Donald Trump was no fan of Obama's red line on chemical weapons in Syria. Soon after Syrian President Bashar al-Assad killed over a thousand innocent people in Ghouta, Trump tweeted:

> Again, to our very foolish leader, do not attack Syria—if you do many very bad things will happen & from that fight the U.S. gets nothing![32]

Trump's preference was to focus on "America first." One hundred days after his inauguration, when videos of a deadly chemical attack on the rebel-held town of Khan Sheikhun surfaced, Trump did an about-face: "That crosses many, many lines, beyond a red line, many, many lines."[33] In a hasty unilateral decision—without proper interagency process, or congressional approval, or consultation with allies, or Security Council authorization,[34] or any legal rationale—Trump launched fifty-nine Tomahawk cruise missiles from warships at Syria's al-Shayrat airfield, the apparent origin of the chemical attack.[35]

Trump's volley hit Syrian-regime targets, not ISIS fighters attacking Iraq. His tactic was to obliterate Obama's international-law rationale for force, and negate the rule of law. Trump's missile strike had no justification under international law: it was not pursuant to an invitation by a state, not in defense of Iraq, and the target was not the ISIS invader. Obama had also requested congressional authorization to expand the US mission in Syria after the 2013 Ghouta chemical attacks, and had been rejected. Trump opted not only to ignore international law, but to ignore Congress as well and rely solely on presidential power. Beyond pounding sand with sixty million dollars' worth of cruise missiles, Trump had no strategy except to do as he pleased until he was stopped.

Dangerously, the positive reactions to Trump's Tomahawk spectacle taught the new president that the individuals whose job it was to enforce the legal checks and balances would overlook his transgressions as long as he broke the law to advance their agendas. Trump's honeymoon period in the White House had been marred by accusations of Russian election collusion and impeachment talk. By attacking Russian interests in Syria, Trump rallied Americans and demonstrated independence. Republican critics praised him, democratic adversaries backed his actions, the United Kingdom, Canada, Israel, Turkey, and Jordan were on side.[36] Trump's rhetorical attacks on NATO, the EU, and the UN caused blowback, but when he got it right, allies and enemies alike applauded his onslaught on the rule of law and praised his accumulation of authoritarian power.

Following the Tomahawk spectacle, rather than enduring daily accountability to the legislature, the judiciary, and the "fake news," Trump would govern by decree and check his ratings with the voters in four years' time.

LAW AND THE WAR MACHINE

Whether attacking, negotiating, or negating the law, leaders' international legal strategies are affecting the conduct of war, even by the most militarily powerful nations in the world.

The seminal debate about the place of international law in the conduct of war was between legal scholars Thomas Franck and Louis Henkin. Franck's explosive article in the *American Journal of International Law* argued that the UN Charter's prohibition on the use of force was dead because the great powers violated the prohibition with impunity and had replaced the post–World War II order with one governed by archaic nineteenth-century principles of balance of power.[37] Henkin replied that Franck's report of the death of the UN Charter's prohibition on force was "greatly exaggerated."[38] Franck judged the law's vitality only by its failures, he said. "In my view, the death certificate is premature and the indictment for legicide must be redrawn to charge lesser though aggravated degrees of assault." He pointed out that states have resorted to war less frequently and less destructively since the UN Charter was created, while acknowledging that war had not been rendered obsolete: "What has become obsolete is the notion that nations are free to indulge it as ever, and the death of that notion is accepted in the Charter."[39]

But neither Franck's nor Henkin's accounts of the law properly explained Bush's, Obama's, or Trump's behavior. International law wasn't dead, as Franck maintained. But to say these presidents were dutiful, law-abiding citizens, as Henkin implied, didn't capture it either.[40] Similarities and differences in these leaders' approaches to international law revealed all three presidents navigating a minefield of treaties, customs, rules, and institutions. They faced the same post–World War II legal terrain, and asked themselves the same strategic questions. "Who will *want* to regulate this transaction? Who will *be able to do so*? What rules will influence the transaction even absent enforcement? And they assess opportunities . . . to influence the rules, or to use them in new ways to achieve their strategic objective."[41] All three presidents behaved like chief executive officers (CEOs) assessing the strategic repercussions of the law for their company. But they would learn that even without centralized enforcement, the law had its own authority and, one way or the other, had to be considered.

President Bush's first term was characterized by what appeared to be a dramatic repudiation of international law.[42] Bush withdrew the United States from the 1972 Anti-Ballistic Missile (ABM) Treaty with Russia, "unsigned" the Rome Statute, illegally invaded Iraq, authorized torture and other violations of the Geneva Conventions, created an archipelago of black sites where the detained were interrogated,[43] failed to "prevent or punish" the genocide in Darfur in violation of US obligations under the 1948 Genocide Convention, and refused to sign any treaties, old or new, limiting violence in war.[44]

This adversarial approach to the rule of law and embrace of "the dark side" played well with nationalistic domestic audiences and the far right of the Republican Party, but created institutional blowback at home and abroad.[45] Generals and Defense Department officials testified in Congressional hearings that Bush's approach was souring relationships with key allies in the "war on terror," harming US effectiveness, and creating voids of contact quickly filled by powerful adversaries, including China.[46] Bush changed tack in his second term, when John Bellinger III became legal advisor to the State Department. Bellinger reaffirmed US commitments to international law, increased US engagement with international institutions such as the ICC, and justified US foreign policy in legal terms.[47] Like a Texas oil tycoon expanding into a new market, Bush began with jingoistic swagger but calibrated his behavior to function more efficiently amongst new peers.

Of the three presidents, it was Obama whose relationship with international law was most erudite. Under the first of two competing scholarly accounts of his relationship with international law, Obama recommitted the United States to the rule of law in international affairs.[48] He immediately ended the Bush-era policies that violated the Torture Convention and the Geneva Conventions.[49] Obama's Nobel Peace Prize acceptance speech is described as "the clearest explanation of how and when he has chosen to wage war."[50] In it, he credited post–World War II international law and institutions with preventing World War III. While recognizing the limitations of the post–World War II state-centered legal regime for regulating today's threats, he called for a "gradual evolution of human institutions," based on the principle that "all nations—strong and weak alike—must adhere to standards that govern the use of force."[51] Harold Koh, legal advisor to the State Department, explained the "Obama-Clinton Doctrine": "1. *Principled Engagement*; 2. Diplomacy as a Critical Element of *Smart Power*; 3. *Strategic Multilateralism; and* 4. the notion that *Living Our Values* Makes us Stronger and Safer, by Following *Rules of Domestic and International Law; and Following Universal Standards, Not Double Standards.*"[52] Koh's account made Obama seem like the CEO of Whole Foods, getting rich by saving the world.

Under the competing account, President Obama's approach to international law was a continuation of Bush's second term.[53] Both presidents, the argument goes, built legal regimes that served US interests and sidelined others.[54] Candidate Obama was a supporter of the ICC during the 2008 campaign, but did little for the court once elected. Obama criticized Bush's "enhanced interrogation" of terrorists, but ordered the summary execution of suspected terrorists abroad. Bush invaded Iraq without UN authorization; Obama invaded Syria. Both presidents relied on problematic legal arguments for force and spurned external judicial oversight. Bush's footprint in Afghanistan and Iraq was heavy; Obama left "heavy doses of light-footprint" in new theaters involving drones, special forces, and cyberattacks.[55] "I am convinced," Obama said, accepting his Nobel

Prize, "that adhering to standards, international standards, strengthens those who do, and isolates and weakens those who don't." He called his position "enlightened self-interest."[56] General Dunlap might have called it lawfare.

Unlike his predecessors, Trump's legal strategy was a showy negation of the law to curry public opinion. Harvard professors Steven Levitsky and Daniel Ziblatt dubbed him "a serial norm-breaker."[57] Two months into Trump's presidency, Jack Goldsmith wrote, "We are witnessing the beginnings of the greatest presidential onslaught on international law and international institutions in American history."[58] Trump quickly gutted the State Department and unleashed the military. He slowed down or halted all new international agreements and prepared to terminate the Iran Nuclear Deal, the Paris Climate Agreement, and the North American Free Trade Agreement (NAFTA). He threatened to defund international organizations including the UN, and to quit NATO. He expanded Obama's targeted killing campaign and reduced its oversight. According to Human Rights Watch, Trump "put the postwar human rights system at risk."[59]

University of Vienna legal scholar Ralph Janik described Trump as a Hegelian for his absolutist view of state sovereignty, his belief that state law is paramount to international law, and that treaties are "tainted with contingency." These Hegelian proclivities, "a relic of the past," found new traction with Trump's authoritarian-populist surge.[60]

Historical analogies provided interesting insight, but it is Trump's behavior as a real-estate mogul that best explains his international legal strategy as president. In three decades of business Trump was involved in 4,095 private lawsuits, including litigation with casino patrons, sexual harassment claims, an investigation into alleged misuse of charity funds, refusal to pay contractors, million-dollar real-estate suits, an argument over the location of an ostentatious flagpole at his Mar-a-Lago resort, and a fraud suit brought by students at Trump University over claims of worthless diplomas.[61] These lawsuits paint a portrait of a litigious individual with a cadre of top lawyers who behaves as he pleases until he is blocked. Because of vast power discrepancies between Trump and most of his adversaries, the odds were in his favor. Trump's volley of legally problematic executive actions—travel ban, attempt to reopen black sites,[62] unilateral missile attacks on Syria—reveal a similar approach: press forward until blocked.

In the twenty-first century, law isn't dead. It has infiltrated the war machine and had, in various ways, shaped the military and political decisions of US presidents. The task of the drafters of the crime of aggression was to refit the law of war for the coming age and attract buy-in from the nations of the world. If the behavior of Bush, Obama, and Trump was any indication, leaders would employ a range of legal strategies to avoid constraints on their power to wage war.

CHAPTER 2

Timeslip

INVASION OF THE CRIMEA, COLLAPSE OF THE LEAGUE OF NATIONS

> Hegel says somewhere that all great historic facts and personages
> recur twice. He forgot to add: Once as tragedy, and again as farce.
> —Karl Marx, *The Eighteenth Brumaire of Louis Bonaparte*,
> December 1851–March 1852

> timeslip *n.* a rift or flaw in the fabric of time that allows travel
> between two or more periods of time or timelines.
> —Jeff Prucher, *Brave New Words: The Oxford Dictionary
> of Science Fiction*

> The future is certain; it is only the past that is unpredictable.
> —Old Soviet joke

In the winter of 2014, a timeslip opened in the Crimea. Vladimir Putin caused it at the end of the Sochi Olympics when he occupied and annexed the autonomous Ukrainian republic and the historic city of Sevastopol. The sensation was one of disorientation. Were we in 1938, as Hillary Clinton maintained, with Hitler claiming he was defending ethnic Germans as he annexed the Czechoslovakian Sudetenland? Or, as Putin contended, had we returned to 1944 Ukraine, with Russians bravely battling foreign-backed, anti-Semitic Ukrainian nationalists. Other disoriented policymakers and pundits found themselves in 1999 Kosovo, or 2008 Georgia, wherever time slipped for them. Putin annexed the Crimea without the UN enforcing the prohibition on aggression, and it appeared the rift had opened into the 1930s when the League of Nations failed to enforce its collective security covenant against Hitler's aggression. When the collective security system faltered, World War II began. Would Putin's invasion collapse the UN and, with it, the rule of law?

The crisis in the Crimea caused a flurry of argumentation that proved that international law was still twitching. It was, in fact, influencing the war machine by reconfiguring the attention of world leaders. Putin and Obama presented a panoply of legal arguments with historical analogies intended to support their strategies. These arguments interpreted the law chauvinistically, but because they relied on common legal rules and precedents, the by-product was a buttressing of the authority of law. Now, what was needed was an independent institution and an authoritative legal process to evaluate their divergent claims. The ICC seemed the logical impartial institution—it had a proven track record of independent adjudication of politically charged cases against political and military leaders.

The danger, however, was that any ICC attempt to discipline the leader of a great power such as Russia might cause the court's collapse. There were two obvious ways this could happen. ICC prosecutor Fatou Bensouda or her successor would initiate a case against a powerful leader for aggression, but the ICC's member states would be too intimidated to make the arrest, revealing impotence and snuffing out the court's authority. Alternatively, Bensouda or judges aware of their enforcement limits might invoke technical legal reasons not to arrest or prosecute. This would expose the ICC to accusations of bias, undermining its legitimacy.

The League of Nations collapsed when it failed to confront Hitler's aggression. The fact is, confronting or not confronting could lead to collapse. Given this harsh reality, the successors to the League traded total effectiveness for resilience and survival. For the UN, this was the Security Council veto. The veto allowed Russia and the other four great powers to prevent enforcement action against themselves. For the ICC, this meant having no jurisdiction over the leaders of non-ICC states that had committed the crime of aggression. Although far from ideal, these safety valves allowed the UN and the ICC to avoid the unfortunate fate of the League.

Why consider together the collapse of the League of Nations, the design of the UN and the ICC, and the legal argumentation of Putin and Obama? Putin's invasion and the collapse of the League raise vital questions about the survival of the UN and the ICC, and the condition of the rule of law today.

The connections begin with the invasion of the Crimea.

THE CRIMEA CIRCUS

Crimeans awoke one morning and were unnerved to discover hundreds of little green men in their midst. Still basking in the magic of the televised closing ceremony of the Olympic games in Sochi, Russia's thrilling tribute to its circus heritage occupied their dreams. Now the circus had come to town. Little green men were everywhere—milling around airports, roadblocks, and government buildings, donning balaclavas and military fatigues. Clearly, they were human, not Martian. But without any identifying badges or insignia to speak of, the particular variety of human and the legal character of the operation remained up for debate.

February had not been tranquil in the Ukraine. Ukrainian President Viktor Yanukovich had reneged on a European Association agreement in favor of a Russian one, sparking student protests that escalated into popular revolution in Kiev. The "Euromaidan Revolution" provoked a secessionist backlash in the Crimea, an autonomous Ukrainian republic on the north coast of the Black Sea, populated predominantly by ethnic Russians.

Russian President Vladimir Putin called a press conference, insisting Russian troops were not meddling in a sovereign state: the heavily armed, tightly coordinated groups who took over Crimea's airports and ports at the start of the incursion were merely spontaneous "self-defence groups" who may have acquired their Russian-looking uniforms from local shops.[1] Russian Minister of Defense Sergey Shoygu added, "Regarding the statements about use of Russian special forces in Ukrainian events, I can only say one thing—it's hard to search for a black cat in a dark room, especially if it's not there." He warned that it would be "stupid" to search for the cat if it is "intelligent, brave, and polite."[2] Polish Minister of Foreign Affairs Radek Sikorski asked Putin for the address of a shop in Ukraine or Russia where people can purchase Strela surface-to-air missile systems and T-64 tanks.[3]

What ringmaster had conjured these foreign soldiers? Ukrainians turned to their crafty leader, but he was gone.

President Viktor Yanukovich disappeared from Kiev on February 21, 2014, at the close of the winter Olympics. Police guarding his private home withdrew quietly, allowing Euromaidan protesters to enter and witness the president's opulence. They fingered his gold bathroom fixtures, tinkled his grand piano, admired the ostriches in his private zoo.

Yanukovich's political machinations in Ukraine's 2004 presidential election had included voter intimidation, electoral fraud, and the massive corruption that sparked the 2004 Orange Revolution in which thousands of demonstrators peacefully converged on Kiev's Independence Square to protest the results. Ukraine's Supreme Court ordered a revote and Yanukovich's rival, Viktor Yushchenko, took power in an internationally monitored election. But by 2010 Yushchenko had squandered his goodwill by mishandling the financial crisis. Yanukovich was reelected by a narrow margin and immediately imprisoned his new rival, Yulia Tymoshenko, a heroine of the Orange Revolution, charged with exceeding her powers as prime minister. In civil conflict, as in international conflict, lawfare is endemic, courts are easily cowed by power, and Herculean judges hard to find.

In November 2013, when President Yanukovich reneged on his campaign promise to forge closer ties with Europe, eight hundred thousand protesters took their grievance to Independence Square, where the Orange Revolution had begun, and occupied City Hall. The Yanukovich Government, seen by many in Kiev as a fat-cat fraternity from hometown Donetsk, responded with authoritarian antiprotest laws. Twenty thousand Euromaidan protesters marched to parliament, the Rada, to demand that Ukraine's constitution be restored to its pre-Yanukovich state. Police fired live ammunition into the rowdy crowd, and government forces—including rooftop snipers—killed an estimated hundred protesters, whom Euromaidans called the "Heavenly Hundred."

Less heavenly were the Ukrainian fascists who joined anti-Yanukovich demonstrations, manning roadblocks, protecting opposition leaders, and confronting police with jerry-rigged petrol bombs.[4] Europhiles within the Euromaidan movement cringed at the sight of hooligans with fascist badges in their ranks. The fascists adorned Kiev's City Hall, now an activist base, with symbols of white power: the Nazi Wolfsangel rune; Celtic cross; Confederate flag; a portrait of Ukrainian partisan leader Stepan Bandera, aligned with the fascists during World War II until they turned on him.[5] Far-right leaders from Svoboda and Right Sector parties revived nationalist chants from the 1930s and taught them to protesters. "Glory to the nation," they shouted. "Death to the enemies!" roared the crowd.[6]

Yanukovich's benefactor, Vladimir Putin, had made a last-ditch attempt in December 2013 to rescue Yanukovich in the eyes of his people, buying fifteen billion dollars of Ukrainian debt and dropping natural-gas prices by a third. But not even an emergency deal brokered by Russian Special Envoy Vladimir Lukin and European Union mediators Radek Sikorski of Poland, Laurent Fabius of France, and Frank-Walter Steinmeier of Germany could diffuse the crisis. Demonstrations escalated and protestors demanding the president's removal took control of Kiev's parliament. Yanukovich disappeared like a will-o'-the-wisp.

On February 22, 2014, in a hasty 328-to-0 parliamentary vote, Ukrainian lawmakers impeached Yanukovich and appointed Oleksandr Turchynov as acting president. Yanukovich, whereabouts unknown, appeared on local television in a prerecorded address. "What is happening now is to a great extent . . . vandalism, banditry and a coup d'état," he claimed. "We see the repeat of the Nazi events, when in the 1930s in Germany and Austria the Nazis came to power. This is a repeat of that. They banned parties. The same is happening now. They are . . . chasing, beating people, burning houses, offices."[7] The interwar analogy struck a nerve with Yanukovich supporters. Opponents rolled their eyes at what they considered shameless legal-historical propaganda. Ukrainian Interior Minister Arsen Avakov, without the need to play the historical-legal game, issued an arrest warrant for Yanukovich. His Facebook post was succinct: "A criminal case has been initiated into mass murders of peaceful civilians."[8]

Soon after, the Rada took legislative action that alarmed Ukraine's Russian-speaking population. Delegates elected a provisional government purged of Yanukovich allies and pro-Russian delegates. Representatives from the nationalist Svoboda party pushed moderate lawmakers into revoking a law guaranteeing minority languages, including Russian, equal status and protection.[9] The Rada unanimously voted to release pro-Western, anti-Russian politician Yulia Tymoshenko from prison, whereupon she went directly to Independence Square, invoked the Orange Revolution, and fired up the hundred-thousand-strong Euromaidan crowd.

The White House applauded "constructive work in the Rada," and urged "the prompt formation of a broad, technocratic government of national unity."[10] But this was wishful thinking in a country so starkly divided and hobbled by corruption. Polish Foreign Minister Radek Sikorski, who helped negotiate the February 21 "Agreement on the Settlement of Crisis in Ukraine," tweeted, "No coup in Kiev. Gov. buildings got abandoned. Speaker of Rada elected legally."[11]

German legal scholar Stefan Soesanto was not so sure: "Ascertaining the legitimacy of the interim government in Kiev is quite tricky . . . for an effective impeachment under constitutional rules the 449-seated parliament would have needed 337 votes to remove Yanukovych from office."[12] There were 328 votes. "Thus under the current constitution," Soesanto concluded, "Yanukovych is still the incumbent and legitimate President of the Ukraine." For an impeachment to be beyond reproach, Yanukovich had to be formally charged with a crime, the Constitutional Court had to review the charges, and three-quarters of the Rada had to vote to remove him. Instead, to speed things along, anti-Yanukovich lawmakers maintained that he withdrew from his duties in an unconstitutional manner.[13] They bypassed the Constitutional Court and held the impeachment vote without a quorum.

All the players knew that to legitimize political violence and make it of lasting historical significance, it had to be ratified by law. But with so much legal horseplay and no impartial referee, everyone claimed victory.

The plush towels in Yanukovich's abandoned Kiev residence were still damp when, on February 23, pro-Russian demonstrations mirroring the Euromaidan protests in Kiev erupted in the Crimean port city of Sevastopol. *Guardian* reporter Howard Amos attended the protest and described a crowd of thousands, chanting, "Russia, Russia, Russia."[14] The gathering voted to establish a replacement administration with the grizzled pro-Russian businessman Aleksei Chaly as mayor and its own independent defense squads. Protesters welcomed Ukraine's disbanded riot police, accused of shooting Euromaidan protesters in Kiev, with flowers and hugs. Amos interviewed anti-Maidan protesters, who branded the new administration in Kiev fascist and Banderist.

Within days of the Sevastopol demonstration, little green men fanning out from the Russian naval base in Sevastopol outnumbered Ukrainian army and naval forces.[15] Alarmed Ukrainian border guards reported a build-up of armored equipment across the narrow channel with Russia.[16] Approximately two-dozen badgeless soldiers with assault rifles and missile launchers stormed the Crimean parliament in a predawn raid. Pro-Russian local politician Sergey Aksyonov, nicknamed "Goblin," greeted them a few hours later and mustered lawmakers for a vote on secession from Ukraine.

In Moscow, Putin asked for authorization from the Federation Council, Russia's upper house, to use military force in Ukraine.[17] It took barely thirty minutes for lawmakers to unanimously approve the request. The Federation Council's March 1 authorization was not limited to the Crimea, it included the rest of the Ukraine too. In a tense ninety-minute phone call with Barack Obama the same day, Putin argued that "ultranationalists" were threatening "the lives and health of Russian citizens" in Crimea.[18] Putin's legal-historical allusions would mean nothing to Obama, with legal-historical precedents of his own. For Putin, unchecked by an international arbiter, law was part and parcel of military strategy.

As Putin expounded his historical interpretation, units of little green men supported by thousands of plain-clothes volunteers seized air- and sea-ports and established checkpoints at highway crossings from mainland Ukraine, effectively cutting off the peninsula.[19] Reinforced with armored convoys, cargo aircraft, and combat helicopters, they overran Ukrainian military bases, politely offering Ukrainian troops the opportunity to leave unharmed.[20] Sitting in Putin's shadow and faced with overwhelming force, they accepted. In three days, without a shot fired, Goblin was in de facto control of the Crimean Peninsula. His *de jure* status was more questionable.

On March 16, the Autonomous Republic of Crimea and the local government of Sevastopol held a referendum where voters—with Russian soldiers "keeping the peace"—were asked whether they wanted to join Russia as a federal subject or restore Crimea's status as part of Ukraine. A total of 97% of Crimeans casting ballots voted for integration with Russia. "Under the stage direction of the Russian Federation, a circus performance is underway: the so-called referendum," Ukrainian Prime Minister Arseniy Yatsenyuk seethed. "Also taking part in the performance are 21,000 Russian troops, who with their guns are trying to prove the legality of the referendum."[21]

Barack Obama promised the result would "never be recognized" by the United States. The UN General Assembly held a vote of its own—one hundred in favor, eleven against, fifty-eight abstentions—condemning the referendum as invalid and affirming Ukraine's territorial integrity and political independence.[22] The United States sponsored a draft Security Council resolution reaffirming Ukraine's "sovereignty, independence, unity and territorial integrity," and declaring Crimea's break with Ukraine and union with Russia invalid.[23] Thirteen of fifteen Security Council members backed the resolution, but Russia vetoed it (China abstained). "Russia has the power to veto a Security Council resolution," said US Permanent Representative Samantha Power, "but it does not have the power to veto the truth."[24] Unfazed, the Kremlin officially annexed the Crimean peninsula.[25]

For over a year, Putin denied Russian involvement. The deed was done, but with no effective international arbiter, legal posturing exacerbated the fog of war.

Politicians and pundits struggled to pinpoint our location in time and place, but the legal-historical analogies with Putin's invasion were baffling. For Martin Brown, historian of Central Europe, it was easy to explain the appeal of historical comparisons: "They calm fears of an uncertain future with reassuring reflections back to a comfortably misunderstood parable from the past, while effortlessly transforming 'unknown, unknowns' into 'known, knowns' with supposedly predictable policy outcomes."[26] Unfortunately, the onslaught of competing parables in the Crimean crisis also made the past uncertain. With so much uncertainty to exploit, the temptation to interpret history to validate a preferred policy proved insurmountable.

The Hitler comparison was an obvious landmark, but it was quickly gutted beyond recognition like a strategic town warring armies are eager to seize. John McCain joined Hillary Clinton in the Hitler-era allusions by comparing German Chancellor Angela Merkel to British Prime Minister Neville Chamberlain. Merkel was pressing for a negotiated solution with Putin, while McCain advocated for a military response. "I am firmly convinced this conflict cannot be solved with military means," Merkel told the 2015 Munich Security Conference.[27] "History shows us that dictators will always take more if you let them," McCain shot back.[28]

At the end of the Sochi Olympics, Russian chess master and Putin critic Garry Kasparov tweeted about the possibility of a "Ukrainian Anschluss," and reminded his followers that Russia's invasion of Georgia had taken place during the 2008 Beijing Olympics.[29] Kasparov compared Putin's propaganda methods and invasion tactics to Hitler's, and warned that another former Soviet republic, the Ukraine, would be annexed in 2014 unless the West took decisive action to stop it.

Ultimately, the historical-legal account that mattered most was Putin's. Where he located himself in time and place might reveal useful information about his intentions. Or not.

PUTIN'S CASE

On March 18, 2014, Putin delivered a speech to the Russian State Duma (the lower house) where he asked lawmakers to add two new entities to the Russian Federation, the Republic of Crimea and the City of Sevastopol.[30] In this call for annexation, punctuated by standing ovations, Putin revealed his version of Crimean history. It was an intoxicating fog of shared Russo-Crimean victory and humiliation that began with his namesake, Prince Vladimir, being driven out of Russia by his fratricidal brother in 976, and continued through a litany of Crimean landmarks where historic Russian battles were won and lost over a thousand years. The purpose of Putin's historical exegesis was to make a political point with more emotional resonance than logical consistency: "In people's hearts and minds," he reasoned, "Crimea has always been an inseparable part of Russia."[31]

As a result of its history, Putin proudly explained, "Crimea is a unique blend of different peoples' cultures and traditions. This makes it similar to Russia as a whole, where not a single ethnic group has been lost over the centuries."[32] Putin envisaged Russia as a tolerant, multiethnic state, in contrast to the fascist "Banderists" next door who had usurped the government in Kiev and were stripping Ukrainian minorities, including those of Russian ancestry, of their rights. Throughout the speech, Putin glossed over Russia's sordid history of persecution of ethnic minorities, most conspicuously Stalin's genocides, and trivialized Russia's mistreatment of the Crimean Tatars, approximately two hundred thousand of whom Russia forcibly deported to Central Asia in boxcars during World War II.[33] "True, there was a time when Crimean Tatars were treated unfairly, just as a number of other peoples in the USSR. There is only one thing I can say here: millions of people of various ethnicities suffered during those repressions, and primarily Russians."[34]

In Putin's account, the 1954 transfer of Crimea and Sevastopol from Russia to the Ukraine was a massive blunder, equal parts tragedy and farce. While Nikita Khrushchev's decision was bizarre, it was ultimately a formality since the Crimea and Sevastopol were transferred within the USSR, a single state. But with the collapse of the Soviet Union in 1990, the "impossible became a reality. . . . It was only when Crimea ended up as part of a different country that Russia realised that it was not simply robbed, it was plundered." Crimeans, Putin lamented, felt as if they had been handed over like "a sack of potatoes."[35]

Compounding this "outrageous historical injustice," the Ukrainian authorities milked the country, fought amongst themselves for power, and attempted to deprive Ukrainian Russians of their language and history. When "Nationalists, neo-Nazis, Russophobes and anti-Semites executed this coup [in 2014 Kiev]," Crimeans called on Russia for help. "Naturally," Putin told the Duma, "we could not leave this plea unheeded; we could not abandon Crimea and its residents in distress."[36]

Putin's historical account corresponded neatly with his legal rationale for the annexation of the Crimea. With the United States, the United Kingdom, and France certain to block any UN Security Council resolution authorizing Russia to use force to restore peace and security in the Crimea, and without an armed attack by Ukraine against Russia to justify self-defense, Putin's legal options were dismal. He was left with four conceivable arguments: intervention by invitation, the defense of Russian nationals, humanitarian intervention, and intervention to help vindicate Crimeans' right to self-determination.[37] Putin threw them all against the wall like undercooked spaghetti, hoping something would stick. For good measure and in line with the maxim "the best defense is a good offense," he proceeded to attack as hypocrites those Western officials calling the annexation illegal.

Putin argued first that he had a request from Yanukovich, hiding in Russia, to intervene and restore peace in the Crimea. The problem with this argument was that Putin had undercut himself by telling the press, "under the agreement [of February 21, brokered by Russian and European mediators in Kiev] . . . Mr. Yanukovych actually handed over power."[38] Nor would the request to intervene from the recently appointed pro-Russian Prime Minister of the Crimea, Sergey Aksyonov, a.k.a. Goblin, suffice. Putting aside for a moment the questionable legality of Aksyonov's appointment, it was the Ukrainian national authorities who possessed the power to issue the invitation, not the regional Crimean ones.

Putin's argument that little green men were needed to protect Russian nationals also stretched international law beyond reason. Some international lawyers maintain that states have a limited right to intervene in another state to protect their citizens if three conditions are met: there is an imminent threat, the territorial state is unable to protect them, and the intervening state strictly confines its objective to protecting its nationals.[39] But even presupposing an actual threat, Putin contravened the third prong of the doctrine, which strictly limits the scope of the intervention. The prototypical case, which the Russian intervention did not resemble at all, was the 1976 Israeli raid on Entebbe to rescue Israeli hostages on an Air France jet from Palestine Liberation Organization (PLO) hijackers when Ugandan President Idi Amin, a PLO accomplice, was unwilling to help. A small team of Israeli commandos stormed the airport, killed the hijackers, rescued the hostages, and left the country within ninety minutes. The fact that the Russian Constitution "guarantees its citizens defense and patronage beyond its boundaries"[40] and that the Crimean intervention was legally authorized by the Federation Council did not make it legal under international law, which has its own independent criteria.

Putin was no fan of humanitarian intervention. He saw it as another Western pretext for power grabs, allowing the United States to circumvent the Russian veto in the Security Council, and railed against NATO intervention to protect persecuted communities in Kosovo (1999) and Libya (2011). Nevertheless, he toyed with the idea in his March 4 press conference: "What is our biggest concern? We see the rampage of reactionary forces, nationalist and anti-Semitic forces going on in certain parts of Ukraine, including Kiev."[41]

But there was no large-scale loss of life tantamount to genocide or ethnic cleansing (Putin himself claimed that not a shot was fired during the occupation of the Crimea), diplomatic avenues to peace were not exhausted, there was no serious attempt to implicate the Security Council or any other legitimate international body in a peace enforcement mission, and Russia's use of force, which resulted in the occupation and annexation of the Crimea, was grossly disproportionate to any human protection purpose. The legal argument was, at best, half cooked. Harvard historian Michael Ignatieff, one of the drafters of the Responsibility-to-Protect doctrine, called it a "grotesque caricature."[42]

With intervention by invitation on shaky footing, the defense of nationals a controversial doctrine among international lawyers, and humanitarian intervention a "grotesque caricature," Putin fell back on a legal concept from the interwar period, the right of peoples to self-determination. In Putin's view, Crimeans should have the opportunity to choose whether to secede from the Ukraine. Considering the simmering secessionist tendencies of various minorities in Russia—Chechens, Circassians, Karachay, Balkars, Abazins, Kumyks, just to name a few—this argument was probably ill advised.

When Putin made the case for Crimean self-determination in his speech to the Duma, he was invoking Woodrow Wilson's guiding principle when redrawing the world map in 1919 Paris. However, the historical precedent he drew on was 1999 Kosovo, where NATO, ignoring Russian protestations, had helped the embattled Kosovar Albanians in their armed struggle to secede from Serbia. "I do not like to resort to quotes, but in this case, I cannot help it,"[43] Putin told the Duma. He proceeded to cite the 2010 ruling of the International Court of Justice on Kosovo's unilateral declaration of independence from Serbia: "General international law contains no prohibition on declarations of independence."[44] Putin leapt to the mistaken conclusion that because international law does not prohibit a people from unilaterally *declaring* independence, Crimea was within its rights to unilaterally *secede* from the Ukraine: "Crystal clear, as they say."[45]

What he neglected to mention was that Article 73 of the Ukraine Constitution requires a national referendum for any territorial adjustment.[46] Putin also ignored the Supreme Court of Canada's authoritative 1998 decision on the legality of unilateral secession by Quebec, invariably cited by national and international tribunals contending with secessionist claims. Here, the Canadian Supreme Court conducted a thorough analysis of international law and held that there is, in fact, no legal entitlement to secession. A referendum in favor of secession, at best, creates an obligation on both sides to negotiate the future legal status of the territory.[47]

A decade before the annexation of Crimea, Putin published a book called *Judo: History, Theory, Practice*, where he tells the story of Akayama, the founder of jujitsu, walking amongst the cherry trees in wintertime. Akayama notices that a thick branch has snapped under the weight of the snow, while a small, flexible branch has bent all the way to the ground, set to spring back when the opportunity presents itself. Putin writes: "When Akayama saw this, he fell into contemplation and exclaimed, 'You must first surrender in order to ultimately gain victory!' "[48] Putin used a similar image toward the end of his Duma speech when he warned the West, "If you compress the spring all the way to its limit, it will snap back hard."[49]

Putin perceived Western-backed regime change in Kiev as the spring's limit and seized the opportunity to snap back hard. In both Georgia and Ukraine, protesters in the mid-2000s had ousted pro-Russian administrations in Western-backed color revolutions: the Rose Revolution in Georgia and the Orange Revolution in Ukraine. These regime changes coincided with NATO's eastward expansion toward Russia and the accession into NATO of Bulgaria, Estonia, Latvia, Lithuania, Romania, Slovakia, and Slovenia. Putin saw NATO's eastward enlargement into Russia's Cold War–era strategic zone as "a serious provocation" and a betrayal of American and European post–Cold War security guarantees.[50] He also knew, but ignored the fact, that voluntary accession of former Russian republics into NATO was not a legal justification for war.

Elements of his Duma speech resembled nothing more than an application of the theory and practice of judo to the conduct of international politics. Putin buttressed his position by arguing that the Crimean referendum to secede from Ukraine and join Russia was "in full compliance with democratic procedures and international norms." He proceeded to exploit widespread resentment toward US military intervention abroad to gain traction for his cause. "Our Western partners, led by the United

States of America, prefer not to be guided by international law in their practical policies, but by the rule of the gun," he maintained. "They have come to believe in their exclusivity and exceptionalism, that they can decide the destinies of the world, that only they can ever be right."[51] He cited as examples the 1999 NATO bombing of Serbia, the 2001 use of force against Afghanistan, the 2003 invasion of Iraq, and the 2011 NATO intervention in Libya. Unless Russia sprung back, Putin warned, Ukraine would be absorbed into NATO and he would be visiting US and European troops in Sevastopol instead of Russia's historic Black Sea Fleet.

For Putin the judoka, his best defense was a good offense. He shored up his position in the Crimea using international law as a crucial pivot and harnessed the momentum of the attack against his opponents, leaving them exposed and off-balance. Obama parried Putin's legal arguments, saying "President Putin seems to have a different set of lawyers making a different set of interpretations, but I don't think that's fooling anybody."[52]

Monitoring Crimean developments from afar, a pattern began to emerge. Attempts had been made to ratify every act of political violence with legal and historical justifications. When the time came for a rejoinder, it seemed that it would be fitting for it to be legal and historical as well. Both leaders had acknowledged the authority of international law in their rush to justify their actions by its terms, but neither was prepared to agree to an impartial referee to judge the validity of his claims. Their unchecked legal argumentation presaged the "post-truth" politics that would become a defining feature of the coming period.

A clear, widely accepted definition of the crime of aggression, interpreted by an impartial, objective, and transparent judicial institution was a potential antidote. Inadvertently, by using legal arguments to advance their agendas, the belligerents were fortifying the strictures that would restrain their actions, and the actions of others.

Western and Russian decision making in the Crimean crisis was propelled by the memory of different tragedies. The West was preoccupied with its victimization by Hitler, a "post-truth" leader who, without domestic and international laws capable of checking him, manipulated the German people to support a catastrophic war. The West's argumentative style was primarily formalistic. It accused Russia of violating established international laws and its intervention in the region was meant to compel Russia to comply. Putin's argumentative style was contextual. He explained the annexation of the Crimea in light of past events, tracing Russia's claim to its origins. Putin's international legal arguments were but an element of that story meant to demonstrate that the West was morally bankrupt and its self-righteous rhetoric was hypocritical.

The West and Russia both based their arguments on self-serving analogical reasoning, deciding which events to include, arranging them in a certain order and stressing some while subordinating others. Loudly, dramatically, they exploited the illusion of determinate analogical reasoning to sway populations to their preferred policies, thereby hardening their countries' positions, making a negotiated settlement seem immoral.

Perhaps the most worrisome question was how the Russian incursion would affect the stability of the post–World War II international order, including the UN and the ICC. We had seen the collapse of the League of Nations, unable to stop Germany, a regional European power. We had witnessed the unraveling of peace built on a precarious balance of power. Hints about the relative resilience and stability of the UN and the ICC are found in examining the weaknesses that led to the 1930s collapse of the League of Nations.

COLLAPSE OF THE LEAGUE

The Archduke Franz Ferdinand's assassination was a comedy of errors. Gavrilo Princip's gang, lying in wait for the Archduke's motorcade, blew up the wrong car. When the Archduke, en route to visit the victims in hospital, took a wrong turn, he happened upon Princip, who scrambled to the car with his revolver and finished the job. Princip reported afterwards, "I only know that I fired twice, or perhaps several times, without knowing whether I had hit or missed."[53]

Princip's shots caused a cascade of events that drew the European powers and their colonies into an industrialized slaughter. Austria-Hungary claimed it had been wronged by Serbia and demanded unreasonable concessions that Serbia was unwilling to meet. The international law of the day (the "old order") contained no prohibition on aggressive war. It provided a license to wage war. A president or prince that deemed his state wronged by another, such as Austro-Hungarian Emperor Franz Joseph, could declare war against the alleged wrongdoer and the territory he seized was compensation.[54] Other states were required to remain neutral or risk being dragged in. The assassination triggered a standoff diplomats attempted unsuccessfully to deescalate. Bilateral and multilateral defense alliances entangled the participants, and when Serbian reservists accidentally violated the Austro-Hungarian border, this hodgepodge of agreements dragged the European powers, and eventually the whole world, into war. Killing someone outside of war, as Princip had done, was murder, but a leader killing thousands during war was lawful and glorious.[55]

As the conflict intensified, the great powers threw increasingly dehumanizing technological innovations into the mix—machine guns, tanks, flamethrowers, poison gas—which put an end to the last vestiges of military chivalry and turned killing into a wholesale enterprise. Technological innovations outpaced the political constraints on warfare and the violence spiraled out of control, resulting in over twenty million military and civilian deaths and the collapse of three empires before grinding to a halt in November 1918. Germany, defeated but unbowed, signed an armistice rather than an unconditional surrender, sparing the German people a sense of defeat and opening the door for demagogues to convince them that they were betrayed when they were later treated as a defeated nation. To this day, historians argue over whether the war was inevitable or a random mistake.[56]

When the Allied victors of World War I gathered in Paris in 1919 to draft a treaty of peace, they were there to accomplish two objectives that were not necessarily compatible: to build a new world order based on justice, and to split the spoils. With American President Woodrow Wilson as their champion, the Allies created the League of Nations, inspired by liberal democratic principles, to establish the rule of law in international affairs and safeguard international peace.[57] Wilson rejected the reigning "balance of power" diplomacy, which he viewed as "unstable," based as it was on "jealous watchfulness and an antagonism of interests."[58] He cautioned, "I can predict with absolute certainty that within another generation there will be another world war if the nations of the world do not concert the method by which to prevent it."[59]

Attempts were made in Paris, spearheaded by the British and the French, to assign legal responsibility for the war. German Kaiser Wilhelm II was their prime target.[60] There was, according to English Prime Minister David Lloyd George, "a growing feeling that war itself was a crime against humanity, and that it would never be finally eliminated until it was brought into the same category as all other crimes by the infliction of condign punishment on the perpetrators and instigators."[61] Lloyd George and French President Georges Clémenceau encountered resistance from US Secretary of State Lansing.[62] The United States supported collective security, not individual criminal responsibility for war. If the kaiser was prosecuted, Lansing feared that an American leader might one day be prosecuted as well.[63] He argued that under the existing order, heads of state are answerable only to their own people and that trying the kaiser under an ex post facto law would violate the US Constitution.[64] The Allies reached a compromise in which the kaiser would be tried by an ad hoc tribunal for "a supreme offence against international morality and the sanctity of treaties," but Wilhelm II fled to the Netherlands, which refused to extradite him to an international tribunal that used ex post facto law.[65] Finally, it was not the kaiser who was punished for World War I, but the German people, who were required to pay crippling reparations.[66]

The states parties to the Covenant of the League of Nations agreed "to respect and preserve as against external aggression the territorial integrity and existing political independence of all Members," but "aggression" was not defined.[67] Rather than define and outlaw aggression, the League provided compulsory institutional procedures such as mediation, arbitration, and adjudication to resolve international disputes before they escalated into violence. If any member disregarded League procedures for resolving disputes and resorted to international violence, that member could be "deemed to have committed an act of war against all," and subject to sanctions and dismissal.[68] The League retained dysfunctional vestiges of the old order. Wars, even blatantly unjust ones, remained permissible if the League's institutional procedures failed to resolve the dispute. The League Council could recommend a military response to restore the peace, but with no standing army, it relied on volunteer states to enforce its edicts. This was not reassuring to Germany's neighbors.

Solemn international agreements—including the 1923 Draft Treaty of Mutual Assistance, the 1924 Geneva Protocol for the Pacific Settlement of International Disputes, the 1925 Locarno Treaties, and the 1928 General Treaty for the Renunciation of War (the Kellogg-Briand Pact)—were added to reassure skittish states that their allies would come to the rescue if enemies attacked. Each of these agreements, especially the widely ratified 1928 General Treaty for the Renunciation of War, reinforced the emerging view that conquest was no longer the entitlement of statesmen acting on behalf of their states, but rather an international crime. None included a substantive definition of the crime of aggression. British Foreign Secretary Austen Chamberlain argued to the House of Commons in 1927 that a definition of aggression would be "a trap for the innocent and a signpost for the guilty."[69]

In the 1920s, the League succeeded in peacefully resolving a number of territorial disputes that risked escalating into war. In all, it dealt with thirty international disputes during that decade.[70] In 1929, the world economy collapsed, and Hitler watched nations frustrated by the peace settlement begin to violate its provisions. Japan launched a false-flag attack on the South Manchurian Railway, a major trade route through China that Japan was leased to protect. Japan blamed China and occupied Manchuria. Though the League's investigators identified Japan as the culprit, member states were confused about whether conquest was a right or a crime and unwilling to provide troops to repel the attack. When Mussolini invaded Abyssinia, now Ethiopia, committing atrocities against the civilian population, the League condemned Italy's aggression. Deflated by failure in Manchuria, instead of mobilizing a military response, it settled on feeble sanctions. When General Francisco Franco led his fascist army in a coup d'état against the elected government, the Spanish Government asked for help, but this was sidelined by the 1936 Non-Intervention Agreement, supported by twenty-four nations in contravention of the avowed aims of the League of Nations.

Adolf Hitler had despised the League and its liberal-internationalist ideals since its inception. The democratic Weimar Government had agreed to peace terms that antagonized Germany's conservative and radical right on the basis of assurances from Wilson that Allied demands for reparations would be moderate.[71] But the Europeans who had lost loved ones and property in the war demanded and won punishing war reparations, the kind Wilson prophetically cautioned against: "It [a punitive peace] would . . . leave a sting, a resentment, a bitter memory upon which terms of peace would rest, not permanently, but only as upon quicksand."[72]

In 1933, Hitler was appointed chancellor of Germany on a bellicose platform fired by anger and frustration at the reparations granted by the Treaty of Versailles.[73] Alarmed, Soviet Foreign Minister Maxim Litvinov proposed a draft definition of aggression to the World Disarmament Conference.[74] Litvinov's draft was the most detailed, objective codification of the definition of aggression to date. Under the definition, the aggressor was the first state to: (1) declare war; (2) invade the territory; (3) attack the territory, vessels, or aircraft; (4) blockade the coasts or ports; or (5) support or harbor armed bands that invade the territory of another state.[75] Except for self-defense, the definition specified that no political, strategic, or economic considerations would serve as a justification for aggression.[76]

In its report to the plenary, the Committee on Security Questions, chaired by Greek politician and legal scholar Nikolaos Politis, explained the importance of a definition of aggression "conceived on a universal plane."[77] First, it would help establish the aggressor in a definite, practical and direct manner. And it would forewarn states about what acts constituted aggression, putting an end to doubts and controversies about which state was the aggressor in an armed conflict.[78] A precise definition would make it less likely that an international body would "attempt to shield or excuse the aggressor for various political reasons."[79] Even without intervention by an international body such as the League, a definition would strengthen the prohibition on force "by enabling public opinion and other States to judge [aggression] with greater certainty."[80]

Representatives of the most militarily powerful states, including the United States and Britain, argued that aggression was impossible to define and that the project should be abandoned.[81] They soon undercut their own argument by presenting definitions of their own.[82] The United Kingdom argued that a comprehensive list of aggressive acts was impossible to enumerate, that the Litvinov-Politis definition was easily circumvented by a clever aggressor, and that its prohibition on first strike was unreasonably restrictive. These arguments presaged America's post–Cold War arguments against the criminalization of aggression.

As states debated the details of the Litvinov-Politis draft, Hitler renounced the disarmament clauses of the Treaty of Versailles and began rearming Germany. Gambling on League inaction for his violation of the peace agreement, he dispatched thirty-two thousand soldiers and police to the demilitarized Rhineland, instructing generals to retreat in the face of French mobilization. Hitler later described the unopposed march into the Rhineland, a revelation of the League's enforcement impotence, as the most nerve-racking forty-eight hours of his life. Emboldened, Hitler proceeded to reinforce Franco's fascists in Spain.

Rather than blatantly repudiating the international legal order established by the League, Hitler cynically exploited it. He made nonaggression pacts, only to invade when the timing was right. Hitler convinced France and Britain to betray Czechoslovakia, promising to end German expansion in exchange for Sudetenland. He sent German Foreign Minister Joachim von Ribbentrop to Moscow to negotiate a nonaggression pact to shield Germany from a war on two fronts, then reneged once German forces were in place to invade the Soviet Union.

The invasion of Poland in 1939 finally brought Britain and France into the fight against Hitler. World War II spelled the end of the nascent League and battered the idea that collective security could "safeguard the peace of nations."[83] Emigré international lawyer Wolfgang Friedmann, addressing anxious colleagues in 1940 at the Grotius Society in London, concluded, "A large body of what we know as positive international law no longer exists, because its basis has been shattered."[84] The League headquarters in Geneva remained unoccupied until the end of the war, when it was formally disbanded and its assets auctioned off.

LEAGUE POSTMORTEM

In heated debates on the international implications of Putin's 2014 Crimea invasion, the question of why the League collapsed took on new relevance, largely because politicians and pundits drew parallels with the beginning of World War II. The obvious question was whether the UN would suffer the same fate as the League. A crucial but rarely discussed matter for states parties to the ICC was whether adding a prosecutable definition of the crime of aggression would make the court vulnerable to collapse if the prohibition were defied by a powerful Putin-like aggressor. There were answers to be found in in the texts of relevant theorists: diplomat Henry Kissinger, historian Philip Bobbitt, international law cultural critic Nathanial Berman.

The League's Structure Was Unsound

Rereading Kissinger's *Diplomacy* underscores his distaste for Woodrow Wilson and the League. Kissinger depicted Wilson as a quack: "Never before had such revolutionary goals been put forward with so few guidelines as to how to implement them. The world Wilson envisaged would be based on principle, not power; on law, not interests—for both victor and vanquished; in other words, a complete reversal of the historical experience and method of operation of the Great Powers."[85]

In Kissinger's opinion, a competent statesman like Otto von Bismarck would have never made Wilson's rookie error. Bismarck would have thoroughly defeated his enemy and only then incorporated it into the community of states. The French and the British had warned Wilson, but he was not a good listener. The result was an ill-conceived compromise between American idealism and European paranoia that was, according to Kissinger, "too punitive for conciliation, too lenient to keep Germany from recovering."[86] Making matters worse, collective security under the League Covenant would not work because states that were menaced by Germany, such as France and Poland, would never trust far-flung allies like the United States to come to their rescue when Germany attacked, as it inevitably would. Kissinger's diagnosis was that "the debacle of the Treaty of Versailles was structural."[87] "The Versailles settlement was stillborn because the values it extolled clashed with the incentives needed to enforce it."[88]

This bleak analysis cast doubt on the notion of the rule of law in international affairs. Kissinger's conclusions smacked of the Thucydides line quoted favorably by an entire generation of "realistic" American international relations scholars: "The strong do as they can and the weak suffer what they must." It did, however, provide some hope regarding the predicament in the Crimea. In an interview with *Der Spiegel* in 2014, ninety-one-year-old Kissinger contradicted Hillary Clinton and John McCain when he assured journalists, "The annexation of Crimea was not a move toward global conquest. It was not Hitler moving into Czechoslovakia."[89] He reasoned that unlike Hitlerite Germany, which sought to tear down the international order, Putinite Russia sought to cozy up: "The theme of the Olympics was that Russia is a progressive state tied to the West through its culture and, therefore, it presumably wants to be part of it."[90] Kissinger made a persuasive case that the 2014 Sochi Olympics were not the 1936 Nazi Olympics in Berlin.

According to Kissinger, it was Europe and the United States that had misunderstood the historical significance of Ukraine to Russia, and needlessly provoked Russia with their policies toward Ukraine. "Understanding Russian history and psychology," he lamented, has never "been a strong point of U.S. policymakers."[91] The West, carried away by its own idealistic rhetoric about Ukrainian self-determination and Putin's crimes, had lost sight of the balance of power and foolishly caused a crisis. Russia responded by taking back the Crimea, which had historic meaning to Russians and housed its Black Sea Fleet. Luckily, because 2014 Russia was not 1936 Germany, a negotiated readjustment was possible, with Ukraine nudged into a posture like Finland's—fiercely independent, cooperative with the West, but careful to avoid institutional hostility toward Russia.[92]

Unlike Germany with the League of Nations, Russia had its exceptional status at the UN as incentive to safeguard the authority of the existing international order. Putin relied on Russia's influence as a permanent member of the Security Council to sway events all over the world, most significantly in the civil war in Syria and in the nuclear negotiations with Iran. Furthermore, Putin was counting on UN rules and principles to vindicate Russia's Crimean claim—intervention by invitation, protection of nationals, and the self-determination of peoples. It would be counterproductive to undercut the very system he was relying on.

The trouble was that it was hard to know how much to rely on Kissinger's theory of history. Like Freud's theory of human psychology, Kissinger's appeared too simplistic, causing blind spots. Freud explained the human personality as a mediated struggle between the id and the superego and Kissinger explained international politics as the battle between great powers vying for domination. In Kissinger's account, world history follows the same basic pattern across time and space, and his theory underestimated nonstate actors like al Qaeda and ISIS, as well as depraved leaders advancing their own personal interests rather than earnestly competing in the rational game of global politics. Most gravely, Kissinger downplayed the human costs of his policies, hoping, idealistically, that the balance of power, like some miraculous cure-all, would make everything right.[93]

The League Was Premature

Philip Bobbitt was a dapper Texan law professor, nephew of Lyndon B. Johnson. While Kissinger developed a simple, elegant structural explanation for war and peace everywhere throughout history, Bobbitt unfurls an original, elaborate narrative about war and peace in successive stages.[94]

Bobbitt rejects Kissinger's monolithic conception of the nation-state. He believes the state has evolved over time with six variants since it first arose in Renaissance Italy.[95] In epochal wars—that is, wars embroiling the great powers—one variant eventually achieves dominance by mastering the strategic and constitutional innovations of its era (e.g., gunpowder during the Thirty Years' War, mass conscription during the Wars of the French Revolution).[96] The peace treaties that end these epochal wars (e.g., the Peace of Westphalia in 1648) then ratify a constitutional order for the society of states modeled on the domestic constitutional order of the victors.

In Bobbitt's diagnosis, the League of Nations collapsed because it was premature. The Treaty of Versailles was implemented before the epochal war it was meant to cap came to a decisive end.[97] For him, the First World War, the Second World War, and the Cold War, including all of the seemingly discrete wars between 1914 and 1990, were part of one war called the Long War, fought over a single set of unresolved issues.[98] The Long War was fought because "three models of the nation-state—the parliamentary, the communist, and the fascist—strove for constitutional legitimacy in the domestic arena, and for a validation of that legitimacy in the international sphere."[99] Though Germany had signed an armistice, all three variants were alive and well in 1919 when Versailles was negotiated and the League of Nations was established. It took until 1945 to discredit fascism in the eyes its own people and the world, and until 1990 to discredit communism.[100] Only after parliamentarianism truly won the Long War in 1990 could it ascend to the society of states.

Bobbitt was far more impressed by Woodrow Wilson than was Kissinger. While the oblivious victors of World War I behaved "as though they were drafting a bill to be paid," Wilson realized that the peacemakers at Versailles were drafting an international constitution.[101] For Wilson, the peace conference presented an opportunity to replicate the American system at the international level. Unfortunately, while focusing on the procedural provisions of this parliamentary-style international constitution, Wilson neglected the political consensus it needed as its foundation. Without Bolshevik Russia and protofascist Germany integrated into the society of states, the League of Nations was destined to fail.

For Bobbitt, the UN Charter, drafted after World War II, "was a sort of amendment to that constitution for the society of states."[102] But because communism continued to challenge parliamentarianism as the legitimate basis for the nation-state after fascism was defeated, the UN suffered many of the same weaknesses as the League. Only when communism was discredited could the final amendments to Wilson's parliamentary-style constitution for the society of nation-states be completed. But by then it was too late.

It was not Putin's invasion of the Crimea that would collapse the UN. The UN had simply become irrelevant, but for different reasons. A new variant of the state was emerging; Bobbitt called it the market-state.[103] No longer would a state's legitimacy be based on its self-defeating promise to provide for the welfare of all its citizens. With globalization, too much was outside any state's control for it to deliver. The market-state would promise something else: to maximize the worldwide opportunity of its citizens and provide them with the minimal security necessary to pursue these opportunities. The UN, a constitution for the outdated society of nation-states, was ill suited for this. The UN was geared toward social welfare, not individual opportunity, and the notion of sovereignty upon which it was founded was archaic.

Bobbitt's theory was majestic—relating history, grand strategy, and law—but it suffered from an unfortunate blind spot. Charting the historic transformation of the state, Bobbitt had underestimated another more important parallel change: the transformation of the individual. In *The Shield of Achilles*, Bobbitt wrote, "In contrast to the prevalent view that war is the result of a decision made by an aggressor, I will assume that, as a general matter, it takes two states to go to war . . . the move to war is an act of the State and not of boys."[104]

The individual as a major conduit to war had played large in mid-twentieth-century conflicts and it was looming even larger at the end of the century when military historians and defense consultants began forecasting the rise of the individual as an existential threat to states. Their forecasts presaged the 9/11 attacks. As US counterterrorism-operation planner and commander John Robb explained, the leverage provided by technology will soon culminate *"with the ability of one man to declare war on the world and win."*[105] States were no longer the only relevant actors in global affairs. With their technologically leveraged capacity to wage devastating wars and their ability to travel anywhere and ally with anyone, it would be catastrophic not to incorporate individuals into the global constitution as well.

The reemergence of the individual in global politics in the decades following the Long War brought to the forefront the question of the personal morality of leaders, of states and insurgencies alike. In a follow-up book celebrating Machiavelli, Bobbitt identifies Machiavelli's distinction between a ruler's personal and governing ethos as one of the Florentine's great Renaissance contributions. In Bobbitt's interpretation, Machiavelli is not amoral, as some scholars claim; he is actually an "intense moralist."[106] "It's just that the morality he urges on a prince, when he is acting on behalf of the people and not simply on his own behalf, subordinates the good of the prince to the good of the state."[107] This depersonalization was a mistake. What Bobbitt was downplaying is that Machiavelli, the moralist, also subordinates the good of outsiders, foreigners, and domestic dissenters to the good of the state, turning the state into a selfish monster and justifying all manner of atrocities. As long as the global order shielded powerful individuals from personal responsibility for mass atrocity, even on behalf of their state, it could never be fully legitimate.

Russia's invasion of the Crimea was not about to collapse the UN. Nor did the UN's progressive social welfare mandate make the organization irrelevant, as Bobbitt suggested. It was the UN's fetishization of states as the primary actors in international politics and the old guard's insistence that political leaders would and should behave like selfish monsters on behalf of their nations that posed the existential threat.

International Lawyers Unleashed Forces They Could Not Control

The work of Nathaniel Berman, a respected legal scholar, shed light on the collapse of the League and the fate of the UN. His law article, "Modernism, Nationalism, and the Rhetoric of Reconstruction," surprisingly included a reproduction of a painting, Pablo Picasso's 1907 *Les Demoiselles d'Avignon*.[108] Berman used it to show how interwar cultural shifts that reinvigorated literature, psychoanalysis, political theory, and painting also transformed law. *Les Demoiselles* and the League were both modernist creations, he said, one in art and the other in law.

Picasso and the drafters of the Treaty of Versailles sought to "reinvigorate their respective domains" and free them from "the surface platitudes of nineteenth-century bourgeois culture" by juxtaposing primitive and futuristic elements in a single work.[109] Modernist ideas captured the imagination of the legal theorists in analogous ways. Where the old prewar international law, confronted with explosive and "primitive" nationalism, could only ignore or repress it, the League sought, albeit unsuccessfully, to harness it, deploying new concepts such as the "self-determination" of peoples, ascertained through futuristic techniques such as the plebiscite.[110]

Tragically, the modernist international lawyers' fixation on their futuristic techniques, including the plebiscite, distracted them from the substance of the nationalistic vitriol they sought to give expression to.[111] For their part, the fascists rejected, "with characteristic brutality," the modernist international lawyers' overtures.[112] It followed from Berman's argument that the League collapsed because it could not control the explosive forces it unleashed and then sought to harness. He ended the 1992 piece, written on the eve of Gulf War I, with a sober warning: "By recently resurrecting that historically suspect phrase, the New World Order, the American president has unwittingly reminded us of where the enthusiasm for intellectual and political renewal can lead."[113]

Unlike Bobbitt, who seemed to relish epochal change in international law, Berman was deeply pessimistic about it. And where Kissinger's structural theory was ahistorical, with the same pattern explaining war and peace across time and space, Berman's account was meticulously contextual, explaining the rise and fall of the League of Nations in relation to a

European cultural movement that caught the imagination of artists and intellectuals in the early twentieth century. Thus, Berman's closing warning against being "deafened by the universal clamor for reconstruction" of the 1990s,[114] given without evidence of a compelling parallel between the past and the present, seemed to me more of a historical reflex than a reasoned prognosis.

What Berman did provide, despite his warning, was a blueprint for revitalizing international law using the technological and cultural innovations of the day. This was Bobbitt's inclination, though not Kissinger's. But while the drafters of the League sought to replace the inherited world order with something untried, a more prudent approach would be to build from what already existed. This was the method employed by the Special Working Group on the Crime of Aggression. Between 2005 and 2009, they assembled twentieth-century legal precedents like Lego blocks until they were satisfied, rightly or not, that the crime they had designed would rise to the challenges of the times.

COLLAPSE: THE UN AND THE ICC

Three authors, although a meager scientific sample, provided some assurance that Putin's Crimea invasion would not topple the UN or usher in World War III. They also offered clues about the fate of the ICC, particularly whether or not prosecuting leaders for illegal wars would doom the ICC to League-like collapse.

The research suggested several tentative conclusions, including that Russia's invasion of the Crimea would not destroy the UN, nor would a Putin-type invasion once the crime of aggression was activated collapse the ICC. Given built-in safety valves such as great-power vetoes in the Security Council and the ad hoc mustering of a volunteer army for every enforcement operation, the authority of the UN could never be pitted against a great power with a permanent seat on the council. Although it may be disappointing in terms of absolute justice, the UN Charter has sacrificed institutional effectiveness for resilience. In exchange for privileged treatment, the great powers agree to behave in accordance with the rule of law, knowing UN collective security can never be invoked against them. Although the UN Security Council cannot authorize force against a permanent member, the fact that they have agreed to the rule of law allows enforcement in other ways.

The ICC has safety valves too. ICC membership is voluntary, so the court's jurisdiction over the leaders of nonsignatory states such as the United States and Russia is limited. Jurisdiction is even more limited in aggression cases, where both aggressor and victim must be ICC member states that have not opted out of the aggression amendments. Furthermore, the

ICC Statute (Rome Statute) provides the UN Security Council with a mechanism to delay investigations or prosecutions that threaten international peace.[115]

The hidden strength of the crime of aggression lies not with a court in The Hague or the UN Security Council, but in the way in which its existence reframes international politics. Over time, even the earlier 1928 Kellogg-Briand Pact's "idealistic" outlawry of war resulted in a precipitous decline in the rate and size of territorial conquest.[116] The 1933 Litvinov-Politis definition has endured and evolved into a key component of the new crime of aggression. The definitive 2010 prohibition is capable of disciplining historical analogies such as those proffered by Putin and Clinton during the Crimean crisis. Around the world, this law has begun to infiltrate domestic institutions and practices governing war. This detailed, objective, consensus definition allows cabinet ministers, lawmakers, opposition parties, the judiciary, the press, and the public to test a leader's justifications for war and to resist illegitimate justifications. By shifting responsibility from states to individuals, the new crime of aggression has the potential to leverage law's deterrent effect.

The definition is on the books, but it needs a referee. What will it take for the law to rise above the cacophony of conflicting claims? Hints are found in a 1945 courthouse in Nuremberg. There, in the most important trial of the twentieth century, an international tribunal judged and punished twelve top Nazis for causing World War II.

CHAPTER 3

The Nuremberg Avant-Garde Moment

The history of the world is but the biography of great men.
—Thomas Carlyle, *On Heroes, Hero-Worship, and the Heroic in History: Six Lectures*, 1841

Kings are the slaves of history.
—Leo Tolstoy, *War and Peace*, 1869[1]

The "prohibition" of war and the declaration that war is criminal are as much use as declaring the law of gravity invalid by prohibiting the stones from falling.
—Bernard Röling, Dutch judge on the International Military Tribunal for the Far East, 1947[2]

The Nuremberg precedent foresaw the danger of authoritarian leaders wielding unchecked military power. Unprecedented in legal history, Nuremberg assigned responsibility for war not to states or social forces, but to individuals. The most avant-garde, potentially transformative aspect of the trial with consequences for world order was the legal innovation that held individual Nazi leaders accountable for World War II. US attorney Robert Jackson, more than any other jurist, championed the juridical framework for holding authoritarian leaders responsible for illegal war. Jackson's dogged advocacy defied prevailing wisdom, provoked resistance, and in time became the legal foundation for the crime of aggression.

JACKSON'S ACCOUNTABILITY BREAKTHROUGH

In March 1941, US Attorney General Robert Jackson and President Franklin Delano Roosevelt sat on Roosevelt's yacht off the coast of Florida refining a speech Jackson was on his way to deliver to the Inter-American Bar Association in Havana, Cuba. Roosevelt had a legal problem that Jackson's speech was meant to resolve. With the Nazis conquering Europe, a massive German offensive against Britain underway, and isolationist sentiment rampant in the United States, Roosevelt needed a legal rationale for the military aid he was providing to the British while maintaining America's neutrality.[3] Yet, Jackson's speech would go further than Roosevelt's request. It would provide an early blueprint for the trial of German and Japanese leaders for the Crime Against Peace after World War II, predecessor to the crime of aggression.

Jackson's challenge was how to legally justify American interference "short of war." Would it be the pre–World War I legal order, where all wars were regarded as legal and the leaders of sovereign states were free to wage war as they pleased? Or would Jackson summon a new world order, where international law distinguished between just and unjust wars, and states were legally bound to intervene on the side of justice? Jackson chose the latter, beginning an intellectual journey that would culminate, seventy years later, in the crime of aggression.

His thinking began with the drafting of the 1941 Havana speech.[4] "It does not appear to be necessary to treat all wars as legal and just simply because we have no court to try the accused," he wrote, repudiating the old order.[5] Under the new order he was imagining, in order to support America's European allies, it was necessary to identify German violations of existing international legal rules. Jackson found two relevant sources, the Christian just-war theorists of the seventeenth and eighteenth centuries, and interwar agreements. He maintained that the League of Nations Covenant, the Kellogg-Briand Pact, and other interwar agreements "swept away the nineteenth century basis for contending that all wars are alike and all warriors entitled to like treatment."[6]

The Kellogg-Briand Pact was crucial to Jackson's argument that the Axis powers had violated international law, the legal basis for US military aid to Britain. It was signed by Germany, Japan, Italy, and almost every other nation. American isolationist historian Charles Beard ridiculed the treaty, calling it "a gibbering ghost."[7] Beard argued that interwar precedents criminalizing aggression had died with the League. His isolationist arguments buttressed the more sophisticated international legal position advanced by Germany's leading international lawyer, Carl Schmitt, who argued the pact was "without definition, without sanction, and without organization," and was therefore an illegitimate basis for criminal prosecution.[8] These depictions of the Kellogg-Briand Pact would haunt the Nuremberg trials and subsequent attempts to hold individuals accountable for aggression.

Marooned by bad weather, Jackson's avant-garde argument to the Inter-American Bar Association was read by the US ambassador to Cuba. His moment would come in London, in the summer of 1945. There, with Allied counterparts, he created the legal and institutional framework that would, at Nuremberg, for the first time, judge political and military leaders for aggressive war. In May 1945, Roosevelt's successor, President Harry Truman, appointed Robert Jackson, then sitting Supreme Court justice, to represent the United States in drafting the Nuremberg Charter and preparing the case against the top Nazis for atrocities and war crimes.[9] "Our view," he announced to skeptical Allied delegates at the London Conference, "is that this isn't merely a case of showing that these Nazi Hitlerite people failed to be gentlemen in war; it is a matter of their having designed an illegal attack on the international peace."[10] Jackson realized he had to convince his British, French, and Soviet counterparts, first, that there existed a definition of aggression applicable to all states, and second, that leaders could be held criminally accountable for its violation.

Jackson faced opposition. French delegate André Gros told the London Conference, "We do not consider as a criminal violation the launching of a war of aggression. If we declare war a criminal act of individuals, we are going farther than the actual law."[11] The French proposed trying the Nazis for breaching existing treaties and customary international law, rather than the crime of aggression.[12] Russian delegate Iona Nikitchenko initially sided with the French, preferring a law that could be "turned only against those who have committed the crimes," over a general prohibition that might capture Soviet leaders as well.[13]

Jackson argued that world opinion now favored individual responsibility for war and that the lacuna left by the interwar treaties should be filled.[14] He urged the delegates to include the broader 1933 Litvinov-Politis definition of aggression, rather than the mere treaty violation and moralistic condemnation that France proposed.[15] All other jurists agreed to incorporate a "crime against peace," including individual responsibility for aggressive war—if it included language proposed by Gros about the illegal violation of treaties. They were not willing to criminalize specific acts in general terms, as was done in the 1933 Litvinov-Politis definition. The Nuremberg definition of crimes against peace melded American and French models, including Jackson's general prohibition on force and Gros's reference to existing treaties: "Crimes Against Peace: namely, planning, preparation, initiation or waging of a war of aggression, or a war in violation of international treaties, agreements or assurances, or participation in a common plan or conspiracy for the accomplishment of any of the foregoing."[16]

The Nuremberg Charter also created modes of individual liability for leaders, established a fair process blending common- and civil-law traditions, placed the burden of proof on the prosecution (rejecting the Soviet position), and provided the defendants the right to counsel.[17] The Nuremberg Charter would be tested in an adversarial process by some of the finest German jurists of the day.

Jackson maintained that aggression should be at the heart of the Nuremberg trials. Some scholars have attempted to cast him as parochial and nationalistic, pandering to the American public, which was less affected by Holocaust atrocities than by the attack on Pearl Harbor, and concerned with protecting its privileged postwar position.[18] Yet, Jackson sincerely believed that the trial of the Nazis for aggressive war would create a crucial legal precedent and help prevent World War III. Expressed as early as 1941, his view was that "legal process is the only practical alternative to force."[19] In 1947, when the trial was over, he wrote, "These standards by which the Germans have been condemned will become condemnation of any nation that is faithless to them," including the United States.[20]

JACKSON'S CASE AT NUREMBERG

At Nuremberg, November 1945, Robert Jackson faced eight American, British, French, and Soviet judges and the specter of historical determinism. To win his case, Jackson would need to prove responsibility for World War II rested on the twenty-two Nazi defendants, not the German people, the German state, or historical inertia. This was no easy charge. Until the creation of the League of Nations, presidents and princes had the prerogative to wage war as they pleased. The League Covenant, the Kellogg-Briand Pact, and many other interwar nonaggression pacts addressed violations by states, not statesmen protected by legal immunity. Jackson and the Allied prosecution team would be asking the Nuremberg tribunal to reject the traditional immunities of political and military leaders and expose them to criminal charges.[21] The Allied team would also challenge the soldier's "just following orders" defense. Jackson's ultimate goal was to enshrine in law, at all levels, personal criminal responsibility for aggression. "The idea that a state, any more than a corporation, commits crimes is a fiction," he argued. "Crimes always are committed only by persons."[22]

The defendants included Rosenberg, whom Jackson called the "intellectual high priest of the 'master race'"; Keitel, "weak and willing tool"; Kaltenbrunner, "the grand inquisitor"; Saukel, "the greatest and cruelest slaver since the Pharaohs of Egypt"; Ribbentrop, "salesman of deception."[23] Viewed as a group, they appear a malevolent social force, a by-product of history, not its origin. A closer look reveals individuals, some in fine suits, others in military garb, placed uncomfortably closely despite their conflicting Nazi commitments. The distinction between group and individual is important. The essential point Jackson had to make to win his case was that World War II was caused by powerful individuals, and therefore the Nuremberg trials were a reasonable response to the defendants' criminal acts. If they were slaves of history, individual criminal responsibility makes no legal sense at all.

Jackson's plan for shifting responsibility for the war from the state to the individual was complicated and circuitous. "Count One" of the indictment charted the steps he would take.[24] He began by depicting the individual defendants as members of a criminal conspiracy committed to waging aggressive war. The conspirators established totalitarian control within Germany, he argued, in order to use the nation's military might to conquer Europe. Jackson demonstrated how the Nazis cynically exploited international law and agreements—the Kellogg-Briand Pact, the Locarno Treaties, the Munich Agreement—to lull Europe into passivity. When the moment was ripe, they broke their promises and attacked without warning. The aim of the conspirators was to abrogate the Treaty of Versailles, reunite the German people, and acquire new territories they claimed as *Lebensraum*, living space, for racial Germans.[25] Jackson argued that these attacks were crimes against peace. Of the three crimes contained in the London Charter—war crimes, crimes against humanity, and crimes against peace—the crime against peace was, in his view, "the greatest menace," and the other international crimes were the byproduct.[26] Crimes against peace became the legal tool that allowed Jackson to prosecute German leaders for atrocities against their own people and against people in occupied countries. Jackson demonstrated that the crime against peace was the unifying principle of the Nuremberg trials.

He almost undercut his larger goal of establishing individual accountability in two ways: by asking the Nuremberg tribunal to hold the defendants responsible for one another's criminal acts, and by introducing the even broader legal category of "criminal organizations," whereby any member, on the basis of membership alone, could be found guilty of all its crimes. Both liability doctrines could be seen as running counter to the overall goal of individual accountability, and risked judicial rejection as being tantamount to guilt by association.[27]

British prosecutors buttressed Jackson's position that individuals are responsible for war by arguing that the defendants had committed crimes against peace by violating binding international treaties and agreements in their illegal invasion of counties including Poland, the United Kingdom, France, Denmark, and Norway.[28] But the more difficult claim, that these violations entailed individual responsibility, had no legal precedent. Defeated World War I leader Kaiser Wilhelm had, after all, found asylum in the Netherlands. Instead, the British based their argument on the authority of the Nuremberg Charter and Germany's unconditional surrender, which gave the tribunal for the first time the power to enforce state-centric prohibitions against individuals.[29] "Insofar as the Charter of this Tribunal introduces new law," British prosecutor Sir Hartley Shawcross maintained, "its authors have established a precedent for the future—a precedent operative against all, including themselves."[30]

THE SUPREME JUDGMENT

At the core of the Nazi defense was the question of who caused the war and its atrocities—culpable individuals, the German state, or larger historical forces. The defense argued that the tribunal was illegitimate, that the defendants had been unaware crimes were occurring, they were legally bound by orders from superiors, they had heroically tried to resist, they had been acting not as individuals but on behalf of the state, and they were acting in self-defense. Lawyers for Hess and Streicher argued that their clients were insane and therefore not responsible for their acts.

In the course of the Nuremberg process, the judges rejected defense arguments and hammered out key aspects of what would become the crime of aggression. A sampling of its legal concepts reveals how the Nuremberg DNA informs the crime of aggression, and how the crime of aggression differs from Nuremberg's crime against peace. Nuremberg defined the illegal conduct that would link individuals to the collective act of aggressive war ("planning, preparing, initiating or waging"). The Nuremberg tribunal decided that only *wars* of aggression, not lesser acts, would be punishable, whereas the modern crime of aggression defines the threshold for punishment as *acts* of aggression that by their character, gravity, and scale, constitute "a manifest violation of the Charter of the United Nations."[31] The judgment refocused guilt on individual culpability and ultimately helped Jackson achieve his larger goal.[32] Crucially, for the first time, the Nuremberg tribunal held individuals responsible for aggressive war. Fueled by Jackson's hostility to authoritarianism and his belief in equality under the law, bellicose leaders would become vulnerable to prosecution under the crime of aggression.

Proponents of the crime of aggression worry that its Nuremberg forerunner, crimes against peace, fails to provide a definition of "war of aggression" or a list of illegal acts.[33] They point out that the Nuremberg Charter does not establish whether all Germans, including civilians, are potentially liable for committing the crime against peace, or only political and military leaders.[34] They are concerned that the judgment fails to clearly distinguish legal elements of the conspiracy to commit crimes against peace from the actual perpetration of the substantive crime.[35]

Although initially skeptical of crimes against peace, the judges finally accepted Jackson's position that this crime was the cornerstone of the trial:

> The charges in the Indictment that the defendants planned and waged aggressive wars are charges of the utmost gravity. War is essentially an evil thing. Its consequences are not confined to the belligerent states alone, but affect the whole world.

To initiate a war of aggression, therefore, is not only an international crime; it is the supreme international crime differing only from other war crimes in that it contains within itself the accumulated evil of the whole.[36]

It took the judges only one month to reach a verdict and draft a judgment. Their verdict against Hermann Goering would demonstrate the justice of holding individuals accountable for aggressive war. Goering had assumed credit for the rise of the Third Reich but portrayed himself as a moderate who had fallen out with Hitler, bravely stood up against the führer's excesses, and had no knowledge of many heinous acts. Reams of evidence debunked Goering's alternative facts and implicated him in aggressive war. His claim that Germany always maintained peaceful relations with Yugoslavia, for example, was countered by minutes from key meetings proving Germany's longstanding intentions to invade.[37] Given the weight of evidence, the tribunal decided that Goering was "the leading war aggressor … His guilt is unique in its enormity."[38]

The attacks on Denmark and Norway were planned by Grand Admiral Raeder and Nazi theorist Alfred Rosenberg, and at trial they claimed they had invaded in preemptive self-defense.[39] The problem the judges faced was that, given Norway's strategic location, the British too had been planning an attack to preclude German access to Norwegian ports and Swedish iron-ore mines. To distinguish aggression from self-defense, the judges invoked the 1842 *Caroline Case*, which established a test for self-defense commonly found in international law textbooks of the day: "Preventive action in foreign territory is justified only in case of 'an instant and overwhelming necessity for self-defense leaving no choice of means, and no moment of deliberation.'"[40] Captured documents submitted by the prosecution revealed that the Germans had no "instant and overwhelming necessity" to attack Norway: the defendants had planned the German operation before the British planned the attack upon which the defendants justified their self-defense claim.[41]

The tribunal found that ten of Germany's "wars of aggression" amounted to crimes against peace: Poland, Yugoslavia, Greece, Denmark, Norway, Belgium, the Netherlands, Luxemburg, the Soviet Union, and the United States. The judges, however, considered the "invasion" of Austria and the "seizure" of Czechoslovakia less grave "acts" of aggression, not full-scale "wars" of aggression. These acts did not amount to the crime against peace, though they linked particular defendants to the Nazi conspiracy to commit crimes against peace. Goering, Raeder, Rosenberg, and the other crimes-against-peace defendants were found personally responsible for aggressive war. Most of those found guilty of conspiracy to commit crimes against peace and the substantive crime against peace were hanged or imprisoned for life. On the eve of his execution, Goering killed himself with a cyanide capsule.

NUREMBERG'S LEGACY

The original Nuremberg tribunal and subsequent Nuremberg trials of second-tier Nazis,[42] as well as the International Military Tribunal for the Far East, where Japanese leaders were tried for the same crimes,[43] were the earliest international courts to reach into the state and hold individuals personally responsible. In doing so, they overruled the traditional immunities for leaders and functionaries performing official duties, and abolished the just-following-orders defense raised by soldiers. By rejecting collective guilt for Germany,[44] and limiting organizational guilt for members of criminal organizations,[45] the Nuremberg trials validated the notion of individual culpability. They applied widely accepted standards of evidence and procedure to concrete cases and provided a partial rebuttal of the victors' justice critique, thus ensuring each defendant be judged on his own choices. The trials labeled the crime against peace "the supreme international crime," and held individuals accountable for committing it, thereby framing war as an atrocity committed by criminal conspirators rather than the inevitable product of social forces.

Following a US initiative, the General Assembly of the newly formed United Nations affirmed the principles of international law established by the Charter and Judgment of the Nuremberg tribunal.[46] The first principle was, "Any person who commits an act which constitutes a crime under international law is responsible therefor and liable to punishment."[47] Nuremberg would serve as a precedent for an international criminal court with global jurisdiction over political, military, and industrial leaders.

Little did Jackson know that it would take over fifty years and another epochal war before his vision of international criminal accountability would reemerge.

CHAPTER 4

Cold War *Jus ad Bellum*

LAW OF FORCE VS. RULE OF LAW

Thus the ego, driven by the id, confined by the super-ego, repulsed by reality, struggles . . . [in] bringing about harmony among the forces and influences working in and upon it.
—Sigmund Freud, *New Introductory Lectures on Psychoanalysis*, 1933

This sentence contradicts itself—or rather—well, no, actually it doesn't!
—Douglas Hofstadter, *Gödel, Escher, Bach: An Eternal Golden Braid*, 1979

Free Radicals: In chemistry, a radical (more precisely, a free radical) is an atom, molecule, or ion that has unpaired valence electrons. . . . [These unpaired electrons] make free radicals highly chemically reactive toward other substances, or even toward themselves.
—Paul Wenthold, *Organic Chemistry for Engineers*, 2014[1]

Nuremberg's essential lesson was that men, not abstract entities, cause wars. Intensifying competition between militarized states can create a volatile situation, but it takes a skillful demagogue to mobilize and harness a nation's dormant aggression. During the Cold War, the Nuremberg precedent was brushed aside, and states were once again treated as the primary global actors. Two competing international orders emerged; Ferencz called them the Rule of Force and the Rule of Law. To his dismay, neither criminalized aggression. Fixation on superpower competition and insensitivity to the collateral damage to "peripheral" communities enabled the dangerous emergence of individuals with the technological capacity to render obsolete the very idea of the balance of power.

THE POST–WORLD WAR II LEGAL ORDER

A 1941 wartime agreement between President Franklin Delano Roosevelt (FDR) and UK Prime Minister Winston Churchill on a US warship off Canada's Newfoundland coast was to become the blueprint for the post–World War II legal order. With the United States still claiming neutrality and the surprise Japanese attack on Pearl Harbor still months away, FDR and Churchill nevertheless spelled out their wartime goals: renunciation of the use of force, an end to territorial conquest, disarmament of aggressor nations, restoration of self-government to conquered nations, international cooperation, freedom from fear and of want, free trade.[2] These ideas were debated and revised in a series of meetings between Churchill, FDR, Stalin and their top advisors in Moscow (1943), Dumbarton Oaks, DC (1944), and Yalta, Crimea (1945).[3]

After their victory, the Allies met in San Francisco to establish the rules governing the use of force in international law and the powers of the bodies responsible for enforcing them. A blanket prohibition on the use of force by states with two exceptions became the basis for the post–World War II security regime. The two exceptions were collective peace enforcement authorized by the UN Security Council,[4] and individual or collective self-defense in response to an armed attack.[5] The Allies unequivocally dispatched the old order whereby armed reprisals were a legitimate form of law enforcement. Unfortunately, the drafters of the UN Charter and the Nuremberg Charter failed to coordinate their projects, and the threat of individuals to global security slipped through the cracks.

FDR had supported the League of Nations until the mid-1930s, when he exclaimed, "The League of Nations has become nothing more than a debating society, and a poor one at that."[6] Roosevelt thought there were too many members to satisfy, and envisaged an international organization with "four policemen"— Great Britain, China, the United States, and the Soviet Union—with designated spheres of influence.[7] Every other nation would be disarmed.

FDR's disarmament plan was unrealistic and was dropped early on, but his four-policemen idea was transformed into the UN Security Council. The question became, who would be deputized? The decision would entrench politics in law. FDR insisted on China in order to police defeated Japan, but Stalin objected, arguing that China was weak, embroiled in a civil war against Mao's (Soviet-backed) communists. FDR won the inclusion of China but was shot down when he recommended Brazil to represent Latin America, and dropped his proposal to include a Muslim country. Churchill was wary of Soviet encroachment in Europe and insisted that France be included to offset the Soviets. Britain, China, France, the Soviets, and the United States ended up with permanent seats.

Stalin insisted that the "Permanent Five" each have an absolute veto that would allow them to prevent resolutions from even being discussed.[8] FDR and Churchill were against the veto, which they correctly saw as a recipe for deadlock. FDR maintained that no party to a dispute should be involved in deciding it.[9] Churchill suggested a modification whereby none of the permanent members could veto a resolution directly concerning itself. Stalin was adamant that the Soviet Union not submit to the judgment of lesser powers. The Allies finally agreed on an absolute veto over decisions pertaining to the use of armed force, but the permanent members could not use the veto to shut down discussion. This decision had profound implications for international order during the Cold War and today, and for prosecution of the crime of aggression.

Following a divisive public debate within the United States and Britain around the notion of a standing UN army, all of the parties involved in the conference rejected the idea. The Soviets and the Chinese pushed for a standing air force instead, but the United States quickly killed the idea and threatened to withdraw from talks if it were pursued. The United States argued that a standing air force would be an unacceptable threat to state sovereignty and that Congress would not agree to such an entanglement. The Allies settled on an arrangement that severely diluted the UN's enforcement power, where UN member states would contribute troops on an ad hoc basis.

Attention turned to the question of whether the Security Council would have the monopoly on the legitimate use of international force or whether regional organizations would have the right to act autonomously. The Allies reached a two-pronged compromise. Regional bodies, granted a degree of autonomy to maintain international peace and security, would nonetheless be subject to the edicts of the Security Council.[10] If attacked, however, states would have the right to respond individually *or collectively* in self-defense, even absent Security Council authorization. This satisfied Churchill and the "regionalists" and placated smaller countries chafing against the consolidation of power in the Security Council.

Rather, the Security Council, without principled legal guidelines, was responsible for determining when aggression had occurred.[11] It had "primary," though not exclusive, responsibility for the maintenance of international peace and security, while the General Assembly, the International Court of Justice, and regional organizations had roles as well.[12] The General Assembly, for instance, shared responsibility with the Security Council when it came to the peaceful resolution of international disputes though negotiation.[13] Meanwhile, the International Court of Justice was empowered to judge the legality of armed force between states, among other legal issues.[14] The General Assembly, the International Court of Justice, and regional organizations could not authorize armed peace enforcement or bind member states with their decisions. Only the Security Council could do so. Conspicuously absent was a definition of aggression.

In the view of the Western powers, the United Nations Charter was the established constitution for the new world order. Stalin, encircled by capitalist "allies," saw it as an armistice between rivals. By spring of 1946, Western powers were in open competition with the Soviet Union. In Fulton, Missouri, in his famous Cold War speech, Churchill declared war: "From Stettin in the Baltic to Trieste in the Adriatic an *iron curtain* has descended across the Continent."[15] The main battle was no longer over wartime justice but over security against the looming threat of Soviet power. Political and military leaders forgot Nuremberg and shifted from individuals to states, from law to geopolitics. But Benjamin Ferencz was determined to keep the Nuremberg spirit alive. Had lawmakers listened to him then, Nuremberg and the UN Charter would be in closer harmony, and dangerous individuals possessing weapons of mass destruction would be on the radar.

The distrust created a Cold War impasse and the Allied victors of World War II turned on one another, making self-interested use of their vetoes. Without a legally binding definition of aggression, Security Council resolutions could be shaped primarily by national interests. The Soviet Union was the main culprit, vetoing a 1949 resolution, submitted by France, calling for a reduction of conventional armaments and a disclosure requirement for nuclear weapons information.[16] It vetoed a second resolution the same year that would have granted several European countries UN membership.[17] Between 1946 and 1950, the Soviet Union vetoed a total of twenty-two pro-Western memberships.[18] By the time of the Korean War in 1950, the Security Council was deadlocked and the post–World War II order in question.

Frustrated states saw a solution to the problem of political self-interest in constraining Security Council decisions with a legal definition of aggression. In 1950, the Soviet Union submitted to the UN General Assembly a list of acts that it considered to be aggressive, based closely upon the 1933 Litvinov-Politis draft. Whether the Soviets sought doctrinal clarity or to undermine with law their erstwhile American allies' superior first-strike military capabilities is difficult to know. Readers of Kennan's "Long Telegram" had learned that the Soviets believed they lived in an antagonistic state of "capitalist encirclement"—that is, under siege.[19] In these circumstances, it made strategic sense to strengthen the legal barriers on first strike and outlaw any modalities of armed force favored by the United States. Despite American skepticism about Soviet motives, they nonetheless joined a special General Assembly committee of fifteen states tasked with defining aggression.

The Special Committee met in 1952 and 1953 but failed to produce a draft.[20] Delegates from powerful (mostly Western) states committed to

the status quo rejected external oversight of their leaders' military operations, while those from nonaligned ("Third World") states resisted limits on their neighbors' anticolonial struggles.[21] A second committee of
nineteen representatives was created in 1954, and it spun its wheels for
years, unable to agree on a definition. In 1957, a third committee was
set up "for determining when it shall be appropriate for the General Assembly to consider again the question of defining aggression."[22] The third
committee met in 1959, 1962, 1965, and 1967, but was derailed by members accusing one another's states of aggression.[23] Ignoring the Litvinov-
Politis definition and the Nuremberg and Tokyo precedents, the third
committee concluded that the time was not yet appropriate to define
aggression.

The Soviets would not be dissuaded. A cadre of newly decolonized African, Latin American, and Middle-Eastern states took their rightful seats in
the UN General Assembly and the Soviets intended to win their support.
The Soviets demanded that a fourth, larger, committee be assembled to
finally resolve the aggression question. The expanded General Assembly
acknowledged a "need to expedite the drafting of a definition of aggression in light of the present international situation."[24] Ferencz applied for,
and was granted, credentials to attend the meetings. "With fighting going
on all over the globe—including in India, Pakistan, Cyprus, the Congo,
Cambodia, Vietnam and the Middle East," he lamented, "it was clear that
it was easier to commit aggression than to define it."[25] The fourth and final
committee, composed of thirty-five states' representatives, had its first meeting in 1968. The negotiations would continue until 1974, tracking the Cold
War crises of the period, and culminate in one of international law's most
Byzantine legal documents, a dark horse best understood in light of the
trompe l'oeil creations of the Dutch artist M. C. Escher.

PARALLEL LIVES, OPPOSING PRECEPTS

Benjamin Ferencz, recently returned from prosecuting the Nuremberg trials, followed the aggression debate that would consume him for his entire
life. In 1940s postwar Germany, Ferencz had assisted General Telford
Taylor, right hand to Robert Jackson, in prosecuting the Nazi doctors,
judges, industrialists, minsters, high command, and other perpetrators
at the subsequent Nuremberg trials. During the investigation phase, Ferencz's team discovered a massive underground bunker outside Berlin
containing meticulous records cataloging the atrocities of the *Einsatzgruppen*, mobile death squads responsible for exterminating all Jews, Gyp-
sies, and dissidents they could capture in occupied territories. These records indicated that the Einsatzgruppen had killed over a million people.

When Ferencz petitioned Taylor to hold a separate trial for the exposed leaders, Taylor, short on staff, appointed twenty-seven-year old Ferencz as lead prosecutor. It was Ferencz's first case. "We ask this court to affirm by international penal action, man's right to live in peace and dignity, regardless of his race or creed," he began. "The case we present is a plea of humanity to law."[26] Ferencz built an airtight case on the documentary evidence unearthed, and the judges convicted the twenty-two defendants. After successfully prosecuting the *Einsatzgruppen Case*, Ferencz helped establish reparations and rehabilitation programs for Nazi victims and watched the post–World War II international legal order take shape. Tormented by what he had seen in the concentration camps, he said, "If we did not devote ourselves to developing effective world law, the same cruel mentality that made the Holocaust possible might one day destroy the entire human race."[27]

Ferencz applauded the creation of the UN, though he was frustrated by the failure of the drafters to provide a binding definition of aggression, a standing UN army, and by inequality in the Security Council. In 1948, he watched the General Assembly of the newly founded UN adopt Eleanor Roosevelt's Universal Declaration of Human Rights, thereby granting rights to people, not only states, under international law. He witnessed the creation of a new crime, genocide, and its prohibition in the 1948 Genocide Convention,[28] but lamented the absence of an international criminal court to prosecute it. Ferencz remained convinced that world peace ultimately required a criminal prohibition on aggressive war, enforced by an international criminal court with global jurisdiction.

In 1956, Ferencz returned to the United States and went into private practice with his former boss, Telford Taylor. Happily married, wrestling on the floor with his children, still the death camps and the Nuremberg trials consumed him. In 1975, he published his two-volume, twelve-hundred-page *Defining International Aggression*, arguing that the legal definition of aggression, having evolved over centuries, is complete, and any doubts are the product of cynical governments "too engrossed in advancing their own immediate cause by every means within their power to be hampered by the visions of idealistic dreamers."[29] In *An International Criminal Court* (1980), he cited every precedent required to create an international criminal court with global jurisdiction. *Enforcing International Law* (1983) contains an exhaustive study of international law enforcement and Ferencz's proposals for improving the existing regime: clarifying the norms of international behavior, persuading people and nations to accept judicial authority, making the UN more effective, demilitarizing states, creating an international force, concentrating on social justice.[30] Without the crime of aggression, Ferencz maintained, there can be no lasting peace.

Ferencz's work was largely disregarded during the Cold War. It was dismissed as unrealistic, especially his contention that a consensus definition of aggression existed and simply needed codification and implementation. Ferencz's unifying theme is "Law. Not war."[31] He blames the absence of effective world law on shortsighted nations: "They fail to recognize that unless differences are resolved by peaceful means, violent means will be inevitable."[32] He cautions, "The price for unbridled sovereignty is war, but in a nuclear world it is a price too high to pay."[33]

Henry Kissinger, arch-realist, US national security advisor, secretary of state, champion of the old order, is the counterpoint to Ferencz's idealism. Born in Germany, ten kilometers from Nuremberg, three years after Ferencz's birth in Romania, both he and Ferencz were Jewish children forced to flee European anti-Semitism. Ferencz arrived in New York, only ten months old. Kissinger arrived as a teen having suffered daily attacks. Both families were poor. Both boys were precocious students who attended Harvard, Ferencz in law before the war and Kissinger in political science afterward. Ferencz was scrappy and optimistic; Kissinger droll and calculating. When the war ended, each dedicated his life to building an international order that would prevent World War III.

Kissinger's 1954 doctoral dissertation was, "Peace, Legitimacy, and the Equilibrium (a Study of the Statesmanship of Castlereagh and Metternich)," on the British foreign secretary and the Austrian foreign minister and chancellor who reshaped the international order after the Napoleonic Wars.[34] According to political scientist Francis Fukuyama, this was where Kissinger first "argued his case that international peace was best guaranteed not through law or international organizations but through a distribution of power that moderated the ambitions of the strong."[35] The dissertation reflected Kissinger's conservative view that the fundamental goal of diplomacy is not justice but order, and that the greatest threat to world peace is revolutionary nations like Napoleonic France and the Soviet Union embarking on crusades that challenge the status quo. Rather than design an international system based on cooperation, "at the mercy of the most ruthless member," the goal should be "stability based on an equilibrium of forces," even if that stability entrenches an oppressive system.[36]

After his dissertation, Kissinger taught in Harvard's Government Department, consulted with government agencies, and met with important academics and policymakers. In 1956–57, as director of a Council on Foreign Relations research project on nuclear weapons and foreign policy, he argued that Eisenhower's doctrine of massive retaliation was no longer a credible deterrent now that the Soviets had the atom bomb. In his first book, Kissinger maintained that the United States should prepare tactical nuclear weapons for use in small regional wars,[37] an idea President

Donald Trump resurrected sixty years later in relation to nonstate actors such as ISIS. Kissinger's position was that US influence depended on the perception its adversaries and allies held of its military power and willingness to use it. He downplayed the risk that these "limited" wars could escalate into nuclear Armageddon. The book was a surprise best seller, winning Kissinger the attention of Nelson Rockefeller, John F. Kennedy, Lyndon B. Johnson, and Richard Nixon. In 1965, he framed the Vietnam War as a test of American resolve in the face of Soviet aggression rather than an anticolonial struggle, a threat to the post–World War II international legal order, or a humanitarian catastrophe. Though Kissinger didn't think the United States could win the war, he supported Johnson's escalation as a signal to the Soviets of American resolve.

Kissinger officially entered politics in 1968. As national security advisor and later, concurrently, secretary of state, Kissinger ignored the Nuremberg principles. He escalated anticommunist violence in the small states he considered peripheral, sometimes through genocidal proxies, while working to broker détente among the great powers in order to avert nuclear war.

Nixon and Kissinger supported West Pakistan in its 1971 antisecessionist struggle against the East, in spite of incontrovertible evidence from American officials on the ground that their allies were perpetrating genocide.[38] The victims were collateral damage in Nixon and Kissinger's effort to contain Soviet expansion in South Asia and signal to China the value of an anti-Soviet alliance. According to Princeton historian Gary Bass, "This largely overlooked horror ranks among the darkest chapters in the entire cold war."[39] West Pakistani leader Agha Muhammad Yahya Khan repaid Nixon and Kissinger by brokering visits to China.

Kissinger flew to China via Pakistan in 1971 to meet Premier Zhou Enlai. The men bonded over distrust of the Soviets and arranged for Nixon to visit and begin normalizing relations between the two countries.[40] Just days after Kissinger's visit was revealed in the press, the Soviets sent their ambassador to the White House to propose their own bilateral summit. "To have the two communist powers competing for good relations with us," Kissinger later said, "could only benefit the cause of peace."[41] US rapprochement with China encouraged the Soviets to curry favor, and US-Chinese cooperation had the potential to generate a negotiated solution to the Vietnam War.

Kissinger, now a popular celebrity, secretly advised Nixon to circumvent Congressional approval and escalate the clandestine bombing of enemy sanctuaries in neutral Cambodia, simultaneously a crime against peace and a crime against humanity. The bombing, which killed thousands of civilians, assuaged America's South Vietnamese and Cambodian allies. According to journalist William Shawcross, the bombing campaign also caused a communist backlash in Cambodia and the rise of the geno-cidal Khmer Rouge.[42] "They are murderous thugs," Kissinger told the Thai foreign minister in 1975 about the Khmer Rouge, when America's appetite for war had waned, "but we won't let that stand in our way. We are prepared to improve relations with them."[43]

By improving relations with communist China at a time of increased Sino-Soviet tension, Kissinger hoped to place the United States in a ful-crum position, tipping the balance of power toward American interests. The time was ripe for détente, with American foreign interventions cre-ating a crippling domestic backlash, oil prices skyrocketing, and Soviet nuclear parity inevitable.

In 1970, the Americans and Soviets met to negotiate a Strategic Arms Limitation Agreement (SALT I). Through back channels, Kissinger tied the outcome of the arms agreement to mutually beneficial concessions on the status of Berlin. Weaving a web of compromises that reduced American-Soviet tensions without weakening either power, Kissinger helped usher in an era of détente. Ferencz credits this "new spirit of detente" with the watershed 1974 definition of aggression that would, in 2010, become the backbone of the crime of aggression.[44] According to singer-songwriter Tom Lehrer, "Political satire became obsolete when Henry Kissinger was awarded the Nobel Peace Prize."[45]

Kissinger's policies left a wake of human destruction and anti-American hatred across the five continents. At home, he is celebrated as Ameri-ca's greatest statesman, time and again thwarting Soviet expansion and averting nuclear war. In a new biography reassessing Kissinger's legacy, Harvard historian Niall Ferguson writes, "Arguments that focus on loss of life in strategically marginal countries—and there is no other way of describing Argentina, Bangladesh, Cambodia, Chile, Cyprus, and East Timor—must be tested against this question: how, in each case, would an alternative decision have affected US relations with strategically im-portant countries like the Soviet Union, China, and the major Western European powers?"[46] "The logic is wobbly," replies New York University historian Greg Grandin. "How can it be simultaneously true that Cam-bodia and Bangladesh were strategically marginal and that the outcome of the cold war depended on their destruction?"[47] Kissinger's disregard for "peripheral" states and for his impact on the destiny of individuals ignored the lessons of Nuremberg, with fateful future consequences.

A COLD WAR DEFINITION OF AGGRESSION

While Ferencz and Kissinger were articulating their opposing visions of world order, special committees of the UN General Assembly struggled to articulate a definition of international aggression.[48] Paradox, illusion, and double meaning lay at the heart of the General Assembly's final 1974 definition, techniques necessary to reach a compromise between the Americans, Soviets, and nonaligned states.[49]

On its surface, the definition seems simple. Article 1 defines aggression in its most generic terms as "the use of armed force by a State against the sovereignty, territorial integrity or political independence of another State, or in any other manner inconsistent with the Charter of the United Nations, as set out in this Definition."[50] But like M. C. Escher's trompe l'oeil creations, foreground and background distinctions are obliterated and the viewer can choose one or the other set of shapes as foreground at will.

In *Regular Division of the Plane III*, a woodcut Escher carved between 1957 and 1958, white cavalry march from left to right across a dark background. Turning away and looking back again, perspective flips to dark cavalry marching in the opposite direction. This time, the background is white. The diplomats of the fourth Special Committee use a similar trompe l'oeil to resolve the longstanding quarrel between the Soviets and the Americans over the principle of priority and the principle of intent as the basis for the definition of aggression.[51]

Maxim Litvinov's 1933 view was that the principle of priority, prohibiting first strike, would be the most effective way to deter potential aggressors.[52] Robert Jackson, representing the United States in the negotiations over the London Charter, accepted Litvinov's view, but by 1968 his country had changed course and now considered the intent, or purpose, of the armed attack to be determinative (the principle of intent). The US delegates on the Special Committee argued that: (1) it is often difficult to determine who had struck first; (2) historically, the first use of armed force was often provoked as a pretext for a massive retaliation; and (3) in the context of weapons of mass destruction, it would be too late to defend once the first strike had landed.[53]

The Soviets won over the Arab states, reeling from Israel's preemptive strike in the 1967 War, and they conceded that intent and purpose were more difficult to ascertain than first strike. Professor Julius Stone, capturing the essence of the debate, asked rhetorically, "Is the critical date of the Middle East Crisis 1973 or 1967, or the first attack by Arab states on Israel in 1948, or is it the Balfour Declaration in 1917, or the Arab invasions and conquest of the seventh century, or even perhaps the initial Israelite conquest of the thirteenth century B.C.?"[54] Neither the principle of priority nor the principle of intent provided a clear solution.

According to Ferencz, the technique for arriving at a compromise on the priority versus intent controversy in 1974 was "to employ language that enabled the parties on both sides to interpret the Article to suit their own prior conception": white cavalry marching from left to right or dark cavalry marching from right to left.[55] First strike is decisive so long as the strike is: (1) in contravention of the UN Charter (no further guidance is given as to which interventions amount to a Charter contravention); (2) the Security Council has not determined that the "act of aggression is justified" (i.e., a valid response to provocation, protection against economic aggression, or preemptive self-defense); or (3) the acts concerned or their consequences are of sufficient gravity (no guidance is given as to which acts or consequences surpass the *de minimis* threshold).[56] Rather than resolving the controversy over how to distinguish aggression and self-defense, the 1974 definition tessellated the Soviet and American conceptions into its articles.

Article 3 drew from the 1933 Litvinov-Politis draft, and elaborated on the general definition in the chapeau by providing a list of acts qualifying as aggression: invasion, bombardment, blockade, attacking another state's armed forces, contravening an agreement to station forces in another state (e.g., by refusing to leave), offering one's state as a launching ground for another state to attack a third state, and the sending of armed bands to attack another state. The list was relatively uncontroversial; it reflected the conflicts of the age.

In 1956, when student protests against the communist government ignited Hungary, the Soviet Union invaded with tanks and troops, suppressed the rebellion, and installed a new communist government (violating Article 3[a], had it existed at the time). In Operation Rolling Thunder (1965–68), the United States justified the most intense strategic bombardment of the Cold War (violating Article 3[b]) on the basis of fabricated reports of a North Vietnamese naval attack (allegedly violating Article 3[d]) on an American destroyer stationed in the Gulf of Tonkin. After Cuban exiles trained by the CIA bungled an attempt to overthrow Fidel Castro's communist government in 1961 (violating Article 3[g]), the Soviets began to deploy nuclear missiles to Cuba (not prohibited by the 1974 definition). Though the joint chiefs of staff unanimously recommended a full-scale invasion (which would have violated Article 3[a]), Kennedy opted for a naval "quarantine" where ships would be searched for missiles before being let through to Cuba. This watered-down blockade (did it violate Article 3[c]?) bought Kennedy time to reach out to Soviet Premier Nikita Khrushchev through back channels and broker a solution to the standoff.

Time and again the superpowers and their proxies took aggressive action meant to consolidate their position in the Cold War. They justified their actions with Kissingerian logic, as necessary to maintain global peace and stability, while advancing strategically favorable positions in the aggression working group. This frustrated Ferencz.

A particularly contentious issue in the aggression working group between 1968 and 1974 was whether the list in Article 3 was open or closed.
So-called "economic aggression" was the most contested candidate for
a spot in Article 3. At first glance, the 1974 definition seems to prohibit
only the use of "armed force," not other uses of force such as economic
aggression. All of the acts of aggression listed in Article 3—invasion,
bombing, blockade, etc.—include the use of armed force. Nevertheless, a
protracted debate over the inclusion or exclusion of so-called economic
aggression risked paralyzing the negotiations. The 1967 and 1973 oil
embargoes, whereby the oil-producing Arab states sought to deter Israel's
allies from supporting it militarily by denying them oil, were fresh in the
minds of many delegates.

In the midst of this impasse, the working group once again accommo-
dated competing positions by using the drafting technique that gives the
1974 definition its Escheresque quality. Article 4 qualifies the list of uses
of armed force amounting to aggression: "The acts enumerated above are
not exhaustive and the Security Council may determine that other acts
constitute aggression under the provisions of the Charter." Furthermore,
as Stone points out, no doubt delighting Israel and its allies, the Security
Council is within its powers under Article 2 to decide that the defensive
use of armed force in response to "extreme economic coercion" does not
amount to aggression.[57] The 1974 definition was drafted so that no concept, including economic aggression, could be used as a sword by one
superpower without also being used as a shield by the other, so long as
their international lawyers grasped its Escheresque quality.[58]

The negotiations also took place in the context of divisive anticolo-
nialist independence struggles in Africa, Latin America, and the Middle
East. A team of legal scholars following the negotiations wrote, "China,
the Soviet Union, and some Third World nations vigorously support the
use of force to achieve self-determination. The United States, Japan, and
the European Community abhor the prospect."[59] Stone disapproved of
the Soviet Union and China, who, he felt, "tried to secure the best of both
worlds."[60] While the Soviet Union tried to permit armed force against
"colonial" or "racist" oppressors under Article 7—i.e., armed force against
the interests of Western powers—China sought to authorize armed force
against "imperialist" oppression, which Beijing associated with both the
United States and the Soviet Union.

The deadlock was ended when an unnamed diplomat, grasping the
trompe l'oeil quality of the draft definition, proposed that peoples, "particularly peoples under colonial and racist regimes or other forms of
alien domination," had the right to "struggle" for self-determination and
"to seek and receive support" toward that aim.[61] Ambiguity in the word
"struggle" in Article 7 and the type of "support" allowed the Americans

to read the 1974 definition to permit *peaceful* struggle, while the Soviets could deem *armed* struggle legal under these circumstances and continue to provide military support. According to Ferencz, "Article 7 was the best illustration of the confrontation of ideas which seemed to be irreconcilable, and the achievement of consensus by the insertion of abstract principles which could be interpreted differently by those with opposing views."[62]

Ferencz's commentaries on the 1974 definition of aggression barely restrained his exasperation at the diplomats who he considered shortsighted and wily, intent on advancing national rather than global interests. Inviting the Security Council to determine when aggression had occurred was, to him, "like asking the fox to guard the chicken coop."[63] Ferencz nevertheless maintained his unshakable optimism and faith in progress. "Seen purely as a legal instrument, the consensus definition of aggression may be little better than a sieve, but it does not follow that it therefore has no substance. Although it reflects the fears, the doubts and the hesitations of our time, the definition is a small, cautious and faltering step in the direction of a better world."[64]

The 1974 definition evoked Escher's 1960 sketch *Ascending and Descending*, where a procession of human figures makes its way up an impossible, never-ending, four-sided staircase, while another, moving in the opposite direction, makes its way down. "That staircase is a rather sad, pessimistic subject, as well as being very profound and absurd," said Escher of the piece. "Yes, yes, we climb up and up, we imagine we are ascending; every step is about 10 inches high, terribly tiring—and where does it all get us? Nowhere."[65] Nobody but Ferencz truly expected this 1974 definition to become a crucial building block of the crime of aggression, prosecutable by an international criminal court.

PREVENTING WORLD WAR III: BALANCING FORCE AND LAW

The Escheresque quality of Cold War–era *jus ad bellum* aggravated Ferencz and drew the scorn of Kissinger. Others, such as UN Secretary-General Dag Hammarskjöld, saw an opportunity. Hammarskjöld realized that the UN was navigating an emergent system in which force and law were mingling and shaping each other. He was at the helm of an embattled organization, scapegoated by states for their own diplomatic failures, attacked by the Soviets as an imperialist puppet and by American McCarthyites as a communist hotbed. Between his 1953 election and his 1961 death in a mysterious plane crash over the Congo, Hammarskjöld became masterful at harnessing legal principles and power dynamics to manage degenerating, violent crises. He successfully brokered the release of American airmen captured by Chinese forces during the Korean War. Working with Canadian diplomat Lester B. Pearson, he helped diffuse the 1956 Suez crisis by negotiating an armed UN emergency force between the belligerents, the first of its kind.

Rather than rely on collective peace enforcement after the fact, Hammarskjöld rushed to flash points, earning the trust of the key players, calming situations that risked embroiling the great powers. The UN Observation Group he proposed helped diffuse Lebanon's 1958 electoral crisis, which was drawing in neighboring states and antagonizing the superpowers.[66] "The situation was beclouded by misinformation, rumor, and preconceived ideas," recalls UN official Brian Urquhart, "to an extent that urgently demanded an objective and disinterested go-between and some realistic and unbiased fact-finding."[67]

Law was an asset in Hammarskjöld's diplomacy, not a liability, and he used it to assure the belligerents he was committed to community goals, not partisan ones.[68] Rather than "set law against power," he used widely acknowledged legal principles such as interdependence and reciprocity to find "islands of agreement" within the limits of the realities on the ground.[69] For Hammarskjöld, writes David Kennedy, law "could serve as a general vocabulary of statecraft and toolkit for innovative solutions rather than simply a checklist of obligations, limits, and entitlements."[70] His creative approach, even using seemingly paradoxical principles such as sovereignty and community, to determine the goals and direction of collective action, intrigued legal scholars of his day and ours.[71] "Hammarskjöld made no sharp distinction between law and policy," Columbia law professor Oscar Schachter wrote in 1961. "In this he departed clearly from the prevailing positivist approach."[72]

In this, Hammarskjöld differed from Kissinger, who despised paradox, writing in 1957, "A series of paradoxes may be intriguing for the philosopher but they are a nightmare for the statesman, for the latter must not only contemplate but resolve them."[73] And he differed from Ferencz, who bemoaned the paradoxical quality of Cold War–era *jus ad bellum*. Hammarskjöld reveled in opposing tendencies—for example, human rights versus state sovereignty—which he weighed and balanced in each crisis until an acceptable solution was found. "I use the word [law] in its broadest sense, including not only written law but the whole social pattern of established rules of action and behavior," he explained to the University of Chicago Law School's 1960 graduating class.[74] Hammarskjöld's broad understanding of law allowed him to see Kissinger's law of force and Ferencz's rule of law as aspects of the same world order.

During the night of September 17, 1961, Hammarskjöld was traveling to meet Moïse Tshombé and negotiate a ceasefire with the Congolese Government. Tshombé was the Western-backed secessionist leader who declared the mineral-rich province of Katanga an independent state following Congolese independence. Before Hammarskjöld could reach Tshombé, his aircraft plummeted into the dense Northern Rhodesian forest, killing the secretary-general and his team. Successive UN enquiries, including one in 2015, were unable to establish whether the crash was an accident or an assassination.[75] Many players in the Congo had an interest in Hammarskjöld's demise: the Katangan rebels (Hammarskjöld had authorized a UN force to assist the Congolese authorities to restore order), European mining companies, the British, the Americans.[76] Former US President Harry Truman told the press that Hammarskjöld "was on the point of getting something done when they killed him. Notice that I said 'when they killed him.'"[77] Truman didn't say who "they" were. President John F. Kennedy called Hammarskjöld "the greatest statesman of our century."[78]

Kissinger's balance of power, Ferencz's rule of law, and Hammarskjöld's hybrid concept of the Cold War international order developed a unique personality, albeit a neurotic one. Kissinger's power instinct was offset by Ferencz's commitment to world community, and Hammarskjöld struggled to pragmatically integrate the competing imperatives. This international order contained disquieting blind spots and biases. States, not civilizations, religions, cities, corporations, or individuals, became the focus of world politics. The competitive relationship between the United States and the Soviet Union framed all international interaction. This oversimplified conflicts such as the Vietnam War, casting it as a proxy war when it was also a decolonization struggle, a humanitarian disaster, a crime scene, and myriad experiences for the people whose lives were upended by it.

These blind spots and biases distracted attention from crucial harbingers of the future. The post–Cold War international order would be characterized not only by nuclear war between the great powers or its aversion, but also the decisions of one "peripheral" individual nurturing an idiosyncratic 1970s and 1980s grievance. That individual was the free radical, Abdul Qadeer (AQ) Khan.

A. Q. KHAN: HARBINGER OF WARS TO COME

Born in Bhopal, India, in 1936, son of a Muslim family, A. Q. Khan was "devout, studious, and respectful of his teachers, and for good measure he was also a perfect son."[79] Bhopal was home to large Hindu and Muslim populations at a time when tensions were running high and violence between the communities ignited in other parts of the country. When the British quit India in 1947, the country was cleaved into India and Pakistan, itself divided into Eastern and Western territories. The Khan family home landed in India, and, fearing for their safety, they and millions of other Muslims moved to Pakistan.[80] In 1952, AQ matriculated in India, boarded a Pakistan-bound train full of Muslim émigrés, and was attacked and robbed by Indian railroad officials and police.[81] The experience traumatized him.[82]

In Karachi, Pakistan, AQ lived with his brother, excelling in college science.[83] Pakistan had just fought India and lost the battle for the largely Muslim state of Kashmir, exacerbating AQ's anti-India grievance and corroborating his father's propaganda about crafty, hegemonic Hindus.[84] After graduation, he applied and was admitted to study metallurgical engineering at a respected technical university in West Berlin.

AQ had a knack for languages and adjusted well to Europe, studying in Delft, meeting and wedding Dutch Henny, and completing a doctorate in metallurgical engineering in Belgium. "He was not a brilliant researcher but a willing and hardworking one," writes biographer William Langewiesche.[85] "He was affable and outgoing and, as everyone agreed, just a very nice guy." In 1972, AQ was hired by Physics Dynamic Research Laboratory, an Amsterdam-based consulting firm specializing in the design of ultra-centrifuges, crucial to enriching uranium for atomic energy.

AQ might have led a quiet Dutch life with Henny and their daughters had it not been for additional life-changing traumas. First was the 1971 secessionist rebellion in East Pakistan, which AQ monitored anxiously from afar. Just twenty-four years after Pakistan was created, it was coming undone. Pakistan moved to crush the rebellion, sending millions of refugees fleeing to India. India intervened, routing the Pakistani military, which had been abandoned by its US and Chinese allies in the face of Soviet opposition. East Pakistan broke away, becoming Bangladesh. Three years later, with Pakistan still stung by its 1971 defeat, India successfully detonated its first nuclear bomb near the Pakistani border. It was obvious that the bomb, incongruously called *Smiling Buddha*, was intended for war against Pakistan, and AQ rebelled against the world's complacency.

AQ's first offer to help Pakistan build a "Muslim" bomb was rebuffed by the two Pakistani engineers he approached on their trip to the Netherlands. Undeterred, he wrote to Pakistani Prime Minister Zulfikar Ali Bhutto, and was rewarded with Bhutto's invitation to meet in Islamabad, relayed by the Pakistani embassy in The Hague. They met secretly on AQ's family trip to Pakistan, and he persuaded the prime minister, struggling to build a plutonium bomb, to open a parallel track involving uranium. Returning to work in the Netherlands, AQ translated secret technical instructions into Urdu and sent them to Pakistan, along with centrifuge pieces collected from the trash. Suspicious upper management reassigned AQ away from centrifuges. Two months later, he took his family on vacation to Pakistan and never returned.

With India in his sights, Prime Minister Bhutto provided AQ with resources to build a nuclear bomb. AQ mined his European industrial and
academic connections to procure parts and expertise. Neither the companies nor the scientists selling components and know-how to AQ were un-
duly concerned about long-term repercussions. AQ exploited loopholes
in the international regulation of nuclear technology, and used the cover
of the United States, a Cold War ally of Pakistan, to develop Pakistan's
nuclear capacity. By 1982, AQ's lab had produced its first weapons-grade
uranium. By 1986, it was capable of producing its own bombs.

In May 1998, India conducted its second nuclear test; two weeks later,
Pakistan detonated its own bomb. AQ's Pakistani rival, Samar Mubarakmand, head of the parallel plutonium program, received official credit
while AQ was sidelined—turning him into a free radical.[86] Aggrieved, AQ
became a veritable nuclear Walmart. He delivered seminars to foreign scientists on uranium enrichment, sold Libya's Muammar Qaddafi a turn-
key nuclear program for one hundred million US dollars, and provided
nuclear equipment and expertise to North Korea, Iran, and one other
state, likely Syria or Saudi Arabia.[87] Whether Pakistan encouraged AQ's
nuclear proliferation or was too disorganized to stop it is less important
than the unleashing of an unregulated, unaccountable global threat. By
promiscuously spilling nuclear secrets, AQ single-handedly subverted the
Cold War international order(s) and jeopardized world peace.

The first world-changing occurrence of nuclear proliferation by a radicalized individual was met with a collective blank stare. Sigmund Freud
defined neurosis as "the inability to tolerate ambiguity." The neurosis of
the Cold War saw Pakistan as peripheral, and unitary states as aligned
with either the United States or the Soviet Union. In addition, the post–
World War II failure to coordinate the UN Charter with the Nuremberg
precedent ignored "peripheral" nonstate radicals. These rigidities of mind
distracted the statesmen of the era from the experiences of the people
they considered collateral damage, enabling A. Q. Khan to slip though
the ideological cracks. When he opened Pandora's box, aberrant individuals possessing nuclear weapons ushered in a new age. He demonstrated
that the Cold War international order, focused on sovereign, territorially
bounded states, was incapable of keeping us safe.

Global security required a more potent law.

Nuremberg Renaissance

THE 1990S

> What we may be witnessing is not just the end of the Cold War, or the passing of a particular period of post-war history, but the end of history as such.
> —Francis Fukuyama, *The End of History?* 1989

> Reporters in the Balkan wars often observed that when they were told atrocity stories they were occasionally uncertain whether these stories had occurred yesterday or in 1941, or 1841, or 1441.
> —Michael Ignatieff, "The Elusive Goal of War Trials," 1997

> History is never one story, and the telling of history involves a certain settling of accounts.
> —Martha Minow, *Between Vengeance and Forgiveness: Facing History After Genocide and Mass Violence*, 1998

The 1990s saw the most important shift from politics to law since World War II. Two distinct legal frameworks developed in parallel, one to address individual mass criminality and the other state illegal force. In international criminal law, the individual would become the primary subject of regulation of mass criminality, rather than the state. In the international law of war, the *jus ad bellum*, various camps would vie to define post–Cold War regulation of state illegal force. These two legal frameworks had met briefly at Nuremberg, 1945, when top Nazi aggressors were punished individually for crimes against peace. It would take until 2010 for international criminal law and the *jus ad bellum* to reunite in a full Nuremberg renaissance. After a forty-five-year hiatus, the merging of the two legal frameworks began.

This chapter tells the story of the 1990s Nuremberg renaissance and the struggle of liberals without a unifying communist foe to settle on new legal justifications for war.

CALIBRATION OF THE LAW OF WAR

The end of the Cold War was a festive moment for Western liberals. Mc-Donald's opens in Moscow; everyone checks Hotmail on the World Wide Web. Irony is the leitmotif, racism a faux pas. Cell phones ring. Western liberals had defeated fascism in 1945, and now communism. American political theorist Francis Fukuyama proclaimed "the end point of mankind's ideological evolution and the universalization of Western liberal democracy as the final form of human government."[1] National-security scholar John Mueller heralded the obsolescence of major war.[2] US President George H. W. Bush, invoking Woodrow Wilson, announced a new "New World Order."[3]

The post–Cold War moment was reminiscent of two other moments of the twentieth century, 1918–28 (post-WWI) and 1945–55 (post-WWII). All three decades began as a world war ended, unleashing creative legal energy and an earnest will to use the rule of law to prevent another epochal conflict. The ends of World War I and World War II were marked by the creation of liberal international institutions designed to promote peace—the League of Nations after World War I, the United Nations after World War II—but in both cases the failure of liberalism to win a decisive victory meant that these legal norms existed alongside informal norms hammered out in the conflict between the great powers, lacking the legitimacy of law.[4] The post–Cold War moment was different. Here, liberalism won outright.

This triumph presented the victors with an opportunity to reshape the international order according to their ideals, including a global legal framework regulating the use of force. Without fascism and communism as counterpoints, the liberal political movement was required to look within itself to determine when the use of armed force against other nations was justified. What it discovered was not reassuring.

The shared liberal values of individualism, freedom, equality, universality, and progress had seemed far clearer set against fascist and communist threats, and suddenly appeared amorphous as a guide to action. State-centered Cold War–era thinking was dangerously outdated in an era when ethnic militias, insurgents, mercenaries, rogue leaders, and individuals with unprecedented access to loose Soviet nuclear weapons threatened global security. Liberal views on the use of armed force competed for dominance, and a series of 1990s-era wars were interpreted in self-serving ways by competing camps.

As the decade progressed, each war seemed to discredit one or another of the four liberal camps: that is, law-and-order liberals, democracy promoters, isolationists, and humanitarian interventionists. Law-and-order liberals, including George H. W. Bush, seized on the end of the Cold War as an opportunity to perfect the Westernized post–World War II international legal order previously thwarted by the Soviet Union.[5] Democracy promoters, some of whom identified as neoconservatives, were less committed to perfecting post–World War II international institutions and more committed to liberalizing the domestic political and economic arrangements of foreign states ruled by undemocratic regimes.[6] Isolationists, intellectual heirs to Charles Lindberg's interwar, nationalistic, radical-right America-First movement, sought to strictly limit the use of force to cases in which core American security or economic interests were threatened.[7] Humanitarian interventionists such as Tony Blair were driven to enforce human rights abroad, particularly when leaders committed atrocities against their own people.[8]

Ultimately, the most important development in the law of war was the new focus on the individual in the international sphere. Where states had been the principal subject of international regulation for at least two centuries, key developments in the 1990s shifted the focus onto individuals. Those that sought to regulate the individual and not just the state (the humanitarian interventionists and democracy promoters) emerged from the decade more relevant than those that remained state-centric (the isolationists and the law-and-order liberals).

But, ultimately, no one would escape the 1990s unscathed.

The Individual in the Law of War: Panama

The Cold War–era language of the law of war was inapt for use in the apprehension of an individual. Yet, in the United States, an individual lawbreaker had become the primary focus. Within weeks of the fall of the Berlin wall, President George H. W. Bush launched Operation Just Cause, the first post–Cold War military operation by a liberal state. Between twenty-five and thirty thousand US troops and over three hundred aircraft invaded Panama to arrest Manuel Noriega—general, de facto leader, CIA Cold War asset, turncoat—for trafficking drugs in the United States.[9]

Within hours of his capture, Bush announced that Noriega, scourge of Panama, would be arraigned in district court in Miami for trafficking drugs in the United States. "The United States is committed to providing General Noriega a fair trial," Bush assured Americans.[10] Legal authority for the invasion of Panama was another matter. "The U.S. used its resources in a manner consistent with political, diplomatic and moral principles," he proudly announced, carefully leaving the word "legal" off his list.[11]

The arrest operation was popular in the United States, while unsettling to the rest of the world. Bush had blatantly disregarded the UN Charter and the vote of the Organization of American States, and unilaterally invaded Panama to advance US interests. Human-rights advocates alleged a US cover-up in the deaths of thousands of Panamanian civilians in the carpet bombing of the poor neighborhood of El Chorrillo, supposedly a pro-Noriega stronghold.[12] Disastrous Cold War–era "regime changes," where the United States, under the spell of Henry Kissinger, installed compliant, corrupt, and at times genocidal dictators as a bulwark against communism were fresh in the minds of ordinary Latin Americans. It was no secret that Noriega had originally been a CIA asset permitted to deal drugs in the United States in exchange for his cooperation in the fight against communism.[13]

The justifications for the invasion and its execution were problematic, but the arrest of Noriega helped imagine a revitalized international law of war in which political and military leaders were accountable for their crimes.

Law-of-War Blind Spot: Iraq

Washington's next war was a year later in the Persian Gulf. In 1990, Saddam Hussein's incendiary speech demanded that Iraq's Arab neighbors, primarily Kuwait and Saudi Arabia, forgive thirty billion dollars of Iraqi debt.[14] Iraq, he said, had shouldered the burden of containing their common foe, revolutionary Iran, during the Iran-Iraq war of 1980–88. Saddam also accused Kuwait of "economic warfare," siphoning more than its allotment of oil from a common pool along their border. When his erstwhile ally kept pumping crude oil, Saddam invaded and annexed Kuwait.

US President Bush and leaders of other liberal states considered Iraq's invasion of Kuwait a textbook violation of the UN Charter. Unlike in Panama, in Iraq President Bush was on firm legal footing, and also on firm diplomatic and military footing. US Secretary of State James Baker assembled the largest military alliance since the "united nations" of World War II. Beyond condemning Saddam's violation of the UN Charter, they aimed to prevent him from controlling the bulk of the world's oil.

Saddam refused to quit Kuwait. The coalition invaded and routed his forces. Bush left Saddam in power, unlike Noriega, possibly to avoid another Vietnam, possibly to occupy Iraq's oilfields when Saddam, as expected, violated UN sanctions. The sanctions would punish Iraq—that is, the dictator's oppressed population—rather than Saddam, who had the resources and know-how to avoid their bite.

Proponents of international law and order under the UN Charter saw the Gulf War as the definitive armed conflict of the 1990s. The victory of liberal states and their Arab allies lent credence to the conviction that the state-centric global order had been perfected. Bush's 1991 "New World Order" speech was borrowed from Churchill's 1944 vision of a new League of Nations,[15] with the addition of "overwhelming military power." Bush envisaged:

> a world order in which "the principles of justice and fair play protect the weak against the strong. . . ." A world where the United Nations, freed from cold war stalemate, is poised to fulfill the historic vision of its founders. A world in which freedom and respect for human rights find a home among all nations. The Gulf war put this new world to its first test. And my fellow Americans, we passed that test.[16]

Bush's new world order appealed to proponents of international law and order under the UN Charter, while undermining the arguments of liberal isolationists. Modern American isolationism, which sprang from the radical individualism of Charles Lindbergh and other conservative intellectuals in the "America-First" movement between World Wars I and II, was discredited by the Japanese invasion of Pearl Harbor and the (Kissingerian) logic of the Cold War, which required international engagement to contain communism.[17] It resurfaced in the 1990s under a new champion—Pat Buchanan—who, unimpressed by the Gulf War and Bush's speech, stuck to his guns. "We love the old republic," Buchanan warned, speaking for himself and his followers, "and when we hear phrases like 'new world order,' we release the safety catches on our revolvers."[18] Buchanan's isolationist views on trade, immigration, and interventionism were dismissed by the Republican establishment in the 1990s, only to resurface and propel Donald Trump to the presidency in 2016.[19]

Absent from the triumphant accounts of operations Desert Storm (the air campaign) and Desert Shield (the ground war) is the fact that Saddam Hussein, like Manuel Noriega, was a US asset propped up to advance American interests in some "peripheral" region during the Cold War. As US policymakers did with Noriega, they overlooked Saddam's atrocities, including his gassing and bulldozing of entire Kurdish villages during his genocidal Anfal campaign in 1987–88, so long as he towed the line.[20] President Bush and UK Prime Minister Margaret Thatcher discussed holding Saddam personally accountable for the invasion of Kuwait, but Bush's New World Order ultimately sidelined the Nuremberg precedent and focused on state responsibility for Iraq.[21] In 2003, America attempted to clean up the Iraq mess in the Second Gulf War, only to unleash a more pervasive and resilient nonstate threat, ISIS.

Enforcement Trauma: Somalia

Emboldened by the enforcement of international law in the Gulf, liberal internationalists were soon presented with another conflict relevant to the future definition of aggression.

In Somalia, 1991, rival clans ousted Mohamed Siad Barre, who had united the factious country under his authoritarian rule for twenty years. The clans set upon one another in a bloody struggle for power that exacerbated a humanitarian emergency caused by a nationwide drought. The collapse of governmental authority in Somalia brought the term "failed state" into 1990s use-of-force parlance.[22] The "failed-state" concept would become the basis for the United States' expansive 2014 justification for the use of force against terrorists in Syria.[23]

UN Secretary-General Boutros Boutros-Ghali pressed for UN-authorized force in Somalia and prevailed.[24] The UN-brokered arms embargo grew into a humanitarian assistance mission and then the deployment of peacekeepers to defend humanitarian workers delivering food and medicine in the midst of clan warfare. Twenty-four peacekeepers were killed and mutilated in Mogadishu, and President Bush offered American firepower on the condition that the new mission would be under US command.[25] In Operation Gothic Serpent, eighteen American troops were killed and seventy-three men were wounded attempting to capture clan leaders responsible for murdering the peacekeepers. *Washington Post* journalist Jim Hoagland dubbed the shifting objectives and unplanned military commitments in Somalia "mission creep."[26]

The Gothic Serpent operation introduced the idea of humanitarian intervention alongside Security Council authorization and self-defense as a possible legal justification for force.[27] The question of when it was legal to rescue populations from atrocities would become central to defining the crime of aggression. Disagreement among isolationists and humanitarian interventionists over the lessons to draw remained unresolved throughout the 1990s.

But the failed attempt to arrest the Somali warlords made liberal states reticent to enforce the rule of law, and so traumatized the United States that it would take years for it to intervene for humanitarian reasons again. David Scheffer, senior advisor to Madeline Albright, describes events in Somalia as "a distant scream that penetrated the subconscious thinking of policy-makers."[28] Operation Gothic Serpent would have tragic consequences in Rwanda, which erupted into genocidal violence seven months after US President Bill Clinton announced his intention to withdraw American forces from Somalia. Stung by the murder and mutilation of UN peacekeepers in Somalia, wary of mission creep, unable to see Rwandan violence as anything other than a conventional war between belligerent armies, the liberal democracies stood by as Rwanda's Tutsi were exterminated.[29]

Shame and Responsibility: Rwanda

On April 6, 1994, Rwandan President Juvénal Habyarimana's plane was shot down by a surface-to-air missile over Kigali, igniting the genocide.

News of the president's assassination spread quickly. Soldiers and volunteers erected rudimentary roadblocks across the capital.[30] The presidential guard murdered opposition leaders. Orders from the capital were passed through administrative hierarchies to village leaders, who mobilized the population for "community work projects," a euphemism for the slaughter of every Tutsi they could hunt down. In one hundred days, those perpetrating the genocide killed between eight hundred thousand and one million men, women, and children.

The Rwandan genocide didn't fit the familiar Western liberal scripts. From a Kissingerian perspective, Rwanda wasn't even a sideshow because it didn't provoke great-power competition.[31] The isolationists, confronted by daily television and print images of the murder of men, women, and children in their homes and churches, seemed vulgar and out of touch. The Rwandan genocide was a problem that could not be solved with nuclear deterrence or open markets. Nor was the Rwandan genocide a "clash of civilizations."[32] Hutu and Tutsi were Banyarwanda, cultivators and herders who shared the same language and culture and had lived together in the Rwandan hills for centuries. If the end of the Cold War was the United States' "unipolar moment," as conservative American political scientist Charles Krauthammer claimed, where did the Rwandan genocide fit in?[33]

With no organized political constituency pressing for action, liberal states froze. Samantha Power maintained that it was an explicit policy objective to stay out of Rwanda during the slaughter, adding that in the case of the French, it was worse.[34] They continued to support their genocidal allies.[35]

Having warned the UN of a massacre, Paul Kagame, commander of the insurgent Rwandese Patriotic Front (RPF), launched a disciplined attack intended to oust the genocidal regime and stop the slaughter.[36] His strategy was to encircle Kigali and sever the Rwandan Army from its supplies. The RPF routed the government forces, who were busy killing Tutsi. They occupied the country and stopped the genocide as Western powers sat by.

Largely dismissed in Western capitals at the time, the Rwandan genocide had important consequences for law regulating military force. In the latter part of the 1990s, shame over disastrous liberal inaction in Rwanda had a retributive effect, pushing the law of war toward muscular humanitarianism, as well as toward individual criminal accountability.

NUREMBERG RENAISSANCE

The reevaluation of Cold War liberal doctrine on the use of force was urgent in the Balkans. Michael Ignatieff, in central Croatia in the early

1990s, was stopped by drunk Serb paramilitaries at a roadblock, accused of spying for the Croats, and arrested. "The writ of the 'international community,'" he learned, "ran no further than 150 metres either side of the UN checkpoint."[37] The Cold War had dictated the patterns of global violence according to spheres of influence. Ignatieff's arrest represented a new era of lawless, disaggregated violence. "The key narrative of the new world order," Ignatieff concluded, "is the disintegration of nation states into ethnic civil war; the key architects of that order are warlords; and the key language for our age is ethnic nationalism."[38]

In 1989, Serbian President Slobodan Milošević delivered a nationalist speech to over one million Serbs in the predominantly ethnic Albanian province of Kosovo, introducing hegemonic intentions and a nationalist platform to counter the post–Cold War collapse of the Yugoslav Federation.

In the summer of 1992, human-rights organizations and the Western media publicly revealed Serbian-run concentration camps.[39] The European Community struggled to negotiate a political deal with Milošević to peacefully resolve the competing national agendas in disintegrating Yugoslavia. In the midst of escalating ethnic violence, the UN Security Council settled on a strongly worded but ineffective resolution, creating UN "safe areas" monitored by lightly armed peacekeepers.[40] Bosnian Serb forces led by General Ratko Mladić overran the Dutch peacekeepers in the Srebrenica "safe area" and executed thousands of men and boys as liberal democracies stood by.[41]

The fall of Srebrenica was a disgrace for divided post–World War II liberal internationalists, who had not succeeded in negotiating the principles of a post–Cold War doctrine on the use of force. The Srebrenica massacre strengthened the arguments of humanitarian hawks, including Madeline Albright, Clinton's UN ambassador, and Richard Holbrooke, Clinton's envoy to the Balkans, who had pleaded with the president for a more robust response to Serb aggression.[42] Srebrenica also undermined the credibility of liberals who had put their faith in UN protection of international order.[43] Perversely, the UN had promised the Muslim population safety in Bosnia if it handed over its arms, then failed to honor that promise when its enemies attacked.

The Srebrenica massacre lent weight to the arguments of isolationists such as Pat Buchanan, who claimed that Western intervention does more harm than good, and simultaneous credence to the new humanitarian hawks such as Michael Ignatieff, who argued for a shift in focus from national security to human security. For many liberals, the Srebrenica massacre, a failure of the rule of law, demanded meaningful, legal retribution.

Payam Akhavan, today one of the world's most sought-after international lawyers, recalled the moment when his small investigative mission to Croatia helped resurrect the Nuremberg precedent. Only twenty-six years old, having just completed his Harvard Master of Laws thesis on the enforcement of the genocide convention, he was a UN investigator in Croatia's bombed-out hinterland. In October 1992, he was sitting in a dilapidated schoolhouse in Krajina next to Hans Corell, a Swedish judge and diplomat whom the Conference for Security and Cooperation in Europe had appointed, along with Helmut Türk (Austria) and Gro Hillestad Thune (Norway) to investigate allegations of ethnic cleansing in the Balkans.[44]

"We're scheduled to speak with the 'minister of justice' of the self-proclaimed Republic of Serbian Krajina, a secessionist region of newly independent Croatia who is sending a message by making us wait," Payam remembers. The interlocutor had a peg leg, unkempt beard, and the uniform of a local extremist militia.[45] He seemed as confounded by Payam's team as they were by him. He took a seat and waited for questions.

Did the minster have any information about the murder, torture, and forced displacement of non-Serb families in the region? The investigators' sources claimed that between two and three thousand missing civilians had been executed by the Yugoslav National Army and Serbian irregular forces.[46] Were the police taking steps to ensure the safety of non-Serbs? Were they enforcing their 1991 law allowing for the confiscation of property belonging to an "enemy of the Serbian Republic of Krajina"? What were his comments? "Blissfully oblivious to the limitations of his thuggish audience," Payam recalls, "Ambassador Corell lectured the menacing warlord about human rights law, like a stern schoolmaster scolding a delinquent student."[47]

The "minister of justice" responded with a long history lesson on the excesses of the Ustashe, Croatian fascists who had murdered hundreds of thousands of Serbs, Jews, and Roma during World War II. Payam guessed at the minister's age. If over fifty, he might have experienced these atrocities firsthand, victim before perpetrator. The investigators asked about recent attacks against Croat civilians, and the minister responded with hair-raising accounts of foreign occupation and atrocities against Christians by Ottoman Turks. The team had heard allegations that this man had killed Croats with his bare hands. Deformed by war and prejudice and lacking significant official condemnation of past anti-Serb atrocities, was he actualizing an aberrant notion of justice? What form of justice might mitigate this cycle of violence, if any?

In Vienna, Payam and his team focused on the evidence of ethnic cleansing they had accumulated on their mission. Yugoslavia brought Payam back to his childhood as a Bahá'í minority in post-revolution Iran, where loved ones had been abducted and tortured to death by the Islamist regime. He was tired of the perpetrators and their alibis and wanted more than just another report: "It was time to do the obvious." That is, "arrest and punish the bastards."[48]

The team thought through how this might work. Who would apprehend and try the perpetrators, and under what law? "This wasn't post-War Germany," Payam said. "The war was ongoing. There would be no victor's justice."[49]

He didn't recall who invoked the Nuremberg precedent, but he remembered the team's reaction: "The idea was completely inadequate and wishful thinking," since it had been on the agenda of the UN General Assembly with no effect for more than forty years.[50] "But it had at least to be said." Payam's team would propose a new political reality, "one in which accountability was part of the cost-benefit calculus of power."[51] The team recommended an ad hoc international tribunal for the former Yugoslavia, empowered to prosecute atrocity crimes committed by all sides. The focus was on atrocity crimes within the former Yugoslavia, and the proposal excluded the crime of aggression.

The Nuremberg idea was in the air. In 1989, Trinidad and Tobago, alarmed by the rise of international drug trafficking, asked the UN General Assembly to resume discussions about the creation of an international criminal court with jurisdiction over trafficking and other international and transnational crimes. The UN General Assembly tasked the International Law Commission (ILC) with preparing a draft. The ILC made headway, but was stymied by the crime of aggression and failed to include a definition. Instead, it listed a number of problems with the idea: there was no antiaggression treaty equivalent to the 1948 Genocide Convention upon which to base the crime of aggression; the 1974 General Assembly definition of aggression dealt with acts by states, not individuals; it was intended as a guide for the Security Council, not a criminal court; the UN Charter granted the Security Council primary responsibility for determining whether aggression had occurred and it was doubtful whether an international criminal court could make independent determinations.[52] Other 1990s-era efforts at drafting a definition of the crime of aggression foundered as well, though the ILC's 1996 "Draft Code of Crimes against the Peace and Security of Mankind" contained a promising but oft-overlooked attempt.[53]

A news story on the Balkans accompanied by a black-and-white image of emaciated men behind barbed wire in a Serb concentration camp reminiscent of Auschwitz provoked public outrage.[54] German Foreign Minister Klaus Kinkel proposed an ad hoc tribunal akin to that of Payam's team.[55] In a controversial, unprecedented expansion of its powers, the Security Council created the International Criminal Tribunal for the former Yugoslavia (ICTY).[56] The Security Council granted the tribunal priority over national courts in prosecuting defendants for genocide, war crimes, and crimes against humanity committed in the Yugoslav Wars, though national courts were expected to prosecute leftover perpetrators. Because the tribunal was created by a Chapter VII UN Charter "peace enforcement" resolution, states were obliged to cooperate with its orders.[57] "There is an echo in this chamber today," Albright told the Security Council. "The Nuremberg principles have been reaffirmed."[58]

The ICTY was a triumphant moment in the Nuremberg renaissance. But the Vietnam-era's "intensive reprioritization of legal focus" from aggression to atrocity had outlived the Cold War.[59] Atrocities, not aggression, were the main preoccupation in the disintegrating Yugoslavia, and the crime of aggression was omitted from the ICTY Statute. Nevertheless, key innovations of the tribunal created a new legal framework for the prosecution of the crime of aggression. These innovations were an important step in fulfilling the Nuremberg legacy in 2010, when the crime of aggression once again joined genocide, war crimes, and crimes against humanity as a core component of international law.[60]

In early 1994, on a Saturday, German commandos acting on a tip from a public television station arrested Duško Tadić on a Munich street.[61] President of the local board of the Serb Democratic Party, policeman, army reservist, café owner, Tadić was also the Butcher of Prijedor, who had tortured and killed inmates at the Omarska concentration camp. ICTY Prosecutor Richard Goldstone's indictment accused Tadić, among other crimes, of forcing a Muslim inmate to bite off another's testicles.[62] Tadić was transferred to The Hague for trial, the tribunal's first defendant.

The *Tadić Case* was foundational to modern international criminal law, one of two parallel legal developments underlying the crime of aggression.[63] By defining key international law doctrines, the ICTY created precedents necessary for courts worldwide to try aggression.

ICTY judges established the legitimacy of a criminal court mandated by the UN Security Council and validated this method of establishing international tribunals, which had been challenged by Tadić.[64] Henceforth, international criminal justice would be a recognized facet of the Security Council's international peace and security mandate. The judges created the possibility that nonstate actors, "activists" like Tadić, could be held directly criminally responsible for international crimes.[65] It resurrected a liability doctrine akin to conspiracy, called "joint criminal enterprise," whereby an individual could be held accountable for a collective act, such as war, if the perpetrators shared a common purpose.[66]

Having established the Yugoslavia Tribunal, the Security Council proceeded to establish a similar ad hoc tribunal for Rwanda.[67] Both were modeled on the Nuremberg precedent but, again, internal atrocities were the focus and the crime of aggression was left out. The International Criminal Tribunal for Rwanda (ICTR) shared a prosecutor, initially

Goldstone, and an appeals chamber with the ICTY to conserve resources and harmonize the international case law.[68] The Nuremberg precedent was proliferating. The danger was that by leaving out the crime of aggression, international criminal law would sanitize armed conflict instead of deterring it.

Two weeks after Radovan Karadžić and Mladić's Serb forces slaughtered seven to eight thousand men and boys in Srebrenica, Goldstone indicted them for genocide and crimes against humanity. On the day of the indictment, they invaded the UN safe area of Zepa.[69] Though NATO had provided sporadic close air support to UN peacekeepers in Bosnia and had sparred with Serb fighter jets over Banja Luka, it was Karadžić and Mladić's atrocities that prompted Operation Deliberate Force, a massive NATO bombing campaign of Bosnian Serb positions. Operation Deliberate Force in conjunction with the 1995 Dayton peace process ended the war in Bosnia.[70] Given their ICTY indictments, Karadžić and Mladić avoided negotiations, clearing the way for new negotiators. The post–Cold War interactions between politics and law, peace and justice, were becoming apparent.

In Yugoslavia, the prevention and punishment of atrocity crimes became a potential justification for war. For the first time, international peacekeepers arrested international criminals for violating international law. UK Prime Minister Tony Blair, a humanitarian hawk, instructed British peacekeepers to arrest ICTY fugitives hiding in areas they patrolled. "Their actions," human-rights activist Aryeh Neier recalls, "persuaded (or embarrassed) troops from other NATO countries, among them the United States and France, also to make arrests."[71] These UN-mandated arrests were the beginning of contemporary international-criminal-law enforcement. Yet, according to Scheffer, "excuses, prevarications, and fearful strategizing in the capitals of the major Western democracies" delayed efforts to arrest Karadžić and Mladić, powerful leaders rumored to be protected by elite Serb forces.[72] The same timidity that stymied genuine efforts at enforcement by Scheffer and others in the 1990s might also threaten enforcement of the crime of aggression.

Milošević was a powerful leader successfully arrested for international crimes. ICTY Chief Prosecutor Louise Arbour, the Canadian jurist replacing Goldstone, issued the 1999 Milošević indictment for atrocities in Kosovo.[73] Disaffected Serbs voted him out of power; Milošević refused to recognize the results of the election. Protesters disillusioned by Milošević's authoritarian nationalism stormed parliament and threw him out.[74] He was politically isolated at home and abroad, a condition that would prove common for the successful arrest of powerful leaders and provide a possible prerequisite for the enforcement of the crime of aggression. In 2001, Milošević surrendered to the Serb authorities.[75]

Between 1993 and 2016, Goldstone and the chief prosecutors who succeeded him, Louise Arbour, Carla Del Ponte, and Serge Brammertz, indicted 161 war criminals.[76] Every war criminal sought by the ICTY was captured, surrendered voluntarily, or killed.[77] The ICTR had similar enforcement success. Tribunals were established to end impunity for atrocities in Cambodia (1997), East Timor (2000), Sierra Leone (2002), Bosnia and Herzegovina (2005), Lebanon (2009), and Colombia (2015). States began arresting and trying perpetrators of international crimes in their domestic courts.

Skeptics argued that international criminal trials are costly, slow, and an impediment to negotiated solutions to armed conflicts. They demanded direct evidence of effective deterrence, which proponents of international justice were unable to provide. Proponents countered that international criminal trials are permeating national systems, generating a "justice cascade," causing states to improve domestic human-rights practices and changing world politics.[78]

What nobody questioned was that the Nuremberg precedent had attained a renaissance. International criminal law was a functioning system poised to revitalize the law of war. The trials following the Yugoslav crisis were the beginning of the global diffusion of the Nuremberg principles. They also strengthened the humanitarian interventionists' position in the post–Cold War use-of-force debates, and spurred the 1990s' reappraisal of the law of war.

An independent commission charged with analyzing contested aspects of the NATO military intervention against Serb forces in Kosovo concluded that the campaign had been "illegal but legitimate": illegal because it did not receive prior Security Council approval, but legitimate because all diplomatic avenues were exhausted and intervention was vital to prevent Milošević's atrocities against Kosovar Albanians.[79] The NATO intervention in Kosovo was a victory for humanitarian interventionists and a defeat for law-and-order liberals.[80] Nothing could have been more objectionable to the isolationists than the humanitarian interventionists' push for increased engagement in foreign wars. Humanitarian hawks hoped to bring the Nuremberg precedent and the UN Charter's rules on the use of force into closer harmony by creating a new legal justification, the prevention of atrocity crimes. States would retain primary responsibility for the safety of their populations, but other states, civil-society organizations, regional organizations, and international institutions would shoulder more responsibility to assist in humanitarian emergencies. If a state receiving peaceful humanitarian and diplomatic support nonetheless failed to protect its population or, as in Rwanda and Kosovo, was itself the perpetrator of crimes, other states or coalitions were required to take action, including the use of force.[81] The use of force to prevent atrocity crimes was not called humanitarian intervention but, rather, "responsibility to protect."[82]

UN Secretary-General Kofi Annan, in his 1999 speech to the General Assembly, laid down the challenge for both sides in the debate.[83] To the law-and-order liberals, he cited the Rwandan example, asking if in the days leading up to the genocide, "a coalition of States had been prepared to act in defense of the Tutsi population, but did not receive prompt Council authorization, should such a coalition have stood aside and allowed the horror to unfold?" Annan challenged the humanitarian hawks on Kosovo: "Is there not a danger of such interventions undermining the imperfect, yet resilient, security system created after the Second World War, and of setting dangerous precedents for future interventions without a clear criterion to decide who might invoke these precedents, and in what circumstances?"[84]

The hazy line between humanitarian intervention and aggression was to become a crucial problem in drafting and adjudicating the crime of aggression. Opponents argued that humanitarian intervention provided a pretext for self-interested land grabs and should be rejected as a justification for war. The Nuremberg precedent offered a solution—a definition of aggression and an independent court to judge defendants raising the humanitarian intervention defense—but a definition of aggression and jurisdictional conditions would not be adopted until the definitive 2010 ICC Review Conference in Kampala.

RWANDA'S JUSTICE MASH-UP

In international criminal law, the movement shifting regulation to the individual began to spread worldwide: Yugoslavia, Sierra Leone, Cambodia, Lebanon, East Timor, Bosnia, Kosovo, and Rwanda. Rwanda's community-based *gacaca* (pronounced "ga-cha-cha") trials, especially, showcased the capacity of international criminal law to penetrate the furthest reaches of the world and all levels of society. Village courts tried individuals for what were once considered "political decisions," excluded from criminal accountability as "acts of state."

Gacaca was also important because it represented a constructive attempt by Rwandans to meld the Nuremberg precedent with their own legal traditions to break cycles of violence. Their incorporation of the standards of Nuremberg for condemning atrocities attuned other war-torn societies to experiences shared across cultures, creating empathy and the possibility of other unique applications of the Nuremberg precedent. "Perhaps more unusual than the facts of genocides and regimes of torture marking this era," Martha Minow suggests in *Between Vengeance and Forgiveness*, "is the invention of new and distinctive legal forms of response."[85]

Rwanda struggled to contend with the around 135,000 pretrial detainees suspected of genocide and incarcerated in deplorable conditions all over the country. After a preliminary attempt to try these suspects using ordinary criminal procedures, the government calculated that it would take over two hundred years to judge everyone.[86] Rwanda's leaders met at Village Urugwiro and came up with their own interpretation of the Nuremberg legacy: gacaca.

Rwandan gacaca was originally a local restorative justice tradition traceable to the fourteenth century. Modernized gacaca amalgamated cultural practices and innovations to address Rwanda's emergency. Part Nuremberg trial, part truth commission, and part healing circle, gacaca was meant to empty the prisons and bring justice and reconciliation to postgenocide Rwanda.[87] Unlike the inclusive indigenous process—which was informal, conciliatory, and restorative—modernized gacaca incorporated formal, adversarial, and retributive elements.

I rode to Gishamvu, Rwanda, on the back of my friend Samuel's motorcycle. Rain ruts had hardened the mountain path into scars and our dust was a murky mist. Gishamvu was a hot spot for people interested in gacaca, Rwanda's participative genocide trials.[88] In this little town, only twenty kilometers from Burundi, public participation in the massacres of Tutsi was particularly shocking. Thousands of refugees fleeing massacres in other parts of Rwanda had sought refuge in Gishamvu's historical church, remembering the survival of Tutsi who fled there in the 1960s. But in 1994, when people fled to Gishamvu, the church became the site of some of the most horrific massacres of the Rwandan genocide.

At the trial in Gishamvu's town square, I saw fifteen gacaca judges, or *inyangamugayo*,[89] seated under an awning, a rickety wooden table between them and the villagers. The majority of the judges were women. The charismatic judge who usually directed proceedings was unwell and a young man replaced her as coordinator. He began the speech he had learned in six days of training, listing eight rules for giving evidence: notify the coordinator before speaking; he or she must give you the floor; priority is given to old witnesses, ones with mobility difficulties, and from afar; the person who speaks must be motivated by the spirit of truth; when people give testimony, they cannot be interrupted; violence and threats are not allowed; it is better to keep your testimony short so that others will have a chance to speak; stay on topic. The rules were repeated every Thursday.

The week before, the villagers had listed property that had been stolen or destroyed during the genocide. This week, their job was more challenging. The challenge was not only to individuals confronting memories of violence, but also to the viability of the community. The villagers were legally required to compile information about the thousands of people massacred in their church.

The coordinator read a family name and a woman in her mid-thirties listed her murdered relatives. Two judges recorded the testimony of the witness, who sat down once the list was read. Half a dozen people gathered quietly in front of the seated judges and deposited the names of murdered relatives to be read aloud. In the next phase of gacaca, the perpetrators would be identified and charged.

At gacaca in Gishamvu, I witnessed Nuremberg's renaissance. No Palace of Justice; no lawyers; no law books or precedents; no professional judges. Villagers selected by the community guided the process, and the Nuremberg precedent was at home on that scorched grass. Rwandans hoped gacaca would bring justice and healing, whatever these notions mean in the wake of immense tragedy.

The application of the Nuremberg precedent in Rwanda was a subtle play of forces, as it would be around the world. Tension between peace and justice permeated the process at all levels. The Tutsi-led transitional government drafting the gacaca law had a powerful incentive to appease the Hutu majority by sacrificing retributive justice for the sake of peace. The Kagame regime ultimately settled on a process blending retributive and restorative elements that antagonized survivors' organizations and defiant Hutu community leaders alike. They drafted the gacaca law to exclude crimes their soldiers had committed against Hutu as they stopped the genocide. Meanwhile, villages across the country were called upon to decide whether they would face their past, revisiting divisive memories of sectarian violence, or sweep it under the rug and try to move on. The dangers of "too much memory and too much forgetting" were very real.[90] Either choice could rekindle Rwanda's cycles of violence.

The interplay of politics and law resulted in miscarriages of justice. Gacaca's flimsy due-process protections were necessary to speed the trials, but they made gacaca vulnerable to abuse by government agents wishing to silence critics.[91] Government officials were discovered intimidating defense witnesses and powerful community members were caught bribing gacaca's unpaid lay judges.[92] Genocide accusations were deployed by neighbors to settle personal and political scores. Many communities resisted these intrusions and applied the law fairly, but others succumbed.

The gacaca experiment demonstrated that the Nuremberg precedent did not exist in a vacuum, it was embedded in power politics. This was a vital insight with implications for drafting and adjudication of the crime of aggression. Powerful actors in Rwanda did all they could to insulate themselves and their allies from accountability, and direct legal regulation and enforcement at their adversaries. Independent judges applying robust procedural safeguards were sometimes all that stood between justice and lawfare.

Despite gacaca's vulnerabilities, it represented a robust attempt by a nation to contend, through law, with its history of mass violence. Rather than retaliating or forgetting, Rwandans were trying to confront the aftermath of genocide and find a way forward. In the ICTY; ICTR; Special Court for Sierra Leone; Extraordinary Chambers in the Courts of Cambodia; Special Tribunal for Lebanon; Special Panels of the Dili District Courts; War Crimes Chamber of the Court of Bosnia and Herzegovina; Special Jurisdiction for Peace in Colombia; the Canadian, German, Belgian, and French criminal courts; and in this remote village, I saw the incremental, global penetration of Nuremberg's principles. Still missing, however, was a functioning international criminal court with jurisdiction to try world leaders for "the supreme international crime."

In my 2002 interviews and conversations with Rwandans, the 9/11 attacks were never mentioned. Tutsi, Hutu, villagers, officials, politicians, and community leaders were busy excavating the 1990s, facing history and themselves. Neither the end of the Cold War nor al Qaeda seemed particularly relevant here. Yet they were relevant in the minds of the powerful men and women from Washington, London, Paris, and Brussels who helped create the context for genocide, then dreamed up legal alibis absolving them of responsibility for stopping it. These officials never imagined that something of international legal significance might unfold in a tiny East African state.

Flying out of Kigali, I left a world trying to dig itself out of the 1990s through justice and reconciliation, and returned to a world beyond the 1990s in which individuals acting independently of any state flew passenger planes into the World Trade Center, the Pentagon, and a Pennsylvania field, killing more Americans than the Japanese attack on Pearl Harbor. That blazing instant buried the Nuremberg justice project and the neocons took power. President George W. Bush addressed a September 20 emergency meeting of a joint session of Congress, warning the world, "Either you are with us, or you are with the terrorists."[93]

CHAPTER 6

The Crime of Aggression

FROM ROME TO KAMPALA

> The coming-of-age narrative . . . typically features a young
> protagonist—either male or female—who undergoes a troubled
> search for an adult identity by process of trials, experiences,
> and revelations.
> —Literary Articles[1]

> Most picaresque novels incorporate several defining characteristics:
> satire, comedy, sarcasm, acerbic social criticism; first-person
> narration with an autobiographical ease of telling; an outsider
> protagonist-seeker on an episodic and often pointless quest for
> renewal or justice.
> —William Giraldi, "What's a Picaresque?" 2012

> Definition of **myth** . . . a usually traditional story of ostensibly
> historical events that serves to unfold part of the world view of
> a people or explain a practice, belief, or natural phenomenon.
> —*Merriam-Webster* online dictionary

In the summer of 1998, Milošević ramped up atrocities against civilian "terrorists" in Kosovo. NATO answered with the "Balkan Air Show," a performance for Milošević featuring eighty-five warplanes streaking over neighboring Albania and Macedonia. Diplomats and civil-society leaders met in Rome to establish an international criminal court with worldwide jurisdiction. Around the world, peacekeeping forces were deployed to protect civilians from atrocities, and a hodgepodge of courts, domestic and international, were prosecuting perpetrators. The moment was ripe for a full vindication of the Nuremberg precedent: a shift from state to individual accountability in war, from politics to law in the regulation of force.

Benjamin Ferencz was in Rome tracking the negotiations, suspicious of diplomats who time and again he'd seen resort to narrow notions of sovereignty and national interest to protect their leaders from prosecution.

It was one thing to establish ad hoc tribunals like the ICTY and ICTR to prosecute foreign perpetrators, quite another to create an international criminal court independent of the UN and capable of prosecuting both foreign and domestic leaders.[2] Ferencz was haunted by Robert Jackson's words to President Truman at the conclusion of the International Military Tribunal: "No one can hereafter deny or fail to know that the principles on which the Nazi leaders are adjudged to forfeit their lives constitute law and law with a sanction."[3] Preoccupied by superpower conflict, resistant to legal constraints on their exercise of military force, the victors of World War II proceeded to shelve the Nuremberg precedent for the duration of the Cold War. Now that the Cold War was over, would states embrace it? "The international community," Ferencz remarked in the midst of the negotiations, "is itself on trial in Rome."[4]

The vast majority of delegations at the Rome conference, from states and civil society, pushed for an impartial and independent ICC with global jurisdiction. If the UN collapsed or permanent members of the Security Council became hostile to it, the ICC would endure. Furthermore, it soon became clear that every state signing the Rome Treaty would be committing itself to incorporating the ICC's rules into its domestic law, enabling it to arrest and prosecute perpetrators of international crimes in local courts. If the ICC collapsed, its laws would live on. Ferencz had been working his whole life for this moment.

What almost collapsed were the negotiations in Rome. Beyond the technical debates between common- and civil-law experts about parochial preferences and heated arguments over the appropriate degree of Security Council control over the ICC prosecutor, a familiar issue deadlocked the negotiations at the eleventh hour: the crime of aggression.[5] Many developing countries, as well as major industrialized powers including Canada, Italy, Japan, and Greece, fought for the inclusion of a definition of aggression in the treaty. German delegate Hans-Peter Kaul argued forcefully that not incorporating aggression would be a "regression" and a "refusal to draw an appropriate conclusion from recent history." The United States opposed incorporation unless there was "no theoretical possibility" its leaders could be prosecuted. The Arab states would not endorse an ICC without the supreme international crime, while the permanent members of the UN Security Council resisted any attempts to supplant the council's powers to make aggression determinations.[6]

David Scheffer, now President Clinton's ambassador-at-large for war crimes issues, was between a rock and a hard place. Clinton had assigned him to build an ICC by the end of the twentieth century, "in a manner that would enable U.S. Participation in it."[7] Scheffer, an architect of the ICTY, ICTR, and Cambodia Tribunal and a champion of criminal responsibility for atrocity crimes, was expected to somehow reconcile the demands of the Senate Foreign Relations Committee, the Joint Chiefs of Staff, the intelligence agencies, and a range of Washington constituencies, as well as African, Arab, Asian, and European negotiating partners. This meant advocating for Security Council control over the ICC prosecutor and limiting ICC jurisdiction over Americans. It also meant designing the crime of aggression to target foreign political and military leaders, not American ones. The US position was opposed by the vast majority of African, Western European, Eastern European, South American, and Pacific states. Scheffer's promise of US military and financial support for the ICC failed to persuade foreign states to accept the American conditions. Many of Scheffer's negotiation partners, including European allies, were not on board with America's exceptionalism. Negotiations were deadlocked and Scheffer took the blame.

At four in the morning in the closing hours of the conference, the chairman of the Committee of the Whole, Canadian diplomat Philippe Kirsch, brokered a compromise whereby the crime of aggression was included in the treaty alongside genocide, crimes against humanity, and war crimes.[8] But the definition and jurisdictional conditions were omitted pending agreement at a future review conference.[9] With this, 120 states voted in favor of the Rome Statute, 21 abstained, and 7—the United States, Saddam's Iraq, Sudan, China, Israel, Qatar, and Yemen—voted against.[10] The diplomats' standing ovation shook the chamber. Some broke down in tears of joy and exhaustion. Richard Dicker, Human Rights Watch's representative in Rome, explained, "You had the sense that so much was at stake, so much hung in the balance."[11] A vast majority of the world's states reaffirmed the Nuremberg principles, voting to hold individuals responsible for atrocities and to make international politics subject to law.

Diplomats had chosen between the "realistic" world view of Kissinger and the "idealistic" one of Ferencz, settling on a Hammarskjöldian position blending the two. An investigation could be triggered by the ICC prosecutor, a state party, or the UN Security Council. In the case of the prosecutor or a state party, jurisdiction was limited to crimes committed by the nationals of ICC states parties or on their territory.[12] But with a Security Council referral, ICC jurisdiction extended to everyone, everywhere, as it would in 2005 with Darfur, Sudan, and in 2011 with Libya. The trade-off was that members of the Security Council's Permanent Five could use their veto in the council to prevent the ICC from prosecuting their own or allied political and military leaders.[13] And, unlike the international criminal tribunals for Yugoslavia and Rwanda with primary jurisdiction over perpetrators, a case would only be admissible at the ICC when national courts were unwilling or unable to prosecute.[14]

Despite these compromises, the Rome Treaty was the most important update to international legal order since the end of World War II.[15]

"I am particularly pleased that aggression was included as one of the four core-crimes," Ferencz posted online immediately. He had worried that the failure to define aggression would be used as a pretext to postpone the creation of an international criminal court, as had happened during the Cold War. "I feared," he wrote, "that an ICC built on a foundation from which the cornerstone was missing would topple."[16]

Human-rights groups, women's groups, peace groups, global governance groups, and religious groups attuned to the experiences of victims of atrocities played a pivotal role throughout the negotiations.[17] These groups formed a coalition that coordinated demonstrations, held press conferences, and distributed detailed reports by a slew of monitoring teams.[18] They pressured national delegations and worked closely with like-minded countries to make the Rome Statute fair, effective, and independent. "Had it not been for the *fin de siècle* re-emergence of 'international civil society,'" historian Erna Paris maintains, "the entire enterprise might still have come to nothing."[19] Ferencz wrote to the coalition: "You are hereby entitled (by the authority not vested in me) to inform your grandchildren that you have made a significant contribution toward replacing the law of force by the force of law."[20]

By April 11, 2002, a requisite sixty states had ratified the Rome treaty, triggering its July 1 entry into force. Less than nine months later, the United States illegally invaded Iraq.

FACTORING IN IRAQ

The effect was shock and awe. Dozens of satellite-guided cruise missiles launched from US warships in the Persian Gulf and the Red Sea. The dawn sky in Baghdad lit up as they obliterated hiding places meant to contain Saddam Hussein. They missed.

Saddam's defiant response on Iraqi television was a legal cluster bomb: "The criminal junior Bush committed, he and his aides, his crime that he was threatening Iraq with and humanity as well."[21] Donning full military garb, invoking Nuremberg, Saddam warned that Iraqi resistance would cause the United States to "lose any hope in accomplishing what they were driven to by the criminal Zionists." He ended his call to arms with: "Long live Jihad and long live Palestine!"[22]

In his justifications for war against Saddam, President George W. Bush argued that UN Security Council resolutions dating back to Saddam's 1990 invasion of Kuwait provided legal authorization to invade.[23] China, France, and Russia, however, along with nonpermanent members of the council, insisted that a new Security Council resolution was necessary for the war to be legal.[24] As Bush's ambassador to the UN John Negroponte acknowledged, these states did not authorize an invasion and they would not, unless there was further evidence of Saddam's failure to disarm.[25] Nor had the United States, in line with another Bush administration justification, suffered an armed attack from Iraq, triggering the right of self-defense. Bush's 2002 claim that the United States had the right to use armed force against a strike at some unknown time in the future by unidentified terrorists who may possess weapons of mass destruction was a delusional interpretation of international law.[26] In his warning to Iraqis not to destroy oil wells or obey any command to use weapons of mass destruction, Bush, like Saddam, invoked the Nuremberg precedent: "War crimes will be prosecuted. War criminals will be punished. And it will be no defense to say, 'I was just following orders.'"[27]

Prime Minister Tony Blair and Attorney General Peter Goldsmith agreed that the United Kingdom should not participate in an illegal war.[28] But Goldsmith advised Blair that the legal case for war need not be airtight for the United Kingdom to participate: "a reasonable case was a sufficient lawful basis for taking military action," and the United Kingdom had one.[29] No independent, impartial tribunal had jurisdiction to weigh Blair and Goldsmith's legal arguments. Elizabeth Wilmshurst was deputy legal advisor at the UK Foreign Office and had been the lead UK negotiator in Rome. On the eve of the invasion, she resigned. "I cannot in conscience go along," she wrote to her superiors, "particularly since an unlawful use of force on such a scale amounts to the crime of aggression; nor can I agree with such action in circumstances which are so detrimental to the international order and the rule of law."[30]

Journalist Jan Frel put Ferencz in a difficult spot by asking his opinion on the legality of the Iraq War.[31] The question set Ferencz's patriotic feelings against his commitment to the Nuremberg legacy, and his reply was measured:

> The last Security Council resolution essentially said, "Look, send the weapons inspectors out to Iraq, have them come back and tell us what they've found—then we'll figure out what we're going to do." The United States was impatient, and decided to invade Iraq—which was all pre-arranged of course. So, the United States went to war, in violation of the charter.[32]

The Nuremberg tribunal's insight that aggressive war contains the "evil of the whole" came to pass. American and Iraqi forces committed atrocities including torture and sexual humiliation at Abu Ghraib prison, the use of human shields, cluster munitions, and systematic rape as a weapon. Iraq descended into sectarian chaos. After thirteen years of war, the public record of violent civilian deaths surpassed 180,000.[33] "There's no such thing as a war without atrocities," Ferencz lamented. "But war-making is the biggest atrocity of all."[34]

The period between the 2003 invasion of Iraq and the 2008 election of Barack Obama was fraught for scholars studying justifications for war. The US-led invasion of Iraq produced an intellectual crisis among the intelligentsia, who had made great strides in the 1990s toward defining a legal justification for the use of force based on humanitarian rescue. Had their definition's ambiguity muddied the waters in judging the invasion of Iraq? Nowhere were the intellectual struggles of the day revealed more starkly than in the Intervention Seminar, convened for Harvard faculty.

Michael Ignatieff, director of the Carr Center for Human Rights, convened the seminar. Participants included Carr Center founder Samantha Power, Carr Center fellow Rory Stewart, Bush legal advisor Jack Goldsmith, legal scholar Martha Minow, Roman Catholic priest Bryan Hehir, and political scientist Stanley Hoffmann. The Iraq War presented justification challenges for each.

Ignatieff's journeys into post–Cold War conflict informed the "Responsibility-to-Protect" criteria, a prospective standard to justify force in cases of emergency human protection. Ignatieff helped formulate the criteria necessary before states could counter atrocities with force.[35] The list of requirements was long. Only large-scale loss of life or ethnic cleansing could serve as just cause. The primary intention needed to be to halt or avert human suffering. As a precaution, the commission preferred multilateral operations requested by victims and supported by neighboring states. The use of force had to be a last resort following exhaustion of peaceful measures. The scale, duration, and intensity of the intervention had to be proportional to the human-protection purpose. Military operations could only be undertaken if there were a reasonable prospect of success and if action would make victims safer.

Most controversially, the Responsibility-to-Protect doctrine placed a conditionality on sovereignty. States unwilling or unable to protect their populations from large-scale loss of life or ethnic cleansing would forfeit their sovereign rights. No longer would dictators be permitted to invoke sovereign autonomy as they exterminated their own people. If the Security Council failed to act, the General Assembly, regional organizations, coalitions, or even states interceding unilaterally could step in. The UN Charter already permitted the use of force when authorized by the Security Council or when states responded defensively to an armed attack, but this humanitarian justification added a third possibility to the existent two. Ignatieff hoped the new justification would become an amendment to the UN Charter or a rule of customary international law binding all states.[36]

The responsibility to protect Iraqis from their leader's atrocities and foreigners from Saddam Hussein's alleged weapons of mass destruction became Ignatieff's primary justification for the Iraq War.[37] After his 1992 journey to Iraq and conversations with Kurdish and Shia genocide survivors, Ignatieff felt compelled to respond to the devastating testimonies of Saddam's victims. "The disagreeable reality for those who believe in human rights," he maintained, "is that there are some occasions—and Iraq may be one of them—when war is the only real remedy for regimes that live by terror."[38]

In 2003, Ignatieff's support for the invasion left him alone and vulnerable. Progressives in the 1960s' mold might have followed him into intervention in Kosovo, but not into Iraq where they believed Iraqi oil, not humanitarian motives, fueled the fight. Previous supporters of Ignatieff's 1990s interventionist thinking were disturbed by *Empire Lite*, his 2003 book advocating America's responsibility to build a "humanitarian empire" backed by military force, and labeled him a proponent of American hegemony.[39]

Both Samantha Power and Michael Ignatieff had travelled the Balkans as war reporters and were deeply moved by the ethnic cleansing of innocent populations. Both espoused a muscular humanitarianism, but they disagreed over Iraq. Nine days before the invasion of Iraq, Power was pressed to take a stand on the gathering war: "Is this a just war, Samantha?" the interviewer asked. "It will have a just result locally and probably a very unjust result . . ." Power began, before she was interrupted with the demand for a simple "yes" or "no." "It's not being fought for human rights reasons," she replied. "It would be great if human rights were a necessary condition."[40]

Though not a full-throated rejection of the Iraq invasion, Power was highly critical of the war once she learned that the United States was unwilling or unable to protect civilians. She drew a stark distinction between the 1999 NATO intervention in Kosovo, which she considered justified humanitarian intervention, and the 2003 invasion of Iraq, which she saw as a debacle.[41] Power realized early on that the 1990s-era humanitarian justifications for war were in danger of perversion if appropriated by proponents of the Iraq War, including her respected friend Ignatieff.

Power took into consideration the group justifying war. She maintained the Bush administration could not be trusted because of its selective adherence to international law.[42] Ignatieff disagreed. He argued, "It must be possible for a person to accept an argument as legitimate even when articulated by someone the person has reasons to distrust."[43] Ignatieff doubted that an "impartial" or "objective" institution like the ICC could succeed in persuading parties to an armed conflict of their interpretive account, leaving his humanitarian-intervention doctrine open to self-interested interpretation.[44] Ignatieff ultimately corrected his position on Iraq and acknowledged that the war was a grave humanitarian error.[45]

Rory Stewart, a British Carr Center fellow, had supported the invasion of Iraq on humanitarian grounds. But as deputy regional governor in the Shiite province of Maysan, he realized nation building by foreigners in Iraq was "Mission: Impossible."[46] Stewart argued passionately that Western states should dramatically reduce their military presence in Iraq and Afghanistan because they were doing more harm than good. Though he was not particularly concerned about the legality of interventions because both legal and illegal interventions created a debacle, Stewart had not considered that a prosecutable crime of aggression would likely have at least kept his country out of Iraq.[47]

Jack Goldsmith had been a conservative star in 2003, a "new sovereigntist" opponent of 1990s nation building and "the judicialization of international politics."[48] As legal advisor to Bush's Defense Department after 9/11, Goldsmith warned that the ICC might indict American officials for their conduct in the war on terror. This warning was followed by ardent US attacks on human rights and international law. Goldsmith was soon picked to head the Office of Legal Counsel of the Justice Department, advising the president on the limits of presidential power.

Goldsmith resigned nine months later, not because he objected to US interrogation methods or other questionable antiterror tactics, but because legal authorization was "sloppily reasoned, overbroad, and incautious."[49] He was especially alarmed by Bush's unprecedented accumulation of presidential power to wage war. Goldsmith urged superiors to secure Congressional authorization and act within established legal constraints to avoid undermining US effectiveness in the war on terror. His reasons were institutional, not humanitarian. Goldsmith argued that wars should be justified on the basis of domestic constitutional procedures such as Congressional authorization, not abstract, undemocratic notions of just war.[50]

Though none of the participants had it on their radar, the crime of aggression provided a workable synthesis of their views. Ignatieff's humanitarian intervention justification was vulnerable to abuse without institutional checks and balances. Goldsmith's championing of domestic legal process as a check on aggressive leaders would be strengthened by leadership accountability, enforced by an international criminal court and a network of regional and domestic courts. Criminal courts applying internationally accepted rules of evidence and procedure would be better placed than Power to evaluate a leader's legal justifications for war, distinguishing aggression and self-defense, humanitarian rescue and cynical land grabs. Stewart's call for humility and responsibility in the use of force was not a reason to sideline discussions over the legality of armed force, but to submit to additional legal safeguards.

It was essential, though, that the law not provide an alibi for inaction in the face of genuine humanitarian emergencies such as Bosnia or Rwanda. International law was not an impediment to humanitarian rescue and self-defense, it was the best way to legitimate necessary armed force, providing the courts with missing powers to keep the executive honest. The problem was that leaders were likely to resist additional checks on their power, invoking stock patriotic and nationalistic arguments to avoid new legal constraints. The disastrous invasion of Iraq and the failure of domestic checks and balances in the United States and the United Kingdom had the potential to spur reconsideration of a prohibition on aggression enforceable by an international criminal court.

Martha Minow, an occasional participant in the Intervention Seminar, added insightful commentary about the importance of law in international politics. In her view, law can help societies contend with political violence. Even if trials don't deter violence, they offer society a rejoinder to atrocities and help communities face history and themselves. Trials are an antidote to the destructive, understandable experiences of vengeance—which can cause a downward spiral of violence—and forgiveness, which, when exacted from victims, "institutionalizes forgetfulness, and sacrifices justice in a foreshortened effort to move on" that often backfires.[51] For Minow, trials are a legal expression of society's constructive aspirations. "Idealists need at a minimum to acknowledge the profound critiques and limitations of the trial response to atrocities," Minow writes. "Yet cynics need to ask: What can be imagined and built, even in the face of critiques and limitations? Indeed, how much is cynicism itself the problem?"[52]

The drafters of the crime of aggression would find themselves negotiating countervailing idealistic and cynical impulses as they worked to craft a just and enforceable law. Martha Minow's insight was that the impulse to constrain aggression through law sprang from humanity's perpetual need to contend with war and break the cycles of violence. Could this impulse to build something constructive be realized through the crime of aggression? Were criminal trials an appropriate response to illegal war?

I travelled to The Hague to find out.

EARLY DAYS IN THE HAGUE

I arrived at the ICC in 2004, greenest law clerk to Argentine Chief Prosecutor Luis Moreno Ocampo. I had come from the gacaca trials in Rwanda and was hoping to learn about the investigation, prosecution, and outcome of ICC trials. Facing me in the prosecutor's conference room were rows of investigators, prosecutors, and diplomats politely awaiting my lecture on gacaca and its implications for their work.

The prosecution team was considering whether it should prosecute perpetrators who had undergone a Northern Ugandan process of traditional justice resurrected by communities to reintegrate Lords Resistance

Army (LRA) deserters. As a court of last resort, the ICC was designed to take cases no other court was willing or able to try. But was the *Mato Oput* tradition a court? Its informal, ritualistic procedures fell short of international fair-trial standards. Yet, with decades of impunity and many perpetrators originally abducted as children, Ugandan Mato Oput, like Rwandan gacaca, was a promising grassroots response. Moreno Ocampo would have to decide whether to intervene and prosecute deserters undergoing or having finished the ritual. I was tasked with reporting on how local and international justice systems could work together, and hoped to learn how international justice was evolving, since it was within this system that the crime of aggression would be enforced.

My boss, Luis Moreno Ocampo, had made his name in the mid-1980s as a prosecutor in the Trial of the Juntas, in which Argentina's democratic government prosecuted the deposed military dictatorship for mass killings during the 1976–83 Dirty War. Because the junta still wielded influence, Moreno Ocampo devised unorthodox ways to collect evidence, protect witnesses, and build a case. Impressed by his collaboration with grassroots groups and his talent at navigating power politics, the Assembly of States Parties to the ICC selected him as first ICC prosecutor.

Moreno Ocampo opened his first official ICC investigations soon after I arrived. Surprisingly, both were self-referrals. It became clear that international justice was an ad hoc network of legal responses to mass violence, including gacaca, Mato Oput, and the Argentine junta trials, and was not only an all-powerful world court in The Hague. In this case, the president of Uganda, despite exposing himself and his allies to indictments for international crimes, asked the ICC prosecutor to investigate enemy warlords. He hoped ICC scrutiny would curtail atrocities and generate international momentum to end the violence.

Moreno Ocampo was moved by the possibility of advancing the justice agenda, even by dealing with an ethically questionable leader. Uganda's referral was a public vote of confidence and President Museveni's cooperation would streamline the investigation and ensure protection of ICC investigators from belligerent forces. The self-referral was also beneficial to Museveni, attracting international support for his long-running counterinsurgency against the LRA.[53] Moreno Ocampo's partnership with power rapidly leveraged ICC force and undermined the warlords, forcing them to the bargaining table. According to Payam Akhavan, advising the Ugandan Government at the time, ICC involvement "measurably weakened the LRA's military capability, encouraged significant defections among LRA commanders, and forced otherwise defiant leaders to the negotiating table."[54]

Yet the deal wasn't done. The crisis became acute when LRA leader Joseph Kony demanded amnesty as a condition for peace, raising the recurrent peace-versus-justice dilemma. Should the ICC prosecute Kony and his commanders for atrocities? Or should it give peace negotiations a chance?

I was tasked with writing an analysis of whether legal accountability rather than political deals with individual leaders would advance the cause of international peace. The brief raised contentious issues about whether or not to prosecute the crime of aggression.

Beyond the principled arguments for prosecuting the LRA leaders were pragmatic reasons to proceed.[55] In every LRA peace negotiation since its 1986 beginnings, the insurgents had withdrawn, rearmed, and resumed atrocities. With or without amnesty, it was unlikely Kony and his commanders would settle down quietly. In addition, ICC focus on leadership rather than foot soldiers could encourage rank-and-file defection, and indicting extremist leaders might open the way for more moderate negotiating partners. Although the process seemed tainted by problematic leaders and blackmailing warlords, it would, in the final analysis, encourage peace. I concluded that the decision to prosecute should be maintained, even if it might disrupt the peace negotiations. The peace-versus-justice dilemma raised in this case would become a recurrent debate at the ICC, with special implications for prosecuting and judging the crime of aggression.[56]

Another basic defining issue in the early days of the ICC with implications for the crime of aggression was the historical function of trials versus their narrow deterrent function. When Congolese warlord Thomas Lubanga was arrested and became the first perpetrator transferred to the ICC, Moreno Ocampo had to question the purpose of an ICC trial. He had to decide whether the Lubanga case should be narrow, showcasing the court's efficiency at sending perpetrators to prison, or broader, providing the world with a Nuremberg-style history of wrongdoing in the Congo.

Moreno Ocampo, with Al Capone's pragmatic, expedient tax-evasion trial in mind, was intent on a narrow case. He charged Lubanga with the war crime of enlisting and conscripting children to participate in hostilities, even though ICC investigators had uncovered indictable evidence of other major crimes, including systematic sexual violence. Moreno Ocampo hoped this streamlined approach would deter armies around the world from using child soldiers, even though these narrow charges made victims of Lubanga's other crimes ineligible for compensation and excluded their experiences from the official record. Investigators committed to a historic record of Lubanga's crimes, the idea that justice includes a memorialization of experience, resigned in protest. The trial was riddled with problems, but its result was to make international law more effective. Lubanga came to symbolize the brutality of using children as soldiers. His prosecution served as a deterrent in the recruitment of children to armies such as the Revolutionary Armed Forces of Colombia (FARC) in Colombia and the Maoists in Nepal (CPN-M).[57] It also demonstrated how an ICC prosecutor facing a politically unpopular aggression referral could make use of his or her discretion to sidestep the issue and prosecute less controversial crimes instead.

In the next case, that of Sudanese President Omar al-Bashir, politics would have needed strategic management in order to successfully enforce international law. It was to prove an object lesson for the effective enforcement of international criminal law, with particular relevance to the crime of aggression.

In 2009, the ICC issued an arrest warrant for al-Bashir. Al-Bashir retaliated by expelling a dozen international aid agencies including Oxfam, Care, and Save the Children from Sudan, seizing their assets, calling them spies.[58] This left hundreds of thousands of internally displaced people encircled by genocidal militias, without clean water or medical care, dependent on his protection. Al-Bashir crisscrossed the country in traditional garb, consolidating his supporters against the ICC, and reaching out to friendly African and Arab leaders. He was vulnerable to a palace coup if weakened. Most importantly, he needed to assure China, Sudan's major oil customer, that he would remain a reliable supplier. At a Khartoum rally, al-Bashir called the ICC a stooge of the imperialist West. "We have refused to kneel to colonialism," he told the cheering crowd. "That is why Sudan has been targeted . . . because we only kneel to God." "Down with USA," they chanted back.[59] By successfully politicizing his indictment, al-Bashir threatened the efficacy of the ICC and of international law.

Al-Bashir's lawyers rejected the court's jurisdiction, ignoring the Security Council mandate, and claiming Sudan was not a member state. They established special national courts to preempt the ICC and claimed that the Darfur tribes wanted indigenous justice processes rather than Western imperialist courts.[60] Al-Bashir pointed to his peace negotiations with the insurgent south, threatening the collapse of the process unless he was granted ICC impunity.[61]

"I cannot be blackmailed, I cannot yield," Moreno Ocampo responded. "Silence never helped the victims. Silence helped the perpetrators. The prosecutor should not be silent."[62]

Yet al-Bashir's strategy worked. His claims that the ICC was biased against Africans attracted the support of African leaders, including Libya's Muammar Qaddafi and Zimbabwe's Robert Mugabe, also vulnerable to ICC indictments. John Dugard and other respected international-criminal-law scholars suggested that the ICC's exclusive focus on Africa was a problem.[63] Where, Dugard asked, were the indictments against Israeli leaders and their Hamas foes for crimes committed in the 2008–9 Gaza War?

"This court does not intend to focus only on Africans, it will prove that in the future," Gambian Deputy Prosecutor Fatou Bensouda told a

New York Times reporter. "But at the moment, Africa clearly presents the gravest situations."[64]

Al-Bashir's manipulation of law and politics showed the vulnerability of the ICC. He remains free and in power. Yet, the al-Bashir case provoked African countries to empower their regional court, the African Court of Justice and Human Rights, to try international crimes. A 2015 protocol to the statute of the African Court included ten new crimes, alongside genocide, crimes against humanity, war crimes, and the crime of aggression.[65] Critics warn that the 2015 protocol was established to usurp ICC jurisdiction, not to advance international justice.[66] It's also possible that the African Court of Justice and Human Rights will one day provide an effective regional venue for prosecuting aggression.

The ICC's early cases showed that international enforcement was vulnerable to political manipulation, but also that law had infiltrated the conduct of international politics. Al-Bashir was free, but major criminals including Congolese Vice President Jean Pierre Bemba and Ivory Coast President Laurent Gbagbo were apprehended in spectacular arrest operations. The ICC could be effective or ineffective, depending on political forces and the strategic choices of the ICC prosecutor. Now the question was which master international law would serve: power or principle. The next battleground would be Kampala, 2010. The world's diplomats met there to add a prosecutable definition of the crime of aggression to the ICC's arsenal.

TRACTION IN PRINCETON

The crime of aggression was added to the ICC's code of crimes in Kampala in 2010. A series of meetings in The Hague, New York, Montreux, and Princeton following the Rome Conference predated the adoption of the final amendment.

The PrepCom was the first group of diplomats and scholars to tackle aggression after Rome. It met ten times and, in 2002, Coordinator Silvia Fernández de Gurmendi, later to become president of the ICC, or chief justice, consolidated the most popular proposals into a succinct "discussion paper," an embryonic definition indicating unresolved points of contention.[67] This was the closest to a justiciable definition of the crime of aggression since Nuremberg and Tokyo. When the PrepCom mandate ended, the Assembly of States Parties passed the torch to the Special Working Group on the Crime of Aggression, chaired by Christian Wenaweser, from Liechtenstein.[68] Benjamin Ferencz advocated for my inclusion as one of a handful of independent experts, useful since aggression was the subject of my doctorate.

To help define aggression, I studied the Covenant of the League of Nations, the General Treaty for the Renunciation of War, the Nuremberg Charter, the UN Charter, the 1974 General Assembly "Definition of Aggression," and the Rome Statute. Ignatieff suggested reading Michael Walzer's 1977 *Just and Unjust Wars*, a classic of just-war theory.[69] "Wars are not self-starting," Walzer wrote, rebutting the idea that wars are caused by historic and social forces. "They may 'break out,' like an accidental fire, under conditions difficult to analyze and where the attribution of responsibility seems impossible. But usually they are more like arson than accident."[70]

Former peacekeeper Frédéric Mégret, an international-criminal-law theorist, summarized three divergent perspectives on the moral wrong of aggression: aggression is a crime against sovereignty, a crime against peace, or a crime against human rights.[71] Explaining the different perspectives, Mégret wrote that aggressors are criminals because they use their state as a weapon and violate the sovereignty, territorial integrity, and political independence of another state, including the people living there.[72] Aggressors threaten the peace of the world by risking a devastating conflagration; aggressors are mass human-rights violators.

These divergent perspectives on the meaning of aggression influenced the language diplomats and scholars fought to include or exclude in the final draft of the law. The wording in the law would effect what could or could not be prosecuted. For example, if one accepted the proposed human-rights perspective then, as Mégret said, "The failure by leading human rights NGOs to condemn the invasion of Iraq [as aggression] on human rights grounds is . . . a dispiriting let down of the ideals of human rights."[73] Another upshot of the human-rights perspective is that wars waged to defend human rights, such as the NATO campaign in Kosovo, do not qualify as aggression.[74]

Crucial as it was to define and implement the crime of aggression, the task seemed insurmountable. To succeed, diplomats would need to strike a new balance between political discretion and legal principle in the use of force. They would need to agree on the basic wrong of aggression, a distinction between a just and an unjust war, and devise a legal mechanism for criminal-law judges to attribute individual responsibility. They would need to cede sovereignty to an independent international court.

When negotiations stalled, Wenaweser invited Ferencz to speak, to remind diplomats why they were there. "It is so obviously correct that law is better than war and that it is better to live in peace with human rights than to live in war, killing people who you don't even know,"[75] Ferencz said. Ferencz depicted Kampala as a turning point in history in which states would have the opportunity to replace the law of force with the rule of law.

With negotiations moving too slowly, Wenaweser introduced speed-up procedures. He supplemented regular UN and Hague meetings with retreats at Princeton University.[76] Diplomats were invited to speak personally to avoid committing their states.[77] Facilitators from Germany, Greece, and Sweden administered thematic questionnaires to the delegations, soliciting their views, rather than requesting potentially polarizing national position papers.[78] The chairman and his team grouped the various views in a comprehensive report adopted by the gathering on the last day of each retreat. The summer-camp atmosphere at Princeton created a camaraderie they called the "spirit of Princeton."[79]

Rather than starting from scratch, the diplomats assembled key precedents into a new law.[80] The definition borrowed language from the UN Charter's prohibition on force: "All Members shall refrain in their international relations from the threat or use of force against the territorial integrity or political independence of any state, or in any other manner inconsistent with the Purposes of the United Nations."[81] The list of prohibited acts—invasion, bombardment, blockade, attacking another state's armed forces, contravening an agreement to station forces in another state (e.g., by refusing to leave), offering one's state as a launching ground for another state to attack a third state, and the sending of armed bands to attack another state—came straight from the 1974 General Assembly "Definition of Aggression." The *actus reus* of the crime, the prohibited conduct—planning, preparing, initiating, or executing an act of aggression—was lifted from the Nuremberg Charter. Wenaweser believed that a definition based on precedent would facilitate agreement on a final draft in Kampala.

Nonetheless, the permanent members of the Security Council and their closest allies balked. They demanded that the ICC prosecutor only be permitted to investigate aggression if the Security Council determined aggression had occurred.[82] This scandalized criminal-law experts at Princeton. They insisted that defendants be able to challenge every aspect of the case for a trial to be fair, including outside determinations by the Security Council.[83]

States pressing for a narrow definition insisted that prohibited acts be limited to those listed in the 1974 General Assembly Definition. Those who advocated a wider, updated prohibition wanted the list open to new acts, sacrificing legal clarity to capture emerging acts of aggression such as cyberattacks.[84] Some delegates, citing the Nuremberg precedent and invoking the Latin maxim *de minimis non curat lex* ("the law does not concern itself with trifles"), argued that only full-scale wars of aggression should be prosecutable.[85] Others said that any use of force violating the UN Charter should be fair game.[86]

Almost imperceptibly, intractable disagreements were resolved and Chairman Wenaweser removed the square brackets denoting competing language from his master draft. Delegates were forced to accept painful compromises, such as the exclusion of explicit language capturing non-state aggressors such as Osama bin Laden in the definition of the crime.[87] The final definition would need to hew closely to customary international law to garner the support required for final adoption in Kampala.

As the Special Working Group came within striking distance of a compromise,[88] critics began to question the wisdom of the project. Some went beyond the ubiquitous nationalistic and "realistic" arguments proffered by militarily powerful states. Former ICTY prosecutor Richard Goldstone argued that the use of armed force by states is "inherently a profoundly political decision," not a legal one.[89] Tufts international law professor Michael Glennon maintained that the emerging definition was too vague: "Every U.S. President since John F. Kennedy, hundreds of U.S. legislators and military leaders, as well as innumerable military and political leaders from other countries could have been subject to prosecution."[90] The US Council on Foreign Relations warned that the crime of aggression would deter states from undertaking emergency humanitarian interventions like NATO's in Kosovo.[91]

Goldstone's argument that the use of force is "inherently" a political decision was unpersuasive to those who had worked for years to achieve a compromise. Genocide, crimes against humanity, and war crimes were also political decisions until states agreed to prohibit them. As legal scholar Kevin Jon Heller said, Glennon's argument was tantamount to saying, "the crime of murder has no content because countries disagree over whether abortion qualifies."[92] Glennon's point that criminal prosecution of aggression could exacerbate political tensions, reinforce positions, and undercut alternative avenues to ending conflicts—such as negotiated solutions—was a reasonable consideration.[93] As for humanitarian intervention, the drafters proposed ways in which judges hearing an aggression case could check aggression while permitting necessary rescue operations.[94]

President Obama, elected in 2008, was keen to reengage with the ICC. By refusing to send a US delegation to the Special Working Group on the Crime of Aggression, President George W. Bush had squandered his opportunity to influence the outcome. The Princeton group was initially enthusiastic when Obama appointed a leading human-rights scholar, former Yale Law Dean Harold Koh, to argue America's case. But in his speech to the American Society of International Law before Kampala, Koh said, "If you think of the Court as a wobbly bicycle that is finally starting to move forward, is this frankly more weight than the bicycle can bear?"[95] Coming from the legal advisor of a military superpower opposing the inclusion of the crime of aggression, the analogy had ominous connotations.

The history of US/ICC relations was fraught. Under George W. Bush, John Bolton, US undersecretary of state for arms control and international security, had led a campaign to destroy the court. He had submitted a letter to UN Secretary-General Kofi Annan "unsigning" the Rome Treaty, which David Scheffer had signed on behalf of the United States before Clinton left office. In 2005, the Bush administration realized it had alienated ICC member states whose cooperation was essential for America's war on terror, and softened its tone on the ICC. The Bush administration opted not to veto a Security Council resolution requesting that Moreno Ocampo open an investigation into atrocities in Darfur.[96] It demanded that the Government of Sudan cooperate fully with the ICC in accordance with the resolution,[97] and Bolton's replacement threatened to veto any attempts by states aligned with the Government of Sudan to use the Security Council to defer the case.[98] Bolton was disturbed by these developments. "If you allow this to happen," he explained, "you legitimize the ICC. My preferred policy is to isolate it and hope it will eventually wither."[99] The Princeton group deliberated, concerned about the position the Obama administration would take.

In February 2009, the Princeton group completed its work. Almost every contentious issue had been resolved.[100] The draft included a generic definition of aggression and a list of prohibited acts. Only "manifest" violations of the UN Charter would qualify, excluding border skirmishes and other minor incursions. The crime would be prosecutable against leaders, but not followers. Criminal responsibility for aggression would be attributed to individuals in the same way it was for genocide, crimes against humanity, and war crimes.[101] What remained unresolved, in square brackets, was the provision on jurisdiction.[102] At stake in the jurisdictional debate was the reach of the ICC; that is, which national leaders could be investigated, prosecuted, and judged by the court. The ICC's jurisdictional rules in aggression cases would establish the new balance between political imperatives and legal principles. Jurisdiction would prove to be Kampala's incendiary flash point.

THE KAMPALA COMPROMISE

In May 2010, I arrived at the Munyonyo Commonwealth Resort in Kampala, the venue for the ICC Review Conference. The African location was significant because all ICC cases had been African and the court's relationship with Africa was on the rocks. Organizers hoped an African

Review Conference would encourage African states and nongovernmental organizations (NGOs) to take ownership.

David Scheffer, now an academic, attended the negotiations as an accredited nonstate delegate, alongside Ben Ferencz, Don Ferencz, William Schabas, Michael Scharf, Jutta Bertram-Nothnagel, and other aggression experts. Scheffer knew from experience that the delegates would need to balance fairness against robust financial and military support if they hoped to reach an agreement between weaker states and great powers such as Russia and the United States.

The United States, an observer state, had sent a large, assertive delegation and was hosting dozens of meetings. Harold Koh and Ambassador-at-Large for War Crimes Stephen Rapp, as well as representatives from the departments of state, justice, and defense; the joint chiefs of staff; and the National Security Council, delivered two messages:[103] under Obama, the United States was serious about cooperating with the ICC and it opposed the activation of the crime of aggression.[104] Their messages contained a carrot and a stick. US engagement and cooperation would be contingent, in part, on a rejection of the Princeton group's aggression draft.[105]

The Princeton group would not be dissuaded. It had built solidarity around a resilient, if imperfect, compromise. The United States tried to exclude humanitarian intervention from the ambit of the crime but, try as it might, was unable to reopen the definition to negotiation.[106] Instead, it pressed to include certain "understandings" in the final compromise. Understandings were not binding on the judges, but could serve as an aid to judicial interpretation. Bill Lietzau, a high-level legal advisor to the US secretary of defense, attempted to include the "purpose" of the act of aggression in any assessment of its legality, but the Iranian delegation, perhaps recalling Cold War–era debates between the Americans and the Soviets over the principles of priority (first strike) and intent (purpose), persuaded the diplomats that purpose was dangerously amorphous.[107]

Lietzau was more successful at inserting an "understanding" into the final compromise concerning the *de minimis* threshold, or minimum level of armed attack allowed before the act could be punished.[108] In a surprising détente, US and Iranian delegations agreed that "in establishing whether an act of aggression constitutes a manifest violation of the Charter of the United Nations, the three components of *character, gravity* and *scale* must be sufficient to justify a 'manifest' determination."[109] The ICC needed more than one component to judge a political or military leader guilty of aggression.[110] The US delegation hoped this "understanding" would influence the judges and create more stringent barriers to prosecution.

But the Princeton group resisted all attempts to push aside the aggression issue or reopen the legally binding definition for debate,[111] recognizing that the United States' motivation was to be free of constraints, with maximum control over the legal regime binding everyone else.[112] The obvious stance for American exceptionalists seemed unjust to anyone else.

For the draft crime to withstand attacks, the Princeton group had designed a conservative law, building from existing precedent.[113] This created its own problems. At a time when warfare was transforming, the Princeton group relied on legal sources designed to regulate the wars of bygone eras. Its fixation on the state was particularly troubling in light of accumulating literature on the transformation of war, which forecast increasing decentralization, the state's loss of its monopoly on combat forces, the diminishing importance of conventional war, and the rise of superpowerful rogue individuals and groups.[114] The Princeton draft was designed to capture a narrow category of perpetrators: military or political leaders who violate the sovereignty of another state. In order to garner the widest possible support and insulate their proposed law from attack, the Princeton group may have built in its obsolescence.

In twelve charged days, two powerful groups came to loggerheads over a poorly drafted ICC amendment provision setting out the rules governing changes to the ICC statute.[115] The interpretation of this amendment provision was crucial to the incorporation of the new crime of aggression.

"Camp Consent" interpreted the language of the provision to require that both aggressor and victim states ratify the Kampala outcome in order for the ICC to prosecute aggression.[116] It was led by the permanent members of the Security Council, Europe, Canada, Australia, and New Zealand.[117] If Camp Consent had its way, only states that ratified the Kampala outcome would be bound. The result would be tantamount to a nonaggression pact excluding the permanent members of the Security Council and their closest allies. A jurisdictional regime excluding the great powers and their close allies would suffer from similar weaknesses as did the League of Nations.

"Camp Protection," supported by most of the global south (Africa, Latin America, and the Caribbean), interpreted the language of the provision to require ratification solely by the victim state to trigger ICC protection.[118] Camp Consent's reading would insulate political and military leaders of any state that didn't ratify the Kampala outcome, even if it attacked a state that had. Camp Protection risked antagonizing the great powers. The amendment issue was key to the reach of ICC jurisdiction; the gulf seemed unbridgeable.

Shuttling between delegations for two weeks, Wenaweser and Prince Zeid of Jordan drafted informal "non-papers" attempting to resolve the divisive jurisdictional issue.[119] A major breakthrough came when Argentina, Brazil, and Switzerland proposed separate jurisdiction and entry-into-force mechanisms for Security Council referrals and state referrals/*proprio motu* investigations.[120] The Argentina/Brazil/Switzerland (ABS) Proposal was a concession by Camp Protection to Camp Consent. Under the ABS Proposal, Security Council referrals, an uncontroversial way to give the ICC jurisdiction over an aggression case, would be available as soon as the first state party ratified the Kampala amendments.[121] The more contentious amendments on state referrals and *proprio motu* investigations would enter into force after seven-eighths of states parties ratified, which could take time. But under the ABS Proposal, patience would be rewarded with a widely accepted protective regime that did not require the consent of the aggressor state or a Security Council referral for the ICC to investigate and prosecute aggression. The Canadian delegation countered with a concession from Camp Consent. Unless the Security Council had determined the existence of an act of aggression, all of the states involved would have to consent to the Kampala amendments by way of an opt-in declaration for the ICC to open a case.[122]

With just two days remaining, Argentina, Brazil, Switzerland, and Canada unveiled a diplomatic compromise: an opt-out mechanism whereby the ICC could by default exercise jurisdiction over an alleged aggressor state unless that state had previously opted out of the Kampala amendments.[123] In a painful concession by Camp Protection, the ICC would have no jurisdiction over the leaders of non-ICC states, even if they attacked an ICC state party. By excluding acts of aggression by nonparty states, the crime of aggression would provide dramatically less protection than the other ICC crimes.

On the final day, Wenaweser and Zeid postponed and repostponed the plenary, circulating successive modifications. In tense private meetings, delegates attempted to cajole holdouts from both camps. The US delegation was ever present. At 8:30 in the evening, the plenary reconvened, only to be delayed by two more hours. Wenaweser circulated a final draft based on the ABS/Canada compromise. The leaders of all ICC member states would automatically be subject to the aggression law once seven years had passed, thirty states had ratified, and the Assembly of States Parties had agreed to activate. ICC member states would automatically be subject to the new aggression law, but a formal opt-out process was included, thereby insulating political and military leaders of ICC states that opted out. The leaders of states that were not parties to the Rome Statute—the United States, Russia, China, Iran, Israel—would not be prosecuted for aggression at the ICC, though the final draft left open the possibility of prosecution in their own or foreign courts.

Wenaweser explained the compromise to the plenary and asked, "Do I take it there is consensus on the adoption of this text?"[124] The room was silent. Heads turned toward Britain and France, concerned they might force a vote. The drafters tracked the departing delegations, worried there would not be a quorum sufficient to pass the law.[125] Japan raised its placard to speak; diplomats whispered nervously. "The delegation of Japan has serious doubts about the legal integrity of the amendment," said the head of the Japanese delegation. It seemed the negotiations would collapse over Japan's distrust of Wenaweser's amendment compromise. "But we will not stand in the way of consensus," he added.[126]

Wenaweser brought down his gavel and, to cheers and applause, the amendment was adopted, alongside genocide (Article 6), crimes against humanity (Article 7) and war crimes (Article 8).[127] Don Ferencz assembled his bagpipes and played *Nkosi sikelel' iAfrika*, Lord Lift Up Africa, as the delegates shook hands and hugged.

I went over to Ben Ferencz, huddled in his chair, looking all his ninety years old.

"Congratulations, Ben," I said, a grin on my exhausted face.

"What do you mean, congratulations?" he barked, thinking of the conditions before ICC prosecutions could start. "There are three new locks on the courthouse door."

After sixty-five years of deadlock, for the first time since Nuremberg, an enforceable definition of the crime of aggression was enshrined in international law. The Kampala agreement shifted regulation from the state to the individual, making criminal leaders accountable for aggressive war. Its detailed prohibitions were more precise than any previous legal injunction on force. The nuanced wording of the new law was an authoritative guide for judges and could potentially be applied not only by the ICC but by any other criminal court around the world. The ICC was empowered to make independent aggression determinations based on commonly accepted legal principles, even if they contradicted the edicts of a politicized Security Council. This historic agreement provided a judicial check on the executive discretion to wage war and buttressed the rule of law.

Some supporters of the crime, including Ferencz, were disappointed with the Kampala compromise. Nonmembers of the ICC were excluded from ICC jurisdiction. ICC member states were provided a formal mechanism to opt out of ICC jurisdiction. With a Security Council referral, anyone could be prosecuted. Without a Security Council referral, ICC jurisdiction was limited to ICC member states that had not opted out. For Ferencz, the limits on jurisdiction and the delaying entry-into-force conditions were too great a concession to the superpowers.

These compromises were necessary for a law on the crime of aggression to exist. The trade-off was that although the superpowers didn't block the agreement, they remained exempt from ICC jurisdiction. It is unknown whether national courts will be bold enough to prosecute powerful leaders. But when the next attack came, it would be impossible to deny that there is an authoritative definition of aggression, that it is a crime, and that leaders who have planned, prepared, initiated, and executed aggressive war are personally responsible.

The devil would be in interpreting the details of the rules, exceptions, and ambiguities.

AMENDMENTS TO THE ROME STATUTE OF THE INTERNATIONAL CRIMINAL COURT ON THE CRIME OF AGGRESSION[128]

Article 8 *bis*
Crime of aggression

1. For the purpose of this Statute, "crime of aggression" means the planning, preparation, initiation or execution, by a person in a position effectively to exercise control over or to direct the political or military action of a State, of an act of aggression which, by its character, gravity and scale, constitutes a manifest violation of the Charter of the United Nations.

2. For the purpose of paragraph 1, "act of aggression" means the use of armed force by a State against the sovereignty, territorial integrity or political independence of another State, or in any other manner inconsistent with the Charter of the United Nations. Any of the following acts, regardless of a declaration of war, shall, in accordance with United Nations General Assembly resolution 3314 (XXIX) of 14 December 1974, qualify as an act of aggression:

(a) The invasion or attack by the armed forces of a State of the territory of another State, or any military occupation, however temporary, resulting from such invasion or attack, or any annexation by the use of force of the territory of another State or part thereof;

(b) Bombardment by the armed forces of a State against the territory of another State or the use of any weapons by a State against the territory of another State;

(c) The blockade of the ports or coasts of a State by the armed forces of another State;

(d) An attack by the armed forces of a State on the land, sea or air forces, or marine and air fleets of another State;

(e) The use of armed forces of one State which are within the territory of another State with the agreement of the receiving State, in contravention of the conditions provided for in the agreement or any extension of their presence in such territory beyond the termination of the agreement;

(f) The action of a State in allowing its territory, which it has placed at the disposal of another State, to be used by that other State for perpetrating an act of aggression against a third State;

(g) The sending by or on behalf of a State of armed bands, groups, irregulars or mercenaries, which carry out acts of armed force against another State of such gravity as to amount to the acts listed above, or its substantial involvement therein.

Article 15 *bis*
Exercise of jurisdiction over the crime of aggression
(State referral, *proprio motu*)

1. The Court may exercise jurisdiction over the crime of aggression in accordance with article 13, paragraphs (a) and (c), subject to the provisions of this article.

2. The Court may exercise jurisdiction only with respect to crimes of aggression committed one year after the ratification or acceptance of the amendments by thirty States Parties.

3. The Court shall exercise jurisdiction over the crime of aggression in accordance with this article, subject to a decision to be taken after 1 January 2017 by the same majority of States Parties as is required for the adoption of an amendment to the Statute.

4. The Court may, in accordance with article 12, exercise jurisdiction over a crime of aggression, arising from an act of aggression committed by a State Party, unless that State Party has previously declared that it does not accept such jurisdiction by lodging a declaration with the Registrar. The withdrawal of such a declaration may be effected at any time and shall be considered by the State Party within three years.

5. In respect of a State that is not a party to this Statute, the Court shall not exercise its jurisdiction over the crime of aggression when committed by that State's nationals or on its territory.

6. Where the Prosecutor concludes that there is a reasonable basis to proceed with an investigation in respect of a crime of aggression, he or she shall first ascertain whether the Security Council has made a determination of an act of aggression committed by the State concerned. The Prosecutor shall notify the Secretary-General of the United Nations of the situation before the Court, including any relevant information and documents.

7. Where the Security Council has made such a determination, the Prosecutor may proceed with the investigation in respect of a crime of aggression.

8. Where no such determination is made within six months after the date of notification, the Prosecutor may proceed with the investigation in respect of a crime of aggression, provided that the Pre-Trial Division has authorized the commencement of the

investigation in respect of a crime of aggression in accordance with the procedure contained in article 15, and the Security Council has not decided otherwise in accordance with article 16.

9. A determination of an act of aggression by an organ outside the Court shall be without prejudice to the Court's own findings under this Statute.

10. This article is without prejudice to the provisions relating to the exercise of jurisdiction with respect to other crimes referred to in article 5.

Article 15 *ter*
Exercise of jurisdiction over the crime of aggression
(Security Council referral)

1. The Court may exercise jurisdiction over the crime of aggression in accordance with article 13, paragraph (b), subject to the provisions of this article.

2. The Court may exercise jurisdiction only with respect to crimes of aggression committed one year after the ratification or acceptance of the amendments by thirty States Parties.

3. The Court shall exercise jurisdiction over the crime of aggression in accordance with this article, subject to a decision to be taken after 1 January 2017 by the same majority of States Parties as is required for the adoption of an amendment to the Statute.

4. A determination of an act of aggression by an organ outside the Court shall be without prejudice to the Court's own findings under this Statute.

5. This article is without prejudice to the provisions relating to the exercise of jurisdiction with respect to other crimes referred to in article 5.

CHAPTER 7

Judging Wars

It is legal because I wish it.
—Louis XIV, speaking before the Parlement de Paris, 1655

Courts are the mere instruments of the law, and can will nothing.
—Chief Justice John Marshall, in *Osborn v. Bank of United States*, 1824

The young man knows the rules, but the old man knows the exceptions.
—Oliver Wendell Holmes Sr., valedictory address to the graduating class of the Bellevue Hospital College, 1871

The 2010 crime of aggression is very similar to Ferencz's concept of the crime as a loose amalgamation of key twentieth-century precedents, but it is more specific.[1] The Kampala agreement establishes the links between the legal precedents, the Lego blocks that constitute the crime, and adds some tweaks. Basically, the definition of the crime of aggression is leadership responsibility for an act of aggression amounting to a "manifest" violation of the UN Charter. The two components of the definition of aggression are the state act and its doctrinal link to the individual perpetrator. The Kampala amendments flesh out the state act by listing seven prosecutable "acts of aggression." These cover every scenario from outright invasion through bombardment and blockade, and, significantly, with the 2014 Crimea example, the "use of armed forces of one State which are within the territory of another State" for purposes not agreed on by the host state. The definition also prohibits any of the enumerated acts when carried out by "armed bands, groups, irregulars or mercenaries" on behalf of a state.[2] The other essential component of the definition is the individual conduct linking the defendant to the state act.[3] Leaders who plan, prepare, initiate, or execute a state act of aggression can be held accountable if they control the military or political actions of a state. The definition and jurisdictional conditions specify which leaders the ICC can investigate and who is outside the court's reach.

Kampala was a compromise, but also a milestone for the rule of law. It provides the ICC and regional and domestic courts with a new role in curbing executive power to wage war. This raises the question of what exactly Kampala will mean on the ground. The interpretive challenges are unknown and untested, as are the legal strategies of defending jurists.

The battle will be waged, as at Nuremberg, in court.

THE ADJUDICATION TRADITION

A criminal trial is a ritual with familiar logic and symbols. Typically, a judge or panel of judges dressed in dark robes sit at an elevated dais looking down at the prosecution and the accused, who occupy matching tables at opposite sides of the room. Sometimes, there are seats for the public, for justice must not only be done, it must be seen to be done. There is a deliberate order to the proceedings dictated by the judges. First, the prosecution speaks, then the defense. In common-law countries, the judge is a referee, while in civil-law jurisdictions, he or she is a scientist searching for the truth. In both traditions, the logic and symbols of the trial are meant to bolster our confidence that the verdict will be fair and impartial. The Kampala amendments subject modern armed conflict to this traditional ritual in the hope it can check the violence of political and military leaders.

Responding to criminal conduct with a trial is to uphold the rule of law. Under the liberal model of government, the legislature makes the laws and the judiciary applies them.[4] This division of power is intended to allow us to live under preexisting rules applicable to all, rather than under the arbitrary edicts of powerful leaders.[5] As Chief Justice John Marshall wrote in an 1824 Supreme Court decision, "courts are the mere instruments of the law, and can will nothing."[6] American jurists in Marshall's time equated the law with Euclidian geometry: "The function of the judge was to discover analytically the proper rules and precedents involved and to apply them to the case as first premises."[7] Harvard law professor Duncan Kennedy describes the judge as a mythic figure in American culture, struggling "to 'rise above' and 'put aside,' to 'resist' and 'transcend,' their personal interest, their instinctive and intuitive sympathies, their partisan group affiliations, and their ideological commitments." This mythic judge lies awake pondering quandaries, and fights for what is right when confronted with "obscure warnings from friends in high places."[8]

Kennedy and other critical legal scholars lost faith in the rule of law after concluding that it reproduces systems of hierarchy and contains gaps, conflicts, and ambiguities resolved by judges pursuing conscious, half-conscious, or unconscious ideological projects.[9] These cynics have not proposed alternatives or improvements. They see international law as part of the battlefield, not a principled constraint on the decisions of political and military leaders.[10] Their cynicism about legal rationality surrenders to the entrenched élites they claim to oppose. David Kennedy acknowledges that "law has infiltrated the war machine" but holds little hope that new sites of legal resistance will check arbitrary military power.[11] His appeal to the ethical conscience of leaders is vulnerable to the same denigrating charge of ambiguity that he levels at law, without the benefit of law's procedural parameters and bite.[12] By exaggerating law's indeterminacy and underestimating the possibilities of societal change, the critical legal scholars reach the same paralyzing conclusion as the rational-choice theorists, their ideological adversaries on the political right, who argue that legal norms never trump self-interest.[13] Both camps agree that "many global problems," including war, "are simply unsolvable."[14]

The drafters of the crime of aggression argue that law will not end war, but can help deter it, judge it, and possibly moderate the excesses of political and military leaders. Criminal law presumes that individuals are free and rational agents who choose to obey the law or violate it. Punishment of criminals is meant to reduce crime by deterring perpetrators, incarcerating culprits, and potentially rehabilitating offenders. Payam Akhavan argues that "Criminal accusations increasingly constitute a serious political impediment to the ambitions of existing or aspiring leaders."[15] According to Akhavan, international criminal justice has begun to change the rules of international relations. Criminal accountability for aggression fortifies domestic and international law so that waging war has consequences for individuals.

Criminal justice has less tangible but equally important goals. Legal scholar Marc Drumbl argues that trials serve an expressive function: "punishment is required to recognize evil, even evil that may not be deterred by the threat of such punishment."[16] According to Martha Minow, "The ideal is equal dignity of all persons."[17] When a court punishes a wrongdoer, it is inflicting a publicly visible defeat meant to correct the wrongdoer's false message that the victim is less worthy.[18] Trials test evidence in a fair process and serve as a bulwark against societal forgetting. "The claim, and the hope," Minow explains, "is that trials create official records of the scope of violence and the participants in it, and that guilty verdicts afford public acknowledgement of what happened, and its utter wrongfulness."[19] The trial's rules of evidence and procedure, though imperfect, provide a bulwark against Goering-like schemes of leaders who would bring their populations to war.[20]

In evaluating the crime of aggression, the question remains whether the assumptions and objectives of criminal justice are applicable to the punishment of leaders for aggressive war. For specific and general deterrence to work, the costs of violating the law must outweigh the benefits. But before incapacitating and rehabilitating a culprit or inflicting a symbolic defeat, that culprit first has to suffer a real one. The criminal trial of a captured leader might be seen as justice by enemies and lawfare by that leader's friends, especially when the individuals judging are from states even marginally affected by the outcome. Finally, judges are not historians and not expected to produce an official historical account of the war when drafting a verdict.[21] The validity of these criticisms depends in large part on the capability and integrity of the judiciary and the credibility of enforcement.

Judges concerned about fair process are scrupulous in assuring their verdicts are beyond reproach. Scholars combing through evidence submitted by prosecution and defense can contextualize the verdict with historical accounts. International cooperation by ICC states parties and allies in providing evidence, arresting fugitives, and surrendering them for trial will increase deterrence, as will domestic enforcement of the crime, most likely by successor regimes. By focusing on the statesman rather than confronting the state, drafters of the crime of aggression may have discovered a way to leverage the force of law and advance the cause of international justice.

That is, if the legal system works.

AGGRESSION JURISDICTION: RULES AND EXCEPTIONS

There are three ways for an aggression case to land on the docket of the ICC: a Security Council referral, a state referral, or a prosecutor's petition to the ICC (*proprio motu*).[22] A Security Council referral allows the court to hear a case against any political or military leader in the world for any of the four international crimes: genocide, crimes against humanity, war crimes, and the crime of aggression.[23] The Security Council can instigate a case without the consent of the states involved. When an ICC state party refers a situation or when the prosecutor initiates one *proprio motu*, the court is restricted to cases against a narrower pool—that is, the leaders of ICC states parties who have not opted out of the Kampala amendments.[24]

This is how the pretrial process works: The Security Council, an ICC state party, or the ICC prosecutor brings a situation to the ICC.[25] If the Security Council is silent and the ICC prosecutor, acting on a state referral or his or her own initiative, concludes that there is reasonable basis to proceed with a full-scale aggression investigation, the prosecutor must notify and provide the relevant information to the UN Secretary-General. If the Security Council, faced with the ICC prosecutor's information, determines that an act of aggression was committed, the prosecutor can proceed with an investigation. If the council is silent—for example, being blocked by a permanent-member veto—the prosecutor must wait six months before requesting the pretrial division of the ICC, in which all six ICC pretrial judges convene in full session, to authorize an investigation.[26] This process is designed to encourage cooperation between the council and the court.[27]

The decision to buttress the ICC's usual three-judge pretrial chamber when the Security Council is silent is specific to aggression cases. It was intended to assuage those states concerned about judicial bias, and the six-judge pretrial division is not used for other ICC crimes.[28] Once the pretrial division authorizes the investigation of a *situation*, the prosecutor investigates *individual defendants* and the trial court applies an even more rigorous standard to establish guilt. Given appeals available at all levels and a Security Council mechanism to defer cases that threaten international peace,[29] skeptics signed on to the Kampala compromise.

The jurisdictional hurdles built into the Kampala agreement would preclude an aggression case against Putin for the 2014 invasion of the Crimea: Russia is not an ICC state party so jurisdiction depends on a Security Council referral, which Russia can veto.[30] Without a Security Council referral, leaders of nonparty states can, however, be tried by domestic, regional, or hybrid courts applying the 2010 definition of the crime of aggression or their own variation. The African Union, for instance, granted its nascent African Court of Justice and Human Rights jurisdiction over a variation of the crime of aggression under which the leaders of nonstate organizations like al Qaeda and Boko Haram can be prosecuted and punished for violations.[31]

The drafters of the crime of aggression struck a delicate compromise between states who demanded a consent-based regime (Camp Consent) and those who wanted the law to provide a deterrent to powerful nonparty states contemplating armed attacks against weaker ICC state parties (Camp Protection). The jurisdictional rules were a great disappointment to Ferencz, who thought they didn't go far enough, and a concern to Harold Koh, who felt they went too far.[32] The drafters consider the jurisdictional rules to be an important evolution in the law of war. By allowing the ICC to make independent legal determinations that may contradict the Security Council's more political resolutions, the Kampala compromise represents an important shift from politics to law in the international order.

Yet, as Oliver Wendell Holmes Sr. said, "The young man knows the rules, but the old man knows the exceptions."[33] ICC judges face three potentially contentious zones of interpretation when deciding whether to hear an aggression case.[34]

First, they must interpret Security Council resolutions related to the situation and discern whether the council determined that aggression occurred. Ascertaining whether the Security Council has determined aggression may be easier said than done. The council rarely calls a military operation "aggression." It prefers to use other terms such as "threat to the peace," "breach of the peace," or "unlawful use of force."[35] The implication is that embattled judges wishing to make a politically sensitive case disappear may find their opportunity in the ambiguous language of a Security Council resolution. ICC judges may also be called upon to determine the temporal and geographic scope of a Security Council resolution. Here, the judges will serve as a check on the legal arguments of government lawyers like John Yoo[36] and Harold Koh,[37] who attempt to use an aging authorization to cover new situations rather than obtaining a new one,[38] an exercise Koh derided in 1995 as a game of "'Find the Statute,' or less colloquially, 'The Hunt for Allegedly Delegated Prior Executive Authority.'"[39]

Ambiguous Security Council resolutions can make leaders vulnerable to prosecution, as happened to UK Prime Minister David Cameron when in 2015, based on the ambiguous Security Council Resolution 2249, he brought the United Kingdom to war against ISIS in Syria.[40] Resolution 2249 was a fraught compromise between the West, who wanted authorization for war after ISIS's 2015 Paris attacks, and Russia, who resisted authorization. The ambiguous language of Resolution 2249 left authorization open to interpretation.[41] Leaders wishing to use force against ISIS in Syria and those wishing to preclude force both found justification in its language.

The second contentious zone of interpretation for ICC judges is contained in a clever argument presented by militarily powerful states and their allies. They maintain that the ICC's amendment provision and the Vienna Convention on the Law of Treaties legally require a consent-based regime in which both aggressor and victim state have ratified the Kampala amendments before the ICC can exercise jurisdiction.[42] This was not the agreement reached at Kampala.[43] At Kampala, all ICC member states agreed to submit to ICC jurisdiction if *either* aggressor or victim state had ratified the amendments, unless they took the steps to formally opt out.[44] Camp Consent's interpretation, if accepted, would allow pretrial judges to reject ICC jurisdiction over leaders of ICC member states that had not opted out, undoing Kampala's delicate compromise.

Finally, ICC judges will have to determine whether other ongoing investigations or prosecutions of the crime of aggression trump ICC jurisdiction. Legal authorities overlap—ad hoc Security Council tribunals (such as the ICTY and ICTR), regional tribunals,[45] hybrid national-international tribunals,[46] federal courts, state/provincial courts, and local restorative justice processes[47]—and ICC judges will be tasked with determining primacy.[48] Many states have now criminalized aggression in their domestic law, thirty-nine by last count, states as diverse as Russia, Ukraine, Germany, Samoa, Finland, and Botswana, and others are in the process.[49] The African Union and the Arab League have criminalized aggression as well.[50]

The opportunities and dangers of domestic enforcement of aggression revealed themselves in April 2016 when a Kiev court used domestic Ukrainian aggression provisions to find captured Russian special forces soldiers Yevgeny Yerofeyev and Alexander Alexandrov guilty of "aggressive war" for their participation in the invasion of the Crimea.[51] The Yerofeyev and Alexandrov verdicts were announced as the trial of Hissène Habré ended in Senegal, and the Chadian dictator became the first world leader sentenced by the courts of another country for international crimes.[52] While the Kiev case raised concern about the dangers of overzealous prosecution and biased judging,[53] by cooperating in designing Habré's trial, Chad and the African Union showed it was possible to render international justice in a domestic court.[54] In 2009, the United Kingdom began the Iraq War (Chilcot) Inquiry of its own former Prime Minister Tony Blair and his administration. Though not a criminal court, the UK inquiry was the closest thing to domestic accountability for the 2003 invasion. Its interrogation and judgment of Blair and his decision to bring the United Kingdom to war in Iraq presaged the possibility of future aggression cases against powerful Western leaders.[55]

ICC jurisdiction over the crime of aggression will conceivably hang on the pretrial judges' interpretation of existing Security Council resolutions, the judges' assessment of the French/UK revisionist argument, and the judges' evaluation of whether the state is genuinely willing and able to judge and prosecute the aggressor.[56] When it comes to establishing wrongdoing, the judges will turn to the definition of the crime.[57]

APPLYING THE DEFINITION OF THE CRIME OF AGGRESSION

Judges hearing an aggression case will be providing answers to three of the twentieth century's most intractable legal questions: Is there a distinction between a just and an unjust war? Can that distinction be defined in universal terms? And, if so, is it possible to hold individuals accountable for an unjust war? When an aggression case lands on the ICC docket, judges will apply the definition of the crime of aggression to rule on the legality of the war and whether to attribute individual responsibility.[58] Their first challenge will be to determine beyond a reasonable doubt if the state has committed an act of aggression amounting to a "manifest" violation of the UN Charter. Their second task will be to establish if the defendant is criminally responsible for the state act.

Conflicting interpretive views of the definitional rules and exceptions of the crime of aggression will govern the application of the new law. If a defendant claims the legal justification of humanitarian intervention or preemptive self-defense, judges will follow a pattern of legal reasoning to determine whether these acts amount to aggression. Judges with shrewd law clerks will locate the interpretive leeway, delineate it with persuasive precedents, and avoid legal arguments that strain credulity. If successful, they will win the support of a majority of judges and have the final word on the aggression decision.

Future legal battle lines are already drawn. The legal disputes begin with Article 2(4) of the UN Charter, "the pivot on which the present day *jus ad bellum* hinges."[59] At first glance, Article 2(4) seems deceptively simple: "All Members shall refrain in their international relations from the threat or use of force *against the territorial integrity or political independence of any state, or in any other manner inconsistent with the Purposes of the United Nations*" (emphasis added). The legal ambiguity of the provision hinges on emphasis of either the first or the second half of the article.[60] The first half suggests a broad prohibition on the use of force. The second half, here in italics, can be read to grant more opportunities for the use of force. The way this segment is interpreted affects the decision on contentious cyberattacks, protection of nationals abroad, hot pursuit, self-defense, and humanitarian-intervention cases.[61]

The legal disputes are further complicated by the wording of the threshold provision of Article 8 *bis* of the definition of the crime of aggression, which says that only "manifest" violations of the UN Charter give rise to criminal responsibility for aggression. The "manifest" qualifier was a compromise between delegations championing the Nuremberg tribunal's all-out "wars of aggression" threshold, and delegations preferring the 1974 General Assembly Definition's more modern "acts of aggression" alternative, which need not involve a full-scale shooting war.[62] The "manifest" threshold, though lower than Nuremberg's "war of aggression" threshold, greatly expands opportunities for the legal use of force. The inclusion of the "manifest" threshold in the definition of the crime of aggression was meant to ensure that only the most serious and unambiguously illegal instances of the use of force by states give rise to individual criminal responsibility. The first judges interpreting the definition of the crime of aggression will consider the character, gravity, and scale of the use of armed force.[63] No one component is sufficient to create liability.[64] A few bullets fired across a border may not qualify as a manifest violation, nor might an unauthorized delivery of emergency medical supplies to a foreign refugee population because the character of the act is humanitarian. Yet, for the Special Working Group on the Crime of Aggression, Saddam Hussein's 1990 invasion of Kuwait was a clear-cut act of aggression. Over time, ICC jurisprudence will hone the meaning of ambiguous terms such as "manifest," "territorial integrity," and "political independence."

Particular uses of force are unambiguously illegal under the definition of the crime of aggression.[65] Reprisals and armed countermeasures—such as the April 7, 2017, US Tomahawk missile barrage against the Shayrat air base in Syria—are illegal under the UN Charter and, therefore, under the definition of the crime of aggression.[66] The unilateral use of force to restore democracy is illegal, absent the consent of the legitimate government.[67] The use of force in support of a secessionist movement, such as the 2014 Russian interference in the Crimea, is illegal as well.[68] These are three clear-cut examples among many.

There are also gray areas in which legality is disputed. Invitations by the legitimate government of a state to intervene against insurgents, such as Yemeni President Hadi's 2015 appeal for aid against Houthi rebels, can generate legal disputes over the validity of the invitation and its scope.[69] Security Council resolutions, such as Resolution 1973 (2011) authorizing force "to protect civilians and civilian populated areas under threat of attack," may give rise to accusations that intervening states have overstepped their mandate.[70] Without the existence of an independent legal authority to judge, militarily powerful leaders usually prevail.

The two key gray areas of humanitarian intervention and self-defense in response to a future attack bear further discussion.

A HYPOTHETICAL CASE OF HUMANITARIAN INTERVENTION

Every December and April, across the United States, law professors produce a subgenre of short story called the "law school hypothetical," an exam prompt to test students' capacity to spot and analyze contentious legal issues. The master of the genre is Rutgers law professor Roger Clark.

Clark has taught international law for forty-five years. He is best known for his scholarship on nuclear weapons and international criminal law, and his representation of small states such as Samoa and the Marshall Islands in multilateral negotiations and international tribunals. Along with his team of lawyers, Clark was nominated for a 2016 Nobel Peace Prize for a lawsuit attempting to hold nine nuclear powers to the terms of the 1968 Nuclear Non-Proliferation Treaty. He was an influential force on the Special Working Group on the Crime of Aggression as a representative of Samoa.

In 2013, Clark crafted a hypothetical called "Alleged Aggression in Utopia: An International Criminal Law Examination Question for 2020" that test-runs many of the issues to come before the ICC.[71] The student role-plays a law clerk at the Office of the ICC Prosecutor and writes a legal memorandum providing advice for the prosecutor on her first aggression case.

General Pickens, chief of the armed forces of the fictional state of Tapu, is the reluctant protagonist. The president and cabinet of Tapu order Pickens to invade the neighboring state of Utopia, capture the capital, and overthrow the regime. They tell Pickens that Utopia is commencing an organized genocide against a minority group. Pickens warns that he may not have enough troops and questions the legality of the operation, whereupon the president presents the general with a short statement drafted by the attorney general of Tapu justifying the intervention under the Responsibility-to-Protect doctrine. Pickens considers his options, to follow the order or resign, and obeys. The invasion is a disaster. Scores of people are killed and Pickens is captured behind enemy lines. The president of Tapu and his entire cabinet commit suicide in a bunker, leaving Pickens to face justice.

What are the legal issues in this aggression hypothetical? The nonbinding guide to interpreting the definition, referred to as "the elements of the crime," attempts to clarify the judging of war:

Elements of the Crime of Aggression:

1. The perpetrator planned, prepared, initiated or executed an act of aggression.
2. The perpetrator was a person in a position effectively to exercise control over or to direct the political or military action of the State which committed the act of aggression.
3. The act of aggression—the use of armed force by a State against the sovereignty, territorial integrity or political independence of another State, or in any other manner inconsistent with the Charter of the United Nations—was committed.
4. The perpetrator was aware of the factual circumstances that established that such a use of armed force was inconsistent with the Charter of the United Nations.
5. The act of aggression, by its character, gravity and scale, constituted a manifest violation of the Charter of the United Nations.
6. The perpetrator was aware of the factual circumstances that established such a manifest violation of the Charter of the United Nations.[72]

Clark answers his own hypothetical. He begins with the state's "act of aggression" and finds that by "invading" Utopia and "attacking" its armed forces, Tapu has perpetrated an act of aggression (Element 3), unless it can provide a legitimate defense of its actions (Element 1). But did General Pickens's actions fit the conduct specified in the definition? Students considering Element 1 will realize that General Pickens didn't plan the invasion, but he executed it, and Clark concludes that two of the six elements of criminal responsibility have been met.[73]

For Pickens to be liable, the prosecutor needs to prove Element 2, that Pickens was a leader, someone "in a position effectively to exercise control over or to direct the political or military action of the State." Though Pickens was not in a position to exercise control over the political action of Tapu, he fulfills Element 2 of the crime of aggression because he was in charge of its military action. Clark's interpretation of the leadership clause includes leaders of bureaucratic organizations like Nazi Germany, while a progressive interpretation would include influential leaders in post-bureaucratic, networked-based organizations like al Qaeda.[74]

Clark argues that Pickens meets the accountability criteria in Element 4: he "was aware of the factual circumstances that established that such a use of armed force was inconsistent with the Charter of the United Nations."[75] Nor is Pickens absolved of responsibility because the attorney general said the operation was lawful.[76] The prosecutor will make the case that "a reasonable statesman or soldier" in Pickens's place should have known that this use of force was a "manifest violation of the Charter of the United Nations."[77]

To determine the fifth element, whether Tapu's invasion and attack of Utopia was a "manifest" violation, Clark looks to the character, gravity, and scale of the operation. He concludes that its gravity and scale surpass the minimal threshold in the crime of aggression, but is troubled by the invasion's "humanitarian" character. Citing the Responsibility to Protect (R2P), he recalls that the legal authority of R2P "was a matter of intense debate when the Kampala amendments were being negotiated."[78] Without hazarding a position on the legality of humanitarian intervention, Clark recalls that humanitarian intervention was a "grey area" flash point in the Kampala negotiations.[79] By calling humanitarian intervention a "grey area," Clark seems to be excluding it from the ambit of the crime, but he nevertheless appears skeptical of unilateral "humanitarian" invasions in response to a genocide that has not yet occurred. Buried in a footnote, Clark says that the preemptive character of Pickens's intervention undermines his humanitarian-intervention defense.[80]

There are other good reasons to be skeptical of leaders who claim to be deploying armed force for humanitarian motives.[81] Intervening states have imposed unwanted conditions on the so-called beneficiaries of their humanitarian action.[82] Humanitarian interventions have exacerbated international and internal conflicts.[83] States rarely use force for humanitarian aims against great powers, creating an imbalance that some consider unjust.[84] "The worst imperialists often claim they are acting from the finest motives," says Princeton political scientist Gary Bass.[85]

But ICC judges interpreting the Kampala amendments are well placed to carve out a limited right of humanitarian rescue with robust safeguards against abuse by powerful nations using humanitarianism as a pretext for conquest.[86] ICC judges are in a position to test humanitarian justifications for the use of force against settled rules of evidence and procedure, institutional checks and balances, and predefined international norms.[87] Applied by an independent and impartial court such as the ICC, R2P would provide the criteria to evaluate humanitarian-intervention claims. This would check dangerous imperialist misadventures and dictators who use sovereignty as an alibi as they exterminate their own people.

The Responsibility to Protect: Principles for Military Intervention (2001)[88]

(1) THE JUST CAUSE THRESHOLD

Military intervention for human protection purposes is an exceptional and extraordinary measure. To be warranted, there must be serious and irreparable harm occurring to human beings, or imminently likely to occur, of the following kind:

A. **large scale loss of life,** actual or apprehended, with genocidal intent or not, which is the product either of deliberate state action, or state neglect or inability to act, or a failed state situation; or

B. **large scale "ethnic cleansing",** actual or apprehended, whether carried out by killing, forced expulsion, acts of terror or rape.

(2) THE PRECAUTIONARY PRINCIPLES

A. **Right intention:** The primary purpose of the intervention, whatever other motives intervening states may have, must be to halt or avert human suffering. Right intention is better assured with multilateral operations, clearly supported by regional opinion and the victims concerned.

B. **Last resort:** Military intervention can only be justified when every non-military option for the prevention or peaceful resolution of the crisis has been explored, with reasonable grounds for believing lesser measures would not have succeeded.

C. **Proportional means:** The scale, duration and intensity of the planned military intervention should be the minimum necessary to secure the defined human protection objective.

D. **Reasonable prospects:** There must be a reasonable chance of success in halting or averting the suffering which has justified the intervention, with the consequences of action not likely to be worse than the consequences of inaction.

(3) RIGHT AUTHORITY

A. There is no better or more appropriate body than the United Nations Security Council to authorize military intervention for human protection purposes. The task is not to find alternatives to the Security Council as a source of authority, but to make the Security Council work better than it has.

B. Security Council authorization should in all cases be sought prior to any military intervention action being carried out. Those calling for an intervention should formally request such authorization, or have the Council raise the matter on its own initiative, or have the Secretary-General raise it under Article 99 of the UN Charter.

C. The Security Council should deal promptly with any request for authority to intervene where there are allegations of large scale loss of human life or ethnic cleansing. It should in this context seek adequate verification of facts or conditions on the ground that might support a military intervention.

D. The Permanent Five members of the Security Council should agree not to apply their veto power, in matters where their vital state interests are not involved, to obstruct the passage of resolutions authorizing military intervention for human protection purposes for which there is otherwise majority support.

E. If the Security Council rejects a proposal or fails to deal with it in a reasonable time, alternative options are:

I. consideration of the matter by the General Assembly in Emergency Special Session under the "Uniting for Peace" procedure; and

II. action within area of jurisdiction by regional or subregional organizations under Chapter VIII of the Charter, subject to their seeking subsequent authorization from the Security Council.

F. The Security Council should take into account in all its deliberations that, if it fails to discharge its responsibility to protect in conscience-shocking situations crying out for action, concerned states may not rule out other means to meet the gravity and urgency of that situation—and that the stature and credibility of the United Nations may suffer thereby.

(4) OPERATIONAL PRINCIPLES

A. Clear objectives; clear and unambiguous mandate at all times; and resources to match.

B. Common military approach among involved partners; unity of command; clear and unequivocal communications and chain of command.

C. Acceptance of limitations, incrementalism and gradualism in the application of force, the objective being protection of a population, not defeat of a state.

D. Rules of engagement which fit the operational concept; are precise; reflect the principle of proportionality; and involve total adherence to international humanitarian law.

    E. Acceptance that force protection cannot become the principal objective.

    F. Maximum possible coordination with humanitarian organizations.

Use of the R2P principles in the interpretation of the crime of aggression can provide nuanced case-by-case decisions in the divisive humanitarian-intervention debate. Independent tribunals could check unilateral humanitarian intervention while opening this possibility for cases that pass the R2P test.[89]

DECONSTRUCTING PREEMPTIVE SELF-DEFENSE

The question of preemptive self-defense is another challenging gray area. The arguments are similar to those of humanitarian intervention, with minor variations. The key question is whether the right of self-defense is triggered by an armed attack that has not yet occurred. The need for a clear legal framework has gained new urgency as states such as Iran and North Korea come closer to pairing nuclear warheads with intercontinental ballistic missiles. "If the American imperialists provoke us a bit, we will not hesitate to slap them with a pre-emptive nuclear strike," warned North Korea in an alarming 2016 YouTube propaganda video.[90] Senior US intelligence officials told *NBC News* that the United States is prepared to launch a preemptive strike if convinced that North Korea is about to conduct a nuclear test.[91]

Legal scholars looking to the plain language and negotiating history of the UN Charter conclude that an actual armed attack is required before a state may lawfully respond with defensive force.[92] Article 51 of the UN Charter, they point out, permits defensive force "if an armed attack occurs."[93] Others maintain that pre–UN Charter international law included the right of anticipatory self-defense and that Article 51 of the UN Charter incorporates that "inherent right" in its language.[94] The former believe a strict rule better promotes international peace, while the latter argue that a looser standard not requiring states to suffer an attack before defending themselves is more in line with the realities of today's weaponry.

Under the limiting interpretation, legitimate self-defense requires: (1) an actual armed attack, (2) the victim state to immediately report the attack to the UN Security Council before responding with (3) necessary and (4) proportional force, (5) until the UN Security Council takes action.[95] A marginally more flexible interpretation of "armed attack" would permit a state to invoke the right of self-defense in response to an attack that has commenced, but not actually crossed the defending state's sovereign borders, such as Japanese ships en route to Pearl Harbor, or a North Korean missile leaving its launcher.[96] According to international law professor Mary Ellen O'Connell, "The right of self-defense is limited to the right to use force to repel an attack in progress, to prevent future enemy attacks following an initial attack, or to reverse the consequences of an enemy attack, such as ending an occupation."[97] The defending state can destroy the attacking force or "tak[e] the defense to the territory of the enemy attacker, if that is necessary and proportional."[98] Though there is some discussion about the meaning of necessity and proportionality, the limiting interpretation of self-defense is still more resistant to abuse than the alternatives.[99]

"We don't want the smoking gun to be a mushroom cloud," US Secretary of State Condoleezza Rice, advocate for a looser standard, famously argued in the run-up to the 2003 invasion of Iraq.[100] Preemptive self-defense in response to possible future attack using weapons of mass destruction became a US government justification for the 2003 invasion of Iraq.[101] In his 2002 National Security Strategy, President Bush argued, "We must adapt the concept of imminent threat to the capabilities and objectives of today's adversaries."[102] President Bush sent Secretary of State Colin Powell to the UN General Assembly and Powell advocated for a defensive war based on falsified intelligence about an imminent threat by terrorists with weapons of mass destruction.[103] By the time Americans learned the truth, the Iraq War was raging and the United States too embroiled to withdraw. The Bush doctrine's fundamental weakness is that it grants a government discretion to deploy military force in another state if it fears an unspecified attack in an unstipulated future.

President Obama, like President George W. Bush, sought to expand the imminence standard to include factors beyond the temporal proximity of the threat. His Justice Department's legal advice factored in "the relevant window of opportunity, the possibility of reducing collateral damage to civilians, and the likelihood of heading off future disastrous attacks on Americans."[104] For both presidents, "imminence" operated as a proxy for myriad factors, unsettling the concept. Without the application of legal safeguards by an objective and independent authority, both presidents' self-defense doctrines risked destabilizing expectations and undermining the imperfect yet resilient world order.

A more promising interpretation of the law of self-defense was based on an obscure 1837 precedent involving a border incident between the United States and Canada. The *Caroline*, a steamship used in the 1830s by American anti-British sympathizers, delivered supplies and arms down the Niagara River to anti-British rebels in Canada. British-backed militiamen crossed into the United States, routed the crew of the *Caroline*, lit her on fire, and sent her down the falls. British Ambassador Henry Fox, Lord Ashburton, claimed self-defense. US Secretary of State Daniel

Webster defined what a state making a self-defense claim would need to prove:

> Necessity of self-defense, instant, overwhelming, leaving no choice of means, and no moment for deliberation . . . [and the defending state] did nothing unreasonable or excessive; since the act, justified by the necessity of self-defense, must be limited by that necessity, and kept clearly within it.[105]

In Webster's formulation, the attack need not have struck for the right of self-defense to be triggered, so long as it was "instant" and "overwhelming" and the response was "necessary" and proportional (not "unreasonable or excessive"). Fox agreed with Webster's definition of self-defense, but not its application to the facts surrounding the *Caroline*.

Though the relevance of the *Caroline* incident has been questioned, it has, in important ways, withstood the test of time. The *Caroline* test has been cited by the Nuremberg tribunal,[106] the Tokyo tribunal,[107] and the International Court of Justice.[108] Many states, including Australia and the United Kingdom, consider the *Caroline* precedent customary law.[109] Critics question its relevance today, describing it as a political agreement brokered by two states in an era when the sovereign right to wage war was not limited by international law.[110] Opponents of the test argue that the precedent had nothing to do with self-defense since the armed conflict was already in progress.[111] Others maintain that the UN Charter supplanted the *Caroline* precedent and granted the Security Council a monopoly on legitimate force absent an armed attack.[112] According to Cambridge professor Christine Gray, "This episode has attained a mythical authority."[113]

Nevertheless, the *Caroline* test charts a course between an unreasonably restrictive rule and one that fails to meaningfully distinguish aggressor and victim. It responds to Condoleezza Rice's argument that requiring states to wait to be hit by nuclear weapons before defending themselves is unjust. But there is a danger in interpreting self-defense to include unilateral preemptive strikes. "Fear that the other may be about to strike in the mistaken belief that we are about to strike gives us a motive for striking, and so justifies the other's motive," warned Nobel laureate Thomas Schelling.[114] The risks of a preemptive nuclear accident are exacerbated when autocratic leaders hostile to legislative and judicial checks on their power ratchet up their rhetoric and prepare their militaries for action.

Since unilateral preventive strikes against fledgling nuclear programs pose massive risks, as in the 2003 invasion of Iraq, it is reasonable that leaders ordering unilateral preemptive war be prepared to take personal responsibility for the decision. A sensible doctrine of self-defense would require a leader launching a preemptive strike to exhaust all viable peaceful means and produce concrete evidence of an imminent attack (with factors set out clearly beforehand), which would be evaluated by the ICC or another authoritative tribunal applying the definition of aggression. Even a relaxed rule such as the Bush doctrine that gives special consideration to the gravity of the threat and the manner in which it would materialize when assessing imminence is more reasonable when applied by an independent judicial institution in accordance with widely accepted rules of evidence and procedure.[115]

Besides the temporal questions, there are other gray areas related to the right of self-defense that judges hearing an aggression case are likely to face. Scholars debate whether a low-scale attack by one state against another gives rise to a right of self-defense, or whether only the "most grave" forms of the use of force trigger that right.[116] The *Nicaragua* (1986) and *Oil Platforms* (2003) cases at the International Court of Justice establish a gravity threshold, without specifying what that threshold is.[117] *Nicaragua, Oil Platforms*, and the 2005 *Case Concerning Armed Activities in the Territory of the Congo* allude to the possibility that a series of low-scale attacks might together surpass the gravity threshold and trigger the right of self-defense.[118]

An unresolved self-defense issue directly relevant to the United States' justification for the use of force in Syria is whether the right is triggered when a state is unable or unwilling to prevent attacks by a third state or nonstate organization (such as ISIS) emanating from its territory. The definition of the crime of aggression prohibits a state from "allowing its territory, which it has placed at the disposal of another State, to be used by that other State for perpetrating an act of aggression against a third State."[119] A state that places its territory at the disposal of another state to launch attacks against a third state is in a weak legal position if it cries "Aggression!" when encountering a forcible defensive response. The legal situation is more murky if the host state simply acquiesces, is genuinely unable to prevent the attacks, or the entity launching the attacks is a nonstate organization.[120] The legal ambiguity was compounded in Syria, when the United States used force in 2014 against ISIS, claiming collective self-defense of Iraq in response to nonstate attacks Syria was unwilling or unable to prevent.[121]

When evaluating novel or gray-area justifications for the use of force, judges will draw on familiar legal sources[122]—the Rome Statute and the court's decisions, the UN Charter, the Nuremberg Charter and Judgment, the Tokyo Charter and Judgment, decisions in Nuremberg's successor trials, the 1974 General Assembly "Definition of Aggression," International Court of Justice decisions, and customary international law, among others—and follow commonly accepted rules of interpretation.[123] If the judges of the ICC and other aggression tribunals are successful, the coming years will see a welcome elucidation of the law of war.

DEGREES OF AMBIGUITY IN THE LAW: ACCEPTABLE AND UNACCEPTABLE

Tufts international law professor Michael Glennon argued that the draft crime of aggression is "blank prose" and that "Prosecution under it would turn upon factors that the law does not delineate, rendering criminal liability unpredictable and undermining the law's integrity."[124] Glennon recommended that the Assembly of States Parties "reject this misbegotten new definition."[125]

A number of international legal scholars have rebuffed Glennon's argument. University of London law professor Kevin John Heller replied that Glennon's argument is tantamount to saying, "the crime of murder has no content because countries disagree over whether abortion qualifies."[126] Columbia clinical professor Jennifer Trahan argued that Glennon's claims "rest on an incorrect construction of the definition, ignorance of the extensive negotiating history and *travaux préparatoires* that exist vis-à-vis the crime, and failure to consult the elements of the crime."[127]

Harold Koh included Glennon's blank-prose argument in the US statement in Kampala, though it was too late for it to influence the outcome.[128] The Special Working Group on the Crime of Aggression had already debated the question and came to the conclusion that the definition was specific enough to survive the legality challenge. Faced with legal gaps and ambiguities, the ICC's legislative body expected the judges to follow the applicable rules of interpretation, fill the gap, resolve the ambiguity, and arrive at a well-reasoned decision, not invalidate the law.[129]

Critics warn that ICC judges hearing an aggression case might attempt to manipulate the law to advance the strategic interests of a particular nation. If so, this would amount to outright bias, providing colleagues with grounds to recuse the offender. If the ICC's normal practice is any indication, judicial interpretation will be influenced by broad legal-policy considerations rather than judicial bias. Various ICC judges will interpret the Kampala outcome emphasizing differing ICC goals, such as deterring threats to the peace, preventing atrocities, ending impunity, and encouraging the national prosecution of international crimes.[130] Depending on their preferred approach to legal interpretation, they will adhere more or less closely to the plain language of the statute, the original understanding of its terms, or its purpose in light of today's realities.

Interpretation does not leave the judges unlimited discretion, nor is it Euclidian geometry. Nobody knows exactly how every aggression case will unfold, but the key zones of interpretation are becoming apparent and international lawyers have a strong sense of the range of legitimate arguments within these zones. These interpretive issues used to be resolved primarily by states arguing their positions between themselves. By according legal interpretation of the law of war to ICC judges, the Assembly of States Parties has set in motion a seminal shift from politics to law in the use-of-force regime. Yet, the moment new laws are implemented, newer arms create unforeseen generations of warfare, complicating the interpretive challenge of the Kampala agreement. In the days to come, the aggression definition will collide with modern warfare and future wars.

Can the law keep up?

CHAPTER 8

Sci-fi Warfare

No sensible decision can be made any longer without taking into account not only the world as it is, but the world as it will be.
—Isaac Asimov, *Asimov on Science Fiction*, 1981

We have no future because our present is too volatile. We have only risk management. The spinning of the given moment's scenarios. Pattern recognition.
—William Gibson, *Pattern Recognition*, 2003

Who controls the past controls the future: who controls the present controls the past.
—George Orwell, *1984*, 1949

Sci-fi writer William Gibson has been called a "visionary,"[1] a "prophet,"[2] and the "sage of the information age."[3] He is credited with anticipating reality television, drones, nanotechnology, Google Glass, the gentrification of San Francisco, and the rise of "competitive unpaid internships."[4] But Gibson gets grumpy when people claim he forecasts the future. "I sit near the tent where they [charlatans] give out bullshit and offer people a different sort of dialogue. My role is to raise questions."[5] When forecasting the future, he says, "We're almost always wrong."[6]

There is an affectation to someone so often right who claims he's almost always wrong. As evidence, he cites the absence of cell phones in *Neuromancer*, his 1984 cyberpunk classic.[7] After the surprise shock of 9/11, Gibson began applying science-fiction techniques to the recent past, to reflect the futuristic speed of contemporary change. "Fully imagined cultural futures were the luxury of another day, one in which 'now' was of some greater duration," says a character in Gibson's 2003 *Pattern Recognition*. "Things can change so abruptly, so violently, so profoundly, that futures like our grandparents' have insufficient 'now' to stand on."[8] But by 2012, Gibson had returned to writing speculative science fiction. "I think science fiction gives us a wonderful toolkit to disassemble and reexamine this kind of incomprehensible, constantly changing present that we live in, that we often live in quite uncomfortably."[9] Still, Gibson's futurism was not a forecast. It was a thought experiment in which he handpicked scenarios from the present and spun them into new patterns, opening the reader's mind to possible futures. When applied to the future of warfare, the most likely "pick" is the paradigm-shifting scenario Gibson imagined in the early 1980s, when he coined the term "cyberspace" before the modern internet existed: "Cyberspace. A consensual hallucination experienced daily by billions of legitimate operators, in every nation, by children being taught mathematical concepts. . . . A graphic representation of data abstracted from the banks of every computer in the human system. Unthinkable complexity."[10] In *Burning Chrome* (1982) and *Neuromancer* (1984), Gibson introduced readers to the possibility of cyber and kinetic war between states, multinational corporations, criminal gangs, superempowered individuals, and the global order. Today, the Pentagon has appropriated Gibson's term and designated "cyberspace," along with land, sea, air, and outer space, as the "fifth military domain," or war zone.[11]

International law can barely keep up, yet it must. To advance international peace, legal standards must imagine the unimaginable, staying true to the legal inheritance of the past and open to the unthinkable complexity of the future.

CYBERATTACK ON RECEIVED LAW

Natanz is a quiet city in the mountains of central Iran, dotted with pear trees and shrines. Nestled in the rugged hills thirty kilometers north of Natanz sits a heavily guarded compound with an underground bunker housing thousands of shiny, upright aluminum tubes. Inside these linked tubes, motors designed by A. Q. Khan spin uranium gas at supersonic speeds until the precious uranium 235 isotope rises from the larger 238 mass and can be skimmed from the top. The process is repeated in an enrichment cascade until the product is pure enough to fuel a power plant (three to four percent) or build a nuclear bomb (ninety percent).

In 2008, Iranian nuclear scientists at Natanz discovered the centrifuges spinning erratically and damaging the delicate machinery inside. The computer system monitoring the cascade gave no indication anything was wrong, but scientists could feel and hear rumbling and explosions in the bunker.[12] Thankfully, nobody was hurt—someone could have been torn to shreds by metal shards had the aluminum tubes burst. Demoralized scientists first blamed these malfunctions on Khan's unreliable equipment and the sloppiness of the local machinists, and began replacing centrifuges. They took approximately one thousand of the five thousand centrifuges offline, delaying Iran's nuclear program by between two and three years.[13]

Iran's centrifuge problems at Natanz began soon after three very different leaders were elected: Barack Obama in the United States, Mahmoud

Ahmadinejad in Iran, and Benjamin Netanyahu in Israel. Obama was committed to improving relations with the Muslim world, Ahmadinejad was dedicated to expanding Iran's nuclear program, and Netanyahu was devoted to stopping Iran from obtaining a nuclear bomb. In 2005, Iranian news quoted Ahmadinejad, "Anybody who recognizes Israel will burn in the fire of the Islamic nation's fury."[14] Obama knew if he failed to assure Netanyahu of Israel's safety from Iranian nuclear attack, Israeli jets would illegally bomb Iran's nuclear installations, as they had bombed Iraq's in 1981 and Syria's in 2007.

But, unlike Iraq or Syria, Iran had buried its nuclear sites deep underground and neither the Israelis nor the Americans knew exactly where they were. An Israeli strike that missed nuclear sites could provoke Iran to speed up secret nuclear-weapon production and cause another Middle East war.[15] Analysts warned that a US war with Iran could dwarf George W. Bush's 2003 debacle in Iraq.[16] Meanwhile, nonforce alternatives including international monitoring and sanctions for noncompliance had failed to curb Iran's nuclear ambitions. Obama's options were limited when the Natanz centrifuges shattered. Iranians eventually suspected US and Israeli sabotage, but were unable to find proof.

In June 2010 in Minsk, computer-security technician Sergey Ulasen discovered the cause of Iran's centrifuge woes.[17] Troubleshooting an Iranian computer that kept crashing and rebooting, he noticed a run-of-the-mill virus that was, upon closer inspection, a futuristic autonomous weapon. This "worm" was planted in free USB flash drives available to Iranian computer scientists running the Windows operating system. It was designed to lay dormant, recording the functioning of the Natanz centrifuge cascade, only to play this back to the Iranian scientists later as it secretly destroyed the rotors.[18]

Former CIA Director Michael Hayden, speaking with *New York Times* journalist David Sanger, was careful not to implicate the United States: "This is the first attack of a major nature in which a cyberattack was used to effect physical destruction. . . . Somebody has crossed the Rubicon."[19] Hayden compared the Natanz cyberattack to August 6, 1945, when the world first saw the capabilities of the uranium bomb, *Little Boy*, dropped on Hiroshima.[20]

During an eighteen-month investigation, Sanger learned that the cyberattacks on Natanz were part of a top-secret, multiyear digital campaign code-named Olympic Games, waged by the United States and Israel to prevent Iran from developing a bomb.[21] With multilateral diplomacy failing to slow or stop Iran's nuclear program and military options too risky, the United States and Israel had found a third path. Sanger concluded from interviews with US, European, and Israeli officials that Obama was personally implicated: "Perhaps not since Lyndon Johnson had sat in the same room, more than four decades before, picking bombing targets in North Vietnam, had a president of the United States been so intimately involved in the step-by-step escalation of an attack on a foreign nation's infrastructure."[22]

Ulasen and his team realized that the worm, though deliberately designed to activate only when it found the network of linked centrifuges at Natanz, had accidentally gotten loose and was spreading to personal computers all over the world.[23] Its physical damage would be limited to Natanz, but this programming mistake meant hackers from around the world now had access to the world's most sophisticated autonomous weapon to modify and repurpose for new attacks.[24] A covert attempt to stop the spread of nuclear weapons had inadvertently led to the proliferation of a sophisticated new weapon that was widely available to individuals and maddeningly difficult to attribute. They called it Stuxnet.[25]

The question was whether Olympic Games amounted to the crime of aggression by the US president and his top military leaders, and what the repercussions would be for international law and order if it did.

QUALIFYING FUTURE FORCE: CHARACTER, GRAVITY, AND SCALE

Ulasen sounded the Stuxnet alarm in June 2010, when diplomats gathered in Kampala, but it was too late to modify the definition of the crime of aggression. Besides, the prevailing view at the ICC Review Conference was that the Princeton group's definition, built from precedents that had survived almost a century of technological innovation in warfare, was perfectly capable of regulating cyberattacks. Not everyone was so sure. For an attack to amount to aggression under the definition, it had to be a "manifest violation" of the UN Charter. For Olympic Games to qualify as aggression, judges had to deem its character, gravity, and scale a manifest violation.[26] Character referred to the quality of the attack. Was the cyberattack more like a nonprosecutable economic attack or was it more like a prosecutable missile attack?[27]

Gravity referred to the seriousness of an act of aggression. International law contained a hierarchy of unlawful uses of force with particular legal consequences.[28] A time-limited border incursion with no physical or human damage, for example, might amount to the illegal "use of force," attracting state responsibility and requiring monetary restitution, but was not as grave as an "armed attack."[29] An "armed attack" was more serious, triggering the right of forcible self-defense.[30] Most serious was an "act of aggression," such as a full-scale invasion (e.g., Saddam's 1990 invasion of Kuwait), grave enough to warrant prosecution and criminal responsibility.[31]

The "scale," or magnitude, of the attack was an issue in Natanz. Olympic Games was a pinprick operation: nobody was killed; no US or Israeli troops violated the territorial integrity of Iran. Physical damage was limited to 984 centrifuges.[32] Nonetheless, the attack was a major violation of Iran's sovereignty and political independence. This would be factored into any *de minimis* assessment, likely under the "gravity" criteria.

The United States promoted additional language in the Kampala "Understandings" to be used as a guide to judicial interpretation. This language described aggression as "the most serious and dangerous form of the illegal use of force."[33] This addition was meant to further raise the *de minimis* threshold so that fewer uses of force could be prosecuted. The United States also attempted to limit the possibilities of prosecution through additional wording stipulating that more than one of the *de minimis* components—character, gravity, or scale—was necessary for prosecution.[34] In the definition itself, judges were free to consider all three components of the *de minimis* threshold in their deliberations.

Without case law on cyberattacks, almost every international law scholar writing about cyberwar was consulting the 2013 *Tallinn Manual*, an independent study of the international law applicable to cyberwar produced by NATO's cybersecurity think tank in Estonia.[35] According to the *Tallinn Manual*, "A cyber operation constitutes a use of force when its scale and effects are comparable to non-cyber operations rising to the level of a use of force."[36] The experts on the Tallinn project were unanimous that Olympic Games was an act of force, but they couldn't agree on the position of the cyberattack on the legal spectrum: whether unlawful "intervention," "armed attack," or "act of aggression."[37]

In September 2012, Harold Koh, legal advisor to the State Department, delivered a seminal speech at US Cyber Command setting out the US government's position: "cyber activities that proximately result in death, injury, or significant destruction would likely be viewed as a use of force."[38] Like the experts drafting the *Tallinn Manual*, Koh focused on the effects of the attack. His examples of illegal force were almost the same as those of the Tallinn experts: cyber operations triggering a nuclear plant meltdown, opening a dam upriver from a populated area, disabling air-traffic control.[39] Koh's list didn't answer the question of whether Olympic Games was an act of aggression.

The US position and the *Tallinn Manual* were at loggerheads on the crucial issue of self-defense. In his 2012 Cyber Command speech, Koh reiterated the longstanding US position: "the inherent right of self-defense potentially applies against *any* illegal use of force. . . . There is no threshold for a use of deadly force to qualify as an 'armed attack' that may warrant a forcible response."[40] Koh was pushing to lower the threshold on "armed attack" so that the United States could respond defensively to the tiniest uses of force, while simultaneously raising the threshold on aggression so American leaders would not be prosecuted if they struck first.

The United States had the most powerful military in the world and wanted the freedom to use it. But the US position could also dangerously lower legal barriers, permitting Iran's leaders to respond to Olympic Games with armed force.[41] Professor Michael N. Schmitt at the US Naval War College, director of the *Tallinn Manual* project, questioned Koh's interpretation of established legal hierarchies governing the use of force: "No member of the International Group of Experts agreed that an armed attack was nothing more than a use of force."[42] Most experts on the *Tallinn Manual* project adopted "serious death, injury, damage, or destruction" as the *de minimis* threshold for an armed attack.[43] Their sensible response to the threshold question would seemingly preclude defensive force by Iran, while excluding the Stuxnet attacks from the ambit of the crime of aggression. Under the Tallinn framework, the United States and Iran would need to resolve their dispute through negotiation, not adjudication or armed force. Despite some confusion resulting from the US position, by 2016 a consensus was forming: only armed attacks causing serious death, injury, damage, or destruction would qualify as manifest violations of the UN Charter.

Then Russia hacked the 2016 US presidential election.

THE UNKNOWN EVOLUTION OF WAR

In June 2016, in the midst of a punishing presidential contest, hackers associated with Russian intelligence broached the Democratic National Committee's computer network and stole sensitive e-mails.[44] A hacker or hacker group called Guccifer 2.0 took credit, and released forty-four thousand e-mails on WikiLeaks days before the Democratic Convention.[45]

Russian hackers also attempted to tamper with US election machinery, but given the nation's fragmented, state-run voting infrastructure they were unable to affect the count.[46] Russian intelligence was more effective in its "fake-news" campaign, deploying an army of internet trolls to disseminate targeted anti-Clinton propaganda in key swing states, including Wisconsin, Michigan, and Pennsylvania, surreptitiously routing stories through captured computers.[47] Falsehoods about Clinton's health, donors, and alleged scandals spread rapidly on social media. Researchers at Stanford explained why the disinformation campaign was so effective: sixty-two percent of US adults were reading their news on social media, popular fake-news stories were more widely shared on Facebook than the most popular conventional news, many people who read fake-news stories believed them, and the most discussed fake-news stories favored Trump.[48] Unexpectedly, the key states targeted by fake news fell narrowly to Trump.[49]

In a tight race with "crooked Hillary," candidate Trump focused on Clinton's use of a private e-mail account while Secretary of State, and implied that her carelessness had compromised American security. "Russia, if you're listening," Trump said at a Florida press conference, "I hope you're able to find the 30,000 emails that are missing."[50] At campaign rallies, Trump fired up his crowds by accusing Clinton of criminality for mishandling classified information. "Lock her up!" the crowds chanted back. Criminal accountability for political leaders was in the air in the United States, but it was divorced from the Nuremberg precedent.

US politicians and pundits called the 2016 hack "unprecedented," but Georgians, Latvians, Ukrainians, and others in the former Soviet republics knew otherwise.[51] "For me, it's déjà vu," said former Georgian President Mikheil Saakashvili.[52] "We've been seeing it already for years," said Janis Garisons, Secretary of State in Latvia's Defense Ministry.[53] These states were the testing ground for Russia's new cyberweapons. No country suffered more cyberattacks or of a greater variety than the Ukraine, whose deepening relationship with Europe provoked a "digital blitzkrieg" from Russia.[54] Waves of Russian incursions shut the power to hundreds of thousands of people, destroyed computers, deleted data, and paralyzed organizations.[55] Russia's hacker army "systematically undermined practically every sector of Ukraine: media, finance, transportation, military, politics, energy."[56] In December 2016, a Russian cyberattack caused a major blackout in Kiev. Ukrainian President Petro Poroshenko reported that in the preceding two months, there had been approximately 6,500 cyberattacks on Ukrainian institutions, including finance and defense ministries and the State Treasury.[57] Poroshenko called the Russian attacks a "cyberwar."[58]

Trump became president elect of the United States. He won the electoral college with 304 votes to Clinton's 227, but lost the popular vote.[59] Upon hearing the election results, the Russian parliament burst into applause.[60]

Republican Senator John McCain called Russian interference "an act of war."[61] If the Russian cyber interference *were* an act of war, the United States could legally respond with armed force under Article 51 of the UN Charter. Furthermore, under the definition of the crime of aggression, if this "act of war" were a manifest violation of the UN Charter as McCain implied, Russian leaders who planned, prepared, initiated, or executed it could be held criminally accountable.

Technological advances in intergroup conflict had begun to outpace law, leaving aggressors unaccountable. But the implications for international order of classifying the 2016 election interference as an "act of war" were deeply unsettling. McCain's depiction of the Russian hacking risked upending the growing consensus that only acts causing "serious death, injury, damage, or destruction" qualify as an armed attack.[62] Allowing ubiquitous cyber interference to trigger the right of forcible self-defense risked opening legal floodgates and increasing shooting wars. Reliably attributing blame and calibrating a proportional response that mitigated escalation were thorny problems in the cyberdomain.

Michael Schmitt, project director for the *Tallinn Manual*, recognized the danger of escalation. "I'm no friend of the Russians," he said, but adding that interference in the 2016 presidential election "is not an initiation of armed conflict. It's not a violation of the UN Charter's prohibition on the use of force. It's not a situation that would allow the United States to respond in self-defense militarily."[63] Nor did election interference amount to an act of aggression under the definition of the crime of aggression. For it to have amounted to a manifest violation of the UN Charter, the character of election interference needed to be qualitatively akin to bombardment, blockade, or the other kinetic acts listed in Article 8 *bis* of the Kampala amendments. *Tallinn Manual 2.0*, released soon after President Trump's 2017 inauguration, began to establish the legal framework for "cyber operations"—as opposed to "cyberwar"—which fall below established thresholds for claiming self-defense or for prosecuting individual perpetrators.[64] In his final weeks as president, Obama weighed large-scale forcible, economic, and cyber retaliation. He opted instead for noncontroversial Cold War–era countermeasures against Russia, including the expulsion of thirty-five suspected Russian intelligence agents from the United States, sanctions against Russian intelligence agencies and officials, and the padlocking of two known Russian intelligence compounds situated on US soil.[65] Given the volatile present situation, presidents and their legal advisors fell back on past analogies and recombined them to interpret and respond to new scenarios.

Russian hacks into the 2016 election sounded alarms, but are just one example of a cluster of destructive tactics called "*systems disruption*" that harm the enemy without bullets and bombs.[66] John Robb, the former US counterterrorism operation planner and commander who coined the term, describes systems disruption as the sabotage of critical systems— such as electricity, telecommunications, gas, water, or transport—to inflict costs on a target state.[67] The 2016 hacks, intended to undermine public faith the US democratic system and install a friendly regime, were a sinister variation.[68] Philip Bobbitt likens the future of warfare to plague prevention and mitigation, with individuals and small groups as transnational pathogens undermining the state.[69]

One way for judges to determine whether ideologically motivated sabotage and plagues unleashed by global guerrillas are legally analogous to bullets and missiles fired by states is to look back to the "moral evil" of aggression.[70] Aggression is qualitatively different from murder and even the other international crimes in that it unleashes widespread evil that includes them all. McGill international law professor Frédéric Mégret explained the moral wrong of aggression as a crime against sovereignty, a crime against peace, and/or a crime against human rights.[71] With this explanation, ideologically motivated sabotage and plagues unleashed by global guerrillas qualify as acts of aggression. The task of judges hearing an aggression case against a nonstate perpetrator launching a nonkinetic attack is to find a defensible way to include the case within the established state- and territory-centric language of the crime of aggression.

In the established language of the crime of aggression, physical territory and kinetic conflict are basic concepts in the regulation of force, but war is changing and the understanding of these concepts needs to change as well.[72] When the main sources and precedents were drafted, armed attacks on territory were the most important method of warfare, and territorial states were the perpetrators and victims of aggression.[73] But as technology transforms conflict, judges will find it necessary to consider whether attacks by private individuals and nonstate groups that lack clearly defined physical boundaries should fall within the scope of the crime of aggression.[74] Judges evaluating new attacks and attackers will need to walk a fine line. For international law to be effective, their interpretation of the crime of aggression must be broad enough to provide adequate deterrence but specific enough to forewarn potential perpetrators, check the discretion of police and prosecutors, and treat like cases alike.

The best way for a judge to include a cyberattack, a biological attack, or systems disruption as an act of aggression is to interpret the word "armed" broadly to include any tool capable of causing massive damage to persons or property. A defendant accused of one of these unconventional attacks is likely to argue that the list of acts amounting to aggression in the definition is closed and that the Rome Statute explicitly prohibits extending the crimes by analogy.[75] In fact, the drafters of the crime of aggression settled the contentious question of whether the list was open or closed by building in what Chairman Wenaweser termed "constructive ambiguity."[76] Under the language of the Kampala agreement, which stipulates, "any of the following acts . . . qualify as an act of aggression," it is left to the judges to decide whether this list is comprehensive or illustrative and whether a cyberattack or another type of system disruption meets the requirements.[77]

To limit the scope of the term "armed attack," only cyberattacks and other unconventional acts of aggression causing damage akin to an armed attack, such as death, injury, damage, or destruction, should be included as an act of aggression.[78] The damage must be physical, to persons or property, of a transnational political nature, and must be tantamount to a manifest violation of the UN Charter. Consistent with Article 2(4) of the UN Charter, the attack must have, as one element, violated the territorial integrity or political independence of the victim state. Under this test, the effects of the attack are of particular significance, rather than the tools used to carry it out.[79]

The prototypical aggressor is Adolf Hitler invading Poland, not "somebody sitting on their bed that weighs 400 pounds," as candidate Trump described the potential perpetrator of the 2016 hacks.[80] The plain language of the definition of the crime of aggression limits its scope to "a person in a position effectively to exercise control over or to direct the political or military action of a State."[81] Despite the frequently discussed attribution challenges posed by cyberattacks, seventeen US intelligence services agreed in a formal assessment that Vladimir Putin ordered the operation.[82] Trump's comment nevertheless raises an important issue with the crime of aggression in light of the transformation of war: the definition focuses on the leaders of states at a time when nonstate aggressors are accumulating powerful new capabilities.

A possible judicial response to this anachronistic limitation, despite the fact that it may at first seem counterintuitive to some jurists, is to read the word "State" dynamically and incrementally to include state-like organizations.[83] This common-law approach to the challenge of social change preserves the character of the original norm while permitting it to adapt.[84] In fact, the properties of the state have never been stagnant.[85] Bobbitt, for example, explains how the modern state has transformed over time, describes its various forms, and forecasts how it will continue to evolve.[86] The definition of the crime of aggression should be adaptable enough to capture conceptual evolution lest it become irrelevant. Eventually, new political-military organizations that do not control territory but that attack states should be included within the ambit of the definition. Whether the definition will one day include acts of aggression against these organizations is an open question that national and international judges hearing aggression cases should resolve on a case-by-case basis. This, after all, is the common-law method: "the proper derivation of general principles . . . arise[s] gradually, in the emergence of a consensus from a multitude of particularized prior decisions."[87]

The main argument against interpreting the definition in this way is that it broadens the definition beyond recognition. There are legitimate concerns that an overly broad definition may dilute its pull to compliance or invite ICC, regional, and national prosecutors to exercise too much discretion in their enforcement of the law. In fact, when the other aspects of the definition are taken into account, such as the *de minimis* clause—specifying that the attack must amount to a "manifest" violation of the UN Charter—and the requirement that the attack must be perpetrated by political or military leaders, the nature of the aggressive organization becomes less relevant. Had the definition been law at the time of the 9/11 attacks, this progressive interpretation would have included Osama bin Laden within its ambit, while a more state-centric interpretation would not because al Qaeda is not a state.

There are dangers in broadening the definition of the crime of aggression to include new technologies of war and new perpetrators of aggression. But there may be more danger in shrinking away from an untested but vital new legal standard.

JUDGING THE POSTMODERN CRIMINAL

Scenario planning can illustrate the changes in warfare that necessitate a shift from state to individual regulation, and from the responsibility of formal leaders in bureaucracies to that of influential network leaders. A scenario is "an internally consistent view of what the future might turn out to be . . . not a forecast, but one possible outcome."[88] Scenario planning allowed the Royal Dutch Shell Company to anticipate the rapid fluctuations in oil prices brought on by the formation and actions of the Organization of Petroleum Exporting Countries (OPEC) and to envisage the collapse of the Soviet Union.[89] Military strategists also try to envision possible futures. Their insight is that many of the most important developments in warfare pertain not to military hardware but to organizational behavior and leadership.

In a groundbreaking article in the *Marine Corps Gazette*, a team of American analysts led by William S. Lind set out a generational theory that describes warfare as heading toward an increasingly decentralized form, resulting in the state's loss of its monopoly on combat forces.[90] Lind and his team, writing as the Soviet Union was collapsing, believed that they were entering a new generation of warfare, which they called the Fourth Generation. The essential idea, according to a 2007 posting on *In Defense and the National Interest*, is that "the world itself has changed, so that terrorism and guerilla warfare—and other elusive techniques that are still being invented—are now ready to move to center stage."[91]

The heralds of fourth-generation warfare are not alone in their forecasts. Military historian Martin van Creveld and US counterterrorism expert John Robb describe the diminishing importance of conventional war and forecast the future irrelevance of state-on-state warfare.[92] According to Robb, "Wars between states are now, for all intents and purposes, obsolete."[93] Robb predicts that the real threat "isn't another state but rather the superempowered group, . . . and as the leverage provided by technology increases, this threshold will finally reach its culmination—*with the ability of one man to declare war on the world and win.*"[94] In 2007, Thomas X. Hammes, a retired colonel in the US Marine Corps, corroborated Robb's findings: "The trend has been and continues to be downward from nation-states using huge, uniformed armies to small groups of like-minded people with no formal organization who simply choose to fight."[95] In the same year, a Marine Corps seminar produced a draft doctrinal manual, in which the authors warned that, "Often, Fourth Generation opponents' strategic centers of gravity are intangible."[96] Unlike Robb, who argues that conventional war is obsolete, the authors of the draft manual add, "Like always, the old generations of war continue to exist even as new ones evolve."[97]

Today we see the main elements of fourth-generation war in the so-called hybrid wars. The US Joint Forces Command defines a hybrid threat as "any adversary that simultaneously and adaptively employs a tailored mix of conventional, irregular, terrorism and criminal means or activities in the operational battle space. Rather than a single entity, a hybrid threat or challenger may be a combination of state and non-state actors."[98] A fourth-generation hybrid warrior "uses all available networks—political, economic, social, and military . . . [and] directly attacks the minds of enemy decision makers to destroy the enemy's political will."[99] By combining kinetic operations with subversive efforts, the aggressor intends "to avoid attribution or retribution."[100]

The transformation of war is related to global shifts in organizational behavior away from bureaucracy, the primary model of the state, and toward new organizational forms. Bureaucracy, with its hierarchies, formal division of labor, and permanent offices, typified by the Nazi state, was once seen as the most efficient and rational way to organize complex human activity.[101] Today, bureaucracies are criticized for squandering the intelligence of the functionaries within, and for their failure to adapt efficiently when rapid change is required.[102] In the context of modern warfare, bureaucracies present additional problems: they are an easy target and not particularly resilient when struck. Permanent infrastructure and specialization of function increase productivity, but also make the entire organization vulnerable when a single part is disabled. Consequently, war-making organizations are restructuring.

Scholars of organizational behavior forecast the rise of the "post-bureaucratic organization." Rutgers management professor Charles Heckscher and his research team describe the post-bureaucratic organization as including broad-based participation, informal decision making, and increased intra- and interorganizational interaction.[103] It is less Pentagon, more al Qaeda. Crucially, the leaders of post-bureaucratic organizations will rely on informal influence rather than formal authority.[104] "But the influence hierarchy is not embedded in permanent offices," observes Heckscher, "and is to a far greater degree than bureaucracy based on the consent of, and the perceptions of, other members of the organization."[105]

The crime of aggression is based on responsibility of state leaders such as Goering. Given the changes in organizations waging war, a new interpretation of the "leadership clause" of the crime of aggression is needed.[106] Formal position and effective control over the action of subordinates, key criteria in international criminal law since Nuremberg, are no longer as important. Increasingly relevant to the concept of leadership is, rather, an individual's centrality within a social network and his or her influence upon that network.[107] Centrality is defined in terms of degree ("the number of direct ties one point has with others"),[108] betweenness ("falls on the shortest path between pairs of other points"),[109] and closeness ("distances among points").[110] Influence, according to Harvard government professor Joseph Nye, rests on the combination of hard power (carrots and sticks) and soft power (attraction and co-option).[111]

The vital role of centrality and influence rather than formal authority in post-bureaucratic organizations has important implications for judges interpreting the crime of aggression. Focusing on centrality and influence rather than formal authority distinguishes a crime that captures leaders such as Abu Bakr al-Baghdadi inciting wars online from a provision limited to the top political and military leaders of bureaucracies. The Kampala amendments define a leader as "a person in a position effectively to exercise control over or to direct . . . political or military action."[112] A judge reading this clause narrowly to require the defendant hold a "formal" position in the aggressive organization (e.g., minister of defense) and exercise "effective" control (i.e., the defendant's commands are almost always obeyed by subordinates) will limit the scope of the crime to the leaders of bureaucracies at a time when bureaucracy, as an organizational form, is fading.

Given the evolution of post-bureaucratic leadership, it seems logical that judges wishing to progressively interpret the leadership clause of the crime of aggression focus primarily on the central "position" and "influence" of the defendant.[113] Forward-leaning judges might read the leadership clause in this way: A leader is a person in a position [i.e., in a bureaucracy or social network] effectively to exercise control over or to direct [i.e., with formal authority or informal influence] the political or military action of a state [or state-like organization]. These interpretive elements can be incorporated independently of one another or in conjunction. They would allow judges hearing an aggression case to capture charismatic leaders such as influential cleric Anwar al-Awlaki,[114] intermediaries between official and criminal organizations such as Serb paramilitary leader Željko Ražnatović (better known as Arkan),[115] and catalysts such as Nazi propagandist Julius Streicher.[116] They would allow the crime of aggression to capture aggressors like bin Laden whose influence within a social network brings the world to war. The Nuremberg-era concept does not cover these criminal categories.[117]

The definition of the crime of aggression will face countervailing criticisms: that it is rigidly anachronistic or that it is dangerously vague. There is some truth to each criticism, exaggerated by each opponent. Those who argue the definition entrenches a series of outdated precedents underestimate the continuity of human culture, including the cultural artifacts of law and war.[118] Iranians, for example, understood the cyber operation at Natanz, their nuclear site, as an attack, even if the weapon was an intangible pattern of zeroes and ones.

Critics arguing that the definition is dangerously vague disregard the accumulated legal wisdom and experience of previous generations.[119] As US Supreme Court Justice Oliver Wendell Holmes Jr. wrote in 1881, "In order to know what [law] is, we must know what it has been, and what it tends to become."[120] Treaties, judgments, opinions, practices, and commentaries provide a rich and nuanced repository of accumulated knowledge for a tribunal judging an aggression case.

For the law of aggression to remain relevant to security and our sense of justice, judges must balance competing imperatives of fidelity to the past and preparedness for the future. If they succeed, they buttress the rule of law worldwide; fail, and they reinforce the demoralizing notion that the law is powerless in the face of rapid technological change.

DRONES: THE FOREVER WAR

During the night of October 7, 2001, US surveillance satellites over Afghanistan identified the Kandahar compound where Mullah Omar, director of the Taliban insurgency, was holed up with a council of top commanders. As the US Combined Air Operations Center prepared to deploy F-16s armed with thousand-pound bombs, to—in the words of one Air Force officer—"sen[d] Mullah Omar and the senior Taliban leadership to the nether regions," the CIA called them off.[121] The CIA had a futuristic weapon to test, the MQ-1 Predator drone. The F-16s stood by while a CIA technician in Virginia, manipulating what appeared to be video-game controls, flew the drone over Mullah Omar's Kandahar compound, zeroed in on a truck, and pulled the trigger. It was a direct hit, but Mullah Omar was not in the truck and in the confusion he escaped.[122] Commanders at the Air Operations Center were livid, having missed their opportunity to incinerate Omar, but another threshold in modern warfare had been crossed. Civil servants sitting in air-conditioned offices ten thousand miles away from their targets could play a video game that rained real death upon the bad guys—and whatever human beings happened to be there at the time.

After this initial strike, drone use multiplied under George W. Bush's administration. President Obama expanded the program at an even greater rate. By the end of Obama's second term, the United States had drones circling overhead in Afghanistan, Algeria, Iraq, Iran, Libya, Somalia, Pakistan, and Yemen, changing America and the world.[123] According to the

Bureau of Investigative Journalism, Obama authorized 506 strikes, killing an estimated 3,040 terrorists and 391 civilians.[124] Other estimates put the number of strikes and the civilian deaths much higher.[125] Either way, drones had ushered in a new era of worldwide, remote-controlled, extrajudicial killing.

What this meant in legal terms landed on the desk of the State Department's top legal advisor, Harold Koh. When Koh joined the Obama administration in 2009, he was one of America's leading human-rights lawyers and scholars. But as a government official, he drafted the legal justification for America's drone program. In a seminal 2010 speech to the American Society of International Law, Koh explained the rationale:

> As a matter of international law, the United States is in an armed conflict with al-Qaeda, as well as the Taliban and associated forces, in response to the horrific 9/11 attacks, and may use force consistent with its inherent right to self-defense under international law. As a matter of domestic law, Congress authorized the use of all necessary and appropriate force through the 2001 Authorization for Use of Military Force (AUMF). These domestic and international legal authorities continue to this day.[126]

During the George W. Bush presidency, Koh had spoken eloquently against torturing suspected terrorists; new information as legal advisor to the State Department under Obama convinced him to draft legal opinions justifying the elimination of terrorists by drones.[127] With Congress unwilling or unable to agree on a new Authorization to Use Military Force against ISIS, and Russia and China certain to block a Security Council resolution authorizing force, Koh simply extended the 9/11-era justifications further.[128]

When Koh returned to civilian life after four years in government, he delivered a speech at Oxford called "How to End the Forever War."[129] "Our overriding goal," he told the audience, "should be to *end* this Forever War, not to engage in a perpetual 'global war on terror,' without geographic or temporal limits."[130]

Reactions to Koh's postadministration public appearances were mixed, ranging from attacking him for breathing new life to the global war on terror to hailing him for trying to bring an end to the Forever War. When New York University (NYU) hired Koh to teach international human rights, students circulated a petition demanding the university disassociate itself from him, calling him "a key legal architect of the Obama Administration's extrajudicial killing program."[131] Allies countered that Koh fought to bring US policy in line with domestic and international law, and that without him things would have been worse.[132]

A joint Stanford-NYU independent investigation into the drone strikes in Pakistan found that the population felt helpless, terrorized, and angry at the United States.[133] Remote-controlled drones circling day and night over communities were striking homes, vehicles, and public spaces without warning.[134] Worse, the United States began to "double tap"—hitting the target and then the rescuers.[135] Obama's so-called "signature strikes," drone attacks based merely on patterns of suspicious activity by groups rather than the identification of particular individuals, turned at least eight weddings into funerals.[136] David Kilcullen, counterinsurgency adviser to US General David Petraeus, warned, "every one of these dead noncombatants represents an alienated family, a new desire for revenge, and more recruits for a militant movement that has grown exponentially even as drone strikes have increased."[137]

By 2014, over seventy countries—including China, Iran, Israel, and Russia—had drones.[138] It will not be long before every state possesses armed drones capable of firing missiles or delivering a chemical, biological, or nuclear payload to a major city.[139] Today's drones suggest potential targets to their operators; tomorrow's drones will strike autonomously, without the intervention of a human operator.[140] "The difference in the current era," warned Bobbitt, "is that now terrorists are about to acquire the weapons and strategies previously reserved to states at war, and thus will acquire also the potential to affect the basic constitutional order."[141]

In August 2015, a British drone in Raqqa, Syria, killed Reyaad Khan (twenty-one years) and Ruhul Amin (twenty-six years).[142] Both were British citizens. Without parliamentary authorization for war in Syria, British Prime Minister David Cameron justified the drone strike as emergency self-defense under Article 51 of the UN Charter. Cameron did not define the enemy to whom self-defense was limited nor what the geographic and temporal boundaries of his military operation were. According to University College London law professor Philippe Sands, "It appears that the United Kingdom is adopting a broader and more expansive vision of what the right of self-defence means—which connects to the approach taken by the United States in its 'global war on terror.' It appears to be a departure from established British practice."[143]

THE END OF THE BEGINNING: SYRIA 2017

The war on terror was winding down and a new era of great-power conflict poised to begin. Donald Trump, Vladimir Putin, Bashar al-Assad, Recep Tayyip Erdoğan, and Ayatollah Ali Khamenei could resolve their differences peacefully or were one mistake away from a great-power war, and drones were a treacherous flash point. Competing forces with new technologies—Syrian Kurdish fighters, Kurdish-allied Arab forces, US Special Operation forces, Syrian regime elements, Russian special forces,

Iranian units, Turkish military units, and Turkish-allied forces—corralled what was left of the ISIS army into ungoverned swaths of territory in Syria, establishing overlapping front lines, intensifying the risk of a great-power conflagration.[144] With the endgame in sight, external forces were becoming increasingly assertive within a smaller battlefield as they vied to win the peace and dictate the future of the region.

Inconspicuous and ubiquitous, deployed by state and nonstate actors alike, drones blurred the front lines in Syria. Physically and legally, drones were an advancing fog: it was unclear whether they fell below the *de minimis* threshold, who was controlling them, whether they were aggressor or observer, if they were on track or off course. The fact that they were unmanned and relatively inexpensive lowered the threshold for downing them, but this risked escalation.

In April, Trump unilaterally launched a barrage of fifty-nine Tomahawk missiles at Shayrat air base in Syria, a reprisal for Assad's use of chemical weapons against Syrian civilians, causing Russia to announce that it was suspending the "deconfliction line" meant to prevent collisions between US and Russian fighter planes streaking through Syrian airspace.[145] In retaliation for ISIS terrorists attacks on parliament and the tomb of Iran's revolutionary founder, Iran fired a volley of ballistic missiles across the border at ISIS forces in Syria.[146] The United States shot down a Syrian warplane attempting to strafe US-backed ground forces, and Russian fighter jets over the Baltic Sea responded by buzzing within five feet of an American spy plane.[147] The United States claimed self-defense, a dubious excuse considering it was waging an unauthorized, uninvited war in Syrian territory. Russia responded by declaring "all flying objects, including planes and drones of the international coalition," potential targets.[148]

On June 8, an Iranian-made Shahed 129 drone dropped a bomb on American-backed Syrian fighters patrolling with coalition advisors, but missed.[149] The legality of American warfare and Iranian drone operations in Syria were both dubious under the UN Charter and customary international law. The unmanned Shahed 129 drone attracted a manned American F-15 fighter jet that shot it down. Undeterred or unaware, a Syrian-piloted Soviet-era SU-22 warplane showed up to bomb the American-backed ground forces, and was chased away by an American F/A-18 Hornet.[150] Great-power conflict was narrowly averted, but with drones peppering Syria's skies, it was only a matter of time before the next encounter.

With drones expanding battlefields and increasing the likelihood of confrontations, a clear legal standard was needed to stabilize expectations and help prevent a catastrophic mistake. No regulation would stop the proliferation of drones, but the law might help mitigate their use. Though imperfect, Obama's 2013 drone-policy reforms measurably reduced civilian casualties and were a step in the right direction.[151] Under these self-imposed constraints, lethal force could only be used against individuals who represent a "continuing and imminent threat," where "capture is not feasible," and "in a manner consistent with applicable law of war principles," such as necessity (target has definite military value), proportionality (collateral damage cannot be excessive), discrimination (between civilian and military targets), and humanity (use of weapons not intended to inflict unnecessary suffering).[152] Obama also transferred the drone program from the CIA to the military, subjecting it to additional principled checks, but ultimately left himself (and successors) with the final say over who lives and dies.[153] "We have to create an architecture for this," Obama said before leaving office, "because [of] the potential for abuse."[154] Obama's regulatory architecture corresponded with fewer civilian deaths,[155] but failed to set territorial or temporal limits on the Forever War.[156] If universalized, Obama's rules would sanitize war without limiting its occurrence.

When Donald Trump took office in 2017, he ordered a review of Obama's reforms with the goal of rolling them back. Trump's review would make it easier for military technicians to launch drone strikes anywhere in the world. It would lower the threshold on acceptable civilian deaths, reauthorize secretive CIA drone strikes, and eliminate the imminence requirement.[157] Though candidate Trump had promised to keep the United States out of foreign wars, he dramatically escalated US strikes in nonbattlefield settings in Pakistan, Yemen, and Somalia.[158] The leaders of states, insurgencies, and corporations took the cue.

A new global arms race had begun.

In the volatile, constantly changing present, there was no settled future, only pattern recognition and reconfiguration within the limits of human imagination. Whether the terror wars had given way to a new era of great-power conflict was anyone's guess. But, at least in one area, it didn't take the speculative mind of William Gibson to see what was coming. When cyber operations met drones, an "individual sitting on a bed weighing 400 pounds" could potentially commandeer entire armies from states, wage war against the world, and win. The next A. Q. Khan would not need the infrastructure of an industrialized state to threaten global security, just a laptop and the technical expertise to use it, expertise that could be stolen online.

What was needed for human security was an international legal standard to check expansionist legal arguments that justify dangerous innovations in warfare. Drones were proliferating and America's legal arguments were too. The result was an expanding battlefield including more actors and targets without geographic or temporal parameters or an authoritative judicial body to establish them. Unless international law evolved and set reasonable limits with credible consequences for violations, the global free-for-all was set to become a forever war.

CHAPTER 9

You're under Arrest, Mr. President

> Where there is no common power, there is no law, where no law, no injustice.
> —Thomas Hobbes, *Leviathan*, 1651

> A state is a human community that (successfully) claims the monopoly of the legitimate use of physical force within a given territory.
> —Max Weber, *Politics as a Vocation*, 1918

> These myriad instantiations of law are fragmented, inconsistent, and contradictory. They are a bricolage built up from practice, history, and the legacy of efforts to solve earlier problems.
> —Sally Engle Merry, Graduation Address on Legal Pluralism to the McGill Faculty of Law, 2013

Enforcement of the crime of aggression in future wars will not require a global monopoly on the use of force. The UN and the ICC are not the only potential enforcers. Future arrest scenarios can be found by examining the successful arrests of previously untouchable leaders. A key factor lies in the precarious hold on power of many leaders who commit international crimes. A lesson learned from arrest operations to date is that a monopoly on force within a defined territory is not an arrest prerequisite; what is necessary is just enough force to apprehend the perpetrator. Although the ICC does not have its own police force, arrests can be generated. UN peacekeepers, regional coalitions, private military contractors, successor regimes, militarily powerful states, and even weaker states have apprehended international criminals. States may be reticent to endanger their soldiers,[1] but they are increasingly willing to cooperate with local authorities or the UN. Ivory Coast President Laurent Gbagbo's arrest for other international crimes is an object lesson. The first aggression defendants at the ICC will likely be handed over by successor regimes.

Four light French Gazelle attack helicopters and two massive Ukrainian-piloted UN MI-24 gunships sped toward the gated residence of deposed Ivorian President Laurent Gbagbo. In the streets below, troops loyal to newly elected president Alassane Ouattara, supported by French special forces, tightened the noose on the former president.[2] Gbagbo, a Sorbonne-educated historian, had spent a decade stoking xenophobia against Ivorians whose ancestors had come from abroad to work in the Ivory Coast's cocoa industry.[3] He had been defeated by Ouattara in the November 2010 elections, but refused to concede. Instead, he launched a campaign of state terror including mass torture, rape, and murder against anyone designated as a political opponent.

Responding to escalating postelection violence between Gbagbo and Ouattara camps, the UN Security Council unanimously adopted peace-enforcement Resolution 1975 (2011), legal authorization for the arrest of the first president to face justice at the ICC.[4] The resolution condemned international crimes by all sides,[5] called for an immediate transfer of power to Outarra, and reaffirmed that UN forces could use "all necessary means" to protect civilians.[6] Gbagbo's violation of an African Union deadline to step down set the arrest in motion.

Machine-gun fire was drowned out as helicopter air-to-ground missiles struck Gbagbo's residence and shook the city. According to a source from the Ivorian opposition, tanks advanced, black plumes of smoke poured out of the palace, and the commandos went in. "They were special forces trained to capture hostages. Gbagbo was taken following a heavy fight, although a lot of his guards ran away. In the end Gbagbo surrendered."[7] Gbagbo was placed in custody under the protection of the UN, lest Ouattara's men take justice into their own hands.[8] France, former colonial master, wisely gave credit for the arrest to the new president and his forces.[9] The Ivory Coast transferred Laurent Gbagbo to the ICC for trial.[10]

The Gbagbo arrest helped international-justice hawks imagine the execution of an effective enforcement operation. UN Secretary-General Ban Ki-moon declared the operation had respected the parameters of Resolution 1975 by protecting civilians.[11] The operation was backed by the African Union, the European Union, the UN, and the Economic Community of West African States (ECOWAS) and hailed as an international-justice victory by the United States.[12] Russian Foreign Minister Sergei Lavrov voiced doubts about the legitimacy of the use of force by UN peacekeepers, but Russia did not block the arrest.[13]

Gbagbo became the first president of a sovereign state to face justice at the ICC.

ENFORCEMENT SETBACKS

While the arrest of President Gbagbo reveals the possibilities of international law enforcement, the failure to apprehend Sudanese President

Omar al-Bashir exposed its limitations. In 2005, the Security Council voted to refer the situation in Darfur to the ICC: eleven states for, none against, four abstaining (Algeria, Brazil, China, and the United States).[14] In 2009, the pretrial chamber of the ICC issued an arrest warrant for al-Bashir. He remains at large, president of Sudan.

Leaders evading arrest for international crimes draw strategic lessons from al-Bashir, who amassed more political leverage than Gbagbo. He is strongman of a country with close allies in Africa; China is his satisfied investor and oil client; the United States and the EU cooperate with him in counterterrorism,[15] and he holds thousands of vulnerable Darfuri civilians hostage in camps. The Security Council asked the ICC to investigate and prosecute, and the ICC judges found cause to issue an arrest warrant for genocide and crimes against humanity. Al-Bashir used the warrant for nationalist propaganda. By labeling the ICC a neocolonialist institution that targeted African leaders, he fanned arrest fears in other African leaders. Al-Bashir's crimes were outrageous, but his political leverage was too great to compel states, domestic rivals, or even Security Council members. Despite the warrant, Security Council members failed to apprehend al-Bashir.

Soon after the ICC issued its warrant, al-Bashir left Sudan, first to visit trusted allies, then further afield, testing the credibility of the warrant. Less than three weeks after the ICC issued its warrant, al-Bashir travelled to Sudan's tiny neighbor, Eritrea, to discuss regional security and generate opposition to the ICC.[16] From Eritrea, he flew to Hosni Mubarak's Egypt, Libya, and then the Arab League Summit in Doha to convince the sympathetic leaders of Arab states to oppose his arrest.[17] He won over members of the African Union by tarring the ICC as neocolonialist, and persuaded Chinese leaders with the promise of a steady supply of oil. In the seven years following the ICC warrant, al-Bashir travelled seventy-four times to twenty-one countries, of which seven were ICC member states legally obliged to arrest him.[18] None did.

While some governments made a point of welcoming al-Bashir, others warned that they intended to arrest him if he landed, or were unable to guarantee his freedom. Botswana, a strong ICC supporter, announced arrest if he entered its territory.[19] Al-Bashir had travelled to Kenya to celebrate the country's new constitution, and Kenyan courts ordered the government to arrest him should he return.[20] Fearing arrest, al-Bashir cancelled trips to the Central African Republic, China, France, Indonesia, Malaysia, Malawi, Nigeria, Turkey, Uganda, UN Headquarters, and Zambia.[21] He fled multilateral meetings in Nigeria[22] and South Africa after their courts proceeded against him, despite their governments having assured him of freedom.[23]

In 2014, after multiple unfulfilled ICC requests to the UN Security Council, as well as ICC formal condemnation of eleven states for shirking arrest obligations,[24] Prosecutor Fatou Bensouda announced she was regrettably suspending the case.[25] "Given this council's lack of foresight on what should happen in Darfur," she said, "I am left with no choice but to hibernate investigative activities in Darfur as I shift resources to other urgent cases."[26]

Al-Bashir was triumphant: "They wanted us to kneel before the international criminal court but the ICC raised its hands and admitted that it had failed."[27] Yet the warrant remains in place and, if arrested, al-Bashir is subject to ICC prosecution.

HOW TO ARREST A HEAD OF STATE

Key factors in successful arrests of leaders who commit atrocities are the instability of their domestic and international political power, and their geographic isolation. The arrest of former Yugoslav President Slobodan Milošević was facilitated by students protesting his corrupt, authoritarian leadership.[28] Street protests escalated into a political movement demanding Milošević's removal and the rule of law. Serbs fed up with his autocratic ways and the ruin he had made of their country finally voted him out, physically removing him from parliament when he refused to cede power.[29] The EU provided incentives for his arrest, and Serbia's new authorities surrendered Milošević to The Hague for trial.[30]

The conditions are ideal when both political and geographic isolation are present. Congolese Vice President Jean Pierre Bemba, one of the richest men in the Democratic Republic of the Congo, travelled to Portugal for medical care. Fearing for his safety in the Congo after his private militia clashed with government forces, he made the mistake of remaining in Europe to visit his wife in Brussels, and was arrested in Belgium, a state that aggressively enforces international criminal law.[31]

Nongovernmental cooperation can undermine autocratic political power and spur the arrest of criminal leaders. Amnesty International and an alliance of human-rights organizations, working concertedly with Spanish lawyers and judges, overcame British resistance and issued an arrest warrant for Chilean President Augusto Pinochet.[32] Pinochet was recovering from back surgery in London when Scotland Yard served an arrest warrant alleging the torture and killing of Spanish citizens in Chile. Using the Spanish warrant, British police detained Pinochet in London. Although Home Secretary Jack Straw subsequently released him back to Chile on medical grounds,[33] Pinochet spent the rest of his days in court answering accusations related to his abuse of power.

Victims may not personally arrest perpetrators, but they can generate the momentum for official action. Austrian Jewish Holocaust survivor

Simon Wiesenthal inspired victims of other state-sponsored international crimes to hunt down their oppressors. Following Wiesenthal's lead, Souleymane Guengueng, Chadian victim of President Hissen Habré's torture dungeons, vowed to bring the ex-president to justice. Partnering with Canadian Human Rights Watch lawyer Reed Brody, Guengueng led a campaign for Habré's arrest for crimes against humanity and was repeatedly blocked.[34] Guengueng and other victims filed the case in Senegal, but bowing to political pressure, the courts refused the case. Guengueng and Brody had more success in Belgium, where a court indicted Habré for international crimes, but Senegal refused to extradite him for trial. Undeterred, Guengueng approached the African Union and convinced it that Habré should be tried. Only then did Senegal agree to put the US-backed dictator on trial. The African Union and Chad partnered with Senegal to ensure fair proceedings.

The arrest of Radovan Karadžić demonstrates how successor regimes, which may be amenable to incentives, are well placed to arrest indicted leaders. Karadžić, the former Bosnian Serb leader and psychiatrist accused of masterminding the siege of Sarajevo and the Srebrenica massacre, was arrested by Serbian security forces on a Belgrade bus. Although indicted by the ICTY, Karadžić had evaded arrest for a decade. Disguised as an Orthodox priest and folk healer, he lived openly under the eyes of NATO and Serb authorities. Only after the European Union made Karadžić's arrest a condition of Serbian membership did the Belgrade government finally detain him and ship him to The Hague. "Without pressure, things do not really move forward," explained ICTY Prosecutor Serge Brammertz. "Linking EU enlargement to the arrest of the fugitives has been a really successful tool."[35]

Powerful nations can help shelter indicted leaders, but they can also help secure their arrests. Liberian President Charles Taylor was granted asylum in Nigeria as part of a deal ending the gruesome fourteen-year civil war in Sierra Leone. A joint United Nations and Sierra Leonean war-crimes tribunal issued an indictment and requested his arrest. The American, Liberian, and Sierra Leonean governments persuaded Nigeria to transfer Taylor to the Special Court for Sierra Leone. Taylor fled his luxury villa in a Range Rover with diplomatic plates, carrying sacks of cash; he made it to the Nigeria-Cameroon border but was identified by customs officials. Nigerian security arrested Taylor and sent him to Liberia. From Liberia, he was flown to Sierra Leone for trial.[36] Uneasy about Taylor's escape attempt and his residual political influence, tribunal officials moved the trial to The Hague. Taylor joined other deposed African and Balkan leaders in a Dutch prison overlooking the North Sea.

UN peacekeepers from NATO countries carried out most of the arrests of Yugoslavia's 161 indicted war criminals. When militarily powerful states are involved, political and geographic isolation is less essential in arrest operations. Polish special forces carried out the first arrest of a war-crimes suspect in Croatia in 1997, and this arrest shamed larger NATO powers into action.[37] The next arrests were carried out by UK SAS special forces. An SAS team posing as Red Cross officials arrested Prijedor's anti-Muslim mayor at work and transferred him to The Hague. Prijedor's anti-Muslim police chief Simo Drljaca pulled a gun on the arresting SAS team, who had interrupted his fishing trip, and he was shot dead. By July 2011, every political and military leader indicted by the ICTY had been captured or killed. According to investigative journalist Julian Borger, "It has arguably been the most successful manhunt in history."[38]

The international criminal cases prosecuted so far underscore the importance of political will in enforcing the rule of law. At first glance this may distinguish international from domestic law enforcement, but both systems require political will to arrest powerful perpetrators. Domestic laws against weak perpetrators are easily enforced, but a domestic campaign against political corruption, high-level white-collar crime, or organized crime requires political courage and cooperation among individuals and organizations. The common weakness of both domestic and international law, from domestic bankers to powerful presidents, lies in the power imbalance that enables unequal enforcement.

The important question then becomes: How can the rule of law be enforced equally against weakened and powerful wrongdoers?

THE IMMUNITY GAMBIT

Powerful leaders, in a fraternal bargain, have long granted themselves immunity from criminal accountability in one another's courts.[39] They have three stock reasons to explain why they should be above the law. The first is metaphysical: conceptually, a head of state personifies the state, and it would be an affront to the dignity of the state itself to try him or her.[40] Second, they argue reciprocal immunities are necessary, especially in moments of crisis, to maintain channels of communication and ensure the smooth conduct of international relations.[41] The third is patriotic: without immunity from prosecution in foreign courts, heads of state might be reticent to make difficult but necessary national-security decisions on behalf of their state for fear of being held criminally accountable.[42] Through state practice and an emergent belief that the practice was legally binding, immunities for heads of state, heads of government, and foreign ministers became customary international law.[43]

International-law immunities pose a unique challenge for prosecution of the crime of aggression.[44] The crime of aggression is, by definition, perpetrated by top leaders, but immunities shield them from prosecution. Yet, the victors of World War II created a necessary exception in the Nuremberg Charter. The Charter deemed the official position of the defendants irrelevant when it came to international crimes, including crimes against peace.[45] The 1990s codified the Nuremberg precedent, and its wording in the Rome Statute was unambiguous: "Immunities or special procedural rules which may attach to the official capacity of a person, whether under national or international law, shall not bar the Court from exercising its jurisdiction over such a person."[46] By ratifying the Rome Statute, 124 states stripped their political and military leaders of immunities for ICC crimes, even stripping the leaders of non-ICC states of their immunities when the situation was referred by the UN Security Council (such as Darfur and Libya).[47] "It is now axiomatic," concluded Beth van Schaack, Deputy US ambassador-at-large for war crimes, "that state officials are not entitled to any form of immunity before the various international tribunals."[48] The "troika"—heads of state, heads of government, and foreign ministers—does however still enjoy immunity from *domestic* prosecution in foreign courts, which ends when they leave office.[49]

With the 2010 inclusion of the crime of aggression in the Rome Statute, the leaders of powerful states and their advocates reopened the immunities debate in an effort to shield the troika from international and post-tenure prosecution. An important battlefield for these debates was the International Law Commission in Geneva. Law commissioners attempting to shield the troika argued that aggression was different from other international crimes and immunities should remain in place.[50] Supporters of the crime of aggression responded that the Nuremberg tribunal prioritized aggression as "the supreme international crime" and the Rome Statute reaffirmed the importance of the crime of aggression by adding it to its three core international crimes. They argued that approximately forty states and a number of regional organizations have criminalized aggression and the Kampala amendments contemplate national as well as international prosecution.[51]

If powerful aggressors are to be held to account, they cannot be permitted to carve out additional privileged zones of impunity. Under Kampala, leaders of non-ICC states who attack ICC member states are now excluded from ICC prosecution. "It would be laughable if it wasn't so tragic," said Ben Ferencz. Granting leaders immunity from foreign criminal jurisdiction, as proposed by powerful members of the International Law Commission, would further weaken the enforcement regime. Those who believe that anyone should be above the law are inviting an international legal system that indemnifies powerful perpetrators, ratifies the law of force, and sows the seeds of future wars.

FUTURE ARREST SCENARIOS

The most promising way to enforce the rule of law fairly and effectively is to strengthen the existing system. If ICC member states fulfill their legal obligations to arrest and surrender perpetrators of international crimes, the territory of 123 member states (2018 count) becomes a single arrest zone. If signatories that have not yet ratified the Rome Statute are included, the arrest zone expands to 139 states. The reason arrests fail is that the leaders of some states are unable or unwilling to fulfill their country's legal commitments.

David Scheffer has proposed a protocol to the Rome Statute that would create an international arrest force with the power to conduct operations within sovereign states.[52] Signatory states would agree in advance to an enforcement team comprising experienced, highly trained police and military personnel responsible for apprehending indicted war criminals on their territory.[53] ICC states parties would be invited to sign, but so would any UN member state, defense alliance (such as NATO), or regional organization (such as the European Union, African Union, or Arab League) approved by the ICC's Assembly of States Parties.[54]

The parties to Scheffer's protocol would select, train, govern, and fund the arrest team.[55] The ICC arrest team could enter a state pursuant to a request from the ICC prosecutor, the written consent of the host state, and the approval of the Protocol Supervisory Group.[56] The Protocol Supervisory Group would be required to respond to all inquiries of the receiving party "so that misunderstandings are avoided and the operation can proceed efficiently."[57]

The strength of Scheffer's innovative proposal is that it establishes a standing force to conduct complex arrest operations and, without a UN army, strengthens the rule of law. Its weakness is that it requires reluctant, sluggish states to commit significant financial and military resources, and an engaged population to make it happen. Nor will this consent-based regime solve the problem of states unwilling to arrest or surrender fugitives.

Another possibility for states that are powerless to arrest is to ask powerful allies to assist in their territory on an ad hoc basis. In 2011, Uganda asked the United States to send military advisors to help track LRA leader Joseph Kony and his top commanders. As Jeffrey Gettleman of the *New York Times* reported, "One hundred of America's elite Special Operations troops, aided by night vision scopes and satellite imagery, are helping African forces find a wig-wearing, gibberish-speaking fugitive rebel commander named Joseph Kony who has been hiding out in the jungle for years with a band of child soldiers and a harem of dozens of child brides."[58] By 2017, US and African Union assistance to Uganda had helped deplete Kony's forces, which fled across Northern Uganda, the Central African

Republic, South Sudan, and the Congo.[59] With fewer than one hundred fighters, LRA attacks and abductions dwindled. Four of five LRA leaders indicted by the ICC were killed, captured, or defected, but Kony remains at large in the vast jungle spanning these countries. Scholars familiar with the region argued that a Ugandan amnesty program that lured approximately thirty thousand fighters out of the bush was the real reason the LRA was depleted, but their argument was undercut when US and Ugandan forces quit the manhunt and LRA attacks resumed with renewed vigor.[60]

President Obama's congressionally authorized decision to participate in the hunt for Kony was inspired by bipartisan grassroots activism in the United States.[61] President George W. Bush had sent seventeen military advisors to assist the Ugandan defense forces in apprehending Kony, but it was an internet video, "Kony 2012," produced by San Diego–based NGO Invisible Children, that propelled Obama and the Republican-controlled Congress into decisive action.[62] "Kony 2012" was "the most viral [Internet] video ever."[63] Despite criticisms that the video simplified a complex problem, fueled a white-savior complex, and was produced by an unstable man running a self-serving organization, "Kony 2012" motivated a bipartisan resolution condemning the LRA's "unconscionable crimes against humanity."[64] "If not ending up dead," John McCain said, "[Kony] could end up in the International Criminal Court, and it'd be a wonderful thing."[65] It also proved that effective advocacy can galvanize international law enforcement.

Another civil-society initiative hinting at the potential for effective international law enforcement teaches partners in war zones how to capture top-secret documents that tie political and military leaders to atrocity crimes.[66] The Commission for International Justice and Accountability (CIJA), founded by Bill Wiley, a former ICTY and ICC war-crimes investigator, "employs about as many investigators as the International Criminal Court has working on all its cases combined."[67] Leakers in Syria and other states where leaders perpetrate atrocities against their people help Wiley's organization collect evidence on the inner workings of criminal regimes for use in prosecution. Wiley has shown that it is possible to privatize the investigative work of the ICC and, without a monopoly on force, expand international justice into hostile states.

It is one thing to privatize international criminal investigations, another to privatize arrests. The short-term risk is that private citizens will act unprofessionally and jeopardize the rule of law. This occurred in the 2007 Nisour Square massacre in Iraq, when Blackwater employees guarding a US State Department convoy opened fire on Iraqi civilians.[68] According to the UK-based NGO War on Want, "Private military contractors ran amok in Iraq and Afghanistan, leaving a trail of human rights abuses in their wake. Now we are seeing the alarming rise of mercenaries fighting on the frontline in conflict zones across the world: it is the return of the 'dogs of war.' "[69] The long-term danger is that private companies deploying force on behalf of states, international organizations, and private interests will become influential political actors, influencing states to wage unnecessary wars for corporate profit.

The possibility of harnessing the market to arrest international criminals arises at a time when states are reticent to act. The ubiquitous state use of private military contractors in the various functions of many of today's wars presages an era of privatized enforcement.[70] For policymakers serious about arrests and willing to risk hiring private contractors, the question becomes how to ensure that these contractors remain democratically accountable.

Under one model, the state remains the focal point for legitimate force, hiring private military contractors to arrest indicted international fugitives and transfer them to the ICC. The strategic-enforcement advantage of this approach is that private contractors paid by states but kept at arm's length are not under the state's "effective control," and may violate the sovereignty of another state to conduct an arrest without legally implicating the arresting state. The risk is that this arms-length relationship will insulate private contractors from democratic oversight and embolden them to violate domestic and international laws.

Risk became reality in September 2001 when President George W. Bush issued an executive order transferring the authority to approve assassinations from the president to the CIA. The CIA then subcontracted assassinations to private military contractor Blackwater.[71] According to journalist Evan Wright, "By removing himself from the decision-making cycle, the president shielded himself—and all elected authority—from responsibility should a mission go wrong or be found illegal."[72]

Private military contractors employed by the United States have carried out assassinations, massacred unarmed civilians, and tortured detainees.[73] In 2014, the US Senate Select Committee on Intelligence concluded that eighty-five percent of CIA interrogations were conducted by private contractors.[74] After the Nisour Square massacre, Blackwater was taken off the list of US military contractors and some employees were prosecuted for manslaughter.[75] Blackwater changed its name to Xe Services and was back in business.

To guard against excessive force by private contractors, states can subcontract aspects of the arrest, not necessarily all. In cases where capacity is the issue and weak states are unable to locate and arrest, private contractors can hunt the fugitive and advise authorities during stakeout and apprehension. Although this is a more promising model from the perspective of democratic accountability, it fails to resolve the problem of arrest in a state unwilling to surrender an indicted criminal.

Under another model, the ICC issues an arrest warrant to be carried out by any state or private actor willing and able to do it. The legal principle of *male captus bene detentus* (wrongly captured, properly detained) draws a distinction between the means of apprehension and the jurisdiction to prosecute, making it possible for FBI agents to arrest fugitives abroad for violating US laws, even without the consent of the custodial state. In a 1989 opinion, the Office of Legal Counsel of the US Justice Department advised the FBI that it can conduct arrests "even if those actions contravene customary international law . . . [or] unexecuted treaties or treaty provisions, such as Article 2(4) of the United Nations Charter."[76] According to the Justice Department, "An arrest that is inconsistent with international or foreign law does not violate the Fourth Amendment," the constitutional guarantee against unreasonable search and seizure.[77] The implication is that US courts can try a defendant who was kidnapped abroad.

International legal scholar Beth van Schaack says the ad hoc international tribunals have largely adopted the same *male captus bene detentus* principle as the United States.[78] Serb concentration-camp commander Dragan Nikolić claimed he was kidnapped in Serbia by Serb bounty hunters and smuggled to the NATO Stabilization Force in Bosnia-Herzegovina, which transferred him to The Hague.[79] The ICTY refuted Nikolić's argument that it condoned illegal kidnapping on the basis of *male captus bene detentus* and it proceeded with the trial.[80] The prosecutor and the judges agreed that legal recourse might be appropriate if the prosecutor's office was directly involved in the violation of a defendant's rights, or in cases of egregious illegal arrest conduct.[81] Neither exception applied to Nikolić's case.

Male captus bene detentus and the Nikolić precedent open the possibility, with attendant dangers, that private actors will one day conduct arrest operations against perpetrators of the crime of aggression. It is not difficult to imagine corporations or NGOs funding investigations by Wiley's Commission for International Justice and Accountability to collect evidence against leaders for the crime of aggression. Armed with an arrest warrant from the ICC and no state willing to enforce it, an organization such as Invisible Children might raise enough money to fund a private military contractor such as Academie (previously Blackwater and Xe) to make the arrest. Working with local collaborators, Academie kidnaps the wrongdoer and smuggles him to The Hague. Investigation and arrest are undertaken without the direct involvement of a single state. The risk is the thin line between enforcement and aggression.

Whenever political and military leaders of states undertake an arrest operation against a foreign aggressor, they risk committing aggression to punish aggression. Unless the use of force is authorized by the Security Council or the receiving state, the leaders planning, preparing, initiating, or executing the operation may be violating the territorial integrity or political independence of the receiving state, even if they intended to arrest a criminal indicted for international crimes.[82] If the arrest amounts to an "act of aggression" and surpasses the *de minimis* threshold—that is, a manifest violation of the UN Charter—it has the potential to attract criminal responsibility.

Leaders who wish to shield themselves from legal responsibility have an incentive to distance themselves from sovereignty-violating operations through executive orders, as President Bush did after 9/11 by delegating authority to the CIA. The results of Bush's legal contortions—including massacres, torture, and assassination by loosely regulated private military contractors—serve as a lesson to international-justice advocates about the risks of outsourcing military force.

With private enforcement of the crime of aggression, it doesn't take much to insulate presidents from the actions of contractors. Under the definition of the crime of aggression, "sending . . . of armed bands, groups, irregulars or mercenaries" establishes legal attribution, but arming, advising, and funding do not.[83] According to the authoritative *Nicaragua* and *Tadic* decisions, states are not accountable for the acts of nonstate groups unless the state had "effective" or "overall" control.[84] Cautious government lawyers will no doubt advise their leaders to delegate planning, preparation, initiation, or execution of an arrest operation to subordinates, or, to distance them further, to subdelegate arrests to private military contractors. Article 25(3) of the Rome Statute describes various ways besides direct participation by which crimes can be committed, including ordering, soliciting, and assisting.[85] It remains to be seen if ICC judges can use Article 25(3) to curb and prosecute the leaders of states who order, solicit, and assist criminal mercenaries.

As Nietzsche warned in *Beyond Good and Evil*, "He who fights with monsters should be careful lest he thereby become a monster."[86] Ultimately, without ICC states parties fulfilling their duty to arrest, leaders enforcing the law of aggression may look like those violating it. The moral and legal questions surrounding international justice enforcement by private military contractors become moot when states fulfill their obligations to arrest.

YOUR TURN, MR. PRESIDENT

Russia, the United States, China, India, and Israel are not states parties to the Rome Statute or signatories to the Kampala amendments, and their leaders are not subject to arrest and trial for the crime of aggression at the ICC. These leaders are, nevertheless, vulnerable to prosecution for international crimes in their own courts if domestic legislation exists, or prosecutable in the courts of other states willing and able to arrest them.

Article 353 of the Russian Criminal Code prohibits "Planning, Preparation, Unleashing or Waging of Aggressive War."[87] The Russian legislation is very similar to Kampala's definition of aggression, both including references to the UN Charter and similar lists of prohibited acts of aggression. The Russian definition targets more aggressors and is not limited to cases with a manifest threshold or a leadership clause. Article 354 prohibits even "Public Appeals to Unleash an Aggressive War."[88] With this legislation, the possibility exists for domestic prosecution of Russian aggressors by successor regimes and also the domestic prosecution of foreign aggressors in Russian courts. There is little chance President Putin will be arrested and tried while in power. Putin commands the police, and President Yeltsin erected barriers to legislative impeachment after a 1993 coup attempt. But foreign aggressors could conceivably be arrested and tried in Russian courts. It would require Putin's political isolation before accountability became a possibility.

It is easy to forget that the greatest threat to leaders of powerful states is usually from within. As the arrests of Slobodan Milošević and Laurent Gbagbo show, successor regimes are sometimes prepared to arrest political rivals and surrender them to tribunals for their crimes. The leaders of powerful states are vulnerable to electoral defeat, impeachment, and coup d'état. Weakened or deposed, they can be arrested and tried by domestic, regional, or international tribunals.

The impulse to hold former leaders to account for international crimes, present in Serbia and the Ivory Coast, also exists in liberal democracies including the United States and the United Kingdom. In 2008, when Barack Obama was elected, he presided over tense discussions about whether or not to hold the Bush regime accountable for war crimes. A 2009 *USA Today*/Gallup poll found that sixty-two percent of Americans favored a criminal investigation or an independent panel to probe the regime's use of torture, illegal wiretapping, and other alleged abuses of power.[89]

Chairman of the Senate Judiciary Committee Patrick Leahy and House Speaker Nancy Pelosi pushed for the establishment of a truth commission to investigate the Bush administration, including top Justice Department lawyers who crafted the legal justifications for illegal anti-terrorism policies.[90] Republican leaders objected. With a nod to the South African Truth and Reconciliation Commission, Leahy proposed immunity for officials who testified truthfully.[91] President Obama initially considered the proposal but changed tack and, to the disappointment of many Americans, said, "I'm more interested in looking forward than I am in looking backwards."[92]

Meanwhile, UK Prime Minister Gordon Brown, Tony Blair's successor, announced the creation of an official inquiry into the UK decision to go to war in Iraq.[93] The Chilcot Inquiry was not a trial, but it resembled one. On January 29, 2010, a single bell announced the arrival of former UK Prime Minister Tony Blair's convoy at the back of the Queen Elizabeth II Conference Centre. For six hours, Blair faced a panel of commissioners approved by the House of Commons and defended his decision to make war in Iraq.[94] By late afternoon, hundreds of angry English protesters had massed outside wearing rubber Blair masks and T-shirts with the slogan, "Jail Tony." A man shouted, "Tony Blair," and the crowd called back, "War Criminal!" Inside the packed chamber, Sir John Chilcot repeated a question to Blair:

> "Any regrets?" he asked.
> "Not a regret for removing Saddam," Blair answered.
> "Come on," someone yelled from the public gallery, and was silenced by Sir John.
> Blair continued, "I believe he was a monster and threatened not just the region but the world."[95]

The Iraq War Inquiry was granted broad authority to question and investigate political and military leaders, but no power to punish.[96] Before the results were released,[97] Labour leader Jeremy Corbyn announced that Blair should be prosecuted if evidence showed the war was illegal and that Blair had committed international crimes.[98] When the inquiry delivered its 2016 report, Blair, voice cracking with emotion, attempted to rebut many of the findings: "I express more sorrow, regret and apology than you can ever know or believe."[99]

Military defeat and domestic action facilitate arrest of great-power leaders. Another mechanism is arrest and prosecution by authorities of foreign states. Many examples exist of successful third-party arrests: Pinochet by the United Kingdom, Taylor by Nigeria, Bemba by Belgium, and Rwandese Prime Minister Jean Kambanda by a multinational team in Kenya. Attempts by states with broad jurisdiction to arrest and try American officials for international crimes have been less successful, but they suggest a path toward third-party arrests of great-power leaders.

In this arrest scenario, lawyers from NGOs such as Amnesty International, the Center for Constitutional Rights, or the International Federation for Human Rights would file charges against a powerful political or military leader with the domestic prosecutor or in the courts of a state with wide jurisdictional laws for international crimes. This has occurred in Belgium, Germany, South Africa, and Spain. A local prosecutor or court evaluates the evidence and determines there is a reasonable basis to proceed.

An arrest warrant can be sealed, providing police with the element of surprise, or unsealed, forewarning the accused perpetrator of the charges.

German attempts to arrest US Secretary of Defense Donald Rumsfeld show the possibilities and pitfalls of third-party arrests of great-power leaders. In 2004, Berlin-based lawyer Wolfgang Kaleck, supported by a coalition of international human-rights organizations, filed suit against Rumsfeld and twelve other US officials for international crimes.[100] Rumsfeld was scheduled to attend a high-level security conference in Munich. German federal prosecutor Kay Nehm stopped the investigation, arguing that Germany could only prosecute Rumsfeld if the United States was unable or unwilling, and there was insufficient evidence to prove this was the case. Rumsfeld was forced to cancel his trip, and only rescheduled after receiving German assurances that he would not be arrested. In 2006, Kaleck filed another case after Rumsfeld had left office, but the case was rejected on the debatable grounds that Rumsfeld did not reside or have plans to reside on German soil.[101]

In 2012, a Malaysian human-rights court tried George W. Bush; Dick Cheney; Donald Rumsfeld; and legal advisers Alberto Gonzales, David Addington, William Haynes, Jay Bybee, and John Yoo in absentia and found them guilty of international crimes.[102] The five-judge tribunal heard witness statements and saw documents presented by the prosecution team, which included American law professor Francis Boyle. "At the very least," wrote journalist Charles Pierce, "this court parceled out the blame for the torture program in a fair manner and all the way up the chain of command."[103] Whether Malaysia will attempt to arrest these powerful Bush-era leaders remains an open question.

These forays into the arrest of powerful leaders by foreign states reveal a shift from politics to law in the international order. Official decisions once insulated from prosecution because they were labeled "acts of state" are now fair game. The failed 2015 arrest of Omar al-Bashir in South Africa demonstrates that political leaders who interfere with judicial decisions about prosecuting international crimes are liable to be disciplined by their own courts and potentially impeached by lawmakers.

When al-Bashir was in Pretoria, the nongovernmental South African Litigation Center requested that the High Court issue an emergency warrant for his arrest. The High Court issued an order banning al-Bashir from leaving the country, in order to hear his case. Defying the order, the South African Government helped al-Bashir to flee. South Africa's High Court of Appeal ruled the government's actions "disgraceful," and said South Africa had a duty to arrest al-Bashir on his return.[104] The Office of the President threatened to review South Africa's participation in the ICC Treaty. A South African judge asked prosecutors to prosecute officials who defied the order to detain al-Bashir.[105] The ICC requested an explanation for

South Africa's failure to fulfill its legal obligation.[106] A bid by lawmakers to impeach President Zuma for failing to arrest garnered considerable parliamentary support but was voted down.[107] President Zuma and his cabinet attempted to revoke South Africa's ICC membership, but the South African High Court found the instrument of withdrawal "unconstitutional and invalid."[108] Having lost the support of his party and facing a no-confidence vote in parliament, Zuma resigned. South Africa retains its obligation to arrest perpetrators of international crimes.

The interaction of the executive, the judiciary, and the legislature of South Africa concerning the ICC indictment against the president of Sudan is a reminder that a state is not a unitary actor. This division of authority provides new avenues for the enforcement of international arrest warrants, potentially even against the leaders of great powers. The key to an arrest has been the political and geographic isolation of the accused, but the South African example indicates that a principled judiciary committed to international justice may ultimately provide another hope for the effective enforcement of international law.

The ICC's indictment against al-Bashir also provides a reminder that the administration of international justice must be fair to be effective. An important reason al-Bashir has been able to evade arrest was his propagandistic use of Europe's colonial history to bias Africa against the ICC. Al-Bashir was able to make a persuasive case because the ICC's twenty-three cases in nine situations and thirty-two individuals indicted so far were all African. Louise Mushikiwabo, foreign minister of Rwanda, spoke for many African opponents of the ICC when she observed, "Who would not support international justice? But the practice is that the lighter skin you are, the less guilty you are."[109]

THE IMPUNITY PLAYBOOK

Even in the United States, the notion that top leaders could be subject to punishment for criminal acts became a preoccupation during and after the 2016 presidential race. Candidate Trump made Clinton's prosecution and punishment for mishandling classified information a hallmark of his campaign. By so doing, he perverted the Nuremberg principle of leadership accountability for self-interested political ends. "It's just awfully good that someone with the temperament of Donald Trump is not in charge of the law in our country," Clinton said. "Because, you'd be in jail," Trump shot back.[110]

But when President Trump became the subject of multiple investigations for alleged collusion with Russia, the ensuing saga showcased tools available to powerful leaders avoiding criminal accountability in their own courts. Trump turned the tables on Clinton, inciting his supporters and recasting criminal law as victor's justice. Political capital was crucial to victory in the House and the Senate, but not a fail-safe protection against civil and criminal lawsuits. As long as Republicans controlled the House and the Senate, and as long as the president retained their support, he was protected from impeachment and removal from office.[111] To protect himself against a potential criminal lawsuit, Trump pressured FBI Director James Comey to drop the investigation. When Comey didn't comply, Trump fired him, raising new prospects of criminal charges for obstruction of justice. Lawyers for President Trump argued, "Mr. Trump is immune from suit because he is President of the United States."[112] This misrepresented the Supreme Court's 1997 *Clinton v. Jones* decision, which held that presidents enjoy immunity from *civil* suits in *federal* court during their time in office, but not for actions taken beforehand.[113] Testing his legal position [presidential power] in the court of public opinion, the president tweeted:

> As has been stated by numerous legal scholars, I have the absolute right to PARDON myself, but why would I do that when I have done nothing wrong?[114]

Trump's gamble was that by stacking the Supreme Court with sympathetic judges, he would ensure a favorable interpretation of the constitution and the scope of presidential power. By rousing his base, blaming his opponents, exploiting his powers, pandering to his party, misstating the law, and transforming America's judiciary, Trump hoped to retain power. But what might an authoritarian-leaning leader do if his grip on power slipped? The time-tested solution lay in committing a crime, the crime of aggression. The besieged leader would seize upon or instigate a crisis to force his populace to rally.[115] It could be a terrorist attack, a preemptive strike on a nuclear program, or direct conflict with an adversary.

"Donald Trump needs a war," wrote Professor Thomas Homer-Dixon.[116] Whether President Trump or another embattled leader would press the button, and whether aggressive war would lead to presidential accountability or preclude it, the possibility of criminal accountability for political leaders was an imminent threat.

CHAPTER 10

Activation

The crisis consists precisely in the fact that the old is dying and the new cannot be born; in this interregnum a great variety of morbid symptoms appear.
—Antonio Gramsci, *Prison Notebooks*, 1929–35

A man devoid of hope and conscious of being so has ceased to belong to the future.
—Albert Camus, *The Myth of Sisyphus and Other Essays*, 1942

When written in Chinese, the word "crisis" is composed of two characters – one represents danger and one represents opportunity.
—John F. Kennedy, remarks at the Convocation of the United Negro College Fund, 1959

THE HOSTAGE CRISIS

Seven years after Kampala, the required number of state ratifications for activation had been deposited. The crucial decision to activate ICC jurisdiction over individuals for the crime of aggression was scheduled for December 2017. Benjamin Ferencz had turned ninety-eight years old in March 2017, and it seemed possible that having witnessed every major milestone toward the criminalization of aggressive war—1919 League of Nations, 1928 Treaty for the Renunciation of War, 1945 Nuremberg trials of German aggressors, 1945 United Nations Charter, 1946 Tokyo trials of Japanese aggressors, 1974 General Assembly "Consensus Definition of Aggression," 1990s Nuremberg renaissance, 1998 International Criminal Court, 2010 Kampala amendments—he would also witness the culmination of his mission to enshrine individual responsibility for aggressive war in the rule of law. That is, if militarily powerful states and their allies did not derail the activation decision.

In March 2017, the first signs of trouble landed on the desk of Nadia Kalb, the Austrian diplomat assigned by the ICC's Assembly of States Parties to ensure a smooth activation process. Canada, Colombia, France, Japan, Norway, and the United Kingdom sent Kalb a legal opinion intended to narrow the scope of the law and limit ICC jurisdiction over aggressors.[1] In contradiction to the plain language and recorded negotiating history, they argued that individuals from unratified states would not be prosecutable at the ICC without a UN Security Council resolution. The deal reached in Kampala stated that unratified states were required to opt out of the Kampala amendments if they wished to remove their leaders from the reach of ICC accountability.[2] If accepted, the revisionist interpretation of the Kampala compromise would insulate political and military leaders including those of Canada, Colombia, France, Japan, Norway, and the United Kingdom, thereby diluting the law's deterrent effect.[3] The legal opinion provoked a battle certain to stymie the activation process, squander a century of legal gains, and obstruct Ferencz's hopes for the rule of law.

Participation at UN Headquarters in 2017 was more restricted than at Kampala in 2010. Only ICC states parties were entitled to participate, excluding nonparties to the ICC Treaty like the United States, Russia, China, and North Korea. Also, Catherine Boucher, Canada's newly appointed head delegate, had pressured Kalb into excluding civil society and academics from formal negotiations. This meant shutting out the legal scholars who had decades of experience in drafting the crime. Significantly absent was Ben Ferencz. His son Don, convener of the Global Institute on the Prevention of Aggression, would later explain this unsettling lacuna.

Delegates hurried from one meeting to the next, fretting about the onslaught on the historical record, the exclusion of experienced experts, and the obstructionist legal submission. Diplomats struggled to understand why Canada, Colombia, France, Japan, Norway, and the United Kingdom intended to narrow the aggression regime or collapse the negotiations. The basis of their legal argument was that treaties do not create obligations for states without their consent. Therefore, Kampala's opt-out compromise was illegal because states did not have to opt out since they were not legally bound. They argued against the negotiating history and plain language of the compromise, claiming that the agreement required states to opt in to the regime before being legally bound. The *Convention on the Law of Treaties* that they relied on in their legal argument did require an opt-in procedure for amendments to existing treaties, but the revisionists ignored a key caveat that stated, "unless the treaty otherwise provides."[4] Article 5(2) of the Rome Statute, concerning exercise of jurisdiction over the crime of aggression, along with the Rome Statute's amendment clauses, provided Kampala negotiators with the power to implement an opt-out provision. What the revisionists downplayed was the Rome Statute's unique amendment procedure for the crime of aggression, and the historical record underpinning the opt-out. The strained legal arguments appeared to serve covert geopolitical aims.

Although French and UK judges sat in judgment of Nazi aggressors at Nuremberg, in 2017 they had extensive foreign military deployments potentially vulnerable to aggression investigations. As permanent members of the Security Council they had unsuccessfully pushed for self-protective Security Council control over aggression cases.[5] France and the United Kingdom's push to water down the prohibition on aggression or frustrate its activation was self-serving. Japan had expressed misgivings in 2010 in Kampala about the amendment process, perhaps concerned that hosting US military bases on its territory might implicate its leaders in an aggressive US war in North Korea or the South China Sea. In the end, Japan joined the Kampala compromise. The motivations of Colombia and Norway were mysteriously obscured by their legal arguments. Both behaved as staunch US allies. Most mysterious of all was Canada.

Canada's unexpected attempts to narrow ICC jurisdiction over aggression or obstruct the negotiations began just as Liberal Foreign Affairs Minister Chrystia Freeland delivered her first major foreign-policy speech, which committed Canada to "the renewal, indeed the strengthening, of the postwar multilateral order" and "the principled use of force." I queried Canadian delegate Catherine Boucher about our government's rationale for narrowing the reach of the crime of aggression, and was met by a hostile barrage: non–state delegates were not permitted to participate in the activation decision or to read the legal opinion of Colombia, France, Japan, Norway, the United Kingdom, and Canada. That excluded me, but having shared a decade of drafting negotiations and searching to understand Canadian obstructionism, half a dozen alarmed state delegations leaked the Canadian position to me.

Obviously, Freeland's rhetoric was at odds with Canada's activation position. Boucher was marginalizing Canada at a time when fifteen NATO partners and UN allies had ratified the Kampala amendments and Canada needed all the support it could get to win a seat on the Security Council. I met with disappointed delegates trying to understand why Canada was attempting to dilute or sink the compromise it had helped broker in Kampala. Was Boucher confused by the Kampala amendments? Was she genuinely convinced of the revisionist legal position? Had she been instructed by Ottawa to act as proxy for US interests and curry favor with the new Trump administration, Canada's dominant trading partner?

Shuttling from meeting to meeting, I argued that the legal position of Canada, Colombia, France, Japan, Norway, and the United Kingdom would dial back Kampala's deterrent power, provide avenues for rogue leaders to use force as they please, and weaken an enforcement system that should be buttressed. The only delegations I encountered who disagreed were Canada, Colombia, France, Japan, Norway and the United Kingdom, though Denmark and Australia had quietly shifted to the revisionist camp. The opt-out majority had the numbers to prevail, but all major ICC decisions since its inception had been taken by Assembly of States Parties consensus. Delegates were concerned that if they outvoted the powerful revisionist states, they would withdraw support for the ICC on other crucial matters.

As negotiations entered the final days, three activation options remained.[6] The first was a simple activation of the Kampala amendments, by consensus or two-thirds vote. Under this option, the ICC judges would be left to interpret whether the Kampala compromise was an opt-out or an opt-in regime. Impartial judges were likely to interpret the Kampala amendments as binding ICC member states unless they opted out, the majority position. The second option was an explicit endorsement of the Canada, Colombia, France, Japan, Norway, and UK position that the ICC would not exercise jurisdiction over crimes of aggression committed by the nationals or on the territory of states that had not formally opted in. The most promising was the third, a face-saving option: Canada and the other states that now rejected the opt-out requirement would be *deemed* to have opted out without having to do so formally. Without diluting the law for other ICC states, this option would shield Canadian and other revisionist leaders from accountability to their populations should they attempt to exempt their leaders from accountability for aggressive war.

In the final hours of the negotiations, the majority coaxed and cajoled individual revisionists, one by one, into variations of the third option. Alen Kessel, legal advisor to Canada's Department of Global Affairs, instructed a resistant Boucher to abandon the revisionist position. Fearing ostracism, Colombia, Japan, and Norway agreed not to stand in the way of consensus. As the midnight deadline loomed, Kalb ceded her chair to the vice presidents of the Assembly of States Parties, Sergio Ugalde of Costa Rica and Sebastiano Cardi of Italy. Clocks were stopped for a last-ditch attempt at compromise. France and the United Kingdom refused to budge. Isolated, up against the wall, they demanded consensus, holding activation hostage to their demands. Fearing that France and the United Kingdom would kill activation over a kerfuffle about opting in or out, Ugalde and Cardi proposed a resolution submitting to their opt-in demand. There was an audible groan as France and the United Kingdom objected to a standard provision safeguarding the independence of the ICC judges from political influence. Only after multiple delegates publicly ridiculed their position in the UN amphitheater did France and the United Kingdom agree to the offered terms they had pushed for all along.

The activation resolution was adopted and the room erupted into applause, cheers, hugs—exuberant, emotional joy.[7] Delegates had worked for the activation of the crime of aggression for decades. Now, for the first time since Nuremberg, individuals could be prosecuted internationally for illegal war. With a Security Council resolution, the crime of aggression would be prosecutable against political and military leaders worldwide. The limits of the achievement were subsumed by the accomplishment. Without a Security Council resolution, acts of aggression by the leaders of nonparty states such as the United States and Russia, or acts on their territory, would not be prosecutable at the ICC. ICC judges were left to determine the extent of ICC jurisdiction over acts of aggression by nationals of nonratifying states parties or on the territory of nonratifying states parties.[8] Their decision would determine which would prevail, the 2010 Kampala amendments or the 2017 activation resolution.

I was unsettled by the fact that Ben Ferencz had not attended the final activation gathering and approached his son Don for an explanation. Don said Ben had been "boiling with anger" because states that sat in judgment at Nuremberg had led the opposition to activation of ICC jurisdiction over the crime of aggression. Rather than leave his wealth to the Global Institute on the Prevention of Aggression and the Planethood Foundation, peace initiatives led by Don, Ben now intended to gift it to the Holocaust Memorial Museum. Instead of advocating for activation of ICC jurisdiction over the crime of aggression, Ben proposed aggression be prosecuted as a crime against humanity, which would, if adopted by prosecutors and judges, widen the scope of ICC jurisdiction so that nationals of nonparty states—such as the United States and Russia—who attacked a state party would be prosecutable in The Hague.[9] When I asked Ben about his rationale, he winked and whispered conspiratorially, "If you can't go through the front door, go through the back."

MORBID SYMPTOMS

Years have passed since ISIS conquered Mosul, enslaved the Sinjar Yezidi, beheaded James Foley, and advanced upon the Kobani Kurds. Years since UN ambassador Samantha Power delivered Obama's controversial legal rationale for war.[10] The terror wars are winding down and mutating into dangerous future wars. Politics, force, and law each seem incapable of forestalling the unknown threat. "We're going to war in the South China Sea in five to ten years," declares Donald Trump's chief strategist.[11] Nations elect leaders who promise to secure their borders, while transnational cyberattacks on governments, corporations, and individuals increase in frequency and sophistication. China and the United States race to produce and export the most drones, arming both state and nonstate actors.

Leaders denigrate the judiciary, public servants, scientists, the media, and wage "info-war," clearing the way for their own alternative facts. They seize discretionary authority and act outside and against democratic rules.[12] Post–World War II institutions falter: the UN, the EU, NATO. On the eve of September 11, John Bolton, President Trump's national security advisor, declares, "The ICC is already dead to us."[13] Accountability becomes a liability and timid ICC states pull their funding. The ICC's Appeals Chamber misguidedly acquits Congolese Vice President Bemba for widespread, systematic murder and rape by his private army in the Central African Republic, dialing back the doctrine of command responsibility.[14]

Meanwhile, international law continues its penetration of politics and searches for opportunities to forestall the proliferating violence. Sir John Chilcot, head of the United Kingdom's inquiry into the Iraq War, scathingly rebukes Tony Blair, a dress rehearsal for future aggression cases and front-page news around the world.[15] A landmark Senegal judgment against Chadian President Hissene Habré rejects Habré's head-of-state-immunity defense and showcases an internationalized form of universal jurisdiction, potentially useful in aggression cases.[16] The ICC prosecutor launches investigations into the murder of civilians and torture of detainees in Georgia and Afghanistan, potentially implicating previously unaccountable Russian and US leaders. Obama travels to Hiroshima and calls for a "moral revolution," though he is careful not to apologize for the United States dropping atomic bombs on largely civilian targets.[17] He warns that "Technological progress without an equivalent progress in human institutions can doom us."[18] If Obama has moral precepts or specific institutions in mind, he does not say.

INTERNATIONAL LAW: CYNICS, DREAMERS, AND PEOPLE IN BETWEEN

At the turn of the millennium, human society changed, like a crystalline structure that snaps into a new configuration when heated. In an extraordinary instant, technological progress provided individuals with the capacity to effect the kind of permanent global change previously only possessed by states. Nobody knows what this reconfiguration presages for the prospects of global survival. NATO forges ahead, recognizing cyberspace, along with land, sea, air, and outer space as the "fifth military domain," while armed drones patrol the skies in the Forever War on terror. Science-fiction visionary William Gibson warns, "We have no future because our present is too volatile."[19]

Cynics submit, as they always do, to the law of force. The strong, they maintain, do what they can and the weak accept what they must.[20] The cynics deride the attempts of Ferencz and other "dreamers" to make the international legal order more just and effective, confidently declaring these naïve efforts will accomplish nothing or make matters worse.[21] As anthropologist of cynicism Rebecca Solnit observes, cynics take pride "in not being fooled and not being foolish," but their dismissive attitude that it's all corrupt "pretends to excoriate what it ultimately excuses."[22]

Meanwhile, Ferencz's ideas, born in Nuremberg and largely disregarded during the Cold War, have inspired a new cadre of diplomats who see the structural shift from state to individuals as an opportunity to advance global peace and justice. Yet, glancing up from their law books at the brutalities of ISIS, the illegal Russian seizure of the Crimea, China's militarization of the South China Sea, North Korean nuclear buildup, and US opposition to increased judicial oversight on war, these idealists wonder whether their efforts are futile. Ferencz warns that cynicism and indifference are as fatal as nuclear weapons, and urges the next generation to "never give up."[23]

The drafters of the crime of aggression hope that the modifications to the international order that tailor the law of war to the individual and strengthen judicial oversight of executive power will help make the law more just and effective. But they worry that these changes to the status quo are too little, too late. They marshal their arguments that the crime of aggression promotes peace and the rule of law, protects human rights and prevents suffering, protects soldiers from being killed or maimed in illegal wars, provides protection against aggression by another state, signals a renewed commitment to peaceful resolution of disputes, completes the Rome Statute, and makes the Rome Statute fully compatible with the UN Charter.[24] Once again, the major problem is enforcement, but the shift to individual regulation; the proliferation of overlapping spheres of local, national, regional, international, and transnational legal authority; and new purveyors of nonstate military force generate new potential.

Opponents repeat the cynic's familiar chant with increased urgency. They say all efforts will backfire, they won't make a dent, they will jeopardize previous accomplishments: leave things as they are.[25] If the crime of aggression is indeed a futile effort, the dreamers wonder why opponents waste their energy trying to tip the bike instead of just sitting back and watching it fall.[26]

Lawyers whose job it will be to defend their clients' wars are already searching for loopholes and gaps to turn the law to their advantage, or at least shield their clients from accountability. But these lawfare mercenaries know they do not have the field to themselves; their arguments will be challenged by skilled prosecutors and weighed by independent, impartial judges.

For people who believe the current system for sanctioning and judging wars is ineffective and unjust, the drafters propose five interventions that defy cynicism. They encourage vacillating private individuals and government officials to test the proposed military intervention against the definition of the crime of aggression. They advise voters and civil-society groups to demand increased judicial oversight of war, starting with ratification of the Kampala amendments. They exhort teachers to elucidate the history and logic of the crime of aggression, encouraging students to weigh law against force in conflict resolution. They call on religious congregations to reaffirm their commitment to peace and support the new crime of aggression in light of spiritual commitments. Finally, they urge bold innovation to thwart Goering-like leaders using fear to goad populations into war.

FACING THE WORLD TO COME

I remember strolling outside Princeton University with Benjamin Ferencz, approaching the Woodrow Wilson School where he is scheduled to address diplomatic delegations about lessons of law and war learned in the seventy-two years since he studied at Harvard. As he speaks, I am transported through a century of hope and despair. The birth of world law, Paris 1919, the year before Ferencz was born in the ruins of the Austro-Hungarian empire. The 1920s formation of the League of Nations and its dissolution in the 1930s, followed by the barbarism of World War II. The Nuremberg trials and the hopeful moment at war's end with the creation of the UN Charter. The dashing of hope with the sidelining of the Nuremberg precedent and UN collective security by great-power conflict throughout the Cold War. The Nuremberg renaissance of the 1990s and its jettison during the war on terror by the United States and other previous champions. The culmination of a consensus definition of the crime of aggression in 2010, followed by committed opposition by powerful leaders who prefer to dodge accountability rather than building an effective international order.

For Ferencz, there is a clear solution to the challenge posed by ISIS. The UN Security Council declares ISIS a threat to international peace and security, and authorizes an international peace-enforcement operation to defeat it. The United States and Russia negotiate their respective roles to avoid an escalated confrontation. The Security Council refers the situation to the ICC to investigate international crimes committed by individuals on all sides of the conflict. The ICC issues indictments against leaders such as Syria's Bashar al-Assad and Abu Bakr al-Baghdadi whenever concrete evidence ties criminal leaders to international crimes. Plied with incentives and wary of sanctions, the nations of the region meet to negotiate an end to the conflict and a resolution of their remaining grievances through legal means. Having successfully cooperated to deplete and scatter ISIS, the allies establish permanent international criminal-law institutions charged with preventing and punishing international crimes, including the crime of aggression.

The future is full of "ifs" for the crime of aggression. The ICC prosecutor may choose to put resources toward softer targets, rather than indicting a victorious aggressor in a trial run of an untested crime. If the prosecutor is courageous enough to initiate a case, ICC states parties might refuse to cooperate with the investigation. If ICC states parties cooperate with the investigation and apprehend an indicted defendant, the judges may balk and devise formalistic reasons to drop the case. If the judges proceed with the case, powerful allies of the defendant might join together to attack the charges or the overall legitimacy of the ICC. If the judges stand firm, they may strengthen the rule of law, but deter necessary humanitarian operations and undermine negotiated avenues for resolving international disputes.

Yet, somehow, Ferencz knows if human society doesn't choose law over war, we'll be condemned to business as usual, the triumph of lunacy over law, the despoliation of the planet. Even he can be tempted by despair, his memories weighted by dark images of World War II and ground gained and lost in the struggle to reach a just, enforceable rule of law:

> I have been pushing this rock up a hill. I know I'll not see the top of the hill. I know that. I may be crazy, but I'm not stupid. I push the rock a little bit further up the hill, knowing that there will be times when I get kicked in the head and it slips back. That happens too. Pick up the rock and keep pushing it. And if there are enough people who keep pushing it long enough, we'll reach the top of the mountain.[27]

Whether history is a mountain to climb, a battle between cynicism and idealism, or a series of accumulating precedents updated when the crystalline structure snaps into a new configuration, I know Ferencz is right. The forces of hatred and injustice are encroaching and our best hope is a coordinated, global legal response. What began as an idealistic dream has culminated in a surprisingly functional, promising legal innovation. The crime of aggression will not get us to the top of the mountain, vanquish cynicism, or put an end to war. It is something more modest: a sensible step in the right direction, a memorial to the victims of a violent century, a reminder of humanity's higher aspiration that only our reason can save us from ourselves.

Notes

INTRODUCTION

1. "International Military Tribunal (Nuremberg), Judgment and Sentences," *American Journal of International Law* 41 (1947): 186 (hereinafter Nuremberg Judgment).

2. Matthias Schuster, "The Rome Statute and the Crime of Aggression: A Gordian Knot in Search of a Sword," *Criminal Law Forum* 14 (2003): 1.

3. G. M. Gilbert, *Nuremberg Diary* (New York: Farrar, Straus, 1947), 278.

4. Ibid., 278–79.

5. International Military Tribunal (Nuremberg), *Trial of the Major War Criminals before the International Military Tribunal*, vol. 1 (Nuremberg: author, 1947), 223, https://www.loc.gov/rr/frd/Military_Law/pdf/NT_Vol-I.pdf.

6. Payam Akhavan, "Beyond Impunity: Can International Criminal Justice Prevent Future Atrocities?" *American Journal of International Law* 95 (2001): 7, 9.

7. Benjamin Wittes and Gabriella Blum, *The Future of Violence: Robots and Germs, Hackers and Drones—Confronting a New Age of Threat* (New York: Basic Books, 2015), 5.

8. See UN Charter, arts. 24, 39.

9. See Martha Minow, *Between Vengeance and Forgiveness: Facing History after Genocide and Mass Violence* (Boston: Beacon, 1998), 12; Jeanne Hampton, "Correcting Harms versus Righting Wrongs: The Goal of Retribution," *UCLA Law Review* 39 (1991–92): 1683.

10. Mark A. Drumbl, "Punishment, Postgenocide: From Guilt to Shame to 'Civis' In Rwanda," *New York University Law Review* 75 (2000): 1255 (explaining retributivism).

11. Andrew Natsios, "Waltz with Bashir: Why the Arrest Warrant against Sudan's President Will Serve Neither Peace Nor Justice," *Foreign Affairs* (March 23, 2009), http://www.foreignaffairs.com/articles/64904/andrew-natsios/waltz-with-bashir?page=show; but see Juan E. Méndez, "The Importance of Justice in Securing Peace," Review Conference of the Rome Statute, May 31–June 11, 2010, Kampala, Uganda, UN Doc. RC/ST/PJ/INF.3 (May 30, 2010), 1: "Less than 85 per cent of negotiations end in an agreement and far less are implemented. In Sudan, there was no peace process before the ICC. All attempts at agreement failed. All attempts at appeasing President Al Bashir failed. The idea that the ICC stopped an 'emerging' peace process is pure invention."

12. Natsios, "Waltz with Bashir"; but see Permanent Representatives of Finland, Germany, and Jordan to the United Nations, letter dated June 13, 2008, addressed to the Secretary-General, Annex to "Nuremberg Declaration on Peace and Justice," UN Doc. A/62/885 (June 19, 2008), https://undocs.org/A/62/885:

"Mediators bear a responsibility to contribute creatively to the immediate ending of violence and hostilities while promoting sustainable solutions. Their commitment to the core principles of the international legal order has to be beyond doubt."

13. "South Sudan: Widespread Atrocities in Government Offensive," Human Rights Watch, July 21, 2015, https://www.hrw.org/news/2015/07/21/south -sudan-widespread-atrocities-government-offensive; "Scorched Earth, Poisoned Air: Sudanese Government Forces Ravage Jebel Marra, Darfur," Amnesty International, September 29, 2016, https://www.amnesty.org/en/documents/afr54/4877 /2016/en/.

14. Akhavan, "Beyond Impunity," 8.

15. Ibid., 17–18 (after twenty years of failed negotiations with Joseph Kony and the top commanders of the Lord's Resistance Army, ICC indictments were an impetus to coordinated international action that reduced and scattered the LRA); see also Reed Brody, "Playing it Firm, Fair and Smart: The EU and the ICC's Indictment of Bashir," Human Rights Watch, March 19, 2009, http://www.hrw .org/en/news/2009/03/19/playing-it-firm-fair-and-smart-eu-and-iccs-indictment -bashir; see also David Tolbert and Marieke Wierda, "Stocktaking: Peace and Justice," Rome Statute Review Conference, June 2010, Kampala, International Center for Transnational Justice Briefing (May 2010), 1, http://ictj.org/sites/de fault/files/ICTJ-RSRC-Global-Peace-Briefing-2010-English.pdf: "There are early indications that the issuing of arrest warrants may strengthen motivations to negotiate. There are also signs that the existence or threat of arrest warrants can spur parties to examine a broader array of justice measures than might otherwise have been the case."

16. Harold Hongju Koh and Todd F. Buchwald, "The Crime of Aggression: The United States Perspective," *American Journal of International Law* 109 (2015): 273.

17. Sarah Sewall, under secretary for civilian security, democracy, and human rights, remarks at the Annual Meeting of the American Society of International Law, April 9, 2015, https://2009-2017.state.gov/j/remarks/240579.htm.

18. David Kennedy, *A World of Struggle: How Power, Law, and Expertise Shape Global Political Economy* (Princeton, NJ: Princeton University Press, 2016), 276.

19. Jack L. Goldsmith and Eric A. Posner, *The Limits of International Law* (New York: Oxford University Press, 2005), 13 (using rational choice theory to analyze international law).

CHAPTER 1

1. David Kennedy, *Of War and Law* (Princeton, NJ: Princeton University Press, 2006), 33–39.

2. Jack Goldsmith, *The Terror Presidency: Law and Judgment inside the Bush Administration* (New York: W. W. Norton, 2007), 85; see also Charlie Savage, *Takeover: The Return of the Imperial Presidency and the Subversion of American Democracy* (New York: Little, Brown, 2007), 8–9 (describing Cheney's career-

long mission to "expand the power of the presidency"); "Cheney's Law," *Frontline*, October 16, 2007, http://www.pbs.org/wgbh/pages/frontline/cheney/.

3. Office of Legal Counsel, *The President's Constitutional Authority to Conduct Military Operations Against Terrorists and Nations Supporting Them*, Memorandum to the President of the United States (September 25, 2001), 202, https://www.justice.gov/sites/default/files/olc/opinions/2001/09/31/op-olc-v025-p0188_0.pdf.

4. Quoted in Sean Howard, "Trump's Over-the-Top National Security Team," *Cape Breton Spectator*, n.d., accessed September 20, 2018, https://capebreton spectator.com/2018/04/04/trump-security-bolton-pompeo/?print=print. See also Ruth Wedgwood and Morton H. Halperin, "Will the Real John Bolton Please Stand Up?" *Foreign Policy*, July 15, 2005, https://foreignpolicy.com/2005/07/15/will-the-real-john-bolton-please-stand-up/. But see Curtis A. Bradley, "The Bush Administration and International Law: Too Much Lawyering and Too Little Diplomacy," *Duke Journal of Constitutional Law and Public Policy* 4 (2009): 58 (arguing that the Bush administration also "made affirmative contributions to particular areas of international law . . . almost never directly repudiated international law and in many cases advanced perfectly respectable legal arguments to support its controversial actions").

5. Silvia A. Fernández de Gurmendi, "Completing the Work of the Preparatory Commission: The Working Group on Aggression at the Preparatory Commission for the International Criminal Court," *Fordham International Law Journal* 25 (2002): 589.

6. See Philippe Sands, *Lawless World: America and the Making and Breaking of Global Rules from FDR's Atlantic Charter to George W. Bush's Illegal War* (New York: Viking, 2005), 174 (quoting President Bush: "I don't care what the international lawyers say, we are going to kick some ass."); House Committee on the Judiciary Majority Staff Report to Chairman John Conyers Jr., *Reigning in the Imperial Presidency: Lessons and Recommendations Relating to the Presidency of George W. Bush* (New York: Skyhorse, 2009), 76–78, 110–29, https://fas.org/irp/congress/2009_rpt/imperial.pdf; "U.S.: 'Hague Invasion Act' Becomes Law," Human Rights Watch, August 3, 2002, https://www.hrw.org/news/2002/08/03/us-hague-invasion-act-becomes-law; "United States 'Unsigning' Treaty on War Crimes Court," Human Rights Watch, May 6, 2002, https://www.hrw.org/news/2002/05/06/united-states-unsigning-treaty-war-crimes-court; Uri Friedman, "Targeted Killings: A Short History," *Foreign Policy*, August 13, 2012, https://foreignpolicy.com/2012/08/13/targeted-killings-a-short-history/.

7. Benjamin Ferencz, "Epilogue: The Long Journey to Kampala: A Personal Memoire," in *The Crime of Aggression: A Commentary*, ed. Claus Kress and Stefan Barriga (Cambridge, UK: Cambridge University Press, 2017), 1516–17.

8. Tim Arango and Eric Schmitt, "U.S. Actions in Iraq Fueled Rise of a Rebel: Baghdadi of ISIS Pushes an Islamist Crusade," *New York Times*, August 10, 2014, http://www.nytimes.com/2014/08/11/world/middleeast/us-actions-in-iraq-fueled-rise-of-a-rebel.html.

9. Charles J. Dunlap, Jr., *Law and Military Interventions: Preserving Humanitarian Values in 21st Century Conflicts*, Working Paper (Cambridge, MA: Carr Center for Human Rights, John F. Kennedy School of Government, Harvard University, 2001), 2, http://people.duke.edu/~pfeaver/dunlap.pdf.

10. See generally John Yoo, *War by Other Means: An Insider's Account of the War on Terror* (New York: Atlantic Monthly, 2006).

11. David M. Crane, "The Take Down: Case Studies Regarding 'Lawfare' in International Criminal Justice—The West African Experience," *Case Western Reserve Journal of International Law* 43 (2010): 201.

12. Barack Obama, "Statement by the President," White House, August 7, 2014, https://obamawhitehouse.archives.gov/the-press-office/2014/08/07/statement-president.

13. Barack Obama, "Statement by the President on ISIL," White House, September 10, 2014, https://obamawhitehouse.archives.gov/the-press-office/2014/09/10/statement-president-isil-1.

14. UN Charter, arts. 39–50.

15. Ibid., art. 51.

16. Barack Obama, "Remarks by the President to the White House Press Corps," Press Release, White House, August 20, 2012, http://www.whitehouse.gov/the-press-office/2012/08/20/remarks-president-white-house-press-corps.

17. "Syria Chemical Attack: What We Know," *BBC News*, September 24, 2013, http://www.bbc.com/news/world-middle-east-23927399.

18. "Syria: Groups Call for ICC Referral," Human Rights Watch, May 15, 2014, https://www.hrw.org/news/2014/05/15/syria-groups-call-icc-referral.

19. Ibid.; Barack Obama, "President Obama's Remarks on Syria," Speech, US Embassy in Chad, August 31, 2013, https://td.usembassy.gov/president-obamas-remarks-syria/.

20. Vladimir V. Putin, "A Plea for Caution from Russia," *New York Times*, September 11, 2013, http://www.nytimes.com/2013/09/12/opinion/putin-plea-for-caution-from-russia-on-syria.html?pagewanted=all.

21. Constanze Letsch, "Foreign Jihadis Change Face of Syrian Civil War," *Guardian*, December 25, 2014, http://www.theguardian.com/world/2014/dec/25/foreign-jihadis-syrian-civil-war-assad.

22. Obama, "Statement," August 7, 2014.

23. UN General Assembly (GA), "2005 World Summit Outcome," GA Res. 60/1, para. 79, UN Doc. A/RES/60/1 (October 24, 2005).

24. Oona A. Hathaway and Scott J. Shapiro, *The Internationalists: How a Radical Plan to Outlaw War Remade the World* (New York: Simon and Schuster, 2017), xv, xvii; Michael J. Kelly, "Time Warp to 1945: Resurrection of the Reprisal and Anticipatory Self-Defense Doctrines in International Law," *Journal of Transnational Law and Policy* 13 (2003): 4, 9–10, 12.

25. UN Charter, art. 51.

26. The use of force in self-defense is only permitted where the attack has a traditional military character and, by its "scale and effects," causes a significant amount of harm. See Military and Paramilitary Activities in and against Nicaragua (Nicaragua v. United States), Judgment, 1986 ICJ Rep. 14, para. 195 (June 27) (hereinafter *Nicaragua*); see also David A. Sadoff, "A Question of Determinacy: The Legal Status of Anticipatory Self-Defense," *Georgetown Journal of International Law* 40 (2009): 546.

27. Permanent Representative of the United States to the UN, letter dated September 23, 2014, addressed to the Secretary-General, UN Doc. S/2014/695

(September 23, 2014); Michael P. Scharf, "How the War against ISIS Changed International Law," *Case Western Reserve Journal of International Law* 48 (2016): 34–35.

28. "Vitaly Churkin Against Strikes at ISIS without Consent from Damascus," TASS, September 10, 2014, http://tass.com/russia/748963.

29. Kevin Jon Heller, "The 'Unwilling or Unable' Standard for Self-Defense," *Opinio Juris* (blog), September 17, 2011, 2:42 a.m., http://opiniojuris .org/2011/09/17/the-unwilling-or-unable-standard-for-self-defense-against-non -state-actors/.

30. Tom Ruys, *"Armed Attack" and Article 51 of the UN Charter: Evolutions in Customary Law and Practice* (New York: Cambridge University Press, 2010), 531.

31. Howard Koplowitz, "ISIS Airstrikes in Syria: 'France Cannot Do Everything,' Foreign Minister Says," *International Business Times*, September 23, 2014, http://www.ibtimes.com/isis-airstrikes-syria-france-cannot-do-everything-for eign-minister-says-1693420.

32. Ashley Hoffman, "18 Times Donald Trump Said the U.S. Shouldn't Bomb Syria," *Time*, April 7, 2017, http://time.com/4730219/syria-missile-attack -donald-trump-tweets/.

33. Luke Harding, "'It Had a Big Impact on Me': Story behind Trump's Whirlwind Missile Response," *Guardian*, April 7, 2017, https://www.theguar dian.com/world/2017/apr/07/how-pictures-of-syrias-dead-babies-made-trump -do-unthinkable.

34. Ryan Goodman, "What Do Top Legal Experts Say about the Syria Strikes?" *Just Security*, April 7, 2017, https://www.justsecurity.org/39712/top-legal-experts -syria-strikes/; David Frum, "Seven Lessons from Trump's Syria Strike," *Atlantic*, April 7, 2017, https://www.theatlantic.com/politics/archive/2017/04/seven-lessons -from-trumps-syria-strike/522327/.

35. Michael D. Shear and Michael R. Gordon, "63 Hours: From Chemical Attack to Trump's Strike in Syria," *New York Times*, April 7, 2017, https://www .nytimes.com/2017/04/07/us/politics/syria-strike-trump-timeline.html?.

36. Harding, "Big Impact."

37. Thomas M. Franck, "Who Killed Article 2(4)? Or, Changing Norms Governing the Use of Force by States," *American Journal of International Law* 64 (1970): 837.

38. Louis Henkin, "The Reports of the Death of Article 2(4) Are Greatly Exaggerated," *American Journal of International Law* 65 (1971): 544.

39. Ibid., 544–45.

40. See generally ibid.; Louis Henkin, *How Nations Behave: Law and Foreign Policy*, 2nd ed. (New York: Columbia University Press, 1979), 47 (emphasis omitted): "Almost all nations observe almost all principles of international law and almost all of their obligations almost all of the time."

41. Kennedy, *Of War and Law*, 35.

42. Jane Mayer, *The Dark Side: The Inside Story of How the War on Terror Turned Into a War on American Ideals* (New York: Doubleday, 2008), 8–9; but see Bradley, "Bush Administration," 58: "The Administration was *too* focused on the law and failed to take adequate account of other, non-legal considerations that are often central to good diplomacy."

43. Dana Priest, "CIA Holds Terror Suspects in Secret Prisons," *Washington Post*, November 2, 2005, http://www.washingtonpost.com/wp-dyn/content/article/2005/11/01/AR2005110101644.html.

44. Eric Posner, "Think Again: International Law," *Foreign Policy*, September 17, 2009, http://foreignpolicy.com/2009/09/17/think-again-international-law/.

45. Mayer, *Dark Side*, 7, 9, 292–93. Mayer attributes the approach to Vice-President Cheney, who believed "There was too much international law, too many civil liberties, too many constraints on the President's war powers, too many rights for defendants, and too many rules against lethal covert actions."

46. General Bantz J. Craddock, Commander, United States Army Committee on House Armed Services, "Posture Statement of General Bantz J. Craddock, United States Army Commander, United States Southern Command, before the 109th Congress House Armed Services Committee, 9 March 2005," 6–7, https://www.globalsecurity.org/military/library/congress/2005_hr/050309-craddock.pdf; Senator John Cornyn questioning Vice Admiral Lowell Jacoby, Senate Armed Services Committee Hearing (March 17, 2005), https://docs.wixstatic.com/ugd/e13974_f85837e734f540548182dfab9c79c741.pdf; Rick Maze, "New Rules May Hinder U.S. Training for Foreign Troops," *Defense News*, May 9, 2005, http://www.amicc.org/docs/Defense%20News%205-9-05.pdf.

47. John B. Bellinger III, "Remarks at The Hague, Netherlands: The United States and International Law" (June 6, 2007), transcript available at https://2001-2009.state.gov/s/l/2007/112666.htm; "Prisoners in War: Contemporary Challenges to the Geneva Conventions," Embassy of the United States in London, Press Release, Lecture at the University of Oxford (December 10, 2007), http://www.usembassy.org.uk/ukpapress72.html.

48. Harold Hongju Koh, "The Obama Administration and International Law," Keynote Speech at the Annual Meeting of the American Society of International Law (March 25, 2010), transcript available at https://www.state.gov/documents/organization/179305.pdf, 4; "Retrospective on International Law in the First Obama Administration," *American Society of International Law Proceedings* 107 (2013): 131.

49. Exec. Order No. 13,491, 3 CFR 199 (2010) (signed January 22, 2009).

50. Greg Jaffe, "How Obama's Nobel Prize Speech Became a Guide to His Wartime Decision-Making," *Washington Post*, June 3, 2016, https://www.washingtonpost.com/graphics/national/obama-legacy/nobel-peace-prize-oslo-2009-speech.html.

51. Barack Obama, Nobel Lecture, Oslo, December 10, 2009, transcript available at https://www.nobelprize.org/nobel_prizes/peace/laureates/2009/obama-lecture_en.html.

52. Koh, "Obama Administration and International Law," 3–4.

53. John B. Bellinger III, "More Continuity Than Change," *New York Times*, February 14, 2010, http://www.nytimes.com/2010/02/15/opinion/15iht-edbellinger.html; E. Posner, "Think Again"; Bradley, "Bush Administration," 76; Jack Goldsmith, "The Contributions of the Obama Administration to the Practice and Theory of International Law," *Harvard International Law Journal* 57 (2016): 455-474 (arguing that in many ways it was an expansion).

54. E. Posner, "Think Again."

55. Goldsmith, "Contributions of the Obama Administration," 458; see also David E. Sanger, *Confront and Conceal: Obama's Secret Wars and Surprising Use of American Power* (New York: Crown, 2012), 243–46.

56. Obama, Nobel Lecture.

57. Steven Levitsky and Daniel Ziblatt, "Is Donald Trump a Threat to Democracy?" *New York Times*, December 16, 2016, https://www.nytimes.com/2016/12 /16/opinion/sunday/is-donald-trump-a-threat-to-democracy.html?_r=0.

58. Jack Goldsmith, "The Trump Onslaught on International Law and Institutions," *Lawfare* (blog), March 17, 2017, 10:09 a.m., https://www.lawfareblog .com/trump-onslaught-international-law-and-institutions.

59. "World Report 2017: Demagogues Threaten Human Rights," Human Rights Watch, January 12, 2017, https://www.hrw.org/news/2017/01/12/world-report -2017-demagogues-threaten-human-rights.

60. Ralph Janik, "Trump and International Law: Making Hegel Great Again?" *Opinio Juris* (blog), February 27, 2017, 7:21 a.m., http://opiniojuris.org /2017/02/27/trump-and-international-law-making-hegel-great-again/.

61. "Donald Trump: Three Decades 4,095 Lawsuits," *USA Today*, n.d., accessed July 20, 2017, https://www.usatoday.com/pages/interactives/trump-law suits/; Vanessa Romo, "Lawsuits Force Alleged Trump Affairs, Sexual Misconduct Claims Back into Public Eye," *Two-Way*, *NPR*, March 20, 2018, https://www.npr .org/sections/thetwo-way/2018/03/20/595348166/lawsuits-force-alleged-trump -affairs-sexual-misconduct-claims-back-into-public-e; David A. Fahrenthold, "New York Files Civil Suit against President Trump, Alleging His Charity Engaged in 'Illegal Conduct,'" *Washington Post*, June 14, 2018, https://www.washington post.com/politics/new-york-files-suit-against-president-trump-alleging-his-char ity-engaged-in-illegal-conduct/2018/06/14/c3cbf71e-6fc9-11e8-bd50-b80389a4e569 _story.html?noredirect=on&utm_term=.62c85c63efc3; Steve Reilly, "USA TODAY Exclusive: Hundreds Allege Donald Trump Doesn't Pay His Bills," *USA Today*, June 9, 2016, last updated April 25, 2018, https://www.usatoday.com/story/news /politics/elections/2016/06/09/donald-trump-unpaid-bills-republican-president -laswuits/85297274/; Fred Grimm, "Uh-Oh, the Litigious Scoundrel You Sued Might Get to Be President," *Miami Herald*, July 20, 2016, updated July 21, 2016, https://www.miamiherald.com/news/local/news-columns-blogs/fred-grimm/arti cle90871347.html; Doug Criss, "A Judge Has Finalized a $25 Million Settlement by Students Who Claim They Were Defrauded by Trump University," *CNN*, April 10, 2018, https://www.cnn.com/2018/04/10/politics/trump-university-settlement-final ized-trnd/index.html.

62. Charlie Savage, "White House Pulls Back from Bid to Reopen C.I.A. 'Black Site' Prisons," *New York Times*, February 4, 2017, https://www.nytimes .com/2017/02/04/us/politics/black-site-prisons-cia-terrorist.html?_r=0.

CHAPTER 2

1. "Vladimir Putin Answered Journalists' Questions on the Situation in Ukraine," President of Russia, March 4, 2014, http://en.kremlin.ru/events/presi dent/news/20366 (hereinafter Putin, "Situation in Ukraine").

2. "Kiev's claims over special forces 'resemble paranoia': Russia," *Zee News*, May 17, 2014, http://zeenews.india.com/news/world/kievs-claims-over-special -forces-resemble-paranoia-russia_932885.html.

3. "Сикорский попросил Путина показать ему магазин, где можно купить 'Бук'" (Sikorsky asked Putin to show him a store where you can buy "Бук"), Unian.net, July 28, 2014, https://www.unian.net/politics/944762-sikorskiy-pop rosil-putina-pokazat-emu-magazin-gde-mojno-kupit-buk.html [in Russian].

4. David Speedie, "Rein In Ukraine's Neo-fascists," *CNN*, March 6, 2014, http://www.cnn.com/2014/03/06/opinion/speedie-ukraine-far-right/.

5. "Ukraine's Revolution and the Far Right," *BBC News*, March 7, 2014, http://www.bbc.com/news/world-europe-26468720.

6. Alec Luhn, "The Ukrainian Nationalism at the Heart of 'Euromaidan,'" *Nation*, January 21, 2014, http://www.thenation.com/article/ukrainian-nationalism -heart-euromaidan/.

7. "Ukrainian President Viktor Yanukovych Refuses to Quit," *BBC News*, February 22, 2014, http://www.bbc.com/news/world-europe-26306886.

8. Quoted in Sergei Loiko, "Ukraine Interim Government Issues Arrest Warrant for Yanukovich," *LA Times*, February 24, 2014, http://articles.latimes .com/2014/feb/24/world/la-fg-wn-ukraine-yanukovich-arrest-warrant-20140224.

9. "Ukraine: Speaker Oleksandr Turchynov Named Interim President," *BBC News*, February 23, 2014, http://www.bbc.com/news/world-europe-26312008.

10. "Statement by the Press Secretary on Ukraine," White House, February 22, 2014, https://www.whitehouse.gov/the-press-office/2014/02/22/statement -press-secretary-ukraine.

11. Radosław Sikorski, comment on *Twitter*, February 22, 2014, 6:18 a.m., https://twitter.com/sikorskiradek/status/4372299921170350096.

12. Quoted in Ashley Deeks, "Russia in Ukraine: A Reader Responds," *Lawfare* (blog), March 5, 2014, 1:30 p.m., http://www.lawfareblog.com/russia-uk raine-reader-responds.

13. Ibid.; Information Department of the Verkhovna Rada of Ukraine Secretariat, "The Verkhovna Rada of Ukraine adopted the Resolution 'On self-withdrawal of the President of Ukraine from performing his constitutional duties and setting early elections of the President of Ukraine,'" *Verkhovna Rada of Ukraine*, February 22, 2014, http://iportal.rada.gov.ua/en/news/News/News/88138.html.

14. Howard Amos, "Ukraine Crisis Fuels Secession Calls in Pro-Russian South," *Guardian*, February 23, 2014, http://www.theguardian.com/world/2014 /feb/23/ukraine-crisis-secession-russian-crimea.

15. "Ukraine Crisis: Russia Vows Troops Will Stay," *BBC News*, March 3, 2014, http://www.bbc.com/news/world-europe-26414600.

16. Ibid.; Alissa de Carbonnel, "How the Separatists Delivered Crimea to Moscow," Reuters, March 12, 2014, https://www.reuters.com/article/us-ukraine -crisis-russia-aksyonov-insigh/how-the-separatists-delivered-crimea-to-moscow -idUSBREA2B13M20140312.

17. Kathy Lally, Will Englund, and William Booth, "Russian Parliament Approves Use of Troops in Ukraine," *Washington Post*, March 1, 2014, https://www .washingtonpost.com/world/europe/russian-parliament-approves-use-of-troops-in -crimea/2014/03/01/d1775f70-a151–11e3-a050-dc3322a94fa7_story.html.

18. Kathy Lally, William Booth, and Will Englund, "Russian Forces Seize Crimea; Ukraine's Interim President Decries Aggression" *Washington Post*, March 1, 2014, https://www.washingtonpost.com/world/a-deeply-concerned -obama-warns-russia-against-action-in-crimea/2014/03/01/c56ca34c-a111–11e3 -a050-dc3322a94fa7_story.html.

19. John Simpson, "Russia's Crimea Plan Detailed, Secret and Successful," *BBC News*, March 19, 2014, http://www.bbc.com/news/world-europe-26644082.

20. Anshel Pfeffer, "Ukraine's Crimea Falls to Putin, without a Shot Fired," *Haaretz*, March 1, 2014, http://www.haaretz.com/news/world/.premium-1.577321.

21. Associated Press, "Crimea Votes on Whether to Secede from Ukraine," *New York Post*, March 16, 2014, http://nypost.com/2014/03/16/crimea-votes -on-whether-to-secede-from-ukraine/.

22. "Territorial Integrity of Ukraine," GA Res. 68/262 (March 27, 2014); United Nations Bibliographic Information System, Voting Record Search, A/RES/68/262, http://unbisnet.un.org:8080/ipac20/ipac.jsp?profile=voting&index=.VM&term =ares68262.

23. "UN Security Council Action on Crimea Referendum Blocked," *UN News*, March 15, 2014, https://www.un.org/apps/news/story.asp?NewsID=47362#.WWZ rLcbMwnU.

24. "UN Security Council Action on Crimea Referendum Blocked," *UN News*, March 15, 2014, https://news.un.org/en/story/2014/03/464002-un-security-coun cil-action-crimea-referendum-blocked.

25. More specifically, under Russian constitutional law, there were a number of steps required to annex the Crimea as a new federal subject of Russia. They were all accomplished within a few days, and the official date of annexation was retroactively set as March 18, 2014.

26. Martin D. Brown, "Ukraine Crisis Is Nothing Like Invasions of Czech-oslovakia," *Conversation*, April 4, 2014, http://theconversation.com/ukraine-crisis-is -nothing-like-invasions-of-czechoslovakia-25169.

27. Quoted in Tom Parfitt and Justin Huggler, "Ukraine Crisis: Do Not Try to Scare Putin, Warns Merkel," *Telegraph*, February 7, 2015, https://www.telegraph .co.uk/news/worldnews/europe/ukraine/11397900/Ukraine-crisis-Do-not-try-to -scare-Putin-warns-Merkel.html.

28. Quoted in Justin Huggler, "Ukraine Crisis: US Officials Compare Peace Ef-forts to Appeasing Hitler," *Telegraph*, February 8, 2015, http://www.telegraph.co .uk/news/worldnews/europe/ukraine/11398762/Ukraine-crisis-US-officials-com pare-peace-efforts-to-appeasing-Hitler.html.

29. Garry Kasparov, "Vladimir Putin and the Lessons of 1938," *Politico Maga-zine*, March 16, 2014, http://www.politico.com/magazine/story/2014/03/vladmir -putin-crimea-hitler-1938-104711.html.

30. Vladimir Putin, "Address by President of the Russian Federation: Vladimir Putin Addressed State Duma Deputies, Federation Council Members, Heads of Russian Regions and Civil Society Representatives in the Kremlin," President of Russia, March 18, 2014, http://en.kremlin.ru/events/president/news/20603 (here-inafter "Address in the Kremlin").

31. Ibid.

32. Ibid.

33. Norman M. Naimark, *Stalin's Genocides* (Princeton, NJ: Princeton University Press, 2010), 97.

34. Putin, "Address in the Kremlin."

35. Ibid.

36. Ibid.

37. Putin, "Situation in Ukraine."

38. Ibid.

39. Tom Ruys, "The 'Protection of Nationals' Doctrine Revisited," *Journal of Conflict and Security Law* 13 (2008): 234–35, 248–50.

40. The Constitution of the Russian Federation (1993), art. 61(2). The Constitution of the Russian Federation (adopted at national voting on December 12, 1993) came into force on the day of its official publication. The text of the Constitution was published in *Rossiiskaya Gazeta* newspaper on December 25, 1993.

41. Putin, "Situation in Ukraine."

42. Michael Ignatieff, "The End of Intervention? The Responsibility to Protect as International Norm—and Now, Parody," Talk at London's Chatham House, March 19, 2014, transcript available at http://www.michaelignatieff.ca/assets/pdfs/Intervention.pdf.

43. Putin, "Address in the Kremlin."

44. "Accordance with International Law of the Unilateral Declaration of Independence in Respect of Kosovo," Advisory Opinion, 2010 ICJ 141, para. 84 (July 22).

45. Putin, "Address in the Kremlin."

46. Конституція України [КУ] [Constitution] June 28, 1996, art. 73 (Ukr.), http://www.legislationline.org/documents/section/constitutions/country/52.

47. "Reference re Secession of Quebec," [1998] 2 SCR 217, para. 91–92 (Can.).

48. Vladimir Putin, Vasiliĭ Shestakov, and Alexey Levitsky, *Judo: History, Theory, Practice* (Berkeley, CA: North Atlantic Books, 2004), 2.

49. Putin, "Address in the Kremlin."

50. Rajan Menon and Eugene Rumer, *Conflict in Ukraine: The Unwinding of the Post–Cold War Order* (Cambridge, MA: Massachusetts Institute of Technology, 2015), 71–73: "Russian opposition to NATO enlargement is well known."

51. Putin, "Address in the Kremlin."

52. Barack Obama, "Remarks by the President Announcing the FY2015 Budget," White House, March 4, 2014, https://obamawhitehouse.archives.gov/the-press-office/2014/03/04/remarks-president-announcing-fy2015-budget.

53. Joachim Remak, *Sarajevo: The Story of a Political Murder* (New York: Criterion Books, 1959), 137.

54. See Hathaway and Shapiro, *Internationalists*, xv, 3–98, describing the "Old World Order" and its evolution from the seventeenth century to 1928.

55. Ibid., xvi.

56. Christopher Clark, *The Sleepwalkers: How Europe Went to War in 1914* (London: Allen Lane, 2012), xxiii–xxxi.

57. Preamble to Covenant of the League of Nations (1919).

58. Woodrow Wilson, President of the United States of America, Speech at Guildhall, London, December 28, 1918.

59. "League of Nations," President Woodrow Wilson House, n.d., accessed April 24, 2016, http://www.woodrowwilsonhouse.org/league-nations.

60. William A. Schabas, *The Trial of The Kaiser* (Oxford: Oxford University Press, 2018), 14–16.

61. David Lloyd George, *Memoirs of the Peace Conference* (New Haven, CT: Yale University Press, 1939), 55.

62. Kirsten Sellars, "The First World War, Wilhelm II and Article 227: The Origin of the Idea of 'Aggression' in International Criminal Law," in Kress and Barriga, *Crime of Aggression*, 29.

63. Ibid., 33.

64. Ibid., 34.

65. Treaty of Peace between the Allied and Associated Powers and Germany (June 28, 1919), 225 Consol. TS 188, art. 227; see also Commission on the Responsibility of the Authors of the War and on Enforcement of Penalties, "Report Presented to the Preliminary Peace Conference (1919)," reprinted in *American Journal of International Law* 14 (1920): 116–17; James Brown Scott, "The Trial of the Kaiser," in *What Really Happened in Paris: The Story of the Peace Conference, 1918–1919*, ed. Edward Mandell House and Charles Seymour, 242–45 (New York: Charles Scribner's Sons, 1921).

66. Treaty of Versailles (1919), art. 232–33.

67. Covenant of the League of Nations (1919), art. 10.

68. Ibid., art. 16.

69. Quoted in Edwin Borchard, "The Multilateral Pact: 'Renunciation of War,'" Address delivered at the Williamstown Institute of Politics, August 22, 1928, http://avalon.law.yale.edu/20th_century/kbbor.asp.

70. Martyn Housden, *The League of Nations and the Organisation of Peace* (Harlow, UK: Longman, 2012), 39.

71. Eric D. Weitz, *Weimar Germany: Promise and Tragedy* (Princeton, NJ: Princeton University Press, 2007), 109–11, 331–33.

72. Woodrow Wilson, "Address to the US Senate (January 22, 1917)," in *The Messages and Papers of Woodrow Wilson*, vol. 1, ed. Albert Shaw, 352 (New York: Review of Reviews Corporation, 1924).

73. Christopher R. Browning, "Lessons from Hitler's Rise," *New York Review of Books*, April 20, 2017, http://www.nybooks.com/articles/2017/04/20/lessons-from-hitlers-rise/.

74. "Definition of 'Aggressor' at the League of Nations Conference for the Reduction and Limitation of Armaments On the 6th February 1933," *Records of the Conference for the Reduction and Limitation of Armaments, Minutes of the Cen. Com.*, vol. 1, *Geneva, 1932* (September 1933), 237–38, http://www.letton.ch/lvx_33sdn.htm.

75. "London Convention Relating to the Definition of Aggression: No. 3391— Convention for the Definition of Aggression, Signed at London, July 3rd, 1933," art. 2, Derechos Human Rights, February 23, 2015, http://www.derechos.org/nizkor/aggression/doc/aggression89.html.

76. Ibid., preamble, art. 3; "Definition of 'Aggressor' at the League of Nations Conference."

77. M. N. Politis, "Report of the Committee on Security Questions," League of Nations Doc. Conf.D./C.G./108 (Geneva, May 24, 1933), pt. I, para. 1–2, Equipo Nizkor, March 26, 2013, http://www.derechos.org/peace/dia/doc/dia17.html.

78. Ibid., para. 2–3.

79. Ibid., para. 2–3.

80. Ibid., para. 2.

81. Kirsten Sellars, *"Crimes Against Peace" and International Law* (Cambridge, UK: Cambridge University Press, 2013) 37–38.

82. Ibid.

83. Covenant of the League of Nations, art. 11.

84. Wolfgang Friedmann, "International Law and the Present War," *Transactions of the Grotius Society* 26 (1940): 211.

85. Ibid., 225–26.

86. Ibid., 239.

87. Kissinger, *Diplomacy* (New York: Simon and Schuster, 1995), 242.

88. Ibid., 238, 244.

89. Juliane von Mittelstaedt and Erich Follath, "Interview with Henry Kissinger: 'Do We Achieve World Order through Chaos or Insight?' " *Spiegel Online*, November 13, 2014, http://www.spiegel.de/international/world/interview-with-henry-kissinger-on-state-of-global-politics-a-1002073.html.

90. Ibid.

91. Henry A. Kissinger, "To Settle the Ukraine Crisis, Start at the End," *Washington Post*, March 5, 2014, http://www.washingtonpost.com/opinions/henry-kissinger-to-settle-the-ukraine-crisis-start-at-the-%20end/2014/03/05/46dad868-a496-11e3–8466-d34c451760b9_story.html.

92. Ibid.

93. See, for example, Henry Kissinger, *World Order* (New York: Penguin, 2014), 295–302 (downplaying the human costs); Michiko Kakutani, "Long View of History Includes Today," *New York Times*, September 8, 2014, https://www.nytimes.com/2014/09/09/books/in-world-order-henry-kissinger-sums-up-his-philosophy.html; see also William Shawcross, *Sideshow: Kissinger, Nixon and the Destruction of Cambodia* (New York: Simon and Schuster, 1979), 396; Christopher Hitchens, *The Trial of Henry Kissinger* (London: Verso, 2001), xxiv.

94. Philip Bobbitt, *The Shield of Achilles: War, Peace and the Course of History* (New York: Alfred A. Knopf, 2002), 344–47.

95. Ibid., 346–47.

96. Ibid., 346–47.

97. Ibid., 32.

98. Ibid., 24–25.

99. Ibid., 41.

100. Ibid., 43, 61.

101. Ibid., 575.

102. *"The Shield of Achilles*: Mr. Bobbit Discusses His Book *The Shield of Achilles: War, Peace, and the Course of History*," C-SPAN, March 19, 2003, http://www.c-span.org/video/?174728-1/book-discussion-shield-achilles.

103. Bobbitt, *Shield of Achilles*, 228–235.

104. Ibid., 8.

105. John Robb, *Brave New War: The Next State of Terrorism and the End of Globalization* (Hoboken, NJ: John Wiley, 2007), 8.

106. Philip Bobbitt, *The Garments of Court and Palace: Machiavelli and the World That He Made* (New York: Grove, 2013), 37.

107. Ibid.

108. Nathaniel Berman, "Modernism, Nationalism, and the Rhetoric of Reconstruction," *Yale Journal of Law and the Humanities* 4 (1992): 359.

109. Ibid., 354–55.

110. Ibid., 363, 368.

111. Ibid., 370.

112. Ibid., 372.

113. Ibid., 380.

114. Ibid.

115. Rome Statute of the International Criminal Court, July 17, 1998, 2187 UNTS 90 (1998), art. 16 (hereinafter Rome Statute).

116. Hathaway and Shapiro, *Internationalists*, 313–14.

CHAPTER 3

1. Leo Tolstoy, *War and Peace*, trans. Richard Pevear and Larissa Volokhonsky (New York: First Vintage Classics, 2008; originally published 1869), 605.

2. B.V.A. Röling, "Interpretation of the Charter," c. January 23, 1947, 6: 3DRL 2481 Series 1/2/10 (Webb papers, Australian War Memorial, Canberra), quoted in Kirsten Sellars, "The Legacy of the Tokyo Dissidents on 'Crimes against Peace,'" in Kress and Barriga, *Crime of Aggression*, 115.

3. Roosevelt had declared US neutrality in September 1939. Franklin Roosevelt, "Neutrality of the United States," Proclamation 2348 (September 5, 1939), published online by Gerhard Peters and John T. Woolley, *The American Presidency Project*, 1999–2018, http://www.presidency.ucsb.edu/ws/?pid=15802.

4. Jackson consulted with Professors Hersch Lauterpacht and Hans Kelsen, and other legal scholars, who helped him to envision crimes against peace as the linchpin of the Nuremberg Trial. See Hathaway and Shapiro, *Internationalists*, 267–69.

5. Robert H. Jackson, Address to the Inter-American Bar Association in Havana, Cuba, March 27, 1941, 350, https://www.roberthjackson.org/wp-content/uploads/2015/01/International_Order.pdf.

6. Ibid, 350–51.

7. Charles A. Beard, *Giddy Minds and Foreign Quarrels: An Estimate of American Foreign Policy* (New York: Macmillan, 1939), 27.

8. Carl Schmitt, "The International Crime of the War of Aggression and the Principle 'Nullum Crimen, Nulla Poena Sine Lege,'" in *Writings on War* (Cambridge, UK: Polity, 2011), 155–64.

9. Harry S. Truman, "Providing for Representation of the United States in Preparing and Prosecuting Charges of Atrocities and War Crimes against the Leaders of the European Axis Powers and Their Principal Agents and Accessories," Exec.

Order No. 9547, 10 FR 4961 (May 2, 1945), http://www.loc.gov/rr/frd/Military
_Law/pdf/jackson-rpt-military-trials.pdf (announced Jackson's appointment).

10. Robert H. Jackson, *Report of Robert H. Jackson, United States Representative, to the International Conference on Military Trials*, US Dept. of State
Publication 3080 (Washington, DC: US Dept. of State Division of Publica-
tions, 1945), 299, http://www.loc.gov/rr/frd/Military_Law/pdf/jackson-rpt-military
-trials.pdf.

11. Ibid., 295.

12. Ibid., 293.

13. Ibid., 298.

14. Ibid., 299.

15. Ibid., 273–74.

16. "Nuremberg Trial Proceedings Vol. 1: Charter of the International Military Tribunal," art. 6(a), Yale Law School, Lillian Goldman Law Library, Avalon Project, 2008, http://avalon.law.yale.edu/imt/imtconst.asp#art6 (hereinafter
Nuremberg Charter).

17. Ibid., arts. 6–10, 13, 16.

18. Sellars, *"Crimes against Peace"*, 88–89, 118–19.

19. Jackson, Address to the Inter-American Bar Association, 349; Hathaway
and Shapiro, *Internationalists*, 261–68.

20. Robert H. Jackson, quoted in Emily Rajakovich, "London Agreement and
Charter, August 8, 1945," Robert H. Jackson Center, September 1, 2015, https://
www.roberthjackson.org/article/london-agreement-charter-august-8-1945/.

21. Nuremberg Charter, art. 7: "The official position of defendants, whether as
Heads of State or responsible officials in Government Departments, shall not be
considered as freeing them from responsibility or mitigating punishment."

22. "The Law of Individual Responsibility," in "Nazi Conspiracy and Aggression Volume 1, Chapter 5," Yale Law School, Lillian Goldman Law Library,
Avalon Project, 2008, http://avalon.law.yale.edu/imt/chap_05.asp.

23. "Nuremberg Trial Proceedings Vol. 19: One Hundred and Eighty-Seventh
Day, 26 July 26, 1946," Yale Law School, Lillian Goldman Law Library, Avalon
Project, 2008, http://avalon.law.yale.edu/imt/07-26-46.asp.

24, "Nuremberg Trial Proceedings Vol. 1: Indictment: Count One," Yale Law
School, Lillian Goldman Law Library, Avalon Project, 2008, http://avalon.law
.yale.edu/imt/count1.asp.

25. Ibid.

26. Jackson, *Report*, 331; "Nuremberg Trial Proceedings Volume 2: Second
Day," 98, Yale Law School, Lillian Goldman Law Library, Avalon Project, 2008,
http://avalon.law.yale.edu/imt/11-21-45.asp.

27. Ann Tusa and John Tusa, *The Nuremberg Trial* (London: Macmillan London, 2003) 451–52.

28. "Nuremberg Trial Proceedings Vol. 1: Indictment: Count Two," Yale Law
School, Lillian Goldman Law Library, Avalon Project, 2008, http://avalon.law
.yale.edu/imt/count2.asp.

29. Nuremberg Charter, arts. 6 and 7.

30. Hartley Shawcross, in "Nuremberg Trial Proceedings Volume 3: Twelfth
Day, Tuesday, 4 December 1945, Morning Session," Yale Law School, Lillian

Goldman Law Library, Avalon Project, 2008, http://avalon.law.yale.edu/imt/12 -04-45.asp.

31. Rome Statute, art. 8(1) *bis*.

32. Telford Taylor, *The Anatomy of the Nuremberg Trials: A Personal Memoir* (New York: Alfred A. Knopf, 1992), 580–97.

33. For an account of crimes against peace holdings against particular defendants, see Roger S. Clark, "Nuremberg and the Crime Against Peace," *Washington University Global Studies Law Review* 6 (2007): 527, 544–49. http://open scholarship.wustl.edu/law_globalstudies/vol6/iss3/6; but see Carrie McDougall, "The Crimes Against Peace Precedent," in Kress and Barriga, *Crime of Aggression*, 49, 52–55.

34. R. Clark, "Nuremberg", 531–33; but see Kevin Jon Heller, "Retreat from Nuremberg: The Leadership Requirement in the Crime of Aggression," *European Journal of International Law* 18 (2007): 477, 480.

35. R. Clark, "Nuremberg," 544.

36. "Nuremberg Trial Proceedings Volume 22: Two Hundred and Seventeenth Day," 426, Yale Law School, Lillian Goldman Law Library, Avalon Project, 2008, http://avalon.law.yale.edu/imt/09-30-46.asp.

37. "Nuremberg Trial Proceedings Volume 22: Two Hundred and Eighteenth Day," 524, Yale Law School, Lillian Goldman Law Library, Avalon Project, 2008, http://avalon.law.yale.edu/imt/10-01-46.asp; "Nuremberg Trial Proceedings Volume 9: Eighty-Seventh Day," 603, Yale Law School, Lillian Goldman Law Library, Avalon Project, 2008, http://avalon.law.yale.edu/imt/03-21-46.asp.

38. Ibid.

39. "Judgment: The Invasion of Denmark and Norway," Yale Law School, Lillian Goldman Law Library, Avalon Project, 2008, http://avalon.law.yale.edu /imt/juddenma.asp.

40. Ibid.

41. Ibid.

42. A new set of trials, collectively called the Subsequent Nuremberg Trials, began in the Allied-occupied zones in Germany. Four of the twelve trials conducted by the United States brought charges of crimes against peace and the fate of the so-called second-tier Nazis was determined in the I. G. Farben, High Command, Krupp, and Ministries cases. Kevin Jon Heller, *The Nuremberg Military Tribunals and the Origins of International Criminal Law* (New York: Oxford University Press, 2011), 179.

43. R. J. Pritchard, ed., *The Tokyo Major War Crimes Trial: The Transcripts of the Court Proceedings of the International Military Tribunal for the Far East*, 124 vols. (Lewiston, NY: Edwin Mellen, 1998); see also Sellars, "*Crimes against Peace*," 234–59.

44. See Henry Morgenthau Jr., *Germany is our Problem* (New York: Harper and Brothers, 1945).

45. Murray C. Bernays, "Subject: Trial of European War Criminals, 15 September 1944, Document 16," in *The American Road to Nuremberg; The Documentary Record 1944–1945*, ed. Bradley F. Smith (Stanford, CA: Hoover Institution Press, Stanford University, 1982), 33–37; see also Shane Darcy, *Collective Responsibility and Accountability under International Law* (Leiden: Transnational, 2007), 199.

46. "Affirmation of the Principles of International Law Recognized by the Charter of the Nürnberg Tribunal, G.A. Res. 95 (I), U.N. GAOR, 1st Sess., pt. 2, at 1144, U.N. Doc. A/236 (1946)," University of Minnesota Human Rights Library, n.d., https://www1.umn.edu/humanrts/instree/1946a.htm.

47. UN International Law Commission, "Principles of International Law Recognized in the Charter of the Nürnberg Tribunal and in the Judgment of the Tribunal" (UN, 1950), http://legal.un.org/ilc/texts/instruments/english/draft _articles/7_1_1950.pdf.

CHAPTER 4

1. Paul Wenthold, *Organic Chemistry for Engineers* (Perdue University, 2014), ch. 5, https://chem.libretexts.org/LibreTexts/Purdue/Purdue_Chem_26100%3A _Organic_Chemistry_I_(Wenthold)/Chapter_05%3A_The_Study_of_Chemical _Reactions/5.3.%09Free_Radicals/Free_Radicals.

2. Declaration of Principles (Atlantic Charter), 204 LNTS 384 (signed and entered into force August 14, 1941).

3. For an account of these negotiations, see Hathaway and Shapiro, *Internationalists*, 199–213, 250.

4. UN Charter, arts. 36–51.

5. Ibid., art. 51.

6. Quoted in Robert A. Divine, *Roosevelt and World War II* (Baltimore, MD: Johns Hopkins Press, 1969), 57.

7. John Lewis Gaddis, *The United States and the Origins of the Cold War, 1941–1947* (New York: Columbia University Press, 1972), 24–27.

8. Brian C. Rathbun, *Trust in International Cooperation: International Security Institutions, Domestic Politics and American Multilateralism* (New York: Cambridge University Press, 2012), 147.

9. Hathaway and Shapiro, *Internationalists*, 200.

10. Kennedy Graham and Tânia Felício, *Regional Security and Global Governance: A Study of Interaction between Regional Agencies and the U.N. Security Council with a Proposal for a Regional-Global Security Mechanism* (Brussels: VUB University Press, 2006), 57–61.

11. UN Charter, art. 39.

12. Ibid., arts. 24 ("primary responsibility"), 9–22 ("The General Assembly"), 52–54 ("Regional Arrangements"), 92–96 ("The International Court of Justice").

13. Ibid., arts. 33, 35.

14. Ibid., arts. 92–96; Statute of the ICJ, arts. 34–38 (ch. II: "Competence of the Court").

15. Winston Churchill, "*Iron Curtain Speech*," History Guide, last updated December 27, 2014, http://www.historyguide.org/europe/churchill.html.

16. Security Council (SC) Res. S/1408/Rev.1 (1949), http://www.un.org/en/ga /search/view_doc.asp?symbol=S/1408/Rev.1.

17. *Report of the Open-Ended Working Group on the Question of Equitable Representation on and Increase in the Membership of the Security Council and*

Other Matters Related to the Security Council, UN Doc. A/58/47 (New York: UN, 2004), 17, http://www.un.org/ga/search/view_doc.asp?symbol=A/58/47(SUPP).

18. Ibid.

19. George Kennan to George Marshall, Telegram, February 22, 1946, Harry S. Truman Library and Museum, http://www.trumanlibrary.org/whistlestop/study _collections/coldwar/documents/pdf/6-6.pdf.

20. Benjamin Ferencz, *Defining International Aggression: The Search for World Peace; A Documentary History and Analysis*, vol. 2 (Dobbs Ferry, NY: Oceana, 1975), 4–5; Thomas Bruha, "The General Assembly's Definition of the Act of Aggression," in Kress and Barriga, *Crime of Aggression*, 147–54.

21. Sellars, "Tokyo Dissidents," 117.

22. "Question of Defining Aggression," UN GA Res. 1181 (November 29, 1957), 12th session, http://legal.un.org/docs/?symbol=A/RES/1181(XII).

23. Ferencz, *Defining International Aggression*, 7–9.

24. "Need to Expedite the Drafting of a Definition of Aggression in the Light of the Present International Situation," UN GA Res. 2330 (XXII) (December 18, 1967), https://unispal.un.org/DPA/DPR/unispal.nsf/0/7B5760D830995C2F8525 732C004C4751.

25. Benjamin B. Ferencz, "The United Nations Consensus Definition of Aggression: Sieve or Substance?" *Journal of International Law and Economics* 10 (1975): 708.

26. "Einsatzgruppen Trial: US Prosecution Opens Case against Einsatzgruppen Members Nuremberg, Germany, September 29, 1947," US Holocaust Memorial Museum, n.d., accessed September 13, 2016, https://www.ushmm.org/wlc/en /media_fi.php?ModuleId=10007080andMediaId=184, quote at 0:23–0:45.

27. "Bio," BenFerencz.Org, n.d., accessed April 24, 2016, http://www.benfer encz.org/#bio.

28. For an account of the invention of the concepts of genocide and crimes against humanity, see Philippe Sands, *East West Street: On the Origins of "Genocide" and "Crimes Against Humanity"* (New York: Vintage Books, 2016).

29. Author's Preface to Ferencz, *Defining International Aggression*.

30. Benjamin B. Ferencz, *Enforcing International Law: A Way to World Peace* (London: Oceana, 1983), 479–89.

31. Federica D'Alessandra, *'Law, Not War': Ferencz' 70-Year Fight for a More Just and Peaceful World* (Brussels: Torkel Opsahl Academic, 2018), http://www .toaep.org/ops-pdf/7-dalessandra.

32. Benjamin B. Ferencz, *An International Criminal Court: A Step Toward World Peace* (Dobbs Ferry, NY: Oceana, 1980), xi.

33. Ibid.

34. Henry Kissinger, "Peace, Legitimacy, and the Equilibrium (a Study of the Statesmanship of Castlereagh and Metternich)" (PhD thesis, Harvard University, 1954).

35. Francis Fukuyama, "A World Restored: Europe after Napoleon," *Foreign Affairs* (September/October 1997), https://www.foreignaffairs.com/reviews /capsule-review/1997-09-01/world-restored-europe-after-napoleon.

36. Walter Isaacson, *Kissinger: A Biography* (New York: Simon and Schuster, 2005; originally published 1992), 75.

37. Henry Kissinger, *Nuclear Weapons and Foreign Policy* (New York: Harper, 1957), 180–82.

38. See generally Gary J. Bass, *The Blood Telegram* (New York: Alfred A. Knopf, 2013).

39. Gary J. Bass, "Nixon and Kissinger's Forgotten Shame," *New York Times*, September 29, 2013, http://www.nytimes.com/2013/09/30/opinion/nixon-and -kissingers-forgotten-shame.html?_r=0.

40. Isaacson, *Kissinger*, 345–46.

41. Ibid., 349.

42. Shawcross, *Sideshow*, 391, 396.

43. "Secretary's Meetings with Foreign Minister Chatchai of Thailand," Memorandum of Conversation (November 26, 1975), National Security Archive at George Washington University, http://nsarchive.gwu.edu/NSAEBB/NSAEBB193 /HAK-11-26-75.pdf.

44. Ferencz, "Sieve or Substance," 708.

45. Tom Lehrer, "Stop Clapping, This Is Serious," *Sydney Morning Herald*, March 1, 2003, http://www.smh.com.au/articles/2003/02/28/1046407753895.html.

46. Niall Ferguson, *Kissinger: 1923–1968: The Idealist* (New York: Penguin, 2015), 24.

47. Greg Grandin, "*Kissinger 1923–1968: The Idealist* by Niall Ferguson Review—a Case of Wobbly Logic," *Guardian*, October 15, 2015, http://www .theguardian.com/books/2015/oct/15/kissinger-1923-to-1968-the-idealist-niall -ferguson-review-biography.

48. Bruha, "General Assembly's Definition," 147.

49. "Definition of Aggression," GA Res. 3314 (XXIX) (December 14, 1974), https://documents-dds-ny.un.org/doc/RESOLUTION/GEN/NR0/739/16/IMG /NR073916.pdf (hereinafter 1974 Resolution).

50. Ibid.

51. Noah Weisbord, "Conceptualizing Aggression," *Duke Journal of Comparative and International Law* 20 (2009): 31–32.

52. "Definition of 'Aggressor' at the League of Nations Conference."

53. Weisbord, "Conceptualizing Aggression," 31–32.

54. Julius Stone, "Hopes and Loopholes in the 1974 Definition of Aggression," *American Journal of International Law* 71 (1977): 236.

55. Ferencz, "Sieve or Substance," 711.

56. Weisbord, "Conceptualizing Aggression," 32.

57. Julius Stone, "Hopes and Loopholes," 230.

58. Weisbord, "Conceptualizing Aggression," 38.

59. Vernon Cassin, Whitney Debevoise, Howard Kailes, and Terence W. Thompson, "The Definition of Aggression," *Harvard International Law Journal* 16 (1975): 599–600.

60. Julius Stone, "Hopes and Loopholes," 234.

61. 1974 Resolution, 144.

62. Ferencz, "Sieve or Substance," 714.

63. Ibid., 706.

64. Ibid., 717.

65. Steven Poole, "The Impossible World of MC Escher, " *Guardian*, 20 June 2015, https://www.theguardian.com/artanddesign/2015/jun/20/the-impossible-world-of-mc-escher.

66. Brian Urquhart, *Hammarskjöld* (repr. New York: W. W. Norton, 1994; originally published 1972), 261.

67. Ibid.

68. Oscar Schachter, "Dag Hammarskjöld and the Relation of Law to Politics," *American Journal of International Law* 56 (1962): 1–2.

69. Ibid., 7; see generally Gabriella Blum, *Islands of Agreement: Managing Enduring Armed Rivalries* (Cambridge, MA: Harvard University Press, 2007).

70. David Kennedy, *World of Struggle*, 234.

71. Ibid., 234–35.

72. Schachter, "Dag Hammarskjöld."

73. Ferguson, *Kissinger*, 294.

74. Dag Hammarskjöld, "The Development of a Constitutional Framework for International Cooperation: Address at the University of Chicago, Chicago, Illinois, May 1, 1960," UN Press Release SG/910 (April 29, 1960), http://www.un.org/depts/dhl/dag/docs/chicagospeech.pdf.

75. UN Secretary-General to the President of the General Assembly, Letter dated July 2, 2015, UN Doc. A/70/132 (July 2, 2015), https://digitallibrary.un.org/record/796005/files/A_70_132-EN.pdf; "Commission of Investigation into the Conditions and Circumstances Resulting in the Tragic Death of Mr. Dag Hammarskjold and of Members of the Party Accompanying Him," UN Doc. A/5069 (1962), http://www.hammarskjoldcommission.org/wp-content/uploads/2012/02/Report-of-the-U.N.-Commission-of-Investigation.pdf.

76. Susan Williams, *Who Killed Hammarskjöld?: The UN, the Cold War and White Supremacy in Africa* (London: Hurst, 2011); Julian Borger and Georgina Smith, "Dag Hammarskjöld: Evidence Suggests U.N. Chief's Plane Was Shot Down," *Guardian*, August 17, 2011, http://www.theguardian.com/world/2011/aug/17/dag-hammarskjold-un-secretary-general-crash.

77. Nina Strochlic, "Who Killed U.N. Secretary-General Dag Hammarskjöld?" *Daily Beast*, July 12, 2015, http://www.thedailybeast.com/articles/2015/07/12/who-killed-u-n-secretary-general-dag-hammarskjold.html.

78. Roger Lipsey, *Hammarskjöld: A Life* (Ann Arbor: University of Michigan Press, 2013), 585.

79. William Langewiesche, "The Wrath of Khan," *Atlantic*, November 2005, http://www.theatlantic.com/magazine/archive/2005/11/the-wrath-of-khan/304333/.

80. Ibid.

81. Ibid.

82. William Langewiesche, *The Atomic Bazaar: The Rise of the Nuclear Poor* (New York: Farrar, Straus, and Giroux, 2007), 80.

83. Ibid.

84. Ibid.

85. Langewiesche, "Wrath of Khan."

86. Ibid.

87. "Nuclear Black Markets: Pakistan, A.Q. Khan and the Rise of Proliferation Networks—A Net Assessment," International Institute for Strategic Studies, accessed April 24, 2016, https://www.iiss.org/en/publications/strategic%20dossiers/issues/nuclear-black-markets—pakistan—a-q—khan-and-the-rise-of-proliferation-networks—-a-net-assessmen-23e1.

CHAPTER 5

1. Francis Fukuyama, "The End of History?" *National Interest* 16 (summer 1989): 4.

2. John Mueller, *The Obsolescence of Major War* (New York: Basic Books, 1989), 6.

3. George H. W. Bush, "Address before a Joint Session of the Congress on the Persian Gulf Crisis and the Federal Budget Deficit," September 11, 1990, published online by Gerhard Peters and John T. Woolley, *The American Presidency Project*, 1999–2018, http://www.presidency.ucsb.edu/ws/?pid=18820.

4. Bobbitt, *Shield of Achilles*, 609–10.

5. G.H.W. Bush, "Address Before a Joint Session."

6. Irving Kristol, *Neoconservatism: The Autobiography of an Idea* (New York: Free Press, 1995).

7. Franklin Foer, "Once Again, America First," *New York Times*, October 10, 2004, http://www.nytimes.com/2004/10/10/books/review/10FOERL.html.

8. Tony Blair, "Doctrine of the International Community," Speech to the Economic Club of Chicago, April 22, 1999, https://www.econclubchi.org/speakers/ (under 1999 on timeline, as "The Right Honorable Tony Blair, Prime Minister of Great Britain, speaks to The Economic Club on April 22, 1999").

9. John Dinges, *Our Man in Panama: The Shrewd Rise and Brutal Fall of Manuel Noriega* (New York: Times Books, 1991), 308; Steve Albert, *The Case against the General: Manuel Noriega and the Politics of American Justice* (New York: Charles Scribner's Sons, 1993), 69–92; Manuel Noriega and Peter Eisner, *America's Prisoner: The Memoirs of Manuel Noriega* (New York: Random House, 1997).

10. "Noriega Surrenders to U.S.," *ABC News* (video), January 3, 1990, https://abcnews.go.com/Archives/video/jan-1990-noriega-surrenders-us-12501505, at 4:04–4:11.

11. Ibid., 4:39–4:48.

12. "The Issue of Civilian Casualties Revisited," Human Rights Watch, April 7, 1991, https://www.hrw.org/legacy/campaigns/iraq/panama91_appen.htm; Norman Cousins, "What's the Truth on Panama Casualties?" *Christian Science Monitor*, October 16, 1991; Ellen Quigley, "Estimates of Panamanian Casualties Not a Secret," Letter to the Editor, *Christian Science Monitor*, November 16, 1990; Kenneth Freed, "Panama Tries to Bury Rumors of Mass Graves," *Los Angeles Times*, October 27, 1991; Godfrey Harris, "Casualties in Panama," Letter to the Editor, *Los Angeles Times*, November 12, 1990; Lee Hockstader, "In Panama, Civilian Deaths Remain an Issue," *Washington Post*, October 6, 1990.

13. See generally Dinges, *Our Man in Panama*; Albert, *Case against the General*; Noriega and Eisner, *America's Prisoner*.

14. Thomas C. Hayes, "Confrontation in the Gulf: The Oilfield Lying below the Iraq-Kuwait Dispute," *New York Times*, September 3, 1990, http://www.ny times.com/1990/09/03/world/confrontation-in-the-gulf-the-oilfield-lying-below -the-iraq-kuwait-dispute.html?pagewanted=all; Reza Ekhtiari Amiri and Fak-hreddin Soltani, "Iraqi Invasion of Kuwait as Turning Point in Iran-Saudi Rela-tionship," *Journal of Politics and Law* 4, no. 1 (2011): 189.

15. "Churchill Proposes an Armed League," *Milwaukee Journal*, May 24, 1944, 1.

16. George H. W. Bush, "Address Before a Joint Session of the Congress on the Cessation of the Persian Gulf Conflict," March 6, 1991, published online by Ger-hard Peters and John T. Woolley, *The American Presidency Project*, 1999–2018, http://www.presidency.ucsb.edu/ws/?pid=19364.

17. Foer, "Once Again, America First"; Chris Woltermann, "What Is Paleocon-servatism?" *Telos*, fall 1993, 9–20.

18. David Brooks, "Buchanan Feeds Class War in the Information Age," *Los Angeles Times*, October 31, 1999, http://articles.latimes.com/1999/oct/31 /opinion/op-28187.

19. Tim Alberta, "The Ideas Made It, But I Didn't," *Politico Magazine*, May/June 2017, http://www.politico.com/magazine/story/2017/04/22/pat-buchanan-trump -president-history-profile-215042.

20. "Whatever Happened to the Iraqi Kurds?" Human Rights Watch, March 10, 1991, http://www.refworld.org/docid/47fdfb1b0.html; Shane Harris and Mat-thew M. Aid, "Exclusive: CIA Files Prove America Helped Saddam as He Gassed Iran," *Foreign Policy*, August 26, 2013, http://foreignpolicy.com/2013/08/26/exclusive -cia-files-prove-america-helped-saddam-as-he-gassed-iran/?utm_content=bufferec2f bandutm_medium=socialandutm_source=facebook.comandutm_campaign=buffer; Samantha Power, *A Problem from Hell: America and the Age of Genocide* (repr., New York: Basic Books, 2013), 172: "In 1987–1988 Saddam Hussein's forces destroyed several thousand Iraqi Kurdish villages and hamlets and killed close to 100 000 Iraqi Kurds, nearly all of whom were unarmed and many of whom were women and children."

21. William A. Schabas, "Issue #15: Should Saddam Hussein Be Prosecuted for the Crime of Aggression?" *Grotian Moment Blog*, Iraqi High Tribunals Trials, Case Western Reserve University School of Law, October 19, 2005, ac-cessed October 11, 2007, https://law.case.edu/Academics/Centers-and-Institutes /Cox-International-Law-Center/Grotian-Moment/ArtMID/804/ArticleID/504.

22. Gerald B. Helman and Steven R. Ratner, "Saving Failed States," *Foreign Policy*, winter 1992–93 (published online June 15, 2010): 3, https://foreignpolicy .com/2010/06/15/saving-failed-states/ (the "failed nation-state" is "utterly inca-pable of sustaining itself as a member of the international community").

23. Permanent Representative of the United States of America to the Secretary-General of the United Nations, letter dated September 23, 2014, UN Doc. S/2014/695 (September 23, 2014). https://www.securitycouncilreport.org/atf/cf /%7B65BFCF9B-6D27-4E9C-8CD3-CF6E4FF96FF9%7D/s_2014_695.pdf.

24. SC Res. 794 (December 3, 1992), http://unscr.com/en/resolutions/doc/794.

25. SC Res. 751 (April 24, 1992), establishing UNOSOM I, United Nations Operation in Somalia (April 1992–March 1993).

26. Jim Hoagland, "Prepared for Non-combat," *Washington Post*, April 15, 1993; "Beware 'Mission Creep' in Somalia," *Washington Post*, July 20, 1993.

27. David Scheffer, "Toward a Modern Doctrine of Humanitarian Intervention," *University of Toledo Law Review* 23 (1992): 253.

28. David Scheffer, *All the Missing Souls: A Personal History of the War Crimes Tribunals* (Princeton, NJ: Princeton University Press, 2012), 47.

29. Power, *Problem from Hell*, 329–89.

30. Alison Des Forges, *Leave None to Tell the Story* (New York: Human Rights Watch, 1999), 183.

31. But see Gérard Prunier, *The Rwanda Crisis: History of a Genocide* (New York: Columbia University Press, 1997), 105 (discussing geostrategic analysis, stating that "according to the Fashoda syndrome, the whole world is a cultural, political and economic battlefield between France and the 'Anglo-Saxons' ").

32. Samuel Huntington, "The Clash of Civilizations," *Foreign Affairs* (summer 1993), https://www.foreignaffairs.com/articles/united-states/1993-06-01/clash-civilizations.

33. Charles Krauthammer, "The Unipolar Moment," *Foreign Affairs* (1990–91), 23–33.

34. Samantha Power, "Bystanders to Genocide," *Atlantic*, September 2001, http://www.theatlantic.com/magazine/archive/2001/09/bystanders-to-genocide/304571/; see also Power, *Problem from Hell*, 329–89.

35. Ibid., 380; Alissa J. Rubin and Maia de la Baume, "Claims of French Complicity in Rwanda's Genocide Rekindle Mutual Resentment," *New York Times*, April 8, 2014, http://www.nytimes.com/2014/04/09/world/africa/claims-of-french-complicity-in-rwandas-genocide-rekindle-mutual-resentment.html: "In the years leading up to the genocide, the French government supported the government of Rwanda, which was then dominated by the Hutu majority, helping to equip, arm and, according to many, train the Rwandan military. Many of those same military forces later spearheaded the slaughter of Tutsis after Rwanda's president at the time, Juvenal Habyarimana, was killed in April 1994. As the genocide unfolded and France continued to support the Hutu government . . ."

36. Roméo Dallaire, *Shake Hands with the Devil: The Failure of Humanity in Rwanda* (Toronto: Random House Canada, 2004), 269.

37. Michael Ignatieff, *Blood and Belonging: Journeys into the New Nationalism* (Toronto: Viking, 1993), 2.

38. Ibid.

39. Roy Gutman, "Ethnic Cleansing: Yugoslavs Try to Deport 1800 Muslims to Hungary," *Newsday*, July 3, 1992, http://www.newsday.com/news/nationworld/world/ny-gutman070392,0,966015.story; "Prisoners of Serbia's War: Tales of Hunger, Torture at Camp in North Bosnia," *Newsday*, July 19, 1992, http://www.newsday.com/news/nationworld/world/ny-gutman071992,0,2407814.story.

40. SC Res. 819, UN Doc. S/RES/819 (April 16, 1993).

41. "The Fall of Srebrenica and the Failure of UN Peacekeeping," Human Rights Watch, October 15, 1995, https://www.hrw.org/report/1995/10/15/fall-srebrenica-and-failure-un-peacekeeping/bosnia-and-herzegovina.

42. Richard Holbrooke, *To End a War* (New York: Random House, 1998), 64, 68–72, 209, 226–27; Ivo H. Daalder, "Decision to Intervene: How the War in

Bosnia Ended," Brookings, December 1998, http://www.brookings.edu/research/articles/1998/12/balkans-daalder.

43. Ibid.

44. Hans Corell, Helmut Türk, and Gro Hillestad Thune, "Report: Rapporteurs (Corell – Türk – Thune) under the Moscow Human Dimension Mechanism to Croatia" (n.p., 1992), 51, http://www.havc.se/res/SelectedMaterial/19921007cscereportoncroatia.pdf.

45. Payam Akhavan, *In Search of a Better World: A Human Rights Odyssey* (Toronto: House of Anansi, 2017), 122.

46. Corell et al., "Report," 19.

47. Akhavan, *Better World*, 122.

48. Payham Akhavan, interviewed by the author in Montreal in March 2014.

49. Ibid.

50. Ibid.

51. Akhavan, *Better World*, 124.

52. Roger S. Clark, "Negotiations on the Rome Statute, 1995–1998," in Kress and Barriga, *Crime of Aggression*, 245–46.

53. ILC, "Draft Code of Crimes against the Peace and Security of Mankind," Yb ILC (1996), vol. II, art. 16: "An individual who, as leader or organizer, actively participates in or orders the planning, preparation, initiation or waging of aggression committed by a State shall be responsible for a crime of aggression."

54. UN, *The Path to the Hague: Selected Documents on the Origins of the ICTY* (The Hague: ICTY, 2001; originally published 1995), 83; Tara John, "The Story of This Shocking Image from a Prison Camp in Bosnia Continues 25 Year Later," *Time*, November 22, 2017, http://time.com/5034826/fikret-alic-time-cover-bosnia/.

55. Scheffer, *All the Missing Souls*, 16: "Though the UN Security Council would soon leapfrog their initiative," recalls Scheffer, "Corell's group nonetheless submitted important draft concepts to the United Nations that helped frame the ultimate statute of the Yugoslav Tribunal."

56. The ICTY was created by a Chapter VII resolution rather than trusting to states to negotiate a treaty that could be delayed or diluted. SC Res. 827 (May 25, 1993).

57. Scheffer, *All the Missing Souls*, 12.

58. Ibid., 7.

59. Samuel Moyn, "From Aggression to Atrocity: Rethinking the History of International Criminal Law," in *Oxford Handbook of International Criminal Law*, ed. Kevin Jon Heller, Frédéric Mégret, Sarah M. H. Nouwen, Jens David Ohlin, and Darryl Robinson, 4 (forthcoming).

60. UN, *Principles of International Law Recognized in the Charter of the Nürnberg Tribunal and in the Judgment of the Tribunal* (UN, 2005; originally published 1950), 3 (Principle VI), http://legal.un.org/ilc/texts/instruments/english/draft_articles/7_1_1950.pdf.

61. Carol Off, *The Lion, the Fox and the Eagle* (Toronto: Vintage Canada, 2001), 271–72; Stephen Kinzer, "Germans Arrest Serb as Balkan War Criminal," *New York Times*, February 16, 1994, http://www.nytimes.com/1994/02/16/world/germans-arrest-serb-as-balkan-war-criminal.html.

62. Prosecutor v. Tadić, Case No. IT-94-1-I, Indictment, para. 5.1 (ICTY 1995).

63. *Tadić*, Case No. IT-94-1-T, Decision on Defence Motion for Interlocutory Appeal on Jurisdiction (ICTY October 2, 1995); ibid., Opinion and Judgment (ICTY May 7, 1997); *Tadić*, Case No. IT-94-1-A, Appeals Chamber Judgment (ICTY July 15, 1999).

64. *Tadić*, Case No. IT-94-1-T, Appeals Chamber Decision, para. 135 (ICTY October 2, 1995), "Decision on the Defence Motion for Interlocutory Appeal on Jurisdiction."

65. Ibid., Trial Chamber, Opinion and Judgment, para. 192 (ICTY May 7, 1997).

66. *Tadić*, Case No. IT-94-1-A, Appeals Chamber Judgment, paras. 220, 227–28 (ICTY July 15, 1999); Allison Marston Danner and Jenny S. Martinez, "Guilty Associations: Joint Criminal Enterprise, Command Responsibility, and the Development of International Criminal Law," *California Law Review* 93 (2005): 133; Mark J. Osiel, "The Banality of Good: Aligning Incentives against Mass Atrocity," *Columbia Law Review* 105 (2005): 1786.

67. SC Res. 955 (November 8, 1994).

68. SC Res. 1503 (August 28, 2003) (granting the ICTR its own prosecutor so that it no longer shared one with the ICTY).

69. Gary Bass, *Stay the Hand of Vengeance: The Politics of War Crimes Tribunals* (Princeton, NJ: Princeton University Press, 2000), 230–31.

70. Holbrooke, *To End a War*.

71. Aryeh Neier, *The International Human Rights Movement: A History* (Princeton, NJ: Princeton University Press, 2012), 268.

72. Scheffer, *All the Missing Souls,* 124–59, quote 125.

73. Prosecutor v. Milošević, Case No. IT-02-54, Initial Indictment "Kosovo" (ICTY May 22, 1999) (amended twice 2001).

74. "Milosevic Arrested, Jailed, Sedated," *CBC News*, April 1, 2001, http://www.cbc.ca/news/world/milosevic-arrested-jailed-sedated-1.267788.

75. Steven Erlanger and Carlotta Gall, "The Milosevic Surrender: The Overview; Milosevic Arrest Came with Pledge for a Fair Trial," *New York Times*, April 2, 2001, http://www.nytimes.com/2001/04/02/world/milosevic-surrender-overview-milosevic-arrest-came-with-pledge-for-fair-trial.html?pagewanted=all.

76. "Ninety were sentenced, nineteen were acquitted, thirteen were transferred to national courts for trial, and thirty-seven proceedings were terminated or the indictments withdrawn." "Infographic: ICTY Facts and Figures," UN, n.d., accessed September 15, 2018, http://www.icty.org/en/content/infographic-icty-facts-figures.

77. Ibid.

78. Kathryn Sikkink, *The Justice Cascade: How Human Rights Prosecutions Are Changing World Politics* (New York: W. W. Norton, 2011).

79. Independent International Commission on Kosovo, *The Kosovo Report: Conflict, International Response, Lessons Learned* 4 (Oxford: Oxford University Press, 2000).

80. See Michael Ignatieff, *Virtual War: Kosovo and Beyond* (New York: Picador, 2000), 17–87, for a debate between Michael Ignatieff and Robert Skidelsky.

81. International Commission on Intervention and State Sovereignty, *The Responsibility to Protect* (Ottawa: International Development Research Centre, 2001), viii, http://responsibilitytoprotect.org/ICISS%20Report.pdf.

82. Ibid.
83. Kofi A. Annan, "Annual Report to the General Assembly," Address to the opening meeting of the UN GA, September 20, 1999, SG/SM/7136, https://www.un.org/press/en/1999/19990920.sgsm7136.html.
84. Ibid.
85. Minow, *Between Vengeance and Forgiveness*, 1; and on the same page: "The capacity and limitations of these legal responses illuminate the hopes and commitments of individuals and societies seeking, above all, some rejoinder to the unspeakable destruction and degradation of human beings."
86. Office of the President of the Republic of Rwanda, *Report on the Reflection Meetings Held in the Office of the President of the Republic from May 1998 to March 1999* (Kigali, August 1999), 51, https://repositories.lib.utexas.edu/bitstream/handle/2152/4907/2378.pdf?sequence=1.
87. Noah Weisbord, "The Law and Ethics of Gacaca: Balancing Justice and Healing in Post-Genocide Rwanda" (2004), 51 (unpublished LLM thesis, Harvard Law School; on file with Harvard Law School Library).
88. Urusaro Alice Karekezi, Alphonse Nshimiyimana, and Beth Mutamba, "Localizing Justice: Gacaca Courts in Post-Genocide Rwanda," in *My Neighbor, My Enemy: Justice and Community in the Aftermath of Mass Atrocity*, ed. Eric Stover and Harvey M. Weinstein, 69 (Cambridge, UK: Cambridge University Press, 2004); Weisbord, "Law and Ethics of Gacaca."
89. *Inyangamugayo* is Kinyarwandan for people of integrity.
90. Minow, *Between Vengeance and Forgiveness*, 118.
91. "Justice Compromised: The Legacy of Rwanda's Community-Based Gacaca Courts," Human Rights Watch, May 31, 2011, https://www.hrw.org/report/2011/05/31/justice-compromised/legacy-rwandas-community-based-gacaca-courts.
92. Ibid.
93. George W. Bush, "Address to a Joint Session of Congress and the American People," September 20, 2001, White House, https://georgewbush-whitehouse.archives.gov/news/releases/2001/09/20010920-8.html.

CHAPTER 6

1. "Literary Themes Coming of Age," Literary Articles, August 19, 2012, http://literacle.com/literary-themes-coming-of-age/.
2. Benjamin B. Ferencz, "Needed: A World Criminal Court," BenFerencz.org, June 29, 1998, http://www.benferencz.org/1990–1999.html#needed (appearing originally in the newspaper *Neue Zürcher Zeitung*).
3. Justice Jackson to President Truman, letter dated October 7, 1946, Yale Law School, Lillian Goldman Law Library, February 5, 2016, Perma.cc record https://perma.cc/W9CP-95VN. Thanks to Don Ferencz for reminding me of this quote.
4. Ferencz, "Needed."
5. See R. Clark, "Rome Statute," 260–68; Herman von Hebel and Darryl Robinson, "Crimes within the Jurisdiction of the Court," in *The International Criminal Court: The Making of the Rome Statute, Issues, Negotiations, Results*, ed. Roy S.

Lee, 79, 81, 84–85 (The Hague: Kluwer Law International, 1999); Fernández de Gurmendi, "Completing the Work," 589; Scheffer, *All the Missing Souls*, 163–226 (an insider's discussion of the key issues facing the US delegation); M. Cherif Bassiouni and Benjamin B. Ferencz, "The Crime Against Peace," in *International Criminal Law*, vol. I, ed. M. Cherif Bassiouni, 2nd ed., 346 (Ardsley, NY: Transnational, 1999).

6. Mohamed M. El Zeidy, "The Arab World," in Kress and Barriga, *Crime of Aggression*, 965–67; Philippe Kirsch and John T. Holmes, "The Birth of the International Criminal Court: The 1998 Rome Conference," *Canadian Yearbook of International Law* 36 (1998): 10, 30–31; Niels Blokker, "The Crime of Aggression and the United Nations Security Council," *Leiden Journal of International Law* 20, no. 4 (2007): 874–75.

7. David Scheffer, "Excerpts from *All the Missing Souls: A Personal History of the War Crimes Tribunals*," *Eyes on the ICC* 9, no. 1 (2012–13): 1.

8. R. Clark, "Rome Statute," 264–67; Bassiouni and Ferencz, "Crime Against Peace," 346.

9. Rome Statute, arts. 5(1)(d), 5(2), 121, 123.

10. "UN Diplomatic Conference Concludes in Rome with Decision to Establish Permanent International Criminal Court," Press Release L/2889, UN, July 20, 1998, https://www.un.org/press/en/1998/19980720.l2889.html.

11. Richard Dicker, in "The Reckoning: Law or War: The Creation of the International Criminal Court," Facing History and Ourselves, n.d. (video), https://www.facinghistory.org/reckoning/law-or-war-creation-international-criminal-court-0 (extract of film originally broadcast on *POV*, PBS, July 14, 2009).

12. Rome Statute, arts. 12–13.

13. Ibid., art. 16.

14. Ibid., art. 17.

15. Benjamin B. Ferencz, "Benjamin Ferencz Reflects on the Rome Conference," BenFerencz.org, July 1998, http://www.benferencz.org/1990–1999.html#romeconference.

16. Ibid.

17. See Marlies Glasius, "Expertise in the Cause of Justice: Global Civil Society Influence on the Statute for an International Criminal Court," in *Global Civil Society 2002*, ed. Marlies Glasius, Mary Kaldor, and Helmut Anheier, 137, 142–44 (Oxford: Oxford University Press, 2002); Noah Weisbord, "Civil Society," in Kress and Barriga, *Crime of Aggression*, 1310.

18. W. R. Pace and M. Thieroff, "Participation of Non-Governmental Organizations," in Lee, *International Criminal Court*, 393.

19. Erna Paris, *The Sun Climbs Slow: Justice in the Age of Imperial America* (Toronto: Alfred A. Knopf Canada, 2008), 247.

20. Ferencz, "Benjamin Ferencz Reflects."

21. "Saddam addresses Iraqi people," address to the Iraqi people regarding war in their country, *CNN.com/WORLD*, March 20, 2003, http://www.cnn.com/2003/WORLD/meast/03/20/irq.war.saddam.transcript/index.html.

22. Ibid.

23. George W. Bush, "President Says Saddam Hussein Must Leave Iraq within 48 Hours," Remarks by the president in Address to the Nation, White House, March 17, 2003, http://georgewbush-whitehouse.archives.gov/news/re

leases/2003/03/20030317-7.html; Jeffrey L. Dunoff, Steven R. Ratner, and David Wippman, *International Law: Norms, Actors, Process: A Problem-Oriented Approach*, 4th ed. (New York: Wolters Kluwer, 2015), 740: "In the months leading up to Operation Iraqi Freedom, the U.S. and British governments agreed that a material breach of Resolution 687 could revive Resolution 678's authorization to use force. However, the British Foreign and Commonwealth Office (FCO) believed that revival required a new Security Council finding, subsequent to Security Council Resolution 1441, that Iraq was in material breach of its obligations."

24. Ibid., 736.

25. UN SCOR, 57th Session, 4644th meeting, UN Doc. S/PV/4644 (November 8, 2002), 3: US ambassador to the UN John Negroponte: "This resolution contains no 'hidden triggers' and no 'automaticity' with respect to the use of force. If there is a further Iraqi breach, reported to the Council by U.N.MOVIC, the IAEA or a Member State, the matter will return to the Council for discussions as required in paragraph 12." "Threats and Responses; The Rationale for the U.N. Resolution on Iraq, in the Diplomats' Own Words," *New York Times*, November 9, 2002, https://www.nytimes.com/2002/11/09/world/threats-responses -rationale-for-un-resolution-iraq-diplomats-own-words.html.

26. White House, *The National Security Strategy of the United States of America* (Washington, September 2002), 6, 15, http://www.state.gov/documents /organization/63562.pdf: "For centuries, international law recognized that nations need not suffer an attack before they can lawfully take action to defend themselves against forces that present an imminent danger of attack."

27. G. W. Bush, "Saddam Hussein Must Leave."

28. Dunoff et al., *International Law*, 742.

29. Ibid.; Ewen MacAskill and Julian Borger, "Iraq War Was Illegal and Breached UN Charter, Says Annan," *Guardian*, September 16, 2004, https://www .theguardian.com/world/2004/sep/16/iraq.iraq.

30. "Wilmshurst Resignation Letter," *BBC News*, March 24, 2005, http://news .bbc.co.uk/2/hi/uk_news/politics/4377605.stm.

31. Jan Frel, "Could Bush Be Prosecuted for War Crimes?" AlterNet, July 9, 2006, http://www.alternet.org/story/38604/could_bush_be_prosecuted_for_war _crimes.

32. Quoted in ibid.

33. "Iraq Body Count," https://www.iraqbodycount.org, accessed April 26, 2016.

34. Frel, "Could Bush Be Prosecuted."

35. International Commission on Intervention and State Sovereignty, *Responsibility to Protect*, xi–xiii.

36. Ibid., 15–16; Ignatieff, *Virtual War*, 71–90.

37. Michael Ignatieff, "The American Empire; The Burden," *New York Times Magazine*, January 5, 2003, http://www.nytimes.com/2003/01/05/magazine/05 EMPIRE.html?pagewanted=all.

38. Ibid.

39. See Michael Ignatieff, *Empire Lite: Nation-Building in Bosnia, Kosovo and Afghanistan* (London: Vintage, 2003), 17; Linda McQuaig, "Tears of an Intellectual Warmonger," *Guardian*, September 6, 2007, https://www.theguardian .com/commentisfree/2007/sep/06/intellectualwarmonger.

40. Peter Hart, "What Did Samantha Power Say about Iraq Invasion?" *FAIR*, June 10, 2013, http://fair.org/home/what-did-samantha-power-say-about -iraq-invasion/.

41. Samantha Power, "The Democrats and National Security," *New York Review of Books*, August 14, 2008, http://www.nybooks.com/articles/2008/08/14 /the-democrats-national-security/?pagination=false.

42. Ibid.

43. Michael Ignatieff, "Intervention, Legitimacy and the Moral Status of Prudence," The Intervention Seminar, Kennedy School of Government, Harvard University, April 4, 2005, 3.

44. Michael Ignatieff, "The Elusive Goal of War Trials," *Harper's Magazine*, March 1997: 15.

45. Michael Ignatieff, "Getting Iraq Wrong," *New York Times Magazine*, August 5, 2007, http://www.nytimes.com/2007/08/05/magazine/05iraq-t.html?_r=0.

46. Rory Stewart, *The Prince of the Marshes: And Other Occupational Hazards of a Year in Iraq* (Boston, MA: Houghton Mifflin Harcourt, 2006); Ian Parker, "Paths of Glory," *New Yorker Magazine*, November 15, 2010, http:// www.newyorker.com/magazine/2010/11/15/paths-of-glory-ian-parker.

47. See Rory Stewart, "Iraq Inquiry," Rory Stewarts's website, February 9, 2015, http://www.rorystewart.co.uk/iraq-inquiry/ (Stewart's 2015 testimony at the Iraq War Inquiry).

48. Jeffrey Rosen, "Conscience of a Conservative," *New York Times Magazine*, September 9, 2007, http://www.nytimes.com/2007/09/09/magazine/09rosen .html.

49. Goldsmith, *Terror Presidency*, 10.

50. Jack Goldsmith, "Democracy, Prudence, Intervention," Paper presented at the Intervention Seminar, December 2005, 2–3.

51. Minow, *Between Vengeance and Forgiveness*, 15.

52. Ibid., 29.

53. Payam Akhavan, "The Lord's Resistance Army Case: Uganda's Submission of the First State Referral to the International Criminal Court," *American Journal of International Law* 99 (2005): 404.

54. Ibid.

55. See Noah Weisbord, "When Peace and Justice Clash," *International Herald Tribune*, April 29, 2005.

56. Noah Weisbord, "Judging Aggression," *Columbia Journal of Transnational Law* 50 (2011), 127–34.

57. Harriet Alexander, "Last Child Soldiers in the Americas to Be Freed as FARC Agree to Release Colombia's Children," *Telegraph*, May 16, 2016, http:// www.telegraph.co.uk/news/2016/05/16/last-child-soldiers-in-the-americas-to-be -freed-as-farc-agree-to/; Sarah Crowe and Marty Logan, "Last Group of Maoist Child Soldiers Discharged in Nepal," UNICEF, February 17, 2010, http://www .unicef.org/protection/nepal_52791.html.

58. CTV.ca News Staff, "Sudan's Bashir Call Expelled Aid Groups 'Spies,'" *CTV News*, March 7, 2009, https://www.ctvnews.ca/sudan-s-bashir-calls-ex pelled-aid-groups-spies-1.377176; Xan Rice, "Sudan's President Orders All For-

eign Aid Groups to Leave Country within a Year," *Guardian*, March 16, 2009, https://www.theguardian.com/world/2009/mar/16/sudan-aid-agencies-expelled.

59. "Profile: Omar al Bashir," *Telegraph*, March 5, 2009, http://www.telegraph.co.uk/news/newstopics/profiles/4944799/Profile-Omar-al-Bashir.html.

60. ICC Office of the Prosecutor, "Third Report of the Prosecutor of the International Criminal Court to the UN Security Council Pursuant to UNSCR 1593" (June 14, 2006), 5–7, https://reliefweb.int/sites/reliefweb.int/files/resources/89C3AEAF4A935E47C125718E0037367E-icc-sdn-14jun.pdf.

61. Ibid., 6; Marlise Simons and Neil MacFarquhar, "Court Issues Arrest Warrant for Sudan's Leader", *New York Times*, March 4, 2009, https://www.nytimes.com/2009/03/05/world/africa/05court.html.

62. "ICC Prosecutor on Darfur Charges," *CNN*, July 14, 2008, http://www.cnn.com/2008/WORLD/africa/07/14/icc.transcript/index.html.

63. John Dugard, "Palestine and the International Criminal Court: Institutional Failure or Bias?" *Journal of International Criminal Justice* 11 (2013): 564–69.

64. Quoted in Marlise Simons, "Gambian Defends the International Criminal Court's Initial Focus on Africans," *New York Times*, February 26, 2007, http://www.nytimes.com/2007/02/26/world/africa/26hague.html?_r=2andoref=slogin%20/.

65. Beth van Schaack, "Immunity before the African Court of Justice and Human and Peoples Rights: The Potential Outlier," *Just Security*, July 10, 2014, https://www.justsecurity.org/12732/immunity-african-court-justice-human-peoples-rights-the-potential-outlier/; African Union Specialized Technical Committee on Justice and Legal Affairs, *Draft Protocol on Amendments to the Protocol on the Statute of the African Court of Justice and Human Rights*, Exp/Min/IV/Rev.7, annex art. 28(a) (Addis Ababa: African Union, May 15, 2012), https://africlaw.files.wordpress.com/2012/05/au-final-court-protocol-as-adopted-by-the-ministers-17-may.pdf.

66. Van Schaack, "Immunity before the African Court"; Shantanu Dey, "Protecting the Powerful: The African Union's Response to Allegations of Human Rights Violations," *Cambridge International Law Journal* (February 2, 2015), http://cilj.co.uk/2015/02/02/protecting-powerful-african-unions-response-allegations-human-rights-violations/.

67. Preparatory Commission for the ICC, Working Group on the Crime of Aggression, July 1–12, 2002, *Discussion Paper Proposed by the Coordinator*, PCNICC/2002/WGCA/RT.1/Rev.2 (July 11, 2002). For the views of Fernández de Gurmendi, see "Completing the Work"; Roger S. Clark, "Rethinking Aggression as a Crime and Formulating Its Elements: The Final Work-Product of the Preparatory Commission for the International Criminal Court," *Leiden Journal of International Law* 15 (2002): 859–90; Silvia A. Fernández de Gurmendi, "An Insider's View," in *The International Criminal Court and the Crime of Aggression*, ed. Mauro Politi and Giuseppe Nesi, 180–88 (Aldershot, UK: Ashgate, 2004).

68. The Special Working Group on the Crime of Aggression is a subsidiary body of the Assembly of States Parties to the Rome Statute of the International Criminal Court. It is nevertheless open to all states "on an equal footing." ICC, Assembly of States Parties, *Continuity of Work in Respect of the Crime of Aggression*,

3rd plenary meeting, ICC-ASP/1/Res.1 (September 9, 2002), para. 2, http://www
.un.org/law/icc/asp/1stsession/report/english/part_iv_res_1_e.pdf.

69. Michael Walzer, *Just and Unjust Wars: A Moral Argument with Historical
Illustrations* (New York: Basic Books, 1977).

70. Ibid., 31.

71. Frédéric Mégret, "What Is the Specific Evil of Aggression?" SSRN, March 28,
2012, p. 5, http://ssrn.com/abstract=2546732.

72. Ibid., 5; 1974 Resolution, Annex, art. 1.

73. Mégret, "Specific Evil of Aggression," 30. The philosopher Larry May
wrote a rigorous defense of this third view, arguing that aggression should be
understood not merely as a first strike against another state but as a wrong that
violates human rights. Larry May, *Aggression and Crimes Against Peace* (New
York: Cambridge University Press, 2008), 4.

74. Larry May, "Just War Theory and the Crime of Aggression," in Kress and
Barriga, *Crime of Aggression*, 278–281.

75. Quoted in Dan Skinner, "Introduction to Ferencz Address of Kampala
Conference on ICC," YouTube, June 13, 2011, at 4:20, https://www.youtube
.com/watch?v=qbW53DPLxWk.

76. See Stefan Barriga, "Against the Odds: The Results of the Special Working
Group on the Crime of Aggression," in *The Princeton Process on the Crime of
Aggression: Materials of the Special Working Group on the Crime of Aggres-
sion 2003–2009*, ed. Stefan Barriga, Wolfgang Danspeckgruber, and Christian
Wenaweser, 3–5 (Princeton, NJ: Liechtenstein Institute on Self-Determination, at
Princeton University, 2009).

77. See, e.g., the substantive comments of the representative of Samoa, legal
scholar Roger S. Clark, "Negotiating Provisions Defining the Crime of Aggression, Its Elements and the Conditions for ICC Exercise of Jurisdiction over It,"
European Journal International Law 20 (2009): 1103–15.

78. Phani Livada, of Greece, was in charge of the "basket" on the definition of
the state/collective act of aggression (the distinction between a just and an unjust
war), Claus Kress, of Germany, of the "basket" on the individual component of
the crime (linking the individual defendant to the collective act), and Pål Wrange,
of Sweden, on jurisdiction (the relationship between state sovereignty, the ICC,
and the Security Council).

79. Stefan Barriga, "Negotiating the Amendments on the Crime of Aggression," in *Travaux Préparatoires of the Crime of Aggression*, ed. Stefan Barriga and
Claus Kress, 15–16 (New York: Cambridge University Press, 2012).

80. Claus Kress and Leonie von Holtzendorff, "The Kampala Compromise on
the Crime of Aggression," *Journal of International Criminal Justice* 8 (2010): 1188.

81. Compare UN Charter, art. 2(4), with Rome Statute, art. 8 bis, para. 2: "For
the purpose of paragraph 1, 'act of aggression' means the use of armed force by a
State against the sovereignty, territorial integrity or political independence of another
State, or in any other manner inconsistent with the Charter of the United Nations."

82. Coalition for the ICC (CICC), "Report of the CICC Team Report on Ag-
gression," Informal Inter-Sessional Meeting of the Special Working Group on the
Crime of Aggression, Liechtenstein Institute On Self-Determination, Woodrow
Wilson School, Princeton University, United States, June 8–11, 2006 (August 26,

2006), para. 57, http://crimeofaggression.info/documents/6/2006_Princeton.pdf (hereinafter CICC 2006 Report); see Carrie McDougall, *The Crime of Aggression under the Rome Statute of the International Criminal Court* (New York: Cambridge University Press, 2013), for an account of these debates and the ideas underlying them.

83. CICC 2006 Report, paras. 70–72.

84. ICC, Assembly of States Parties, Special Working Group on the Crime of Aggression (SWGCA), *List of Acts that Qualify as an Act of Aggression*, Resumed 6th Sess., New York, November 30–December 14, 2007, ICC-ASP/6/SWGCA/1 (December 13, 2007), para. 18–23, http://www.iccnow.org/documents/ICC-ASP-6-SWGCA-1_English.pdf (hereinafter SWGCA December 2007 Report). See Nicolaos Strapatsas, "Rethinking General Assembly Resolution 3314 (1974) as a Basis for the Definition of Aggression under the Rome Statute of the ICC," in *Rethinking International Criminal Law: The Substantive Part*, ed. Olaoluwa Olusanya, 155, 160 (Groningen: Europa Law, 2007); see also Roger S. Clark, "Amendments to the Rome Statute of the International Criminal Court Considered at the First Review Conference on the Court, Kampala, 31 May–11 June 2010," *Goettingen Journal of International Law* 2 (2010): 696.

85. CICC 2006 Report, paras 21–24: while only "wars of aggression" were prosecutable at the International Military Tribunal at Nuremberg, "acts of aggression" were prosecutable at the successor trial.

86. Ibid., paras 14–24.

87. Language capturing nonstate actors perpetrating the crime of aggression is included in the Malabo Protocol. "Draft Protocol on Amendments to the Protocol on the Statute of the African Court of Justice and Human Rights," art. 28M, AU Doc. No. STC/Legal/Min. 7(1) Rev.1 (May 15, 2014) (hereinafter Malabo Protocol). The African Union Assembly adopted the Malabo Protocol on June 30, 2014, at its 23rd Ordinary Session. See AU Doc. No. Assembly/AU/Dec.529 (XXIII).

88. Barriga, "Against the Odds," 1.

89. Richard Goldstone, "Prosecuting Aggression," *New York Times*, May 26, 2010, http://www.nytimes.com/2010/05/27/opinion/27iht-edpoint.html.

90. Michael Glennon, "The Blank-Prose Crime of Aggression," *Yale Journal of International Law* 35 (2010): 72–73; for the contrary view, see Jennifer Trahan, "A Meaningful Definition of the Crime of Aggression: A Response to Michael Glennon," *Pennsylvania Journal of International Law* 33 (2012), http://scholarship.law.upenn.edu/cgi/viewcontent.cgi?article=1068andcontext=jil; Andreas Paulus, "Second Thoughts on the Crime of Aggression," *European Journal of International Law* 20 (2009): 1117–28; for a contrary view, see Claus Kress, "Time for Decision: Some Thoughts on the Immediate Future of the Crime of Aggression: A Reply to Andreas Paulus," *European Journal of International Law* 20 (2009): 1129–46.

91. Vijay Padmanabhan, John B. Bellinger III, and Matthew C. Waxman, "From Rome to Kampala: The U.S. Approach to the 2010 International Criminal Court Review Conference," Council on Foreign Relations, April 2010, p. 16, http://www.cfr.org/courts-and-tribunals/rome-kampala/p21934.

92. Kevin Jon Heller, comment posted on January 30, 2010, 9:11 a.m. EST, on "Thoughts on Glennon's 'Blank-Prose Crime of Aggression,'" *Opinio Juris*

(blog), January 29, 2010, 7:48 p.m., http://opiniojuris.org/2010 01 29/thoughts -on-glennons-blank-prose-crime-of-aggression/.

93. Noah Weisbord, "Who Started the Fight?" *New York Times*, May 3, 2010, http://www.nytimes.com/2010/05/04/opinion/04iht-edweisbord.html.

94. Weisbord, "Judging Aggression," 156–167.

95. Koh, "Obama Administration and International Law," 8.

96. SC Res. 1593 (March 31, 2005).

97. UN SCOR, 62nd Sess., 5789th meeting, UN Doc. S/PV.5789 (December 5, 2007), 11–12; see UN SCOR, 63rd Sess., 5912th meeting, UN Doc. S/PV.5912 (June 16, 2008), 2; ibid., 5905th meeting, UN Doc. S/PV.5905 (June 5, 2008), 2.

98. Michael Abramowitz and Colum Lynch, "Darfur Killings Soften Bush's Opposition to International Court," *Washington Post*, October 12, 2008, http://www .washingtonpost.com/wp-dyn/content/article/2008/10/11/AR2008101101964 .html.

99. Quoted in ibid.

100. But see Sean D. Murphy, "Aggression, Legitimacy and the International Criminal Court," *European Journal of International Law* 20 (2009): 1147–56; Padmanabhan et al., "From Rome to Kampala"; Antonio Cassese, "On Some Problematical Aspects of the Crime of Aggression," *Leiden Journal of International Law* 20 (2007): 841–49; James Nicholas Boeving, "Aggression, International Law, and the ICC: An Argument for the Withdrawal of Aggression from the Rome Statute," *Columbia Journal of Transnational Law* 43 (2005): 557–611.

101. Rome Statute, pt. III, "General Principles of Criminal Law."

102. Carrie McDougall, "When Law and Reality Clash: The Imperative of Compromise in the Context of the Accumulated Evil of the Whole—Conditions for the Exercise of the International Criminal Court's Jurisdiction over the Crime of Aggression," *International Criminal Law Review* 7 (2007): 277–333; Blokker, "Crime of Aggression," 867–94.

103. Koh and Buchwald, "Crime of Aggression," 260, 294.

104. Harold Hongju Koh, "Intervention at Kampala," Statement at the Review Conference of the ICC, US Department of State, June 4, 2010, https://2009-2017 .state.gov/s/l/releases/remarks/142665.htm; Stephen J. Rapp, "Statement to the Review Conference of the ICC," Department of State, June 1, 2010, https://2009 -2017.state.gov/j/gcj/us_releases/remarks/2010/142520.htm.

105. Koh, "Intervention at Kampala," and "Remarks at Kampala, Uganda: Closing Intervention at the Review Conference of the International Criminal Court," Department of State, June 11, 2010, https://2009-2017.state.gov/s/l/re leases/remarks/143218.htm.

106. William A. Schabas, "Kampala Diary 7/6/10," *The ICC Review Conference: Kampala 2010* (blog), June 8, 2010, http://iccreviewconference.blogspot .ca (quoting Bill Lietzau, legal advisor to the US secretary of defense, lamenting, "We chose not to be part of that process [the Special Working Group on the Crime of Aggression], and we have to live with the consequences").

107. For perspectives of the negotiators from Iran and the USA, see Djamchid Momtaz and Esmaeil Baghaei Hamaneh, "Iran," in Kress and Barriga, *Crime of Aggression*, 1174–97; Harold Hongju Koh and Todd F. Buchwald, "United States," in Kress and Barriga, *Crime of Aggression*, 1290–99.

108. GA Review Conference (RC), Res. 6, UN Doc. RC/Res.6 (June 11, 2010), Annex III, paras. 6–7, http://crimeofaggression.info/documents/6/RC-Res6-ENG (hereinafter Kampala Compromise).

109. Kress and von Holtzendorff, "Kampala Compromise," 1205–7.

110. Claus Kress, "The State Conduct Element," in Kress and Barriga, *Crime of Aggression*, 507–13.

111. Stefan Barriga and Leena Grover, "A Historic Breakthrough on the Crime of Aggression," *American Journal of International Law* 105 (2011): 519–20: "Reopening the definition of the crime was not supported by U.S. allies among the states parties, however, and was strongly rejected by others; since the definition, with its delicate and deliberate wording, was the product of years of difficult debate, new discussions were simply out of the question."

112. Harold Hongju Koh and Stephen J. Rapp, "U.S. Engagement with the ICC and the Outcome of the Recently Concluded Review Conference," Special Briefing, June 15, 2010, https://2009-2017.state.gov/j/gcj/us_releases/remarks /2010/143178.htm: "We think that with respect to the two new crimes, the outcome protected our vital interests. The court cannot exercise jurisdiction over the crime of aggression without a further decision to take place sometime after January 1st, 2017. The prosecutor cannot charge nationals of non-state parties, including U.S. nationals, with a crime of aggression. No U.S. national can be prosecuted for aggression so long as the U.S. remains a non-state party. And if we were to become a state party, we'd still have the option to opt out from having our nationals prosecuted for aggression. So we ensure total protection for our Armed Forces and other U.S. nationals going forward."

113. But see Koh and Buchwald, "Crime of Aggression," 270: "The absence of an explicit requirement that a state have waged a 'war of aggression' appeared to depart from customary international law and was another point that significantly concerned the United States."

114. Wittes and Blum, *Future of Violence*, 5: "Modern technology enables individuals to wield the destructive power of states"; Weisbord, "Conceptualizing Aggression," 29–32; Martin van Creveld, *The Transformation of War* (New York: Free Press, 1991), 10–18; Robb, *Brave New War*, 7.

115. Rome Statute, art. 121(5); see Stefan Barriga and Niels Blokker, "Entry into Force and Conditions for the Exercise of Jurisdiction: Cross-Cutting Issues," in Kress and Barriga, *Crime of Aggression*, 623–25; Stefan Barriga and Niels Blokker, "Conditions for the Exercise of Jurisdiction Based on State Referrals and *Proprio Motu* Investigations," in Kress and Barriga, *Crime of Aggression*, 655–56; Roger S. Clark, "Ambiguities in Articles 5(2), 121 and 123 of the Rome Statute," *Case Western Reserve Journal of International Law* 41 (2009): 413 (discussing "fundamental ambiguity" of provision); Barriga and Grover, "Historic Breakthrough," 523–24.

116. Ibid., 524: "Those delegations preferring a consent-based regime (in particular, Australia, Canada, New Zealand, most European states, and permanent members of the Security Council) argued for Article 121(5), which had the additional advantage that the exercise of jurisdiction could, in principle, begin after the first ratification. Those arguing for Article 121(4) (in particular, all of the African states, members of the Non-aligned Movement, and most Latin American

and Caribbean countries) stressed that the crime of aggression should be treated equally to the other core crimes: requiring aggressor state consent would depart from the territoriality principle enshrined in Article 12(2) of the Statute and lead to impunity rather than preventing aggression and protecting potential victims of this crime." See also William A. Schabas, "Kampala Diary 8/6/10," *The ICC Review Conference: Kampala 2010* (blog), June 9, 2010, http://iccreviewconference.blogspot.ca.

117. In March 2010 an informal "roll call" was taken on the question. The following countries expressed a preference for a consent-based regime: Albania, Andorra, Australia, Austria, Belgium, Bulgaria, Canada, Columbia, Croatia, Estonia, Fiji, France, Germany, Hungary, Ireland, Italy, Japan, Latvia, Luxembourg, Macedonia (FYROM), Mexico, the Netherlands, Norway, Paraguay, Peru, Poland, Portugal, New Zealand, Slovakia, Spain, Sweden, and the United Kingdom. The following countries expressed a preference for a regime that is not based on the consent of the alleged aggressor state: Argentina, Belize, Bolivia, Botswana, Brazil, Burkina Faso, Chile, Congo, Costa Rica, Democratic Republic of Congo, Djibouti, Ecuador, Finland, Gabon, Ghana, Greece, Guinea, Guyana, Jordan, Kenya, Lesotho, Madagascar, Namibia, Nigeria, Republic of Korea, Romania, Samoa, Senegal, Slovenia, South Africa, Switzerland, Tanzania, Trinidad and Tobago, Uganda, Venezuela, and Zambia. The result of the roll call outlined here is based on the notes of Liechtenstein delegate Stefan Barriga, whose delegation led the negotiations and who was present at that meeting. See Stefan Barriga, "Exercise of Jurisdiction and Entry into Force of the Amendments on the Crime of Aggression," Belgian Interministerial Commission for Humanitarian Law: Colloquium "From Rome to Kampala," Brussels, June 5, 2012 (version with minor updates as of June 2016); Barriga and Grover, "Historic Breakthrough," 524.

118. Kress and von Holtzendorff, "Kampala Compromise," 1213; Barriga and Grover, "Historic Breakthrough," 524.

119. See Barriga and Grover, "Historic Breakthrough," 520: "Ambassador Wenaweser and Prince Zeid pursued 'shuttle diplomacy' with individual delegations and groups, among them the permanent members of the Security Council (who also often met individually with one or both of them), the African Group (which was keenly interested in reaching a consensus on this issue on African soil), the Group of Latin American and Caribbean Countries (with strong leadership from Argentina and Brazil), the Group of Eastern European States, and a largely Western group of "like-minded" countries."

120. Barriga and Blokker, "Exercise of Jurisdiction," 623–26.

121. "Non-Paper Submitted by the Delegations of Argentina, Brazil and Switzerland as of 6 June 2010," in Barriga and Kress, *Travaux Préparatoires*, 740–42.

122. "Non-Paper Submitted by the Delegation of Canada as of 8 June 2010," in Barriga and Kress, *Travaux Préparatoires*, 753.

123. Barriga and Blokker, "Exercise of Jurisdiction," 624.

124. William A. Schabas, "Success!!!," *The ICC Review Conference: Kampala 2010* (blog), June 12, 2010, http://iccreviewconference.blogspot.ca.

125. Apparently a quorum had been met, but just barely. See Barriga and Grover, "Historic Breakthrough," 520: "Article 121(3) of the Rome Statute requires

a two-thirds majority of states parties (111 at the time) for the adoption of an amendment—that is, at least 74 votes. But only 84 states parties to the Rome Statute had made the journey to Kampala, and some delegations left before the final meeting of the conference, thereby handing the blocking minority to a mere half-dozen delegations."

126. Kress and von Holtzendorff, "Kampala Compromise," 1180. See also Schabas, "Success!!!"

127. Rome Statute, arts. 6–8.

128. Kampala Compromise.

CHAPTER 7

1. Benjamin B. Ferencz, "Enabling the International Criminal Court to Punish Aggression," *Washburn University Global Studies Law Review* 6, no. 3 (2007): 559–60.

2. For a nuanced commentary on the state-conduct components of the definition of the crime of aggression, see Kress, "State Conduct Element," 412.

3. For a nuanced commentary on the individual-conduct components of the definition of the crime of aggression, see Roger S. Clark, "Individual Conduct," in Kress and Barriga, *Crime of Aggression*, 565.

4. "Resource Center," "What is Judicial Independence?" Canadian Judicial Council, n.d., accessed August 3, 2016, https://www.cjc-ccm.gc.ca/english /resource_en.asp?selMenu=resource_judges_en.asp: "It is important to remember that the courts do not make new laws; they make decisions based on existing laws that the government has passed."

5. Minow, *Between Vengeance and Forgiveness*, 25.

6. Osborn v. Bank of United States, 22 U.S. (9 Wheat.) 738, 6 Law Ed. 204 (1824).

7. Edward. A. Purcell, *The Crisis of Democratic Theory: Scientific Naturalism and the Problem of Value* (1973), 75; but see Jerome Frank, "Mr. Justice Holmes and Non-Euclidean Legal Thinking," *Cornell Law Review* 17 (1932): 568, http:// scholarship.law.cornell.edu/clr/vol17/iss4/2.

8. Duncan Kennedy, *A Critique of Adjudication: Fin de Siècle* (repr., Cambridge, MA: Harvard University Press, 1997), 3: The mythic judge is not just master of self-control, but he is also "wielder of trained moral intuition" and "scourge of corruption."

9. Ibid., 2 ,14.

10. See David Kennedy, *The Dark Sides of Virtue: Reassessing International Humanitarianism* (Princeton, NJ: Princeton University Press, 2005) 236.

11. David Kennedy, *World of Struggle*, 260.

12. Ibid, 276.

13. See, e.g., Goldsmith and Posner, *Limits of International Law*, 100.

14. Ibid., book jacket.

15. Akhavan, "Beyond Impunity," 9.

16. Drumbl, "Punishment, Postgenocide," 1255.

17. Minow, *Between Vengeance and Forgiveness*, 12.

18. Ibid.; Hampton, "Correcting Harms," 1659.

19. Minow, *Between Vengeance and Forgiveness*, 123.

20. In his essay "The Idler," Samuel Johnson writes, "Among the calamities of war may be justly numbered the diminution of the love of truth, by the falsehoods which interest dictates and credulity encourages." Samuel Johnson, "No. 30. Corruption of News-Writers," in *Essays from the "Rambler," "Adventurer," and "Idler,"* ed. W. J. Bate, 287–90 (originally published in *The Idler*; New Haven, CT: Yale University Press, 1968).

21. Richard Ashby Wilson, *Writing History in International Criminal Trials* (New York: Cambridge University Press, 2011), 1–23; Darrell A. H. Miller, "Text, History, and Tradition: What the Seventh Amendment Can Teach Us about the Second," *Yale Law Journal* 122 (2013): 935: "Judges are not historians, and so, in addition to the risk that they will not understand the materials they are charged to consult, there is the additional risk that they will not conduct a dispassionate examination of the historical evidence and will simply marshal historical anecdotes to achieve what they have already decided is the preferred outcome."

22. Rome Statute, art. 15 *bis* (1) (referring to arts. 13[a] and [c]).

23. Ibid., art. 15 *ter*; for a nuanced commentary, see Niels Blokker and Stefan Barriga, "Conditions for the Exercise of Jurisdiction Based on Security Council Referrals," in Kress and Barriga, *Crime of Aggression*, 646.

24. See ibid., 652; but see Dapo Akande, "Prosecuting Aggression: The Consent Problem and the Role of the Security Council," Oxford Legal Studies Research Paper No. 10/2011, SSRN, February 17, 2011, doi:10.2139/ssrn.1762806.

25. Rome Statute, arts. 15 *bis* and 15 *ter*.

26. Ibid., art. 15 *bis* (8).

27. Under art. 24(1) of the UN Charter, the Security Council has "primary responsibility for the maintenance of international peace and security," and art. 39 gives the Security Council the power to "determine the existence of any threat to the peace, breach of the peace, or act of aggression."

28. CICC 2006 Report, paras. 67–69.

29. Rome Statute (1998), art. 16.

30. Though the Criminal Code of the Russian Federation (art. 353) criminalizes aggression, providing the possibility that Russian courts might one day try Vladimir Putin. See Astrid Reisinger Coracini, "Selected National Laws and Regional Instruments on the Crime of Aggression," in Kress and Barriga, *Crime of Aggression*, 1101.

31. Malabo Protocol, art. 28M, https://www.au.int/web/sites/default/files/treaties /7804-treaty-0045_-_protocol_on_amendments_to_the_protocol_on_the_statute _of_the_african_court_of_justice_and_human_rights_e.pdf.

32. Koh argued that, under a proper interpretation of the Rome Statute's amendment procedure, only states who formally opt in should be bound; see Koh's presentation at "The International Criminal Court and the Crime of Aggression" (video), discussion on the impending activation of the Kampala amendments, at German House, New York, February 23, 2016, German Center for Research and Innovation, n.d., http://www.germaninnovation.org/news-and-events/past-events /past-event?id=f9da87f5-5ada-e511-83dd-00155dcfd969 (at around 7:30).

33. Oliver Wendell Holmes Sr., valedictory address to the graduating class of the Bellevue Hospital College, 1871.

34. I initially identified four zones of interpretation—interpreting the Security Council determination, where the act of aggression took place, complementarity, and the interests of justice—but decided, after looking at the court's practice to date, that the three discussed will be more important. Weisbord, "Judging Aggression," 99–103.

35. Nicolaos Strapatsas, "The Practice of the Security Council Regarding the Concept of Aggression," in Kress and Barriga, *Crime of Aggression*, 180; *Policy Issues under the United Nations Charter and the Rome Statute*, Conference on International Criminal Justice, Turin, Italy, May 14–18, 2007, UN Doc. ICCASP/6/INF.2 (August 21, 2007), 30, http://iccnow.org/documents/Turin_Report_English_21-08-07_ADVANCE_COPY.pdf.

36. John Yoo, "International Law and the War in Iraq," *American Journal of International Law* 97 (2003) 567, http://scholarship.law.berkeley.edu/facpubs/1746: "Two independent sources of law provided the United States and its allies with authority to use force in Iraq: UN Security Council resolutions and the right to self-defense. Resolution 678 authorized member states 'to use all necessary means to uphold and implement resolution 660 (1990) and all subsequent relevant resolutions and to restore international peace and security in the area.'"

37. Harold Hongju Koh, "Obama's ISIL Legal Rollout: Bungled, Clearly. But Illegal? Really?" *Just Security*, September 29, 2014, https://www.justsecurity.org/15692/obamas-isil-legal-rollout-bungled-clearly-illegal-really/.

38. Yoo with SC Res. 660 (1990) and Koh with the 2001 Congressional Authorization for Use of Military Force.

39. Harold Hongju Koh, "War and Responsibility in the Dole/Gingrich Congress," Faculty Scholarship Series Paper 2097 (1996), 14, Yale Law School, Lillian Goldman Law Library, Legal Scholarship Repository, http://digitalcommons.law.yale.edu/fss_papers/2097/ (originally published in the *University of Miami Law Review* 50, no. 1 [October 1995]).

40. SC Res. 2249 (November 20, 2015), http://www.un.org/press/en/2015/sc12132.doc.htm; Dapo Akande and Marko Milanovic, "The Constructive Ambiguity of the Security Council's ISIS Resolution," *EJIL: Talk!* (blog), November 21, 2015, http://www.ejiltalk.org/the-constructive-ambiguity-of-the-security-councils-isis-resolution/#more-13855; David Bosco, "UK's Parliament Debates What the UN Security Council Said," *Lawfare* (blog), December 2, 2015, 12:24 p.m., https://www.lawfareblog.com/uks-parliament-debates-what-un-security-council-said; Ashley Deeks, "Threading the Needle in Security Council Resolution 2249," *Lawfare* (blog), November 23, 2015, 3:25 p.m., https://www.lawfareblog.com/threading-needle-security-council-resolution-2249.

41. Deeks, "Threading the Needle": "Most UNSCRs that authorize force have several features: (1) they contain a preambular paragraph that specifically invokes Chapter VII; (2) they use the word 'decides' as the active verb in the paragraph that authorizes force; and (3) they use the term 'all necessary means' or 'all necessary measures' as the code for force authorization. OP5 is a hybrid, because it lacks the first two features but contains the third – 'all necessary measures.' As a result, Akande and

Milanovic conclude—correctly, I believe—that OP5 likely is not intended to serve as a stand-alone authorization for using force against ISIS in Syria and Iraq."

42. Koh and Buchwald, "Crime of Aggression," 273–77; Akande, "Prosecuting Aggression."

43. Barriga and Blokker, "Entry Into Force," 622–25; R. Clark, "Amendments to the Rome Statute," 704; Kress and von Holtzendorff, "Kampala Compromise," 8; Jennifer Trahan, "The Rome Statute's Amendment on the Crime of Aggression: Negotiations at the Kampala Review Conference," *International Criminal Law Review* 11 (2011): 82–87, 90–93.

44. Rome Statute, art.15 *bis*, paragraph 4.

45. The Criminal Chamber within the African Court of Justice and Human Rights will be capable of trying aggression cases. Malabo Protocol, art. 28M.

46. States have partnered with the UN to establish hybrid courts to try the perpetrators of international crimes in Sierra Leone, Lebanon, Cambodia, and East Timor.

47. Gacaca in Rwanda, Mato Oput in Northern Uganda.

48. A case is inadmissible at the ICC if it is already being investigated or prosecuted by a national or regional court. The exception is when a state or regional court is unwilling or unable to proceed genuinely—e.g., when a state such as Sudan is pretending to prosecute in order to render a case inadmissible at the ICC. Rome Statute, art. 17. The ICC, for example, found that the Government of Sudan had established sham courts for alleged perpetrators of atrocities in an attempt to avert ICC jurisdiction: "Sudan: National Courts Have Done Nothing on Darfur," Human Rights Watch, June 11, 2007, https://www.hrw.org/news/2007/06/11/sudan-national-courts-have-done-nothing-darfur.

49. Astrid Reisinger Coracini, "(Extended) Synopsis: The Crime of Aggression under Domestic Criminal Law," in Kress and Barriga, *Crime of Aggression*, 1038: "A first assessment indicates that at least thirty-nine states and two regional organisations have adopted legislation related to aggression."

50. Ibid.

51. "Ukraine Finds Russian 'Soldiers' Guilty of Waging War," *BBC News*, April 18, 2016, http://www.bbc.com/news/world-europe-36070383; see also Astrid Reisinger Coracini, "Evaluating Domestic Legislation on the Customary Crime of Aggression under the Rome Statute's Complementarity Regime," in *The Emerging Practice of The International Criminal Court*, ed. Carsten Stahn and Göran Sluiter, 734–36, nn. 57–72 (Leiden: Martinus Nijhoff, 2009) (comparing national codes containing domestic variants of the crime of aggression); see also Nidal Nabil Jurdi, "The Domestic Prosecution of the Crime of Aggression after the International Criminal Court Review Conference: Possibilities and Alternatives," *Melbourne Journal of International Law* 14 (2013): 3–6, http://www.austlii.edu.au/au/journals/MelbJIL/2013/5.pdf.

52. "Chad's Ex-Dictator Convicted of Atrocities," Human Rights Watch, May 30, 2016, https://www.hrw.org/news/2016/05/30/chads-ex-dictator-convicted-atrocities; "Q&A: The Case of Hissène Habré before the Extraordinary African Chambers in Senegal," Human Rights Watch, May 3, 2016, https://www.hrw.org/news/2016/05/03/qa-case-hissene-habre-extraordinary-african-chambers-senegal.

53. Isaac Webb, "Ukraine's Uneasy Justice," *Foreign Affairs* (June 1, 2016), https://www.foreignaffairs.com/articles/ukraine/2016-06-01/ukraines-uneasy -justice; see Jennifer Trahan, "Is Complementarity the Right Approach for the International Criminal Court's Crime of Aggression? Considering the Problem of 'Overzealous' National Court Prosecutions," *Cornell International Law Journal* 45 (2012): 586, http://www.lawschool.cornell.edu/research/ILJ/upload/Trahan -final.pdf, for a discussion of the dangers of "overzealous" national court aggres- sion prosecutions; see also Jurdi, "Possibilities and Alternatives"; Julie Veroff, "Reconciling the Crime of Aggression and Complementarity: Unaddressed Ten- sions and a Way Forward," *Yale Law Journal* 125 (2016): 735, http://papers.ssrn .com/sol3/papers.cfm?abstract_id=2716517.

54. Customary international-law immunities are likely to shield heads of state, heads of government, foreign ministers, and some high-ranking officials such as ministers of defense from prosecution by the courts of another state while in of- fice, but they don't shield leaders from accountability at international tribunals. "Case Concerning the Arrest Warrant of 11 April 2000" (Democratic Republic of the Congo v. Belgium), Judgment, 2002 ICJ (February 2002), paras. 58–59; see also Dapo Akande and Sangeeta Shah, "Immunities of State Officials, Interna- tional Crimes, and Foreign Domestic Courts," *European Journal of International Law* 21, no. 4 (2010): 818, http://www.ejil.org/pdfs/21/4/2115.pdf.

55. The Chilcot Inquiry is discussed in more detail in chapter 9.

56. Rome Statute, art. 15 *bis* and *ter.*

57. Ibid., art. 8 *bis.*

58. Ibid., art. 8 *bis* and elements.

59. Yoram Dinstein, *War, Aggression, and Self-Defence*, 4th ed. (Cambridge: Cambridge University Press, 2005), 85.

60. UN Charter, art. 2, para. 4.

61. Hersch Lauterpacht, ed., *Oppenheim's International Law*, vol. II, 7th ed. (London: Longmans, Green, 1948), 154–56; Ian Brownlie, *International Law and the Use of Force by States* (Oxford: Clarendon, 1963).

62. Kress, "State Conduct Element," 413–16; see R. Clark, "Nuremberg," 535–36 (clarifying the legal distinction between a "war of aggression" and the lesser category of "invasion" at Nuremberg).

63. Kampala Compromise, Annex III, Understanding 7.

64. Ibid.

65. Kress, "State Conduct Element," 502–7.

66. Ibid., 504–5 (for an overview and authoritative sources); see also GA, "Declaration on Principles of International Law Concerning Friendly Relations and Co-operation among States in Accordance with the Charter of the United Nations," GA Res. 2625 (XXV) (October 24, 1970); O. Corten, *The Law Against War: The Prohibition on the Use of Force in Contemporary International Law* (Oxford: Hart, 2012), 234.

67. See Kress, "State Conduct Element," 504.

68. Ibid., 502–4.

69. "Statement issued by the Kingdom of Saudi Arabia, the United Arab Emir- ates, the Kingdom of Bahrain, the State of Qatar and the State of Kuwait," UN

Doc. S/2015/217 (March 27, 2015), Annex, 3–5; Kress, "State Conduct Element," 457, n. 229.

70. UN Doc. S/RES/1973 (March 17, 2011), http://www.un.org/ga/search /view_doc.asp?symbol=S/RES/1973%20%282011%29; Claus Kress, "Major Post -Westphalian Shifts and Some Important Neo-Westphalian Hesitations in the State Practice on the International Use of Force," *Journal on the Use of Force and International Law* 1 (2014): 32.

71. Roger S. Clark, "Alleged Aggression in Utopia: An International Criminal Law Examination Question for 2020," in *The Ashgate Research Companion to International Criminal Law: Critical Perspectives*, ed. William A. Schabas, Yvonne McDermott, and Niamh Hayes, 63–64 (Farnham, UK: Ashgate, 2013).

72. ICC, *Elements of Crimes* (The Hague: author, 2011), 43, https://www .icc-cpi.int/NR/rdonlyres/336923D8-A6AD-40EC-AD7B-45BF9DE73D56/0/El ementsOfCrimesEng.pdf.

73. R. Clark, "Alleged Aggression in Utopia," 66.

74. Weisbord, "Conceptualizing Aggression," 46.

75. R. Clark, "Alleged Aggression in Utopia," 67. ICC, *Elements of Crimes*, 43, "Introduction," para 2: "There is no requirement to prove that the perpetrator has made a legal evaluation as to whether the use of armed force was inconsistent with the Charter of the United Nations."

76. Ibid.

77. R. Clark, "Alleged Aggression in Utopia," 67.

78. Ibid., 67, n. 6: "Out of necessity, the matter had to be left to the evolution of general law."

79. Ibid., 67.

80. Ibid.

81. Oscar Schachter, *International Law in Theory and Practice* (Dordrecht: Martinus Nijhoff, 1991), 123–25; Bryan F. MacPherson, "Limited Humanitarian Intervention," *International Legal Theory* 7 (2001): 65; Ian Brownlie, "Thoughts on Kind-Hearted Gunmen," in *Humanitarian Intervention and the United Nations*, ed. Richard B. Lillich, 147–48 (Charlottesville, VA: University Press of Virginia, 1973); Henkin, *How Nations Behave*, 144–45; cf. Nicholas Onuf, "Humanitarian Intervention: The Early Years," *Florida Journal of International Law* 16 (2004): 755; but see Nicholas Tsagourias, "Humanitarian Intervention and Legal Principles," *International Legal Theory* 7 (2001): 85.

82. Schachter, *International Law*, 125.

83. Ibid.

84. See, e.g., MacPherson, "Limited Humanitarian Intervention," 64 ("intervention is an asymmetrical right" that "will mostly be employed by the powerful states against weaker states"); Tsagourias, "Humanitarian Intervention," 84; Thomas M. Franck, *Recourse to Force* (Cambridge, UK: Cambridge University Press, 2002), 189 ("But it is no argument that states willing to intervene in Kosovo may not be equally willing to intervene in Chechnya or Tibet. . . . The ultimate test of a humanitarian intervention's legitimacy is whether it results in significantly more good than harm.").

85. Gary J. Bass, *Freedom's Battle: The Origins of Humanitarian Intervention* (New York: Alfred A. Knopf, 2008), 15; see also Ryan Goodman, "Humanitarian

Intervention and Pretexts for War," *American Journal of International Law* 100 (2006): 107.

86. Jennifer Trahan, "Defining the 'Grey Area' where Humanitarian Intervention May Not Be Fully Legal, but Is Not the Crime of Aggression," *Journal on the Use of Force and International Law* 2 (2015): 42 (arguing that R2P, narrowly construed, is "fully consonant with the crime of aggression, and actions by individual leaders involved in R2P would not fall within the crime": ibid., 43); see also Sean Murphy, "Criminalizing Humanitarian Intervention," *Case Western Reserve Journal of International Law* 41 (2009): 342.

87. According to Professor Nicholas Wheeler, "What is important, then, is to distinguish between power that is based on relations of domination and force, and power that is legitimate because it is predicated on shared norms." Nicholas J. Wheeler, *Saving Strangers: Humanitarian Intervention in International Society* (New York: Oxford University Press, 2000), 2.

88. International Commission on Intervention and State Sovereignty (ICISS), *The Responsibility to Protect* (Ottawa: International Development Research Centre, 2001), xii–xiii, http://responsibilitytoprotect.org/ICISS%20Report.pdf.

89. Trahan, "Defining the 'Grey Area' "; see also Murphy, "Criminalizing Humanitarian Intervention."

90. Choe Sang-Hun, "North Korean Propaganda Video Depicts Nuclear Strike on Washington," *New York Times*, March 26, 2016, https://www.nytimes.com/2016/03/27/world/asia/north-korea-propaganda-video-nuclear-strike.html.

91. William M. Arkin, Cynthia McFadden, and Kenzi Abou-Sabe, "U.S. May Launch Strike if North Korea Reaches for Nuclear Trigger," *NBC*, April 13, 2017, http://www.nbcnews.com/news/world/u-s-may-launch-strike-if-north-korea-reaches-nuclear-n746366.

92. Mary Ellen O'Connell, *The Myth of Preemptive Self Defense* (Washington, DC: American Society for International Law, 2002), 16, https://www.nyccriminallawyer.com/wp-content/uploads/2014/07/oconnell.pdf; Brownlie, *Use of Force by States*; Ahmed M. Rifaat, *International Aggression: A Study of the Legal Concept* (Uppsala: Almqvist and Wiksell International, 1979), 124–27; Lauterpacht, *Oppenheim's International Law*; Hans Kelsen, *Recent Trends in the Law of the United Nations* (supplement to *The Law of the United Nations*; London: Stevens, 1951]), 914: "This right . . . has no other content than the one determined by Article 51."

93. UN Charter, art. 51: "Nothing in the present Charter shall impair the inherent right of individual or collective self-defence if an armed attack occurs against a Member of the United Nations, until the Security Council has taken measures necessary to maintain international peace and security. Measures taken by Members in the exercise of this right of self-defence shall be immediately reported to the Security Council and shall not in any way affect the authority and responsibility of the Security Council under the present Charter to take at any time such action as it deems necessary in order to maintain or restore international peace and security."

94. Derek W. Bowett, *Self-Defence in International Law* (Clark, NJ: Lawbook Exchange, 2009; originally published 1958), 152; Anthony D'Amato, "Israel's Air Strike upon the Iraqi Nuclear Reactor," *American Journal of International*

Law 77 (1983): 584 (concluding that Israeli strike against the Osirik reactor did not compromise Iraq's territorial integrity or political independence and was not inconsistent with the purposes of the UN; therefore, the strike did not violate art. 2(4) of the Charter).

95. UN Charter, art. 51; see also Christine Gray, *International Law and the Use of Force*, 3rd ed., ed. Malcolm D. Evans and Phoebe N. Okowa (New York: Oxford University Press, 2008), 117–19; but see George Fletcher and Jens David Ohlin, *Defending Humanity* (New York: Oxford University Press, 2008), 72–78, for a more expansive reading of art. 51 based on the negotiating history of the UN Charter.

96. Dinstein, *War, Aggression, and Self-Defence*, 182 (so-called interceptive self-defense in response to a "committed," "irrevocable" attack).

97. O'Connell, *Myth of Preemptive Self Defense*, 6–7.

98. Ibid., 7.

99. Michael Newton and Larry May, *Proportionality in International Law* (New York: Oxford University Press, 2014) 15–32; Judith Gardam, *Necessity, Proportionality, and the Use of Force by States* (New York: Cambridge University Press, 2004), 5; see "Oil Platforms" (Islamic Republic of Iran v. United States of America), Judgment, ICJ Reports 2003, 161, paras. 76–77 (November 6, 2003), http://www.icj-cij.org/files/case-related/90/090-20031106-JUD-01-00-EN.pdf, for the ICJ's analysis of necessity and proportionality in the context of a 1987 armed conflagration between Iran and the United States in the Persian Gulf (hereinafter "Oil Platforms").

100. "See Top Bush Officials Push Case against Saddam," *CNN*, September 8, 2002, http://edition.cnn.com/2002/ALLPOLITICS/09/08/iraq.debate/.

101. See, e.g., George W. Bush, "President Bush Outlines Iraqi Threat," White House, October 7, 2002, https://georgewbush-whitehouse.archives.gov/news/releases/2002/10/20021007-8.html: "[Iraq] possesses and produces chemical and biological weapons. It is seeking nuclear weapons. . . . Members of the Congress of both political parties, and members of the United Nations Security Council, agree that Saddam Hussein is a threat to peace and must disarm. We agree that the Iraqi dictator must not be permitted to threaten America and the world with horrible poisons and diseases and gases and atomic weapons."

102. White House, *National Security Strategy*, 15.

103. Colin Powell, *It Worked for Me: In Life and Leadership* (New York: Harper Perennial, 2014; originally published 2012), 223. Powell responds to accusations of "knowing the information was false": "I didn't. And yes, a blot, a failure, will always be attached to me and my UN presentation. But I am mad mostly at myself for not having smelled the problem. My instincts failed me."

104. US Department of Justice, "Lawfulness of a Lethal Operation Directed against a U.S. Citizen Who Is a Senior Operational Leader of Al-Qa'ida or an Associated Force," Draft White Paper (November 8, 2011), 7, fas.org/irp/eprint/doj-lethal.pdf.

105. Daniel Webster to Henry Stephen Fox, letter dated April 24, 1841, in Daniel Webster, *The Papers of Daniel Webster: Diplomatic Papers*, vol. 1, *1841–1843*, ed. Kenneth E. Shewmaker, Kenneth R. Stevens, and Anita McGurn (Lebanon, NH: University Press of New England, 1983).

106. Nuremberg Judgment, 205 (applying the *Caroline* test).

107. See "International Military Tribunal at Tokyo (1948)," in *The Law of War: A Documentary History*, ed. Leon Friedman, vol. 2, 1029, 1157–59 (New York: Random House, 1972).

108. The case law at the International Court of Justice has done little to resolve the debate over the legal authority of the *Caroline* test because the judges have consistently decided cases pertaining to the use of force without recourse to the doctrine of self-defense: Thomas M. Franck, "Some Observations on the ICJ's Procedural and Substantive Innovations," *American Journal of International Law* 81, no. 1 (1987): 120; "Oil Platforms," paras. 73–77; "Armed Activities on the Territory of the Congo" (Democratic Republic of the Congo v. Uganda), 2005 ICJ 168, paras. 146–47 (December 19, 2005) (hereinafter "Armed Activities"); "Legal Consequences of the Construction of a Wall in Occupied Palestinian Territory," Advisory Opinion, 2004 ICJ 136, 139 (July 9, 2004), para. 139 (hereinafter Israeli Wall Case), https://www.icj-cij.org/files/case-related/131/131-20040709 -ADV-01-00-EN.pdf; see generally Terry D. Gill, "The Temporal Dimension of Self-Defense: Anticipation, Pre-emption, Prevention and Immediacy," in *International Law and Armed Conflict: Exploring the Faultlines*, ed. Michael N. Schmitt and Jelena Pejic, 125–28 (Leiden: Martinus Nijhoff, 2007) (surveying the scholarship on the *Caroline* criteria).

109. George Brandis, "The Right of Self-Defence against Imminent Armed Attack in International Law," public lecture at the T. C. Beirne School of Law, University of Queensland, text posted on *EJIL: TALK!* (blog), May 25, 2017, https://www.ejiltalk.org/the-right-of-self-defence-against-imminent-armed -attack-in-international-law/#more-15255; Jeremy Wright, "The Modern Law of Self-Defence," speech at the International Institute for Strategic Studies, text posted on *EJIL: TALK!* (blog), January 11, 2017, https://www.ejiltalk.org/the -modern-law-of-self-defence/#_ftnref24.

110. Sadoff, "Question of Determinacy," 537: Because the *Caroline* doctrine was articulated while these concepts were developing, "Critics question the formula's proper contribution to shaping customary international law at all." See also William V. O'Brien, *The Conduct of Just and Limited War* (New York: Praeger, 1981), 132–33 (finding the *Caroline* doctrine "more rhetorical than substantive" in effect); James A. Green, "Docking the *Caroline*: Understanding the Relevance of the Formula in Contemporary Customary International Law Concerning Self-Defense," *Cardozo Journal of International and Contemporary Law* 14 (2006): 440–41.

111. Dinstein, *War, Aggression, and Self-Defence*, 184–85: "There was nothing anticipatory about the British action against the *Caroline* steamboat."

112. O'Connell, *Myth of Preemptive Self Defense*, 13.

113. Gray, *Use of Force*, 149.

114. Thomas C. Schelling, *The Strategy of Conflict* (Cambridge, MA: Harvard University Press, 1980), 207.

115. Greenwood, "Pre-emptive Use of Force," 36 (arguing that while "international law does not require States wait until it is too late" to engage in self-defense, "it does not give a broad general license for preemptive military action" either).

116. See Kress, "State Conduct Element," 460, n. 248, for a summary with sources.

117. "Oil Platforms, " para. 72 (the ICJ did "not exclude the possibility that the mining of a single military vessel might be sufficient to bring into play the 'inherent right of self-defense' "); *Nicaragua*, paras. 247, 249, 195.

118. Ibid., para. 64; *Nicaragua*, para. 231; "Armed Activities," para. 146.

119. Rome Statute, art. 8 *bis*, para. 2(f).

120. Kress, "State Conduct Element," 460–61.

121. Jack Goldsmith, "Thoughts on the Latest Round of Johnson v. Koh," *Lawfare* (blog), September 16, 2011, 8:43 a.m., http://www.lawfareblog.com /2011/09/thoughts-on-the-latest-round-of-johnson-v-koh/; Heller, " 'Unwilling or Unable.' "

122. Rome Statute, art. 21, "Applicable Law."

123. Leena Grover, "Interpreting the Crime of Aggression," in Kress and Barriga, *Crime of Aggression*, 375.

124. Glennon, "Blank-Prose Crime of Aggression," 72–73: "The definition's ambiguity broadens its potential reach to the point that, had it been in effect for the last several decades, every US President since John F. Kennedy, hundreds of US legislators and military leaders, as well as innumerable military and political leaders from other countries could have been subject to prosecution." The Council on Foreign Relations also adopted Glennon's position in a special report released just before the Review Conference: Padmanabhan et al., "From Rome to Kampala," 13–15.

125. Michael J. Glennon, "The Vague New Crime of 'Aggression,' " *New York Times*, April 5, 2010, http://www.nytimes.com/2010/04/06/opinion/06iht-edg lennon.html?_r=0.

126. Heller, "Thoughts on Glennon's 'Blank-Prose' " (Heller called Glennon's position, that customary international law does not criminalize aggression, "truly bizarre," and took issue with the fact that Glennon cites only his own work in defense of it).

127. Trahan, "Meaningful Definition," 907.

128. Koh, "Intervention at Kampala": "A fourth major question is whether, despite the considered attention that has been given to Article 8bis [*sic*], genuine consensus has been reached regarding the meaning of the proposed definition of the crime of aggression?"

129. See Grover, "Interpreting the Crime of Aggression," 375, for a detailed guide to interpretation.

130. Preamble to the Rome Statute.

CHAPTER 8

1. Thomas Jones, "*Distrust That Particular Flavor* by William Gibson" (book review), *Guardian*, February 17, 2012, http://www.theguardian.com/books/2012 /feb/17/distrust-particular-flavor-william-gibson-review; William Gibson, "If You Liked My Book, You'll Love These," *New York Magazine*, n.d., accessed September 3, 2016, http://nymag.com/arts/books/features/66294/index2.html.

2. Gabriel Winslow-Yost, "William Gibson's Man-Made Future," *New Yorker*, December 8, 2014, http://www.newyorker.com/books/page-turner/william-gibsons -man-made-future.

3. Ned Beauman, "William Gibson," *Guardian*, November 16, 2014, http://www .theguardian.com/books/2014/nov/16/william-gibson-interview-the-peripheral.

4. Winslow-Yost, "Man-Made Future"; Erika Anderson, "William Gibson Talks to EMA about Getting the Future Right," *PaperMag*, October 14, 2015, http://www.papermag.com/william-gibson-talks-to-ema-about-getting-the-fu ture-right-1427658486.html.

5. David Beers, "William Gibson Hates Futurists," *Tyee*, October 18, 2007, http://thetyee.ca/Books/2007/10/18/WillGibson/.

6. Geeta Dayal, "William Gibson on Why Sci-Fi Writers Are (Thankfully) Almost Always Wrong," *Wired*, September 13, 2012, https://www.wired.com/2012 /09/interview-with-william-gibson/.

7. "William Gibson Book Expo 2010 Speech-Part 1 'Zero History' (audio only)," YouTube, June 6, 2010, 7:54–8:14, https://www.youtube.com/watch?v =AJ5duD15P9s.

8. William Gibson, *Pattern Recognition* (New York: G. P. Putnam's Sons, 2003), 57.

9. Geeta Dayal, "William Gibson on Twitter, Antique Watches and Internet Obsessions," *Wired*, September 14, 2012, http://www.wired.com/2012/09 /william-gibson-part-2-twitter/.

10. William Gibson, *Neuromancer* (New York: Ace Books, 1988; originally published 1984), 51.

11. Cyberspace was acknowledged as the fifth military domain by NATO Secretary-General Jens Stoltenberg in June 2016 when he announced that all NATO ministers had also recognized "cyberspace as an operational domain." General Ronald R. Fogleman (Air Force chief of staff), "Information Operations: The Fifth Dimension of Warfare," address to the Armed Forces Communications-Electronics Association in Washington, IWS—the Information Warfare Site, April 25, 1995, http://www.iwar.org.uk/iwar/resources/5th-dimension/iw.htm; "War in the Fifth Domain," *Economist*, July 1, 2010, http://www.economist. com/node/16478792; Catherine Hardy, "Cyberspace Is Officially a War Zone— NATO," *Euronews*, June 15, 2016, http://www.euronews.com/2016/06/15 /cyberspace-is-officially-a-war-zone-nato/.

12. Sanger, *Confront and Conceal*, 199.

13. Yaakov Katz, "Stuxnet Virus Set Back Iran's Nuclear Program by 2 Years," *Jerusalem Post*, December 12, 2015, http://www.jpost.com/Iranian-Threat/News /Stuxnet-virus-set-back-Irans-nuclear-program-by-2-years; William J. Broad, John Markoff, and David E. Sanger, "Israeli Test on Worm Called Crucial in Iran Nuclear Delay," *New York Times*, January 15, 2011, http://www.nytimes.com /2011/01/16/world/middleeast/16stuxnet.html?_r=0 (but some sources maintain that the delay was hardly a setback at all, see Joby Warrick, "Iran's Natanz Nuclear Facility Recovered Quickly from Stuxnet Cyberattack," *Washington Post*, February 16, 2011, http://www.washingtonpost.com/wp-dyn/content/article/2011 /02/15/AR2011021505395.html).

14. "Iranian leader: Wipe out Israel," *CNN International*, October 27, 2005, http://edition.cnn.com/2005/WORLD/meast/10/26/ahmadinejad/.

15. David E. Sanger, "A Spymaster Who Saw Cyberattacks as Israel's Best Weapon against Iran," *New York Times*, March 22, 2016, http://www.nytimes.com/2016/03/23/world/middleeast/israel-mossad-meir-dagan.html: "An Israeli bombing run would provide an illusory solution, temporarily flattening those facilities, only to have them return, this time deep underground."

16. Geoffrey Kemp and John Allen Gay, "The High Cost of War with Iran," *National Interest*, November 24, 2014, http://nationalinterest.org/commentary/the-high-cost-war-iran-8265; Mark Mazzetti and Tom Shanker, "U.S. War Games Sees Perils of Israeli Strike against Iran," *New York Times*, March 19, 2012, http://www.nytimes.com/2012/03/20/world/middleeast/united-states-war-game-sees-dire-results-of-an-israeli-attack-on-iran.html; see Dennis Jett, "If You Liked Iraq, You'll Love Iran," *Huffington Post*, August 26, 2012, http://www.huffingtonpost.com/dennis-jett/liked-iraq-love-iran_b_1832020.html.

17. See Kim Zetter, *Countdown to Zero Day: Stuxnet and the Launch of the World's First Digital Weapon* (New York: Broadway Books, 2014), 5–18. In other accounts, German cybersecurity specialist Ralph Langner discovered Stuxnet and its properties: Mark Clayton, "From the Man Who Discovered Stuxnet, Dire Warnings One Year Later," *Christian Science Monitor*, September 22, 2011, http://www.csmonitor.com/USA/2011/0922/From-the-man-who-discovered-Stuxnet-dire-warnings-one-year-later.

18. Peter Singer, "Stuxnet and Its Hidden Lessons on the Ethics of Cyberweapons," *Case Western Reserve Journal of International Law* 47 (spring 2015): 82.

19. Sanger, *Confront and Conceal*, 200.

20. Ibid.

21. David E. Sanger, "Obama Order Sped Up Wave of Cyberattacks against Iran," *New York Times*, June 1, 2012, http://www.nytimes.com/2012/06/01/world/middleeast/obama-ordered-wave-of-cyberattacks-against-iran.html?pagewanted=alland_r=0.

22. Sanger, *Confront and Conceal*, x.

23. Zetter, *Countdown to Zero Day*.

24. Clayton, "Dire Warnings."

25. Stuxnet was "an alias Microsoft conjured from letters in the name of one of the driver files (mrxnet.sys) and another part of the code": Zetter, *Countdown to Zero Day*, 14.

26. Rome Statute, art. 8 *bis*, para. 1.

27. Marco Roscini, "World Wide Warfare: *Jus ad Bellum* and the Use of Cyber Force," *Max Planck Yearbook of United Nations Law* 14 (2010): 105 (noting that early Charter history and "the travaux préparatoires also reveal that the drafters did not intend to extend the prohibition to economic coercion and political pressures."); Oscar Schachter, "In Defense of International Rules on the Use of Force," *University of Chicago Law Review* 53 (1986): 119–42 (discussing pressures to revise the limits on self-defense drawn by the UN Charter but arguing against moves to do so); Lori Fisler Damrosch, "Politics across Borders: Nonintervention and Nonforcible Influence over Domestic Affairs," *American Journal of International Law* 83 (1989): 1.

28. In ascending order of gravity, they are unlawful "intervention" (*Nicaragua*, Judgment, 1986 ICJ Rep. 14, 65 para. 195 (June 27, 1986); "threat of force" (UN Charter, art. 2[4]); "use of force" (ibid., art. 2[4]); "threat to the peace" (ibid., art.

39); "breach of the peace"(ibid., art. 39); "armed attack" (ibid., art. 51); and "act of aggression"(ibid., art. 39); see Dapo Akande and Antonios Tzanakopoulos, "The International Court of Justice and the Concept of Aggression," in Kress and Barriga, *Crime of Aggression*, 220–21 (for an overview of scholarly views on use-of-force gravity thresholds); Kress, "State Conduct Element," 453–54, 459–88.

29. *Nicaragua*, paras. 228, 231–32; see Gray, *Use of Force*, 177–87 (discussing frontier incidents).

30. UN Charter, art. 51.

31. Kampala Compromise, Annex III, Understanding 6.

32. Sanger, *Confront and Conceal*, 206.

33. Kampala Compromise, Annex III, Understanding 6.

34. Ibid., Understanding 7.

35. The *Tallinn Manual* listed ninety-five nonbinding rules that the experts unanimously agreed reflected customary international law. Michael N. Schmitt, ed., *Tallinn Manual on the International Law Applicable to Cyberwarfare* (New York: Cambridge University Press, 2013).

36. Ibid., 45 (Rule 11).

37. Ibid.: "The clearest cases [of violations of Article 2(4) the UN Charter] are those cyber operations, such as the employment of the Stuxnet worm, that amount to a use of force" (Rule 10, Comment 9); "Acts that injure or kill persons or damage or destroy objects are unambiguously uses of force," so long as the effects are not trivial and the cyber operations have been carried out by a state or are attributable to one (Rule 11, Comment 8).

38. Harold Hongju Koh, "International Law in Cyberspace: Remarks as Prepared for Delivery by Harold Hongju Koh to the USCYBERCOM Inter-Agency Legal Conference Ft. Meade, MD, Sept. 18, 2012," *Harvard International Law Journal Online* 54 (2012): 4, http://www.harvardilj.org/wp-content/uploads/2012/12/Koh-Speech-to-Publish1.pdf.

39. Michael N. Schmidt, "International Law in Cyberspace: The Koh Speech and *Tallinn Manual* Juxtaposed," *Harvard International Law Journal Online* 54 (2012): 19, http://www.harvardilj.org/wp-content/uploads/2012/12/HILJ-Online_54_Schmitt.pdf; see also Weisbord, "Conceptualizing Aggression," 39–41.

40. Koh, "International Law in Cyberspace," 7.

41. So long as that response met the UN Charter's self-defense criteria, including necessity, proportionality, and reporting. UN Charter, art. 51.

42. M. Schmidt, "International Law in Cyberspace," 22.

43. Ibid.

44. Russian hackers also breached the Democratic Congressional Campaign Committee, and the e-mails of Clinton campaign manager John Podesta. Ellen Nakashima, "Russian Government Hackers Penetrated DNC, Stole Opposition Research on Trump," *Washington Post*, June 14, 2016, https://www.washingtonpost.com/world/national-security/russian-government-hackers-penetrated-dnc-stole-opposition-research-on-trump/2016/06/14/cf006cb4–316e-11e6–8ff7–7b6c1998b7a0_story.html.

45. Eric Lipton, David E. Sanger, and Scott Shane, "The Perfect Weapon: How Russian Cyberpower Invaded the U.S.," *New York Times*, December 13, 2016, https://www.nytimes.com/2016/12/13/us/politics/russia-hack-election-dnc.html.

46. Matthew Cole, Richard Esposito, Sam Biddle and Ryan Grim, "Top-Secret NSA Report Details Russian Hacking Effort Days before 2016 Election," *Intercept*, June 5, 2017, https://theintercept.com/2017/06/05/top-secret-nsa-report -details-russian-hacking-effort-days-before-2016-election/.

47. Rachel Roberts, "Russia Hired 1,000 People to Create anti-Clinton 'Fake News' in Key US States During Election, Trump-Russia Hearings Leader Reveals," *Independent*, March 30, 2017, http://www.independent.co.uk/news/world/ameri cas/us-politics/russian-trolls-hilary-clinton-fake-news-election-democrat-mark -warner-intelligence-committee-a7657641.html.

48. Hunt Allcott and Matthew Gentzkow, "Social Media and Fake News in the 2016 Election," *Journal of Economic Perspectives* 31 (spring 2017): 212.

49. Ibid.

50. Jeremy Diamond and Stephen Collinson, "Democrats Accuse Trump of Disloyalty over Clinton Emails," *CNN*, July 28, 2016, http://www.cnn.com/2016 /07/27/politics/donald-trump-vladimir-putin-hack-hillary-clinton/.

51. Adam Schiff, the leading Democrat on the House Intelligence Committee, said, "What we saw the Russians do in our presidential election was just utterly unprecedented in its scope and in its impact," in Uri Friedman, "What the Russians Did Was Utterly Unprecedented," *Atlantic*, December 27, 2016, www.theatlantic.com/international/archive/2016/12/adam-schiff-russia-elec tion-hack/511571/; see also David Smith, "FBI Covered Up Russian Influence on Trump's Election Win, Harry Reid Claims," *Guardian*, December 10, 2016, https://www.theguardian.com/us-news/2016/dec/10/fbi-russia-trump-election -harry-reid-james-comey-wikileaks; Mallory Shelbourne, "Clapper: 'Aggressive- ness' of Russian Interference in Election 'Unprecedented,' " *Hill*, May 30, 2017, http://thehill.com/homenews/news/335575-clapper-aggressiveness-of-russian -interference-in-election-unprecedented.

52. Quoted in Ivan Watson, Antonia Mortensen, and Victoria Butenko, "Ex- Soviet States Tell US 'I Told You So' over Russia Hacking Allegations," *CNN*, December 16, 2016, http://www.cnn.com/2016/12/16/politics/russia-hacking-alle gations-mikheil-saakashvili/index.html.

53. Quoted in ibid.

54. Andy Greenberg, "How an Entire Nation Became Russia's Test Lab for Cyberwar," *Wired*, June 20, 2017, https://www.wired.com/story/russian-hackers -attack-ukraine/.

55. Ibid.

56. Ibid.

57. Natalia Zinets, "Ukraine Hit by 6,500 Hack Attacks, Sees Russian 'Cyber- war,' " *Reuters*, December 29, 2016, http://www.reuters.com/article/us-ukraine -crisis-cyber-idUSKBN14I1QC.

58. Ibid.

59. "Presidential Results," *CNN*, n.d., accessed July 31, 2017, http://www.cnn .com/election/results/president (Clinton won 48.5% to Trump's 46.4%).

60. Peter Walker, "Donald Trump Wins: Russian Parliament Bursts into Ap- plause upon Hearing Result—Country's Jubilant Politicians say 'Grandmother Hillary Can Take Some Rest Now,' " *Independent*, November 9, 2016, http://

www.independent.co.uk/news/world/americas/us-elections/donald-trump-wins -us-election-russia-putin-result-a7406866.html.

61. Theodore Schleifer and Deirdre Walsh, "McCain: Russian Cyberintrusions an 'Act of War,'" *CNN*, last updated December 30, 2016, http://www.cnn .com/2016/12/30/politics/mccain-cyber-hearing/index.html.

62. M. Schmitt, *Tallinn Manual*, 55 (Rule 13, Comment 6).

63. Quoted in Ellen Nakashima, "Russia's Apparent Meddling in U.S. Election Is Not an Act of War, Cyber Expert Says," *Washington Post*, February 7, 2017, https://www.washingtonpost.com/news/checkpoint/wp/2017/02/07/russias -apparent-meddling-in-u-s-election-is-not-an-act-of-war-cyber-expert-says/?utm _term=.39c80a1a3254.

64. Michael N. Schmitt, ed., *Tallinn Manual 2.0 on the International Law Applicable to Cyber Operations* (Cambridge, UK: Cambridge University Press, 2017).

65. Greg Miller, Ellen Nakashima, and Adam Entous, "Obama's Secret Struggle to Punish Russia for Putin's Election Assault," *Washington Post*, June 23, 2017, https://www.washingtonpost.com/graphics/2017/world/national-security /obama-putin-election-hacking/?utm_term=.68545b23bd14.

66. Robb, *Brave New War*, 95.

67. Ibid.

68. Office of the Director of National Intelligence, *Assessing Russian Activities and Intentions in Recent US Elections*, ICA 2017-01D (January 6, 2017), ii, 1,, https://assets.documentcloud.org/documents/3254237/Russia-Hack-Report.pdf (hereinafter Russia Hack Report).

69. Philip Bobbitt, *Terror and Consent* (New York: Alfred A. Knopf, 2008), 3–4.

70. Astrid Reisinger Coracini and Pål Wrange, "The Specificity of the Crime of Aggression," in Kress and Barriga, *Crime of Aggression*, 336–39.

71. Mégret, "Specific Evil of Aggression," in Kress and Barriga, *Crime of Aggression*, 1402.

72. UN Charter, art. 2, para. 4 (prohibiting the "threat or use of force" in international relations); UN Charter, art. 51 (reserving inherent right of self-defense following an "armed attack"); 1974 Resolution, art. 1, 143 (requiring "armed force"), art. 3, UN Doc. A/9631 (listing examples of acts of aggression requiring the deployment of "armed forces"); see Sean P. Kanuck, "Information Warfare: New Challenges for Public International Law," *Harvard International Law Journal* 37 (1996): 288–90.

73. Julius Stone, "Hopes and Loopholes," 230: however, "a substantial body of states continued to press in the Special Committee for inclusion of economic aggression in the [1974] definition."

74. See, e.g., Kanuck, "Information Warfare," 290 ("It is both much easier and more profitable to conduct information warfare against an adversary's knowledge resources than to conduct a conventional war against its armed forces"); Matthew C. Waxman, "Cyber-Attacks and the Use of Force: Back to the Future of Article 2(4)," *Yale Journal of International Law* 36 (2011): 422–23 (noting there is "'growing consensus' that future conflicts may feature 'the use of cyber-warfare to disable a country's infrastructure, meddle with the integrity of another country's

internal military data, try to confuse its financial transactions or to accomplish any number of other possibly crippling aims,'" quoting John Chipman, director-general and chief executive of the International Institute for Strategic Studies, "The Military Balance 2010" (press release).

75. Rome Statute, art. 22 (2).

76. SWGCA, 5th Sess., "Informal Inter-Sessional Meeting of the Special Working Group on the Crime of Aggression," held at the Lichtenstein Institute on Self-Determination, Woodrow Wilson School, Princeton University, United States, June 11–14, 2007, report ICC-ASP/6/SWGCA/INF.1, para. 47.

77. Rome Statute, art. 8 *bis*, para. 2.

78. Weisbord, "Conceptualizing Aggression," 39; Schmitt, *Tallinn Manual*, 50; see also Waxman, "Cyber-Attacks," 427; Koh, "International Law in Cyberspace."

79. See, e.g., National Research Council (NRC) Committee, *Offensive Information Warfare, Technology, Policy, Law, and Ethics Regarding U.S. Acquisition and Use of Cyberattack Capabilities* (Washington, DC: National Academies, 2009), 32–36; Waxman, "Cyber-Attacks," 431–32; Abraham D. Sofaer, David Clark, and Whitfield Diffie, "Cyber Security and International Agreements," in Committee on Deterring Cyberattacks, *Proceedings of a Workshop on Deterring CyberAttacks: Informing Strategies and Developing Options for U.S. Policy* (Washington, DC: National Academies, 2010), 185, http://www.nap.edu/open book.php?record_id=12997andpage=179; Michael N. Schmitt, "Computer Network Attack and the Use of Force in International Law: Thoughts on a Normative Framework," *Columbia Journal of Transnational Law* 37 (1999): 914–16; Horace B. Robertson Jr., "Self-Defense against Computer Network Attack under International Law," *US Naval War College International Law Studies* 76 (2002): 140; Richard A. Clarke and Robert K. Knake, *Cyber War* (New York: Harper Collins, 2010), 178.

80. "2016 Presidential Campaign Hacking Fast Facts," *CNN*, 2018, accessed July 1, 2018, http://www.cnn.com/2016/12/26/us/2016-presidential-campaign -hacking-fast-facts/index.html.

81. Rome Statute, art. 8 *bis*, para. 1.

82. Russia Hack Report; "Joint Statement from the Department Of Homeland Security and Office of the Director of National Intelligence on Election Security," Department of Homeland Security, October 7, 2016, https://www .dhs.gov/news/2016/10/07/joint-statement-department-homeland-security-and -office-director-national.

83. Genocide, crimes against humanity, and war crimes can be perpetrated by the leaders of nonstate organizations (see, e.g., Rome Statute, arts. 7[2][a] and [i]).

84. David Scheffer proposes amendments to the definition of the crime of aggression that would encapsulate "political, *military*, or *cyber* action of a State *or non-State entity*" (italics in original), in "Amending the Crime of Aggression under the Rome Statute," in Kress and Barriga, *Crime of Aggression*, 1494.

85. The 1933 Montevideo Convention on the Rights and Duties of States is taken by some jurists to preclude a dynamic and incremental interpretation of statehood. It was not, however, drafted for the purpose of international criminal law, and should serve as a guide for judicial interpretation, not binding authority.

86. See Bobbitt, *Shield of Achilles*, 344–47, where he sets out six variants of the state.

87. Frederic R. Kellogg, "Law, Morals, and Justice Holmes," *Judicature* 69 (1986): 217.

88. Michael E. Porter, *Competitive Advantage: Creating and Sustaining Superior Performance* (New York: Free Press, 1985), 446–48. Joseph Nye, former head of the US National Intelligence Council, describes scenario planning as a tool in estimative intelligence "to help policymakers interpret the available facts, to suggest alternative patterns that available facts might fit, [and] to provide informed assessments of the range and likelihood of possible outcomes." Joseph S. Nye Jr., "Peering into the Future," *Foreign Affairs* 73 (1994): 83.

89. Gill Ringland, *Scenario Planning: Managing for the Future* (Chichester: John Wiley, 1998), 20–21; Bobbitt, *Shield of Achilles*, 718–19.

90. William S. Lind, Keith Nightengale, John F. Schmitt, Joseph W. Sutton, and Gary I. Wilson, "The Changing Face of War: Into the Fourth Generation," *Marine Corps Gazette* (October 1989): 22. The first generation was characterized by tactics of line and column and culminated in the massed-manpower armies of the Napoleonic era. The second generation used the industrial society to mass-produce firepower and encourage tactics such as indirect fire covering movement. In the third generation, rather than closing with the enemy, successful commanders used mechanized forces to bypass and collapse the enemy's formations (i.e., blitzkrieg). See also Thomas X. Hammes, *The Sling and the Stone: War in the 21st Century* (St. Paul, MN: Zenith, 2004), 1–31.

91. "Is 4GW Simply Using Military Force in New Ways?" *Defense and the National Interest*, November 25, 2007, http://dnipogo.org/strategy-and-force-em ployment/fourth-generation-warfare-articles/.

92. See van Creveld, *Transformation of War*, 10–18; Robb, *Brave New War*, 7.

93. Ibid., 7.

94. Ibid., 7–8; Wittes and Blum, *Future of Violence*, 5.

95. Thomas X. Hammes, "Fourth Generation Warfare Evolves, Fifth Emerges," *Military Review* (May–June 2007): 20, http://www.au.af.mil/au/awc/awcgate /milreview/hammes-4gw_and-5th.pdf.

96. Imperial and Royal (K. u. K.) Austro-Hungarian Marine Corps, "Fourth Generation War," FMFM 1-A, Draft 4.2 (June 18, 2007), 6, http://ics.leeds.ac.uk /papers/pmt/exhibits/3007/fmfm_1-a.pdf.

97. Hammes, "Fourth Generation Warfare," 20.

98. Brian P. Fleming, *The Hybrid Threat Concept: Contemporary War, Military Planning and the Advent of Unrestricted Operational Art* (Fort Leavenworth, KS: School of Advanced Military Studies, 2011), quoting Russell W. Glenn, "Thoughts on Hybrid Conflict," *Small Wars Journal* (March 2, 2009): 2.

99. Hammes, *Sling and the Stone*, 2.

100. Peter Pindják, "Deterring Hybrid Warfare: A Chance for NATO and the EU to Work Together?" *NATO Review*, n.d., accessed September 5, 2016, http://www .nato.int/docu/review/2014/Also-in-2014/Deterring-hybrid-warfare/EN/index.htm.

101. Max Weber, "Politics as a Vocation," in *The Vocation Lectures*, ed. David Owen and Tracy B. Strong, trans. Rodney Livingstone, 34 (Indianapolis: Hackett, 2004; originally published 1919).

102. Charles Heckscher, "Defining the Post-Bureaucratic Type," in *The Post-Bureaucratic Organization: New Perspectives on Organizational Change*, ed. Charles Heckscher and Anne Donnellon, 20, 23–24 (Thousand Oaks, CA: Sage, 1994).

103. "An organic form of organization . . . [is] more team-based, more flexible, and less rulebound than the traditional 'mechanical' hierarchy." Charles Heckscher and Lynda M. Applegate, "Introduction," in Heckscher and Donnellon, *Post-Bureaucratic Organization*, 2–3. See also "Adjusting Organization Forms to Appropriate Conditions: Explanation of Theory of Mechanistic and Organic Systems of Burns and Stalker," 12 Manage, n.d., accessed September 5, 2016, http://www.12manage.com/methods_burns_mechanistic_organic_systems.html (comparing the post-bureaucratic and the organic organizational forms).

104. Heckscher and Applegate, "Introduction."

105. Heckscher, "Defining the Post-Bureaucratic Type," 25.

106. Weisbord, "Conceptualizing Aggression," 47–48; Scheffer, "Amending the Crime of Aggression," 1494.

107. According to organizational-behavior scholars Daniel Brass and Marlene Burkhardt, "a common finding in social network studies is that central positions are often associated with power and influence." Daniel J. Brass and Marlene E. Burkhardt, "Centrality and Power in Organizations," in *Networks and Organizations*, ed. Nitin Nohria and Robert G. Eccles, 191 (Boston, MA: Harvard Business School Press, 1992).

108. Michael D. Irwin and Holly L. Hughes, "Centrality and the Structure of Urban Interaction: Measures, Concepts, and Applications," *Social Forces* 71 (1992): 19.

109. Linton C. Freeman, "A Set of Measures of Centrality Based on Betweenness," *Sociometry* 40 (1977): 35, citing Alex Bavelas, "A Mathematical Model for Group Structure," *Applied Anthropology* 7 (1948): 16.

110. Irwin and Hughes, "Centrality," 20.

111. Joseph S. Nye Jr., *The Powers to Lead* (New York: Oxford University Press, 2008), 31: "Soft power is not merely the same as influence, though it is one source of influence. After all, influence can also rest on the hard power of threats or payments. Nor is soft power just persuasion or the ability to move people by argument, though that is an important part of it. It is also the ability to entice and attract. Attraction often leads to acquiescence."

112. Rome Statute, art. 8 *bis*, para. 1.

113. Weisbord, "Conceptualizing Aggression," 47–48.

114. See James MacGregor Burns, *Leadership* (New York: Harper Colophon, 1979), 243–44; see also Boas Shamir, Robert J. House, and Michael B. Arthur, "The Motivational Effects of Charismatic Leadership: A Self-Concept Based Theory," *Organizational Science* 4 (1993): 577.

115. See, e.g., Christopher S. Stewart, *Hunting the Tiger: The Fast Life and Violent Death of the Balkans' Most Dangerous Man* (New York: St. Martin's, 2007) (discussing the leader of the transnational Serb paramilitary group Arkan's Tigers).

116. Ori Brafman and Rod A. Beckstrom, *The Starfish and the Spider: The Unstoppable Power of Leaderless Organizations* (New York: Portfolio, 2006), 92: "In open organizations, a catalyst is the person who initiates a circle and then fades away into the background."

117. But see Heller, "Retreat from Nuremberg," 477: "The jurisprudence of the International Military Tribunal, Nuremberg Military Tribunal, and International Military Tribunal for the Far East . . . not only assumed that the crime of aggression could be committed by two categories of individuals who could never satisfy the 'control or direct' requirement—private economic actors such as industrialists, and political or military officials in a state who are complicit in another state's act of aggression—they specifically rejected the 'control or direct' requirement in favour of a much less restrictive 'shape or influence' standard."

118. Weisbord, "Conceptualizing Aggression," 7: "As a direct consequence of the method chosen by the diplomats, the definition of the crime of aggression contains anachronistic concepts that undermine its relevance, and therefore its legitimacy, today."

119. Glennon, "Blank-Prose Crime of Aggression," 85–88, 101–2; Paulus, "Second Thoughts," 1128.

120. Oliver Wendell Holmes Jr., *The Common Law*, ed. Mark DeWolfe Howe (Cambridge, MA: Belknap, 1963; originally published 1881), 5.

121. Chris Woods, "The Story of America's Very First Drone Strike," *Atlantic*, May 30, 2015, http://www.theatlantic.com/international/archive/2015/05/america-first-drone-strike-afghanistan/394463/.

122. Ibid.

123. Jack Serle and Jessica Purkiss, "Drone Wars: The Full Data," Bureau of Investigative Journalism, January 1, 2017, https://www.thebureauinvestigates.com/category/projects/drones/drones-graphs/.

124. Ibid.

125. Marina Fang, "Nearly 90 Percent of People Killed in Recent Drone Strikes Were Not the Target," *Huffington Post*, October 15, 2015, http://www.huffingtonpost.com/entry/civilian-deaths-drone-strikes_us_561fafe2e4b028dd7ea6c4ff.

126. Koh, "Obama Administration and International Law."

127. David G. Savage, "Obama Advisor Who Had Decried 'War on Terror' Now Defends Drones," *Los Angeles Times*, January 5, 2013, http://articles.latimes.com/2013/jan/05/nation/la-na-koh-drones-20130106.

128. Matthew C. Weed, *2001 Authorization for Use of Military Force: Issues Concerning Its Continued Application* (Congressional Research Service, April 14, 2015), https://www.fas.org/sgp/crs/natsec/R43983.pdf.

129. Harold Hongju Koh, "How to End the Forever War," speech at Oxford Union, May 7, 2013, https://www.law.yale.edu/system/files/documents/pdf/Faculty/KohOxfordSpeech.pdf.

130. Ibid.

131. "Statement of No Confidence in Harold H. Koh," letter to Dean Trevor Morrison and President John Sexton, in "Reclaiming Human Rights: An Examination of Harold Koh and His Disservice to Global Peace," WordPress, n.d., accessed September 24, 2018, https://rethinkkoh.wordpress.com/; see also International Human Rights and Conflict Resolution Clinic (Stanford Law School) and Global Justice Clinic (NYU School of Law), *Living under Drones: Death, Injury, and Trauma to Civilians from US Drone Practices in Pakistan* (September 2012), 121–22, https://chrgj.org/wp-content/uploads/2016/09/Living-Under-Drones.pdf (hereinafter *Living under Drones*).

132. Michael Posner, professor at NYU Stern School of Business, to members of the NYU Law Community, letter dated March 8, 2015, https://www.justsecurity.org/wp-content/uploads/2015/04/Michael-Posner-response-to-Statement-of-No-Confidence.pdf (responding to the "Statement of No Confidence in Harold Koh"); Ryan Goodman, "Advancing Human Rights from Within: The Footsteps of Harold Koh," *Just Security*, April 10, 2015, https://www.justsecurity.org/21912/harold-koh-nyu-asil-2010-speech-advancing-human-rights/; "Open Letter In Support of Harold Hongju Koh," n.d., accessed July 24, 2017, https://sites.google.com/site/haroldkohletter/; Nahal Toosi, "Koh in the Cross Hairs," *Politico*, April 19, 2015, http://www.politico.com/story/2015/04/harold-koh-in-the-crosshairs-117110.

133. *Living under Drones*, vii.

134. See ibid., 81.

135. See ibid., 74, 76, vii, x; Tara McKelvey, "Drones Kill Rescuers in 'Double Tap', say Activists," *BBC News Magazine*, October 22, 2013, http://www.bbc.com/news/world-us-canada-24557333.

136. Tom Engelhardt, "The US Has Bombed at Least Eight Wedding Parties Since 2001," *Nation*, December 20, 2013, http://www.thenation.com/article/us-has-bombed-least-eight-wedding-parties-2001/; Tom Engelhardt, "The Wedding Crashers," *TomDispatch*, July 13, 2008, http://www.tomdispatch.com/post/174954/engelhardt_the_wedding_crashers; Lucy Draper, "The Wedding that Became a Funeral," *Newsweek*, December 12, 2014, http://www.newsweek.com/wedding-became-funeral-us-still-silent-one-year-deadly-yemen-drone-strike-291403; "US Investigates Yemenis' Charge that Drone Strike 'Turned Wedding into a Funeral,' " *NBC News*, January 7, 2014, http://investigations.nbcnews.com/_news/2014/01/07/22163872-us-investigates-yemenis-charge-that-drone-strike-turned-wedding-into-a-funeral?lite.

137. David Kilcullen and Andrew McDonald Exum, "Death from Above, Outrage Down Below," *New York Times*, May 16, 2009, http://www.nytimes.com/2009/05/17/opinion/17exum.html?_r=0.

138. Lynn E. Davis, Michael J. McNerney, James Chow, Thomas Hamilton, Sarah Harting, and Daniel Byman, *Armed and Dangerous? UAVs and U.S. Security* (Santa Monica, CA: Rand Corporation, 2014), 7, http://www.rand.org/pubs/research_reports/RR449.html.

139. Patrick Tucker, "Every Country Will Have Armed Drones within 10 Years," *Defense One*, May 6, 2014, http://www.defenseone.com/technology/2014/05/every-country-will-have-armed-drones-within-ten-years/83878/.

140. Heather M. Roff and P. W. Singer, "The Next President Will Decide the Fate of Killer Robots—and the Future of War," *Wired*, September 6, 2016, https://www.wired.com/2016/09/next-president-will-decide-fate-killer-robots-future-war/.

141. Bobbitt, *Terror and Consent*, 23.

142. Patrick Wintour and Nicholas Watt, "UK Forces Kill British Isis Fighters in Targeted Drone Strike on Syrian City," *Guardian*, September 7, 2015, http://www.theguardian.com/uk-news/2015/sep/07/uk-forces-airstrike-killed-isis-briton-reyaad-khan-syria.

143. Quoted in Owen Bowcott, Alice Ross, and Vikram Dodd, "Right of Self-Defence Central to Legal Debate over Syria Drone Strike," *Guardian*, September 7,

2015, http://www.theguardian.com/uk-news/2015/sep/07/right-of-self-defence-legal-debate-syria-drone-strike.

144. Aaron Stein, "The ISIS Endgame in Syria Exposes Long-Held Grievances," *Newsweek*, March 14, 2017, http://www.newsweek.com/isis-end-game-syria-exposes-long-held-grievances-567218; Mary Dejevsky, "As Syria's War Enters Its Endgame, the Risk of a US-Russia Conflict Escalates," *Guardian*, June 21, 2017, https://www.theguardian.com/commentisfree/2017/jun/21/syria-war-endgame-us-russia-conflict-washington-moscow-accidental-war.

145. Jon Gambrell, "AP Explains: What Is the U.S./Russia Deconfliction Line?" *AP News*, April 7, 2017, https://apnews.com/9147aa068855466386cf19d dab5bc827/ap-explains-us-russia-line-protected-pilots-over-syria.

146. Kyle Mizokami, "Iran Launched a Salvo of Ballistic Missiles at ISIS," *Popular Mechanics*, June 19, 2017, http://www.popularmechanics.com/military/weapons/a26983/iran-launched-missiles-syria/; Thomas Erdbrink and Mujib Mashal, "At Least 12 Killed in Pair of Terrorist Attacks in Iran," *New York Times*, June 7, 2017, https://www.nytimes.com/2017/06/07/world/middleeast/iran-parliament-attack-khomeini-mausoleum.html.

147. Michael R. Gordon and Ivan Nechepurenko, "Russia Warns U.S. after Downing of Syrian Warplane," *New York Times*, June 19, 2017, https://www.nytimes.com/2017/06/19/world/middleeast/russia-syria.html; Paul D. Shinkman, Russian Jet Flies within 5 Feet of U.S. Spy Plane," *US News*, June 20, 2017, https://www.usnews.com/news/national-news/articles/2017-06-20/russian-jet-flies-within-5-feet-of-us-spy-plane-over-baltic-sea.

148. Ibid.

149. Ibid.

150. Ibid.

151. Spencer Ackerman, "Fewer Deaths from Drone Strikes in 2013 after Obama Policy Change," *Guardian*, December 31, 2013, https://www.theguardian.com/world/2013/dec/31/deaths-drone-strikes-obama-policy-change.

152. Eric H. Holder Jr. (US attorney general) to the Honorable Patrick J. Leahy, letter dated May 22, 2013, https://assets.documentcloud.org/documents/703181/ag-letter-5-22-13.pdf.

153. Daniel Klaidman, "Obama: I Make the Drone Decisions," *Daily Beast*, May 23, 2013, http://www.thedailybeast.com/obama-i-make-the-drone-decisions.

154. Quoted in Greg Jaffe and Karen DeYoung, "Trump Administration Reviewing Ways to Make It Easier to Launch Drone Strikes," *Washington Post*, March 13, 2017, https://www.washingtonpost.com/world/national-security/trump-administration-reviewing-ways-to-make-it-easier-to-launch-drone-strikes/2017/03/13/ac39ced0–07f8–11e7-b77c-0047d15a24e0_story.html?utm_term=.6ec7ede8c5c7.

155. Ackerman, "Fewer Deaths from Drone Strikes."

156. But see Azmat Khan and Anand Gopal, "The Uncounted," *New York Times Magazine*, November 16, 2017, https://www.nytimes.com/interactive/2017/11/16/magazine/uncounted-civilian-casualties-iraq-airstrikes.html: "the air war has been significantly less precise than the coalition claims," and "in terms of civilian deaths, this may be the least transparent war in recent American history."

157. Jaffe and DeYoung, "Trump Administration."

158. Micah Zenko, "The (Not-So) Peaceful Transition of Power: Trump's Drone Strikes Outpace Obama," *Council on Foreign Relations* (blog), March 2, 2017, https://www.cfr.org/blog-post/not-so-peaceful-transition-power-trumps-drone-strikes-outpace-obama.

CHAPTER 9

1. Bass, *Stay the Hand of Vengeance*, 29–30.
2. "Ivory Coast: Gbagbo Held after Assault on Residence," *BBC News*, April 11, 2011, http://www.bbc.com/news/world-africa-13039825 (hereinafter "Gbagbo Held after Assault").
3. Xan Rice and Nicholas Watt, "Ivory Coast's Laurent Gbagbo Arrested—Four Months On," *Guardian*, April 11, 2011, https://www.theguardian.com/world/2011/apr/11/ivory-coast-former-leader-arrested.
4. Security Council, "Security Council Demands End to Violence in Cote d'Ivoire, Imposing Sanctions against Former President and Urging Him to 'Step Aside', in Resolution 1975," coverage of 6508th meeting, SC/10215, UN, March 30, 2011, http://www.un.org/press/en/2011/sc10215.doc.htm.
5. According to Human Rights Watch, "abuses by pro-Ouattara forces reached a comparable level" against "civilians from ethnic groups associated with Gbagbo." "The Laurent Gbagbo and Charles Blé Goudé Trial: Questions and Answers," Human Rights Watch, January 25, 2016, https://www.hrw.org/news/2016/01/25/laurent-gbagbo-and-charles-ble-goude-trial.
6. SC Res. 1975, paras. 6–7 (March 30, 2011), http://www.globalr2p.org/media/files/cotedivoire1975.pdf.
7. Peter Allen, "Ivory Coast: Laurent Gbagbo Captured by French Special Forces, Rival Claims," *Telegraph*, April 11, 2011, http://www.telegraph.co.uk/news/worldnews/africaandindianocean/cotedivoire/8443240/Ivory-Coast-Laurent-Gbagbo-captured-by-French-special-forces-rival-claims.html.
8. Colum Lynch and William Branigin, "Ivory Coast Strongman Arrested after French Forces Intervene," *Washington Post*, April 11, 2011, https://www.washingtonpost.com/world/ivory-coast-strongman-arrested-after-french-forces-intervene/2011/04/11/AFOBaeKD_story.html.
9. Ibid.: "Initial reports indicated that French troops had captured Gbagbo . . . and turned him over to Ouattara's forces. But Ouattara's U.N. envoy subsequently told reporters that the arrest had been carried out by forces loyal to the president-elect."
10. Gbagbo and Blé Goudé Case, ICC-02/11-01/15, ICC, n.d., accessed September 13, 2016, https://www.icc-cpi.int/cdi/gbagbo-goude.
11. "Gbagbo Held after Assault."
12. "Q&A: Ivory Coast Crisis," *BBC News*, April 13, 2011, http://www.bbc.com/news/world-africa-11916590; *CNN* Wire Staff, "Ivory Coast President Urges Calm after Gbagbo Is Arrested," *CNN*, April 11, 2011, http://edition.cnn.com/2011/WORLD/africa/04/11/ivory.coast.crisis/?hpt=T2.
13. "Russia Lashes Out at UN Military Action in Cote d'Ivoire," *RT News*, April 6, 2011, https://www.rt.com/news/cote-ivoire-gbagbo-un/.

14. "While recognizing that States not party to the Rome Statute have no obligation under the Statute, urges all States and concerned regional and other international organizations to cooperate fully." SC Res. 1593, para. 1–2 (March 31, 2005), https://www.icc-cpi.int/NR/rdonlyres/85FEBD1A-29F8-4EC4-9566-48EDF 55CC587/283244/N0529273.pdf.

15. "U.S. Affirms Sudan's Cooperation on Counter-Terrorism Efforts for 2014," *Sudan Tribune*, June 19, 2015, http://www.sudantribune.com/spip.php?article55404; and, later, a secret refugee-stemming agreement with the EU, Jürgen Dahlkamp and Maximilian Popp, "Questionable Deal: EU to Work with African Despot to Keep Refugees Out," *Spiegel Online International*, May 13, 2016, http://www.spiegel .de/international/world/eu-to-work-with-despot-in-sudan-to-keep-refugees-out -a-1092328.html; Mohammed Osman, "How the U.S. and EU's Cooperation with Sudan Rubberstamps Bad Behaviour," *Just Security*, July 30, 2018, https://www .justsecurity.org/59701/u-s-eus-cooperation-sudan-rubberstamps-bad-behavior/.

16. The warrant was issued March 4, 2009; al-Bashir travelled to Eritrea March 23. "Sudan President Al-Bashir Defies Arrest Warrant with Trip to Eritrea," *Telegraph*, March 24, 2009, http://www.telegraph.co.uk/news/worldnews/africaandindian ocean/sudan/5040418/Sudan-President-al-Bashir-defies-arrest-warrant-with-trip -to-Eritrea.html.

17. Arab League Secretary-General Amr Moussa said the Arab league would support al-Bashir against any threats posed by the warrant. "Al-Bashir Defiant at Darfur Rally," *Al Jazeera*, March 8, 2009, http://www.aljazeera.com/news/africa /2009/03/20093845925483192.html.

18. "89 Trips Since 2009: An Indicted War Criminal's Global Travels," n.d., accessed June 26, 2017, https://s3.amazonaws.com/uploads.knightlab.com/story mapjs/bec643e888c2d80434574655a1e32c37/bashir/draft.html; Nuba Reports, "Sudan's President Has Made 74 Trips across the World in the Seven Years He's Been Wanted for War Crimes," *Quartz Africa*, March 4, 2016, http://qz.com/630571 /sudans-president-has-made-74-trips-across-the-world-in-the-seven-years-hes-been -wanted-for-war-crimes/.

19. "Botswana says Sudan's Bashir Will Be Arrested if He Visits," *Sudan Tribune*, June 9, 2006, http://www.sudantribune.com/spip.php?article31449.

20. "Kenyan Court Issues Arrest Order for Sudan's Bashir," Reuters, November 28, 2011, http://www.reuters.com/article/us-kenya-bashir-icc-idUSTRE7AR0 YA20111128.

21. Andy Checkley, "Sudanese President Cancels Trip to Uganda," *Guardian*, July 20, 2009, https://www.theguardian.com/katine/2009/jul/20/omar-bashir-ugandan -trip; "France Invites Sudan, Not Bashir, to Summit," Reuters, March 22, 2010, http:// www.reuters.com/article/us-sudan-france-invitation-idUSTRE62L2B720100322; "ICC Fugitive Al-Bashir's Travel Curtailed," *Global Justice*, April 21, 2015, https:// ciccglobaljustice.wordpress.com/2015/04/21/icc-fugitive-al-bashirs-travel-cur tailed/; Elise Keppler, "Dispatches: Think Again, President Al-Bashir," Human Rights Watch, April 20, 2015, https://www.hrw.org/news/2015/04/20/dispatches-think -again-president-al-bashir; Colum Lynch, "Sudan's Omar Al-Bashir Cancels U.N. Trip," *Foreign Policy*, September 25, 2013, http://foreignpolicy.com/2013/09/25 /sudans-omar-al-bashir-cancels-u-n-trip-2/; Marlise Simons, "Sudan: President Cancels Zambian Trip," *New York Times*, December 15, 2010, http://www.nytimes

.com/2010/12/15/world/africa/15briefs-Bashir.html?_r=0; Sudan; "Central African Republic Convinces Bashir President to Stay Away," *Sudan Tribune*, December 1, 2010, http://allafrica.com/stories/201012070603.html; "Sudan's Al-Bashir Goes Missing on Way to China," *Telegraph*, June 27, 2011, http://www.telegraph.co.uk /news/worldnews/africaandindianocean/sudan/8600895/Sudans-al-Bashir-goes -missing-on-way-to-China.html.

22. "Nigeria Hints It Was Preparing to Arrest Sudan's Bashir During Visit," *Sudan Tribune*, August 19, 2013, http://www.sudantribune.com/spip.php?article47721.

23. Owen Bowcott, "Sudan President Omar Al-Bashir Leaves South Africa as Court Considers Arrest," *Guardian*, June 15, 2015, https://www.theguard-ian.com/world/2015/jun/15/south-africa-to-fight-omar-al-bashirs-arrest-warrant -sudan; Agence France-Presse, "South African Court Rules Failure to Detain Omar Al-Bashir Was 'Disgraceful,'" *Guardian*, March 16, 2016, https://www .theguardian.com/world/2016/mar/16/south-african-court-rules-failure-to-detain -omar-al-bashir-was-disgraceful.

24. Michael Astor, "ICC Prosecutor Knocks Security Council over Sudan," *San Diego Union-Tribune*, June 9, 2016, http://www.sandiegouniontribune.com/sdut -icc-prosecutor-knocks-security-council-over-sudan-2016jun09-story.html.

25. David Smith, "ICC Chief Prosecutor Shelves Darfur War Crimes Probe," *Guardian*, December 14, 2014, https://www.theguardian.com/world/2014/dec/14 /icc-darfur-war-crimes-fatou-bensouda-sudan.

26. Ibid.

27. Ibid.

28. R. Jeffrey Smith, "Anti-Milosevic Protests Sweep Across Yugoslavia," *Washingston Post*, October 3, 2000.

29. "Milosevic Arrested, Jailed, Sedated."

30. "Milosevic Arrest Breaks Ground on International Justice", June 28, 2001, Human Rights Watch, https://www.hrw.org/news/2001/06/28/milosevic-arrest -breaks-ground-international-justice; Anton la Guardia, Ambrose Evans-Pritchard, and Alex Todorovic, "£900m in Aid for Handing Over Milosevic," *Telegraph*, June 30, 2001, https://www.telegraph.co.uk/news/worldnews/1312896/900m-in -aid-for-handing-over-Milosevic.html.

31. "Congo Ex-rebel Chief Bemba Arrested for War Crimes," Reuters, May 24, 2008, https://www.reuters.com/article/us-congo-democratic-bemba-idUS L2454580020080525; Anaga Dalal, "CAR, Part II: Continued Media Cove-rage of Bemba Arrest," Coalition for the ICC, May 27, 2008, http://iccnow.org /?mod=newsdetail&news=2676.

32. "World, Europe: Pinochet Arrested in London," *BBC News*, October 17, 1998, http://news.bbc.co.uk/2/hi/europe/195413.stm.

33. Warren Hoge, "After 16 Months of House Arrest, Pinochet Quits En-gland," *New York Times*, March 3, 2000, https://www.nytimes.com/2000/03/03 /world/after-16-months-of-house-arrest-pinochet-quits-england.html.

34. Klaartje Quirijns, *The Dictator Hunter* (film) (Amsterdam: Pieter Van Huys-tee Film and Television, 2007); "Democracy Now!: *The Dictator Hunter*: Victims of US-Allied Chadian Dictator Hissene Habre Lead Quest to Bring Him to Justice," Democracy Now! online broadcast, June 12, 2008, http://www.democracynow .org/2008/6/12/the_dictator_hunter_victims_of_us.

35. Julian Borger, "The Hunt for the Former Yugoslavia's War Criminals: Mission Accomplished," *Guardian*, August 3, 2011, https://www.theguardian.com/world/2011/aug/03/former-yugoslavia-war-crimes-hunt.

36. Charles Chernor Jalloh, "Introduction: Assessing the Legacy of the Special Court for Sierra Leone," in *The Sierra Leone Special Court and Its Legacy: The Impact for Africa and International Criminal Law,* ed. Charles Chernor Jalloh, 13 (New York: Cambridge University Press, 2014).

37. Julian Borger, *The Butcher's Trail: How the Search for Balkan War Criminals Became the World's Most Successful Manhunt* (New York: Other Press, 2016), 27–30, 43.

38. Ibid.

39. Hazel Fox, *The Law of State Immunity*, 2nd ed. (Oxford: Oxford University Press, 2008), 667–82; Dapo Akande, "International Law Immunities and the International Criminal Court," *American Journal of International Law* 98 (2004): 409.

40. Beth van Schaack, "Immunity Doctrines: The Need for a Systemic Approach," *Just Security*, October 28, 2014, https://www.justsecurity.org/16838/immunity-doctrines-systemic-approach/; Fox, *Law of State Immunity*, 673.

41. Concepción Escobar Hernández, "Second Report on the Immunity of State Officials from Foreign Criminal Jurisdiction," UN Doc. A/CN.4/661 (April 4, 2013), paras. 59–60.

42. Fox, *Law of State Immunity*, 201–4; the "metaphysical rationale" and the "international-relations rationale" are typically raised to explain so-called personal immunities (*ratione personae*), and the "metaphysical rationale" and the "patriotic rationale" to explain functional immunities (*ratione materiae*).

43. See "Case Concerning the Arrest Warrant of 11 April 2000" (Democratic Republic of Congo v. Belgium), 2002 ICJ 121 (February 14, 2002), paras. 51–70.

44. Helmut Kreicker, "Immunities," ch. 21 in Kress and Barriga, *Crime of Aggression.*

45. Nuremberg Charter, art. 7.

46. Rome Statute, art. 27 (2); see also In the Case of the Prosecutor v. Omar Hassan Ahmad Al Bashir, Decision on the Prosecution's Application for a Warrant of Arrest against Omar Hassan Ahmad Al Bashir, ICC-02/05–01/09 (March 4, 2009), para. 43, www.legal-tools.org/doc/e26cf4.

47. Dapo Akande, "The Legal Nature of Security Council Referrals to the ICC and Its Impact on Al Bashir's Immunities," *Journal of International Criminal Justice* 7 (2009): 37–339, 342.

48. Van Schaack, "Immunity before the African Court."

49. Concepción Escobar Hernández, "Fifth Report on Immunity of State Officials from Foreign Criminal Jurisdiction," UN Doc. A/CN.4/701 (June 14, 2016), paras. 20, 219, http://legal.un.org/docs/?symbol=A/CN.4/701 (including the crime of aggression as an exception to immunity *ratione materiae* from foreign criminal jurisdiction); Regina v. Bow Street Metropolitan Stipendiary Magistrate and others, ex Parte Pinochet Ugarte (Amnesty International and others intervening) (No. 1), 4 All E R 897, 939–40, 945–46 (1998) (H. L., per Nicholls, Steyn, L. JJ) (stating that serving heads of state are immune from criminal jurisdiction of foreign states); Naomi Roht-Arriaza, *The Pinochet Effect: Transnational Justice in*

the Age of Human Rights (Philadelphia, PA: University of Pennsylvania Press, 2005), 57, 186–88.

50. Hernández, "Fifth Report on Immunity," paras. 221–22.

51. Charles Jalloh, "ILC Plenary Debate on the Fifth Report on Immunity of State Officials from Foreign Criminal Jurisdiction (A/CN.4/710; June 2016)" (May 23, 2017), para. 16.

52. David Scheffer, "Proposal for an International Criminal Court Arrest Procedures Protocol," *Northwestern Journal of International Human Rights* 12 (2014): 229–52.

53. Ibid., 232.

54. Ibid.

55. Ibid, 232, 236–38.

56. Ibid., 243

57. Ibid., 236.

58. Jeffrey Gettleman, "In Vast Jungle, U.S. Troops Aid in Search for Kony," *New York Times*, April 29, 2012, http://www.nytimes.com/2012/04/30/world/africa/kony-tracked-by-us-forces-in-central-africa.html?pagewanted=all.

59. Conor Gaffey, "Joseph Kony: Rebels Kidnap Civilians Weeks after U.S. Stops Hunting Warlord," *Newsweek*, June 17, 2017, http://www.newsweek.com/kony-2012-joseph-kony-lra-us-military-626944.

60. Ibid.; Conor Gaffey, "Child Soldiers of Africa: Uganda's Search for Lord's Resistance Army Leader Joseph Kony Ends in the Central African Republic," *Newsweek*, April 18, 2017, http://www.newsweek.com/joseph-kony-lords-resistance-army-585736.

61. "The Lord's Resistance Army," Enough Project, n.d., accessed September 3, 2016, http://www.enoughproject.org/conflicts/lra/us-government-and-lra.

62. Invisible Children, "Kony 2012," YouTube, March 5, 2012, https://www.youtube.com/watch?v=Y4MnpzG5Sqc.

63. Nick Carbone, "Top 10 Everything of 2012," *Time*, December 4, 2012, http://entertainment.time.com/2012/12/04/top-10-arts-lists/slide/kony-2012/.

64. Scott Wong, "Kony Captures Congress' Attention," *Politico*, March 22, 2012, https://www.politico.com/story/2012/03/kony-captures-congress-attention-074355; Michael Gerson, "The controversy over 'Kony 2012,'" *Washington Post*, March 10, 2012, https://www.washingtonpost.com/blogs/post-partisan/post/the-controversy-over-kony-2012/2012/03/10/gIQAzc6M3R_blog.html; Robert Mackey, "African Critics of Kony Campaign See a 'White Man's Burden' for the Facebook Generation," *New York Times*, March 9, 2012, http://thelede.blogs.nytimes.com/2012/03/09/african-critics-of-kony-campaign-hear-echoes-of-the-white-mans-burden/; Matt Williams, "Kony 2012 Campaigner Jason Russel: 'I Wasn't in Control of My Mind or Body,'" *Guardian*, October 8, 2012, https://www.theguardian.com/world/2012/oct/08/kony-2012-jason-russell-interview-nbc.

65. Wong, "Kony captures Congress' attention."

66. Ben Taub, "The Assad Files," *New Yorker*, April 18, 2016, http://www.newyorker.com/magazine/2016/04/18/bashar-al-assads-war-crimes-exposed.

67. Ibid.

68. James Risen, "Before Shooting in Iraq, a Warning on Blackwater," *New York Times*, June 29, 2014, http://www.nytimes.com/2014/06/30/us/before-shooting-in

-iraq-warning-on-blackwater.html; Sabrina Tavernise, "U.S. Contractor Banned by Iraq over Shootings," *New York Times*, September 18, 2007, http://www.nytimes .com/2007/09/18/world/middleeast/18iraq.html?pagewanted=all and_r=0; Nicky Woolf, "Former Blackwater Guards Sentenced for Massacre of Unarmed Iraqi Civilians," *Guardian*, April 14, 2015, https://www.theguardian.com/us-news/2015 /apr/13/former-blackwater-guards-sentencing-baghdad-massacre.

69. Richard Norton-Taylor, "Britain Is at Centre of Global Mercenary Industry, Says Charity," *Guardian*, February 3, 2016, https://www.theguardian.com/business /2016/feb/03/britain-g4s-at-centre-of-global-mercenary-industry-says-charity.

70. Conor Friedersdorf, "The Terrifying Background of the Man Who Ran a CIA Assassination Unit," *Atlantic*, July 18, 2012, http://www.theatlantic.com /politics/archive/2012/07/the-terrifying-background-of-the-man-who-ran-a-cia -assassination-unit/259856/; Peter W. Singer, "Corporate Warriors: The Rise of the Privatized Military Industry and its Ramifications for International Security," *International Security* 26 (2001): 186–87; see also Peter W. Singer, *Corporate Warriors: The Rise of the Privatized Military Industry* (Ithaca, NY: Cornell University Press, 2003), 9–17.

71. Evan Wright, *How to Get Away with Murder in America: Drug Lords, Dirty Pols, Obsessed Cops, and the Quiet Man Who Became the CIA's Master Killer* (ebook) (San Francisco: Byliner, 2012), loc. 1432; see also Mayer, *Dark Side*, 39: "To give the President deniability, and to keep him from getting his hands dirty, the finding called for the president to delegate blanket authority to Tenet to decide on a case-by-case basis whom to kill, whom to kidnap, whom to detain and interrogate, and how."

72. Ibid.

73. *Accountability for Abu Ghraib Torture by Private Military Contractors* (New York: Center for Constitutional Rights, n.d., accessed September 3, 2016) http://ccr justice.org/sites/default/files/assets/files/PMC%20factsheet%20january%202015 .pdf; Spencer S. Hsu and Victoria St. Martin, "Four Blackwater Guards Sentenced in Iraq Shootings of 31 Unarmed Civilians," *Washington Post*, April 13, 2015, https://www.washingtonpost.com/local/crime/four-blackwater-guards-sentenced -in-iraq-shootings-of-31-unarmed-civilians/2015/04/13/55b777e0-dee4–11e4 -be40–566e2653afe5_story.html.

74. Senate Select Committee on Intelligence, "Committee Study of the Central Intelligence Agency's Detention and Interrogation Program" (updated April 3, 2014, declassification revisions December 3, 2014), 21, reproduced at *New York Times*, December 9, 2014, http://www.nytimes.com/interactive/2014/12/09 /world/cia-torture-report-document.html; Hunter Stuart, "How We Outsourced CIA Torture and Why It Matters," *Huffington Post*, December 16, 2014, http:// www.huffingtonpost.com/2014/12/12/outsourcing-torture-n_6317236.html.

75. Matt Apuzzo, "Ex-Blackwater Guards Given Long Terms for Killing Iraqis," *New York Times*, April 13, 2015, http://www.nytimes.com/2015/04/14 /us/ex-blackwater-guards-sentenced-to-prison-in-2007-killings-of-iraqi-civilians. html; James Glanz and Alissa J. Rubin, "From Errand to Fatal Shot to Hail of Fire to 17 Deaths," *New York Times*, October 3, 2007, http://www.nytimes .com/2007/10/03/world/middleeast/03firefight.html; Elise Labott, "Official: U.S. Will Not Renew Iraq Contract with Blackwater," *CNN*, January 30, 2009, http:// www.cnn.com/2009/WORLD/meast/01/30/us.blackwater.contract/.

76. "Authority of the Federal Bureau of Investigation to Override International Law in Extraterritorial Law Enforcement Activities," *Opinions of the Office of Legal Counsel* 13 (1989): 163, http://fas.org/irp/agency/doj/fbi/olc_override.pdf.

77. Ibid.

78. Beth van Schaack, "Al-Liby: Male Captus, Bene Detentus?" *Just Security*, October 7, 2013, https://www.justsecurity.org/1739/al-liby-male-captus-bene -detentus/: "A notable exception to this rule was articulated in United States v. Toscanino, 500 F.2d 267 (2d Cir. 1974), which held that jurisdiction should be barred where cruel or outrageous treatment in violation of the due process clause is involved."

79. Malcolm Forbes, "The Manhunt for the Butchers of the Balkans," *Daily Beast*, March 21, 2016, http://www.thedailybeast.com/articles/2016/03/21/the -manhunt-for-the-butchers-of-the-balkans.html.

80. Prosecutor v. Dragan Nikolić, Case No. IT-94–2-Pt, Decision On Defence Motion Challenging the Exercise of Jurisdiction by the Tribunal (ICTY, October 9, 2002).

81. Van Schaack, "Al-Liby."

82. Rome Statute, art. 8 *bis* (1)

83. Ibid., art. 8 *bis* (2)(g).

84. Effective control is the standard the International Court of Justice used in 1986 to assess whether the United States should be held accountable for acts carried out by Contra guerillas in Nicaragua (*Nicaragua*, para 115). The "effective control" standard was later countenanced by the ICTY in the Tadić Case by a more permissive "overall control" test. Prosecutor v. Tadic, Case No. IT-94–1-A, Judgment, para. 146 (July 15, 1999).

85. Rome Statute, art. 25(3)(b)–(c): "A person shall be criminally responsible and liable for punishment for a crime within the jurisdiction of the Court if that person . . . orders, solicits or induces the commission of such a crime which in fact occurs or is attempted."

86. Friedrich Nietzsche, *Beyond Good and Evil: Prelude to a Philosophy of the Future*, trans. Helen Zimmern (Project Gutenberg, ebook last updated February 4, 2013; originally published 1886), para 146, http://www.gutenberg.org /files/4363/4363-h/4363-h.htm.

87. Reisinger Coracini, "Selected National Laws," 1100–1101.

88. Ibid.

89. "A Truth Commission for the Bush Era?" *New York Times*, March 2, 2009, http://roomfordebate.blogs.nytimes.com/2009/03/02/a-truth-commission -for-the-bush-era/?_r=0; Jill Lawrence, "Poll: Most Want Inquiry into Anti-terror Tactics," *USA Today*, February 12, 2009, http://usatoday30.usatoday.com/news /washington/2009-02-11-investigation-poll_N.htm.

90. Carolyn Lochhead, "Pelosi Backs Anti-Terror Truth Commission," *SF Gate*, April 23, 2009, http://www.sfgate.com/politics/article/Pelosi-backs-anti-terror -truth-commission-3163447.php; Jeremy A. Rabkin, "A Bush 'Truth Commission': The Pros and Cons," *Los Angeles Times*, March 12, 2009, http://www.latimes .com/opinion/opinion-la/la-oew-schwarz-rabkin12–2009mar12-story.html.

91. Scott Shane, "To Investigate or Not: Four Ways to Look Back at Bush," *New York Times*, February 21, 2009, http://www.nytimes.com/2009/02/22/week inreview/22shane.html?scp=10andsq=conyers%20commissionandst=cse.

92. Quoted in Brent J. Steele, *Alternative Accountabilities in Global Politics: The Scars of Violence* (London: Routledge, 2013), 163, n. 1; Shane, "To Investigate or Not."

93. "The Inquiry," Iraq Inquiry, n.d., accessed September 14, 2016, http://www.iraqinquiry.org.uk/the-inquiry/, archived November 23, 2017, at The National Archives, http://webarchive.nationalarchives.gov.uk/20171123123857/http://www.iraqinquiry.org.uk/the-inquiry/.

94. Sir John Chilcot (chairman), Sir Lawrence Freedman, Sir Roderic Lyne, Baroness Usha Prashar, and Sir Martin Gilbert. The committee appointed two advisers to help it conduct its work: General Sir Roger Wheeler, a former chief of the general staff, assisted the committee on military matters, and Dame Rosalyn Higgins QC, former president of the International Court of Justice, advised on international law.

95. Matthew Moore, "Tony Blair at the Iraq Inquiry—as It Happened" (video), *Telegraph*, January 29, 2010, http://www.telegraph.co.uk/news/newsvideo/7072427/Watch-Tony-Blair-live-at-Iraq-war-inquiry.html.

96. Prime Minister Brown announced, "no British document and no British witness will be beyond the scope of the inquiry." Quoted in Richard Norton-Taylor, "Back to Baghdad: How—and Why—Did Britain Go to War?" *Guardian*, November 23, 2009, https://www.theguardian.com/uk/2009/nov/23/chilcot-iraq-war-inquiry.

97. Ashley Cowburn, "Chilcot Report: Tony Blair Set to Be Savaged in 'Absolutely Brutal' Iraq War Inquiry Verdict," *Independent*, May 22, 2016, http://www.independent.co.uk/news/uk/politics/chilcot-report-tony-blair-set-to-be-savaged-in-absolutely-brutal-iraq-war-inquiry-verdict-a7041926.html.

98. Michael Holden, "Tony Blair in Spotlight as Report into Iraq War Due to be Published," Reuters, June 30, 2016, https://www.reuters.com/article/us-britain-iraq-inquiry/tony-blair-in-spotlight-as-report-into-iraq-war-due-to-be-published-idUSKCN0ZG2JU.

99. Rowena Mason, Anushka Asthana, and Heather Stewart, "Tony Blair: 'I Express More Sorrow, Regret and Apology than You Can Ever Believe,'" *Guardian*, July 6, 2016, https://www.theguardian.com/uk-news/2016/jul/06/tony-blair-deliberately-exaggerated-threat-from-iraq-chilcot-report-war-inquiry.

100. Ulrike Demmer, "Wanted for War Crimes: Rumsfeld Lawsuit Embarrasses German Authorities," *Spiegel Online International*, March 26, 2007, http://www.spiegel.de/international/world/wanted-for-war-crimes-rumsfeld-lawsuit-embarrasses-german-authorities-a-473987.html.

101. "Rumsfeld Torture Cases," European Center for Constitutional and Human Rights, n.d., accessed September 3, 2016, https://www.ecchr.eu/en/our_work/international-crimes-and-accountability/u-s-accountability/rumsfeld.html; "Prosecuting the US for War Crimes: Legal Fight against Rumsfeld Heads to Spain," *Spiegel Online International*, April 20, 2007, http://www.spiegel.de/international/europe/prosecuting-the-us-for-war-crimes-legal-fight-against-rumsfeld-heads-to-spain-a-480215.html.

102. Yvonne Ridley, "Bush Convicted of War Crimes in Absentia," *Foreign Policy Journal*, May 12, 2012, http://www.foreignpolicyjournal.com/2012/05/12/bush-convicted-of-war-crimes-in-absentia/; Charles P. Pierce, "War Criminals

among Us: Bush, Cheney, and the Eyes of the World," *Esquire*, June 1, 2015, http://www.esquire.com/news-politics/politics/news/a35397/bush-cheney-war-crimes/.

103. Ibid.

104. Agence France-Presse, "Failure to Detain Omar Al-Bashir."

105. "South Africa to Review Membership of World Court after Bashir Row," *Guardian*, June 25, 2015, https://www.theguardian.com/world/2015/jun/25/south-africa-review-international-criminal-court-bashir.

106. Prosecutor v. Omar Hassan Ahmad Al Bashir, "Order Requesting Submissions from the Republic of South Africa for the Purposes of Proceedings under Article 87(7) of the Rome Statute," 7, ICC-02/05–01/09-247 (September 4, 2015), https://www.icc-cpi.int/pages/record.aspx?uri=2044798#search=south%20africa.

107. Thulani Gqirana, "DA's Bid to Impeach Zuma Fails," *Mail and Guardian*, September 2, 2015, http://mg.co.za/article/2015-09-02-das-bid-to-impeach-zuma-fails.

108. *South Africa: Withdrawal of Notification of Withdrawal* (New York: United Nations, March 7, 2017), https://treaties.un.org/doc/Publication/CN/2017/CN.121.2017-Eng.pdf.

109. Caroline Schmitt and Louise Mushikiwabo: "Where Is a White Man Convicted by the ICC?" *Deutsche Welle*, October 28, 2015, http://www.dw.com/en/louise-mushikiwabo-where-is-a-white-man-convicted-by-the-icc/a-18812687; see also Caroline Schmitt, "13 Years, 1 Billion Dollars, 2 Convictions: Is the International Criminal Court Worth It?" *Deutsche Welle*, January 27, 2016, http://www.dw.com/en/13-years-1-billion-dollars-2-convictions-is-the-international-criminal-court-worth-it/a-19006069.

110. Quoted in Will Wilkinson, "Because You'd Be in Jail," *New York Times*, n.d., accessed July 24, 2017, https://www.nytimes.com/interactive/projects/cp/opinion/clinton-trump-second-debate-election-2016/because-youd-be-in-jail.

111. Frank Rich, "Just Wait: Watergate Didn't Become Watergate Overnight, Either," *New York Magazine*, June 25, 2017, http://nymag.com/daily/intelligencer/2017/06/frank-rich-nixon-trump-and-how-a-presidency-ends.html; but see Erin Gloria Ryan, "In Your Dreams: Liberal Impeachment Fantasies Have to Stop," *Daily Beast*, June 29, 2017, http://www.thedailybeast.com/liberal-impeachment-fantasies-have-to-stop.

112. Tal Kopan, "Trump Claims Immunity as President in Lawsuit," *CNN*, last updated April 18, 2017, http://www.cnn.com/2017/04/17/politics/trump-immunity-lawsuits/index.html.

113. Clinton v. Jones, 117 S. Ct. 1636 (1997), 1643–44.

114. Donald J. Trump, "As has been stated by numerous legal scholars, I have the absolute right to PARDON myself, but why would I do that when I have done nothing wrong? In the meantime, the never ending Witch Hunt, led by 13 very Angry and Conflicted Democrats (and others) continues into the mid-terms!" Twitter, 2018, accessed July 1, 2018, https://twitter.com/realdonaldtrump/status/1003616210922147841?lang=en.

115. Masha Gessen, "The Reichstag Fire Next Time: The Coming Crackdown," *Harper's Magazine*, July 2017, https://harpers.org/archive/2017/07/the-reichstag-fire-next-time/; Mark Danner, "What He Could Do," *New York Review of Books*, March 23, 2017, http://www.nybooks.com/articles/2017/03/23/what-trump-could-do/.

116. Thomas Homer-Dixon, "War is the 'Win' Trump Craves to End the Russia Investigation," *Globe and Mail*, updated June 29, 2017, https://www.theglo beandmail.com/opinion/war-is-the-win-trump-craves/article35477538/.

CHAPTER 10

1. ICC Assembly of States Parties, *Report on the Facilitation on the Activation of the Jurisdiction of the International Criminal Court over the Crime of Aggression*, ICC-ASP/16/24 (November 27, 2017), 15–19, https://asp.icc-cpi.int/iccdocs /asp_docs/ASP16/ICC-ASP-16–24-ENG.pdf.

2. Stefan Barriga, "The Scope of the ICC Jurisdiction over the Crime of Aggression: A Different Perspective," *EJIL: TALK!* (blog), September 29, 2017, https://www.ejiltalk.org/the-scope-of-icc-jurisdiction-over-the-crime-of-aggres sion-a-different-perspective/.

3. Oxford international legal scholar Dapo Akande made an impressive effort to shore up Canada, Colombia, France, Japan, Norway, and the United Kingdom's legal arguments, but the vast majority of delegations remained unpersuaded. See Dapo Akande, "The ICC Assembly of States Parties Prepares to Activate the ICC's Jurisdiction over the Crime of Aggression: But Who Will Be Covered by that Jurisdiction?" *EJIL: TALK!* (blog), June 26, 2017, https://www.ejiltalk.org /the-icc-assembly-of-states-parties-prepares-to-activate-the-iccs-jurisdiction-over -the-crime-of-aggression-but-who-will-be-covered-by-that-jurisdiction/; see Nikolas Stürchler, "The Activation of the Crime of Aggression in Perspective," *EJIL: TALK!* (blog), January 26, 2018, https://www.ejiltalk.org/the-activation-of-the-crime-of-aggression-in-perspective/ ("A large majority of States Parties that took the floor (I counted 37 out of 46) spoke out in favor of option 1, dismissed option 2 as not constituting a compromise given the existence of contending legal views, and/or signaled readiness to explore option 3. Seven expressed their continued preference for option 2 or voiced some unease with option 3. Only two States Parties, the most prominent proponents of the restrictive group, openly rejected option 3.").

4. Vienna Convention on the Law of Treaties, May 23, 1969, 1155 UNTS 331, arts. 39 and 40.1.

5. Edwige Belliard, "France," in Kress and Barriga, *Crime of Aggression*, 1143–45; Christopher Whomersley, "United Kingdom," in Kress and Barriga, *Crime of Aggression*, 1285–97.

6. See Claus Kress, "On the Activation of ICC Jurisdiction over the Crime of Aggression," *Journal of International Criminal Justice* 16 (2018): 9–11; also see Stürchler, "Activation."

7. ICC, Assembly of States Parties, "Draft Resolution Proposed by the Vice-Presidents of the Assembly: Activation of the Jurisdiction of the Court over the Crime of Aggression," L10-E-141217, ICC-ASP/16/L.10 (December 14, 2017), http://www.ejiltalk.org/wp-content/uploads/2017/12/ICC-ASP-16-L10-ENG -CoA-resolution-14Dec17-1130.pdf.

8. Jennifer Trahan, "From Kampala to New York: The Final Negotiations to Activate the Jurisdiction of the International Criminal Court over the Crime

of Aggression," *International Criminal Law Review* 18 (2018): 197–243; Stürchler, "Activation"; see also Annegret L. Hartig, "Dubious Negotiations in New York: Did France and the UK Come to Blow it Up?" *IntLawGrrls*, January 18, 2018, https://ilg2.org/2018/01/18/dubious-negotiations-in-new-york-did-france-and-the-uk-come-to-blow-it-up/, for an account of French-UK bargaining practices in New York.

9. Benjamin Ferencz, "Epilogue: The Long Journey to Kampala, A Personal Memoir," in Kress and Barriga, *Crime of Aggression*, 1511–15.

10. "States must be able to defend themselves . . . when, as is the case here, the government of the State where the threat is located is unwilling or unable to prevent the use of its territory for such attacks." Permanent Representative of the United States to the Secretary-General of the UN, letter dated September 23, 2014, UN Doc. S/2014/695.

11. Benjamin Haas and Steve Bannon, "We're Going to War in the South China Sea . . . No Doubt," *Guardian*, February 2, 2017, https://www.theguardian.com/us-news/2017/feb/02/steve-bannon-donald-trump-war-south-china-sea-no-doubt.

12. Robert Diab, *The Harbinger Theory: How the Post-9/11 Emergency Became Permanent and the Case for Reform* (New York: Oxford University Press, 2015), 42.

13. "Full Text of John Bolton's Speech to the Federalist Society," *Al Jazeera*, September 10, 2018, https://www.aljazeera.com/news/2018/09/full-text-john-bolton-speech-federalist-society-180910172828633.html.

14. Prosecutor v. Jean-Pierre Bemba Gombo, ICC-01/05–01/08 A, Judgment on the appeal of Mr. Jean-Pierre Bemba Gombo against Trial Chamber III's "Judgment pursuant to Article 74 of the Statute," 166–94 (June 8, 2018), https://www.icc-cpi.int/CourtRecords/CR2018_02984.pdf.

15. Labor leader Jeremy Corbin calls the 2003 invasion of Iraq an "illegal war" and, when asked about Blair, argues that individuals who made the decisions should face justice. Jon Stone, "Jeremy Corbyn 'Still Prepared to Call for Tony Blair War Crimes Investigation,'" *Independent*, May 23, 2016, http://www.independent.co.uk/news/uk/politics/jeremy-corbyn-still-prepared-to-call-for-war-crimes-investigation-into-tony-blair-a7042926.html; Nigel Pankhurst, "Newspaper Headlines: Iraq War Report and Blair Fallout," *BBC News*, July 7, 2016, http://www.bbc.com/news/blogs-the-papers-36731483.

16. "Hissene Habre Verdict: Landmark Decision Brings Justice for Tens of Thousands of Victims," Amnesty International, May 30, 2016, https://www.amnesty.org/en/latest/news/2016/05/hissene-habre-verdict-landmark-decision-brings-justice-for-tens-of-thousands-of-victims/; Celeste Hicks, "Is Habre's Landmark Conviction a New Model for International Justice?" *World Politics Review*, June 6, 2016, https://www.worldpoliticsreview.com/articles/18983/is-habre-s-landmark-conviction-a-new-model-for-international-justice. Recalling the United States' role in propping up Habré as a bulwark against Muammar Qaddafi, US Secretary of State John Kerry seized this "opportunity for the United States to reflect on, and learn from, our own connection with past events in Chad." John Kerry, "On the Conviction of Hissene Habre for War Crimes, Crimes Against Humanity, and Torture," Press Statement (May 30, 2016), https://geneva.usmission.gov/2016/05/31

/john-kerry-on-the-conviction-of-hissene-habre-for-war-crimes-crimes-against
-humanity-and-torture/.

17. Barack Obama, Speech in Hiroshima, Japan, May 27, 2016, in "Text of President Obama's Speech in Hiroshima, Japan," *New York Times*, May 27, 2016, http://www.nytimes.com/2016/05/28/world/asia/text-of-president-obamas-speech-in-hiroshima-japan.html.

18. Ibid.

19. Gibson, *Pattern Recognition*, 57.

20. Thucydides, *History of the Peloponnesian Wars*, trans. Richard Crawley (New York: J. M. Dent and E. P. Dutton, 1910), 394 (Melian dialogue).

21. Goldsmith and Posner, *Limits of International Law*, 6; Kennedy, *Dark Sides of Virtue*, 21–22.

22. Rebecca Solnit, "The Habits of Highly Cynical People," *Harper's Magazine*, May 2016, http://harpers.org/archive/2016/05/the-habits-of-highly-cynical-people/?single=1.

23. Benjamin B. Ferencz, "The Memory of Hiroshima," Letter to the editor, *New York Times*, May 26, 2016, http://www.nytimes.com/2016/05/27/opinion/the-memory-of-hiroshima.html?smid=tw-share: "Nuclear weapons are not the only enemy. Indifference can be fatal. In our new world, armed conflict threatens all of humanity." Benjamin Ferencz, "Law Not War!: Creating a World of Peace and Tolerance," *Soka Gakkai International Quarterly* 84 (April 2016), 9, http://www.sgi.org/content/files/resources/sgi-quarterly-magazine/1604_84.pdf.

24. *Handbook: Ratification and Implementation of the Kampala Amendments to the Rome Statute of the ICC—Crime of Aggression, War Crimes* (Princeton, NJ: Liechtenstein Institute on Self-Determination, Woodrow Wilson School of Public and International Affairs, Princeton University, n.d.), 4–5, http://crimeofaggression.info/documents/1/handbook.pdf.

25. Albert O. Hirschman, *The Rhetoric of Reaction: Perversity, Futility, Jeopardy* (Cambridge, MA: Belknap, 1991), 7. The perversity thesis: "Any purposive action to improve some feature of the political, social, or economic order only serves to exacerbate the condition one wishes to remedy." The futility thesis: "Attempts at social transformation will . . . 'fail to make a dent.' " The jeopardy thesis: "The cost of the proposed change . . . is too high as it endangers [a] previous . . . accomplishment."

26. Koh, "Obama Administration and International Law," 8.

27. Ferencz, "Law Not War!" 9.

Index

Abu Ghraib, 93

Academie, 161

Addington, David, 165

African Court of Justice and Human Rights, 101, 117

African Union, 117, 119, 152, 153, 155, 158

aggression: act of (see crime of aggression); efforts to define by the United Nations, 56–58, 61–65, 80; examples of superpower, 63; Litvinov-Politis definition, 36–37, 44, 47, 56, 63; 1974 definition, 62–65; perspectives on the meaning of, 102; undefined by international agreements of the 1920s, 35; undefined by the League of Nations, 35

Ahmadinejad, Mahmoud, 134–35

Akande, Dapo, 243n3

Akhavan, Payam, 78–80, 98, 115

Aksyonov, Sergey, a.k.a "Goblin," 26, 29

Albright, Madeleine, 78, 81

Alexandrov, Alexander, 119

America first movements: Buchanan's isolationism, 75; isolationism between the world wars, 73, 75; Trump's isolationism, 16, 75

Amin, Idi, 29

Amin, Ruhul, 148

Amnesty International, 154

Amos, Howard, 25–26

Annan, Kofi, 84

Anti-Ballistic Missile (ABM) Treaty of 1972, 17

Applegate, Lynda M., 230n103

Arab League, 119

Arbour, Louise, 82–83

Aristotle, 9

Asimov, Isaac, 133

al-Assad, Bashar, 15, 149

Assembly of States Parties: activation role of, 108, 169; activation scheduled for 2017, 2; consensus as decision-making norm, 172; Moreno Ocampo selected as first ICC prosecutor, 98; Preparatory Commission, 10; shift from politics to law set in motion by, 131; Special Working Group, initiation of, 101; Special Working Group on the Crime of Aggression, 43, 101–5, 120, 130

Avakov, Arsen, 24–25

al-Awlaki, Anwar, 145

al-Baghdadi, Abu Bakr, 11, 13–14, 145

Baker, James, 74

Balkans, the, 77–84

Bandera, Stepan, 24

Barre, Mohamed Siad, 76

Barriga, Stefan, 211n111, 211n116, 212n119, 212–13n125

al-Bashir, Omar, 6, 100–101, 152–54, 165–66

Bass, Gary, 60, 123

Baume, Maia de la, 200n35

Beard, Charles, 46

Beckstrom, Rod A., 230n116

Bellinger, John, III, 18

Bemba, Jean Pierre, 101, 154, 174

Bensouda, Fatou, 22, 100–101, 154

Berman, Nathaniel, 37, 42–43

Bertram-Nothnagel, Jutta, 106

Bangladesh, 68

Bhutto, Zulfikar Ali, 68–69

bin Laden, Osama, 104, 142, 145

Bismarck, Otto von, 38

Blackwater, 159–60

Blair, Tony: as humanitarian interventionist, 73; ICTY fugitives, instructions to arrest, 82; investigation and judgment of, 119, 164; Iraq War, decision to participate in, 4, 93; rebuke of, 174

Blum, Gabriella, 211n114

Bobbitt, Philip, 37, 39–43, 140, 142, 148

Bolton, John, 10, 105, 174

Borger, Julian, 156

Boucher, Catherine, 170–72

Boutros-Ghali, Boutros, 76

Boyle, Francis, 165

Bradley, Curtis A., 181n4, 183n42

Brafman, Ori, 230n116
Brammertz, Serge, 83, 155
Branigin, William, 234n9
Brass, Daniel J., 230n107
Brody, Reed, 155
Brown, Gordon, 164, 241n96
Brown, Martin, 27
Buchanan, Pat, 75, 78
Buchwald, Todd F., 211n113
Burkhardt, Marlene E., 230n107
Bush, George H. W., 4, 72–76
Bush, George W.: assassination authority
    transferred to the CIA, 160, 162; at-
    tacking international law, 10–11, 17–18,
    181n6; drone use under, 146; hunt for
    Kony, assistance provided for, 159;
    Iraq, on the threat posed by, 220n101;
    justification of the war against Saddam,
    92–93, 127; 9/11, response to, 87;
    Special Working Group, refusal to send
    a delegation to, 104; trial and conviction
    of in Malaysian human-rights court, 165
Bush doctrine, 127, 129
Bybee, Jay, 165

Caesar, Julius, 9
Cameron, David, 118, 148
Camus, Albert, 169
Canada, 31, 169–72
Cardi, Sebastiano, 172
Carlyle, Thomas, 45
Caroline incident, the, 51, 127–28
Case Concerning Armed Activities in the
    Territory of the Congo (2005), 129
Chaly, Aleksei, 25
Chamberlain, Austen, 35
Chamberlain, Neville, 27
Cheney, Dick, 10, 165
Chilcot, Sir John, 164, 174, 241n94
Chipman, John, 228n74
Churchill, Winston, 54–56, 74
Churkin, Vitaly, 15
Clark, Roger, 121–23, 218n75
Clémenceau, Georges, 34
Clinton, Bill, 76, 90
Clinton, Hillary, 21, 27, 38, 138–39,
    166–67
Clinton v. Jones, 167
Cold War: beginning of, 56; defining ag-
    gression during, 56–58, 61–65; Ferencz,
    disregarding of, 59; Hammarskjöld's

diplomacy during, 65–67; Kissinger's,
    59–61; nuclear proliferation by an in-
    dividual, 67–69; Nuremberg precedent
    shelved during, 90; Rule of Force vs.
    Rule of Law, 53
Comey, James, 167
Commission for International Justice and
    Accountability (CIJA), 159, 161
Coracini, Astrid Reisinger, 216n49
Corbyn, Jeremy, 164, 244n15
Corell, Hans, 79
Council on Foreign Relations, 104
Crimea, Autonomous Republic of: vote
    favoring integration with Russia, 26
Crimea, the: annexation of, Russian
    constitutional law and, 187n25; argu-
    mentative styles applying international
    law to the crisis in, 32–33; the circus
    surrounding the Russian invasion of,
    22–28; Kissinger on the Russian an-
    nexation of, 38–39; Putin's historical
    argument regarding Russia and, 28–32;
    timeslip opened by Russian invasion
    of, 21–22
crime of aggression, 2–7; activation of,
    negotiation and adoption of resolution
    for, 169–73; amendments to the Rome
    Statute on the, 110–12; American
    exceptionalism in response to, 106–7;
    crimes against peace as forerunner
    to, 50 (see also crimes against peace);
    cyberattacks, determining the status of,
    136–38; definition under the Kampala
    amendments, 113; early ICC cases
    with implications for, 99; elements
    of, 122; the future, "ifs" in, 177; the
    future and, dreamers and cynics on,
    175–76; hidden strength of, 44; the
    ICC Review Conference at Kampala,
    compromise reached at, 105–10,
    136–37; the ICTY and, 81–82 (see also
    International Criminal Tribunal for
    the former Yugoslavia); immunity and,
    157; Intervention Seminar, as synthesis
    of views expressed at, 96; jurisdiction,
    issues of, 105; leadership clause, need
    for new interpretation of, 144–46; legal
    argumentation of "post-truth" politics,
    as a potential antidote to, 32; new
    technologies/perpetrators and, 139–43;
    PrepCom discussions of, 101; the Rome

conference, action at, 90–92; Russian interference in the 2016 US presidential election and, 140; the Special Working Group on the Crime of Aggression/ Princeton group negotiations, 101–5; veto in the Security Council and, 55. *See also* aggression

crime of aggression, adjudicating the: applying the definition of the crime of aggression, 119–21; degrees of ambiguity in the law and, 130–31; goals of, 115–16; a hypothetical case of humanitarian intervention, 121–26; rules and exceptions, 116–19

crime of aggression, enforcing the: acting with impunity, Trump as an example of, 166–67; arrest and prosecution by foreign states, 164–66; arresting a head of state, 154–56; arrest of Gbagbo, 151–52; committing the crime of aggression in the course of, potential for, 161–62; domestic action to investigate and arrest leaders, 162–64; failure to apprehend al-Bashir, 152–54; future arrest scenarios, 158–62; powerful leaders and immunity, the issue of, 156–57; by private contractors, 159–62

crimes against humanity: arrest warrant issued for al-Bashir for, 153; bipartisan resolution condemning LRA for, 159; campaign for Habré's arrest for, 155; as core international crime, 1, 49, 81, 91, 104–5, 109, 116; ICC prosecution of, 3; ICTY prosecution of, 81–82

crimes against peace: as forerunner to crime of aggression, 50; Nuremberg definition of, 47; the Nuremberg judges' acceptance of Jackson's position on, 50–51; Nuremberg verdict affirming, 52; as the unifying principle of the Nuremberg trials, 49

cyberspace, 134, 174, 223n11

Deeks, Ashley, 215–16n41
Del Ponte, Carla, 83
Dicker, Richard, 91
Dinstein, Yoram, 221n111
Draft Treaty of Mutual Assistance of 1923, 35
Drljača, Simo, 156

drones, 146–50
Drumbl, Marc, 115
Dugard, John, 100
Dunlap, Charles, 11–12, 19
Dunoff, Jeffrey L., 205n23

Entebbe, Uganda: Israeli raid on the airport in, 29–30
Escher, M. C., 57, 62, 65
Euromaidan Revolution, 23–24

Fabius, Laurent, 15, 24
failed states, 76, 124
Ferencz, Benjamin B.: the activation decision and, 169–70, 173; on the Bush administration, 10; the competing international orders during the Cold War, 53; compromise on the priority versus intent controversy, 62–63; concept of the crime of aggression, 113; continued concern with aggression, 58–59; detente and the definition of aggression in 1974, 61; distinguished from Hammarskjöld and Kissinger, 66–67; on exclusion of powerful leaders from prosecution, 157; "idealistic" world view of, 91; ISIS, solution to the challenge posed by, 176–77; jurisdictional rules of the Kampala agreement, disappointment regarding, 117; at Kampala, 106, 109; Kissinger as counterpoint to, 59; law over war, the struggle to promote, 177; on the legality of the Second Gulf War, 93; the next generation, as inspiration for, 175; on the 1974 definition, 65; Nuremberg spirit, commitment to, 56; as prosecutor at Nuremberg, 1, 57–58; remarks to the Special Working Group, 102; on the results of the Rome conference, 92; at the Rome conference, 89–90; on the threat of armed conflict, 245n23; at United Nations' meetings trying to define aggression, 57; the United States, anger at the actions of, 1; war-making as biggest atrocity, 93; Weisbord and, 1–2, 7, 101
Ferencz, Don, 106, 109, 170, 173
Ferguson, Niall, 61
Fernández de Gurmendi, Silvia, 101
Foley, James, 14
Fox, Hazel, 237n42

Fox, Henry, 127–28
Franck, Thomas M., 17, 218n84
Franco, Francisco, 35
Franz Ferdinand (archduke of Austria), 33
Franz Joseph (emperor of Austria-Hungary), 33
Freedman, Sir Lawrence, 241n94
Freeland, Chrystia, 171
Frel, Jan, 93
Freud, Sigmund, 39, 53, 69
Friedmann, Wolfgang, 37
Fukuyama, Francis, 59, 71–72
futurism, 133–34

gacaca, 84–87, 98
Garisons, Janis, 139
Gbagbo, Laurent, 101, 151–53, 163
General Treaty for the Renunciation of War (the Kellogg-Briand Pact) of 1928, 14, 35, 44, 46, 48
Geneva Conventions: violations authorized by Bush, 17
Geneva Protocol for the Pacific Settlement of International Disputes of 1924, 35
Genocide Convention of 1948, 17, 58, 80
Germany: attempt to prosecute Rumsfeld, 165; Nuremberg (see Nuremberg)
Gettleman, Jeffrey, 158
Gibson, William, 133–34, 174
Gilbert, Gustave, 3
Gilbert, Sir Martin, 241n94
Giraldi, William, 89
Glennon, Michael J., 104, 130, 222n124
Goering, Hermann, 3, 51–52
Goldsmith, Jack, 19, 94, 96
Goldsmith, Peter, 93
Goldstone, Richard, 81–83, 104
Gonzales, Alberto, 165
Gopal, Anand, 233n156
Gramsci, Antonio, 169
Grandin, Greg, 61
Gray, Christine, 128
Greenwood, Christopher, 221n115
Gros, André, 47
Grover, Leena, 211n111, 211n116, 212n119, 212–13n125
Guengueng, Souleymane, 155

Gulf War, First, 74–75
Gulf War, Second, 4, 10, 92–97, 127

Habré, Hissène, 119, 155, 174
Habyarimana, Juvénal, 76, 200n35
Hadi, Abdrabbuh Mansur, 121
Hammarskjöld, Dag, 65–67
Hammes, Thomas X., 143
Harvard Intervention Seminar, 93–97
Hayden, Michael, 135
Haynes, William, 165
Heckscher, Charles, 144, 230n103
Hehir, Bryan, 94
Heller, Kevin Jon, 15, 104, 130, 222n126, 231n117
Henkin, Louis, 17, 183n40
Higgins, Dame Rosalyn, 241n94
Hirschman, Albert O., 245n25
Hitler, Adolf, 21, 27, 35–37
Hoagland, Jim, 76
Hobbes, Thomas, 151
Hoffmann, Stanley, 94
Hofstadter, Douglas, 53
Holbrooke, Richard, 78
Holmes, Oliver Wendell, Jr., 146
Holmes, Oliver Wendell, Sr., 113, 117
Homer-Dixon, Thomas, 167
humanitarian concerns as justification for use of force, 6–7, 12, 14, 29–30, 76, 84, 95–96, 123–24
human rights: as component of crime of aggression, 102, 141, 175; as justification for use of force, 73, 95, 102
Human Rights Watch, 19, 234n5
Hussein, Saddam, 4, 11–12, 74–75, 92, 94–95, 120

ICTR. See International Criminal Tribunal for Rwanda
ICTY. See International Criminal Tribunal for the former Yugoslavia
Ignatieff, Michael, 30, 71, 77–78, 94–95, 102
immunity, 156–57
impeachment, 16, 24–25, 163, 165–67
India, 67–69
individual, the: the crime of aggression and (see crime of aggression); criminal responsibility for international crimes,

71, 81–83; nuclear proliferation by, 69; reemergence of in conceptions of global politics, 41; shifting accountability from states to leaders, 3–5, 44, 73, 89
individual responsibility for war: argument made at Nuremberg by Jackson, 48–49; crime of aggression as establishing (see crime of aggression); the development of Jackson's argument for, 45–48; in the law of war, 73 (see also law of war); the verdict at Nuremberg affirming, 51–52
International Court of Justice, 55
International Criminal Court (ICC): adjudicating the crime of aggression (see crime of aggression, adjudicating the); amendments to the Rome Statute on the crime of aggression, 110–12, 145; arrest warrant for al-Bashir, 153–54; Assembly of States Parties (see Assembly of States Parties); defining "crime of aggression" as potential dilemma for, 37; early cases of, 97–101; ICC Review Conference at Kampala, 105–10, 136–37; peace-versus justice dilemma, 98–99; Preparatory Commission of the Assembly of States Parties, 10; the Rome conference and, 90–92; Russian annexation of the Crimea, dilemma posed by, 22; safety valves of, 43–44; South Africa requested to explain failure to fulfill legal obligations, 165–66; the US, history of relations with, 105
international criminal law: adjudicating, 115–16; the crime of aggression as, potential of, 3–4 (see also crime of aggression); enforcement of, 4 (see also crime of aggression, enforcing the); individuals as the primary subject of, 71, 84; state responsibility, limitations of assuming, 3–5
International Criminal Tribunal for Rwanda (ICTR), 4, 202n68
International Criminal Tribunal for the Former Yugoslavia (ICTY), 4, 6, 80–83, 155–56, 161, 201n56
international law: argumentative styles in the Crimean crisis and, 32–33; Cold War era (see Cold War); enforcement of (see crime of aggression, enforcing the); the future and, cynics/dreamers/

people in between on, 174–76; Hammarskjöld's use of, 66; humanitarian intervention, 30; immunity and, 156–57; innovations in warfare and the need for evolution of, 150; the League of Nations (see League of Nations); legal frameworks developed in the 1990s, 71 (see also law of war); post–World War II legal order, evolution of, 54–57; Putin's arguments for Crimean annexation based on, 29–32; right of peoples to self-determination, 30–31; right to intervene in another state to protect citizens, conditions for, 29; the Rome conference, 89–92; the Rwandan gacaca and, 84–87; violence, continued search for opportunities to forestall, 174; war and, seminal debate about, 17. See also law of war
international law, leaders' strategies for contending with, 9, 16–19; attacking the law, George W. Bush and, 10–11, 17–18; negating the law, Trump and, 15–16, 19; negotiating the law, Obama and, 11–15, 18–19
International Law Commission (ILC), 80, 157
International Military Tribunal for the Far East, 52
Iran: Natanz cyberattack, 134–37, 146
Iraq: the First Gulf War, 74–75; Nisour Square massacre, 159; Obama's policy towards, 11–15; the Second Gulf War, 4, 10, 92–97, 127
Islamic State (ISIS), 4, 11–15, 129, 149, 176–77
Israel: Entebbe raid, 29–30

Jackson, Robert: the case made at Nuremberg, 48–49; individual accountability for war, developing an argument for, 45–48; Litvinov's principle of priority, acceptance of, 62; as proponent of holding authoritarian leaders responsible for war, 45; statement at the conclusion of the International Military Tribunal, 90
Janik, Ralph, 19
Japan, 35
Johnson, Lyndon B., 60

Johnson, Samuel, 214n20

Judo: History, Theory, Practice (Putin), 31

justifications for use of force: exceptions to UN Charter's prohibition on the use of force, 12, 94; failed states, 76, 124; humanitarian intervention, 6–7, 12, 14, 29–30, 76, 84, 95–96, 123–24; human rights, defense of, 73, 95, 102; responsibility to protect and prevention/punishment of atrocities, 6–7, 82–84, 94–95, 122–26; self-defense, 14–15, 126–29, 182n26, 205n26

Kagame, Paul, 77

Kalb, Nadia, 169–70, 172

Kaleck, Wolfgang, 165

Kambanda, Jean, 164

Kampala compromise: negotiations to reach, 105–10; statutory results of, 110–12

Kanuck, Sean P., 227n74

Karadžić, Radovan, 82, 155

Kasparov, Garry, 27

Kaul, Hans-Peter, 90

Kellogg-Briand Pact of 1928, 14, 35, 44, 46, 48

Kelsen, Hans, 191n4, 219n92

Kennan, George, 56

Kennedy, David, 66, 115

Kennedy, Duncan, 114, 213n8

Kennedy, John F., 60, 63, 67, 169

Kerry, John, 244n16

Kessel, Alex, 172

Khan, Abdul Qadeer (AQ), 67–69, 134

Khan, Agha Muhammad Yahya, 60

Khan, Azmat, 233n156

Khan, Reyaad, 148

Khrushchev, Nikita, 28, 63

Kilcullen, David, 148

Ki-moon, Ban, 152

Kinkel, Klaus, 80

Kirsch, Philippe, 91

Kissinger, Henry, 37–39, 42–43, 59–61, 66–67, 74

Koh, Harold Hongju: crime of aggression, concerns regarding, 211n113, 222n128; on cyber activities as a use of force, 137; ICC judges as a check on government lawyers like, 118; at the ICC Review Conference (Kampala), 106, 130; jurisdictional limits as protection

for the US regarding crime of aggression, 211n112; Kampala compromise, concerns regarding, 117; legal justification for the use of drones, drafting of, 147; the Obama-Clinton doctrine explained, 18; "opt in" interpretation of the Rome Statute's amendment procedure, 214n32; right of self-defense criteria, US position on, 137–38; speech to the American Society for International Law, 104

Kony, Joseph, 98–99, 158–59

"Kony 2012," 159

Korea, People's Democratic Republic of (North), 126

Krane, David, 12

Krauthammer, Charles, 77

Kress, Claus, 208n78

Kuwait, 4, 12, 74

Langewiesche, William, 68

Langner, Ralph, 224n17

Lansing, Robert, 34

Lauterpacht, Hersch, 191n4

Lavrov, Sergei, 152

law: criminal trials, 114–15; international (*see* international law); rule of buttressed by the crime of aggression, 4–5; as a weapon of war, 11–12

lawfare, 11–12, 19, 116

law of war: the Balkans and reevaluation of, 77–84; enforcement of, Somalia as a challenge for, 75–76; inaction as an issue, the Rwandan genocide and, 76–77, 84; the individual in, Noriega's arrest and, 73–74 (*see also* individual, the); justifications for use of force (*see* justifications for use of force); liberalism in the post-Cold War moment and, 72–73; the Second Gulf War and, 92–93; the Second Gulf War and, Intervention Seminar on, 93–97; state-centric global order, the First Gulf War as, 74–75

League of Nations: collapse of, 7, 37; creation of, 34; Hitler and, 21–22, 33, 36–37; institutional procedures and international agreements of, 35; international disputes and, 35–36; Roosevelt and, 54

League of Nations, reasons for collapse of: international lawyers unleashed forces they could not control, Berman's theory of, 42–43; potential fate of the United Nations and, 37; premature establishment of, Bobbitt's theory of, 39–42; unsound structure, Kissinger's theory of, 38–39

Leahy, Patrick, 163

Lehrer, Tom, 61

Levitsky, Steven, 19

liberalism: the New World Order and, 75; the post-Cold War moment and, 72–73

Lietzau, Bill, 106, 210n106

Lind, William S., 143, 229n90

Lindberg, Charles, 73, 75

Litvinov, Maxim, 36, 62

Livada, Phani, 208n78

Lloyd George, David, 34

Locarno Treaties of 1925, 35

London Conference, 47

Lord's Resistance Army (LRA), 97–99, 159

Louis XIV (king of France), 113

LRA. See Lord's Resistance Army

Lubanga, Thomas, 99

Lukin, Vladimir, 24

Lynch, Colum, 234n9

Lyne, Sir Roderic, 241n94

Machiavelli, Niccolo, 41

Malabo Protocol, 209n87

Malaysia, 165

male captus bene detentus (wrongly captured, properly detained), principle of, 161

Marshall, John, 113–14

Marx, Karl, 21

Mato Oput, 97–98

May, Larry, 208n73

Mayer, Jane, 184n45, 239n71

McCain, John, 27, 38, 139, 159

Mégret, Frédéric, 102, 140–41

Méndez, Juan E., 179n11

Merkel, Angela, 27

Merry, Sally Engle, 151

Miller, Darrell A. H., 214n21

Milošević, Slobodan, 6, 78, 83, 89, 154, 163

Minow, Martha, 71, 84–85, 94, 97, 115, 203n85

mission creep, 76

Mladić, Ratko, 78, 82

Montevideo Convention, 228n85

Moreno Ocampo, Luis, 1–2, 97–100, 105

Moussa, Amr, 235n17

Mubarakmand, Samar, 69

Mueller, John, 72

Mugabe, Robert, 100

Museveni, Yoweri, 98

Mushikiwabo, Louise, 166

Mussolini, Benito, 35

myth: definition of, 89

Natsios, Andrew, 6

Negroponte, John, 92–93, 205n25

Nehm, Kay, 165

Neier, Aryeh, 82

Netanyahu, Benjamin, 135

New World Order, 42, 72, 74–75

Nicaragua, 240n84

Nicaragua v. United States (1986), 129, 162

Nietzsche, Friedrich, 9, 162

Nightengale, Keith, 229n90

Nikitchenko, Iona, 47

Nikolić, Dragan, 161

Nixon, Richard, 60

Non-Intervention Agreement of 1936, 36

Noriega, Manuel, 73–74

nuclear proliferation, 68–69

Nuremberg: aggression, Jackson's stance on, 47–48; "crimes against peace," as unifying principle of the trials, 49; "crimes against peace," definition of, 47; irrelevance of official position of defendants, 157; Jackson's case at the trial, 48–49; judgment of the tribunal, 1; legacy of, 52; legal and institutional framework of the Nuremberg Charter, development of, 46–47; the Nazi defense, 50; renaissance of in the 1990s, 71, 79–81, 83–87; responsibility for war assigned to individuals at, 45; Rome conference, principles reaffirmed at, 91; Subsequent Nuremberg Trials, 193n42; the verdict, 50–52

Nye, Joseph, Jr., 145, 229n88, 230n111

Obama, Barack: accountability of Bush regime for war crimes, consideration of pursuing, 163; authorization for participation in hunt for Kony by, 159; drone policy reforms, 149–50; drone use under, 146–48; "moral revolution"

Obama, Barack (*continued*)
  called for at Hiroshima, 174; the Muslim world and Netanyahu, relations with, 134–35; negotiating international law, 11–15, 18–19; Nobel Peace Prize acceptance speech, 18–19; Olympic Games cyber operation and, 135–36; reengagement with the ICC, 104, 106; Russian annexation of the Crimea, legal arguments in response to, 21–22, 26–27, 32; Russian interference in the 2016 presidential election, response to, 140; self-defense doctrine of, 127
Obama-Clinton Doctrine, 18
O'Brien, William V., 221n110
O'Connell, Mary Ellen, 127
Olympic Games cyber operation, 135–37
Omar, Mullah, 146
Operation Deliberate Force, 82
Operation Desert Storm, 12
Operation Gothic Serpent, 76
Operation Just Cause, 73
Orange Revolution, 23–25, 31
Orwell, George, 133
Ouattara, Alassane, 151–52

Pakistan, 67–69
Panama, 73
Paris, Erna, 92
peace-versus-justice dilemma, 2, 7, 98–99
Pearson, Lester B., 66
Pelosi, Nancy, 163
Picasso, Pablo, 42
Pierce, Charles, 165
Pinochet, Augusto, 154
Podesta, John, 225n44
Politis, Nikolaos, 36
Poroshenko, Petro, 139
post-bureaucratic organization, 144–45
Powell, Colin, 127, 220n103
Power, Samantha, 14, 27, 77, 94–96, 199n20
Prashar, Baroness Usha, 241n94
preemptive strikes, 126–29
Princip, Gavrilo, 33
Prosecutor, The v. Duško Tadic, 162
Prunier, Gérard, 200n31
Putin, Vladimir: American intervention in Syria, legal argument against, 13; arrest of, unlikelihood of, 163; the Crimea, invasion of, 21, 23, 26; Crimean invasion, jurisdictional hurdles precluding

aggression case for, 117; Russian annexation of the Crimea, legal arguments supporting, 21–22, 26–32; Russian interference in the 2016 US presidential election, 142; Yanukovich, support of, 24

Qaddafi, Muammar, 69, 100

Raeder, Erich, 51
Rapp, Stephen J., 106, 211n112
Ratner, Steven R., 205n23
Ražnatović, Željko (a.k.a. Arkan), 145
responsibility to protect as justification for use of force, 6–7, 82–84, 94–95, 122–26
Ribbentrop, Joachim von, 37
Rice, Condoleezza, 127–28
Robb, John, 41, 140, 143–44
Rockefeller, Nelson, 60
Röling, Bernard, 45
Rome conference, 89–92
Rome Statute: amendments on the crime of aggression, 110–12; Article 5(2), 170; Article 25(3), 162, 240n85; Bush's "unsigning" of, 17; on immunity not barring exercise of jurisdiction, 157; international civil society coalition supporting, 92; proposed enforcement protocol, 158
Rome Treaty, 90–91
Roosevelt, Eleanor, 58
Roosevelt, Franklin Delano, 45–46, 54–55, 191n3
Roscini, Marco, 224n27
Rosenberg, Alfred, 51
Rose Revolution, 31
Rubin, Alissa J., 200n35
Rumsfeld, Donald, 165
Russia: annexation of the Crimea, pressure on international organizations and law posed by, 21–22; annexation of the Crimea, Putin's speech calling for, 28–32; annexation of the Crimea, Russian constitutional law and, 187n25; Constitution of the Russian Federation, adoption of, 188n40; crime of aggression in the Russian Criminal Code, 163; US presidential election of 2016 and, 138–40
Ruys, Tom, 15
Rwanda: gacaca and Nuremberg, 84–87, 98; the genocide, 76–77
Rwandan Patriotic Front (RPF), 77

Saakashvili, Mikheil, 139
Sadoff, David A., 221n110
Sands, Philippe, 148
Sanger, David E., 135, 224n15
Schabas, William, 106
Schachter, Oscar, 66
Scharf, Michael, 106
Scheffer, David: arrest of Serb leaders, on timid enforcement delaying, 82; on the Corell group's contributions to the ICTY statute, 201n55; cyber action, proposed amendments including, 228n84; at the ICC Review Conference, 106; proposed enforcement protocol for the Rome Statute, 158; at the Rome conference, 90–91; Rome Treaty, signing of, 105; Somalia, description of events in, 76
Schelling, Thomas, 128
Schiff, Adam, 226n51
Schmitt, Carl, 46
Schmitt, John F., 229n90
Schmitt, Michael N., 138, 140
self-defense as justification for use of force, 14–15, 126–29
Shawcross, Sir Hartley, 49
Shawcross, William, 60
Shoygu, Sergey, 23
Sikorski, Radek, 23, 24–25
Soesanto, Stefan, 25
Somalia, 76
South Africa, 165–66
South African Litigation Center, 165
Special Working Group on the Crime of Aggression: Clark as an influential force on, 121; definition of crime of aggression, conclusion a regarding, 130; Kuwait invasion a clear-cut act of aggression for, 120; method used by, 43; negotiations and conclusions of, 101–5; as a subsidiary body of the Assembly of States Parties, 207n68; Weisbord's inclusion in, 2, 101
Stalin, Joseph, 54–56
state, the: evolution of, 39–40
Steinmeier, Frank-Walter, 24
Stewart, Rory, 94–96
Stoltenberg, Jens, 223n11
Stone, Julius, 62, 64
Strategic Arms Limitation Agreement (SALT I), 61
Straw, Jack, 154

Streicher, Julius, 145
Stuxnet, 136, 224n25
Sudan, 6, 100, 105, 152–53, 179n11, 216n48
Sutton, Joseph W., 229n90
Syria: collective self-defense of Iraq as justification for use of force in, 129; drones and the fog or war in, 148–49; "failed-state" concept as justification for use of force in, 76; Obama's policy towards, 11–15; opposing legal arguments over intervention in, 12–15; Trump's policy towards, 15–16
systems disruption, 140

Tadić, Duško, 81
Tallinn Manual, 137–38, 225n35, 225n37
Taylor, Charles, 12, 155
Taylor, Telford, 57–58
Thatcher, Margaret, 4, 75
Thune, Gro Hillestad, 79
timeslip: definition of, 21; in the reaction to Russian annexation of the Crimea, 27; threats to international organizations and law posed by aggression, analogous cases of, 21–22
Tolbert, David, 180n15
Tolstoy, Leo, 45
Trahan, Jennifer, 130, 219n86
Trinidad and Tobago, 80
Truman, Harry, 46, 67
Trump, Donald J.: criminal liability, acting with impunity to avoid, 166–67; Kissinger's position on tactical nuclear weapons, resurrection of, 60; missile strike in Syria ordered by, 149; negating international law, 15–16, 19; the 2016 presidential campaign, 138–39, 142; rolling back of Obama's reforms on use of drones, 150; wrongdoing, denial of, 242n114
Tshombé, Moïse, 66–67
Turchynov, Oleksandr, 24
Türk, Helmut, 79
Tymoshenko, Yulia, 23, 25

Ugalde, Sergio, 172
Uganda, 97–99, 158–59
Ukraine: Crimean crisis (see Crimea, the)
Ulasen, Sergey, 135
UN Charter: Article 2(4), 120; Article 51, 15, 126, 219n93; effectiveness of,

UN Charter (*continued*)
disagreement over, 17; institutional
effectiveness sacrificed for resilience,
43; Nuremberg principles and, lack
of coordination between, 54, 56, 69;
prohibition on use of force, 103; prohibition on use of force, exceptions to,
12, 94; Security Council given primary
responsibility for determining if aggression has occurred, 80, 83, 214n27; state
responsibility, focus on, 3
United Kingdom: the *Caroline* incident,
127–28; definition of aggression, opposition to, 36–37; drone use justified
by self-defense, 148; Iraq War Inquiry,
164; participate in the Second Gulf
War, decision to, 93
United Nations (UN): aggression, efforts
to define, 56–57, 61–65, 80; aggression
cases, the Security Council's role in pursuing, 5, 116–18; in the Balkans, 78–84;
Bobbitt's view of, 40–42; charter of (*see*
UN Charter); establishment of, 54–56;
exceptions to the blanket prohibition
against the use of armed force, 12–13,
54; General Assembly affirmation of
Nuremberg principles, 52; Hammarskjöld as Secretary-General, 65–67;
the ICC and the Security Council of,
91; International Criminal Tribunal
for Rwanda (ICTR), 81–83, 202n68;
International Criminal Tribunal for the
former Yugoslavia (ICTY), 4, 6, 80–83,
155–56, 161, 201n56; Russian annexation of the Crimea, dilemma posed by,
21–22, 27; safety valves, limits and
resilience supplied by, 43; Security
Council, politicized decisions of, 5, 56;
Security Council Resolution 1973, 121;
Security Council resolution authorizing
arrest of Gbagbo, 152; Security Council
resolutions concerning the Second Gulf
War, 92–93; Security Council's role in
the responsibility to protect justification
for military intervention, 124–25; in
Somalia, 76; Syria, legal maneuvering
over intervention in, 12–15
United States: accountability for acts
carried out by Contra guerillas in Nicaragua, 240n84; accountability of Bush
regime for war crimes, consideration

of pursuing, 163; assisting Uganda
in attempted apprehension of Kony,
158–59; the *Caroline* incident, 127–28;
Cold War (*see* Cold War); crime of
aggression, positions regarding, 36–37,
62, 90–91, 106-7, 137–38; Cuban Missile Crisis, 63; drone use by, 146–50;
Ferencz's anger at the actions of, 1;
the First Gulf War, 74–75; the ICC
and, 43, 105; Iran, cyber attack on,
135–36; isolationism in (*see* America
First movements); Kissinger, foreign
policy under, 59–61 (*see also* Kissinger,
Henry); *male captus bene detentus*
(wrongly captured, properly detained),
principle of, 161; Noriega, arrest of,
73–74; North Korea and, 126; Nuremberg, Jackson at, 46–51; post-World
War II security regime, construction
of, 54–55; private military contractors
employed by, 159–60; prosecution of
an American leader, fear of/objection
to, 34, 90; Russian annexation of
the Crimea, response to, 27; Russian
interference in the 2016 presidential
campaign, 138–40; Rwanda and, 77;
the Second Gulf War, 92–93, 95, 127
(*see also* Bush, George W.); Somalia
and, 76; Sudan, actions regarding, 6;
Syria and, 12–16, 129, 148–49; World
War II, justifying interference in while
remaining neutral, 45–46. *See also*
Bush, George H. W.; Bush, George W.;
Obama, Barack; Trump, Donald
Universal Declaration of Human Rights,
58
Urquhart, Brian, 66

van Creveld, Martin, 143
van Schaack, Beth, 157, 161, 240n78
Vienna Convention on the Law of Treaties,
118
Vladimir I/Vladimir the Great (Grand
Prince of Kiev), 28

Walzer, Michael, 102
war: American presidents' approach
to international law regarding (*see*
international law, leaders' strategies for
contending with); cyberspace as a zone
for, 134–36, 223n11; drones as an in-

strument of, 146–50; individual responsibility for (*see* individual responsibility for war); international law and, seminal debate about, 17; law as a weapon of, 11–12; opposing legal arguments over action in Syria, 12–15; Russian interference in the 2016 US presidential election as an act of, 139–43; the transformation of, 143–44
War on Want, 159–60
Waxman, Matthew C., 227–28n74
Weber, Max, 151
Webster, Daniel, 127–28
Wenaweser, Christian, 101–4, 107–9, 141
Wenthold, Paul, 53
Wheeler, Nicholas, 219n87
Wheeler, Sir Roger, 241n94
Wierda, Marieke, 180n15
Wiesenthal, Simon, 155
Wiley, Bill, 159, 161
Wilhelm II (Kaiser of Germany), 34, 49
Wilmhurst, Elizabeth, 93
Wilson, Gary I., 229n90
Wilson, Woodrow, 30, 34, 36, 38, 40
Wippman, David, 205n23

Wittes, Benjamin, 211n114
World War I: legal responsibility for, attempts to assign, 34; origin, fighting, and end of, 33–34
World War II: beginning of, 37; post-war legal order debated at meetings of Allies' leadership, 54
Wrange, Pål, 208n78
Wright, Evan, 160

Xe Services, 160

Yanukovich, Viktor, 23–25, 29
Yatsenyuk, Arseniy, 26
Yeltsin, Boris, 163
Yerofeyev, Yevgeny, 119
Yoo, John, 10, 12, 118, 165, 215n36
Yugoslavia, the former, 77–84
Yushchenko, Viktor, 23

Zeid al-Hussain, Zeid bin Ra'ad (prince of Jordan), 107–8
Zhou Enlai, 60
Ziblatt, Daniel, 19
Zuma, Jacob, 166

Human Rights and Crimes against Humanity
Eric D. Weitz: Series Editor

A World Divided: The Global Struggle for Human Rights in the Age of Nation-States, Eric D. Weitz

The Crime of Aggression: The Quest for Justice in an Age of Drones, Cyberattacks, Insurgents, and Autocrats, Noah Weisbord

The Killing Season: A History of the Indonesian Massacres, 1965–66, Geoffrey B. Robinson

Evidence for Hope: Making Human Rights Work in the 21st Century, Kathryn Sikkink

"They Can Live in the Desert but Nowhere Else": A History of the Armenian Genocide, Ronald Grigor Suny

Child Migration and Human Rights in a Global Age, Jacqueline Bhabha

The Young Turks' Crime against Humanity: The Armenian Genocide and Ethnic Cleansing in the Ottoman Empire, Taner Akçam

The International Human Rights Movement: A History, Aryeh Neier

All the Missing Souls: A Personal History of the War Crimes Tribunals, David Scheffer

Against Massacre: Humanitarian Interventions in the Ottoman Empire, 1815–1914, Davide Rodogno

Stalin's Genocides, Norman M. Naimark

"If You Leave Us Here, We Will Die": How Genocide Was Stopped in East Timor, Geoffrey Robinson

Terror in Chechnya: Russia and the Tragedy of Civilians in War, Emma Gilligan

Torture and the Twilight of Empire: From Algiers to Baghdad, Marnia Lazreg

Cannibal Island: Death in a Siberian Gulag, Nicolas Werth, translated by Steven Rendall, with a foreword by Jan T. Gross

Echoes of Violence: Letters from a War Reporter, Carolin Emcke